Sports Address Bible

The Comprehensive Directory of Sports Addresses

Edward T. Kobak, Jr.

GLOBAL SPORTS PRODUCTIONS, LTD.
1223 Broadway, Suite 102
Santa Monica, CA 90404

Seventh Edition

Revised Edition IIa

© Edward T. Kobak, Jr.,

First published and copyrighted in the United States in 1980, with subsequent publication in 1983, 1987, 1989-90, 1991, 1993 and 1994.

1994-95 Fall/Winter Revised 7th Edition

ISBN 0-9619181-5-2
ISSN 0-743-4561

Introduction

Welcome to the seventh edition of `The Sports Address Bible` now subtitled The Comprehensive Directory of Sports Addresses. The book is rapidly becoming the most informative sports resource directory of its kind.

The Bible has continually grown since its inception back in 1980 following my return from the Lake Placid Winter Olympics. Since then, the book has changed over the course of the years, due to the increase in information that you, the readers, have requested.

What was once a book primarily for the sports collector, has now become a valuable resource bible for the sports executive, the media director, the student searching for a sports management program at college, the college student looking for a sports career, the librarian, from the college professor and guidance councelor to the administrator and instructor in the physical education field - as well as the average sports fan. The Bible has become a resource tool to a much broader audience since its inception.

Each year the book changes a little, adding new sections and information that has been requested by you, the reader. This is why your input is very important. The responses I receive help me shape each future edition. So, if there is information you would like to see in future editions, feel free to voice your interests.

With the recent arrival of the Arizona Fall Baseball League, the Northern, Frontier and Hawaii Winter Baseball, the newly revived Central Hockey League, the Sunshine Hockey League, the Continental Indoor Soccer League, the birth of the NBL on the heels of the demise of the World and Global leagues, the new Atlantic Basketball League along with a slew of proposed leagues and the recent NBA & NFL expansion, the sports world is ever increasingly changing, creating an even bigger need for the **Sports Address Bible**!

Lastly, I'd like to express my sincere "thank you" to those who have supported the book. A "thank you" to my advertisers as well as the administrators and publicists I have called upon. Finally, a special "thank you" to my mother who has spent most of her vacation in California helping me with the data entry for the Bible.

A "Special thank you" to a few people who have been directly involved in the production of the Bible.

Firstly, to my **mother** who spent long hours of data entry on the Bible, among other responsibilities, to **Mike Boylan** of Boylan Printing who has spent long hours on the printing and bindery of the Bible.

Lastly to my friends **Warren Walk** and **Bristo Loving**, who provided valuable insight and hours working with *The Sports Address Bible.*

TABLE OF CONTENTS

New Sports Leagues

Listed in this section are new or prospective leagues that have recently announced formation.

Chinese Taipei Professional Baseball League
No. 51, 8F, Sec. 4
Nanking East Road
Taipei, Taiwan
Republic of China
Pres: P.P. Tang
011 (02) 752.1006

Pro Baseball Association of Puerto Rico
P.O. Box 4091
Old San Juan Station,
Puerto Rico 00901
(809) 725-4375
Pres.: Francisco Guell
(809) 725-9036 (PR #)

Hawaii Winter Baseball League

1210 Auahi Street
Suite 231
Honolulu, HI 96814
(808) 592-2255
Fax (808) 592-2260
President: Robert berg
PR/Mkt: Rubin Chappins
Mkt/Adv: Dave Rolf
(808) 593-1533
Fax (808) 593-0569

Hilo Stars
76 Terrace Circle
Hilo, Hawaii 96720
(808) 969-9033
G.M.: Clyde Nekoba

Honolulu Sharks
1210 Auahi Street
Suite 231
Honolulu, Hawaii 96814
(808) 592-2255
G.M.: Eric Tokunaga

Kauai Emeralds
P.O. Box 67
Hanapepe, Kauai, Hawaii 96716
(808) 335-6430
G.M.: Ross Kagawa

Maul Stingrays
P.O. Box 1193
Wailuku, Maui, Hawaii 96793
(808) 242-2950
G.M.: Lane Fujii

The Hawaii Winter Baseball League is in its inaugural season

Colorado Silver Bullets
Wittle Communications
333 Main Street
Knoxville, TN 37902
(800) 278-2772
Fax (615) 595-5177
GM: Phil Niekro
PR: Kathleen Christie

Women's professional touring team

Hollywood Legends
22349 La Palma Avenue
Suite 112
Yorba Linda, CA 92687-7247
(310) 281-7354

Barnstorming club made up of former major leaguers.

National Cycle League

532 La Guardia Place
Suite 162
New York, NY 10012
(212) 871-7472
Fax (212) 260-7424
Comm: Pete O'Neil

Amsterdam Flying Dutchmen
Walstro 24
3831 WX Leusden,
The Netherlands
011 (31) 33.94.6261
GM: Rene Lith

Houston Outlaws
4400 Memorial Drive
Suite 3098
Houston, TX 77007
(713) 869-2718
GM: Jack Gott

Independent Leagues

1020 Seventh Street
Portsmouth, OH 45662
(614) 353-7647
Fax (614) 353-5842
President: Steve Sturgill

Chillicothe Paints
PO Box 1583
59 N. Paint Street
Chillicothe, OH 45601
(614) 773-8326
Fax (614) 773-8338
GM: Chris Hanners

Erie Sailors
Yorktown Center
2501 West 12th Street
Erie, PA 16505
(814) 835-1213
Fax (814) 838-6334
GM: Pat Brown

Kentucky Rifles
PO Box 351
415 Second Street
Pikeville, KY 41501
(606) 432-2148
Pres: Mike Weisbart

Lancaster Scouts
306 E Chestnut Street
Lancaster, OH 43130
(614) 687-1077
Fax (614) 653-3030
Pres: Bill Sidwell

Newark Buffalos
31 N. Fourth Street
Newark, OH 43055
(614) 349-9866
Fax (614) 349-9758
Pres: Jim Lacrone

Ohio Valley Redcoats
325 7th Street
Parkersburg, WV 26102
(304) 422-0426
Fax (304) 485-0715
Pres: Mike Raber

Portsmouth Explorers
402 Bank One Plaza
PO Box 950
Portsmouth, OH 45662
(614) 354-3453
Fax (614) 353-5709
GM: Steve Sturgill

Zanesville Greys
331 Parkway Drive
Zanesville, OH 43701
(614) 453-8531
Fax (614) 454-8900
Pres: Bob Wolfe

The league began its inaugural
season in 1993. This is an
independent league.

Texas-Louisiana League
13455 Noel Road, Suite 1650
Galleria Tower II
Dallas, TX 75240
(214) 991-3332
Fax (214) 991-8887
Dir. of Oper: Jack Lazorko

Alexandria Aces
PO Box 6005
Alexandria, LA 71307
(318) 473-ACES
Fax (318) 473-2229
GM: Craig Brasfield

Amarillo Dillas
PO Box 31241
Amarillo, TX 79109
(806) 342-DILA
Fax (806) 374-2269
GM: Eric Sawyer

Beaumont Bullfrogs
PO Box 20574
Beaumont, TX 77720
(409) 83FROGS
Fax (409) 832-2397
GM: Mike Patrick

Corpus Christi Barracudas
PO Box 271129
Corpus Christi, TX 78427
(512) 857-CRAB
GM: Michael Schiff

Mobile Bay Sharks
PO Box 81214
Mobile, AL 36689
(205) 342-0188
GM: Matt Riley

**Rio Grand Valley
White Wings**
PO Box 530007
Harlingen, TX 78553
(210) 412-WING
Fax (210) 412-9479
GM: Brian Borchardt

San Antonio Tejanos
PO Box 791611
San Antonio, TX 78279
(210) 434-JANOS
GM: Mike Marek

Tyler Wildcatters
PO Box 7807
Tyler, TX 75711
(903) 597-WILD
Fax (903) 597-6464
GM: Lee Smith

The Tx-La League began its inaugural
season in 1994. They will operate as
an independent league.

North Central League

Brainerd Bears
304 S. 6th Street
Brainerd, MN 56401
(218) 828-9197

Huron Heaters
115 Third Street S.E.
Huron, SD 57350
(605) 352-7515

Marshall Mallards
230 Lyon Street
Theatre Bldg., Suite 102
Marshall, MN 56258
(507) 537-4144

Minneapolis Loons
2021 E. Hennepin Avenue
Suite 240
Minneapolis, MN 55413
(612) 379-7404

Regina Cyclones
PO Box 3433
Regina, Saskatchewan S4P 3J8
(306) 949-2255

Saskatoon Riot
1235 Avenue P South
Saskatoon, Saskatchewan S7M 5P9
(306) 653-BALL

1994 is the North Central League's
inaugural season.

Baseball

The Arizona Fall League
10201 S 51st Street
Suite 230
Phoenix, AZ 85044
(602) 496-6700
Fax (602) 496-6384
Comm.: Mike Port

Chandler Diamondbacks
1435 W Ocotillo Road
Chandler, AZ 85245
(602) 895-5115

Grand Canyon Rafters
Tempe Diablo Stadium
2200 W. Alameda
Tempe, AZ 85282
(602) 350-5205

Phoenix Saguaros
HoHoKam Park
1235 N. Center Street
Mesa, AZ 85201
(602) 964-4467

Scottsdale Scorpions
7402 E. Osborne
Scottsdale, AZ 85251
(602) 941-1930

Sun Cities Solar Sox
13440 N. 111th Avenue
Sun City, AZ 85351
(602) 977-1718

Tucson Javelinas
Hi-Corbett Field
Randolph Park
Tucson, AZ 85726
(602) 795-7880

Northern League
12712 Parkwood Drive
Burnsville, MN 55337
(612) 894-4048
Fax (612) 894-4070
Pres: Miles Wolf
Ex Dir: Top Leip

Duluth-Superior Dukes
PO Box 205
Duluth, MN 55801
(218) 727-4525
Fax (218) 727-4533
GM: Tom Van Schaack

St. Paul Saints
1771 Energy Park Drive
St. Paul, MN 55108
(612) 644-6659
Fax (612) 644-1627
GM: Bill Fanning

Sioux City Explorers
3400 Line Drive
Sioux City, IA 51106
(712) 277-9467
Fax (712) 277-9406
GM: Tim Utrup

Sioux Falls Canaries
PO Box 84412
Sioux Falls, SD 57118
(605) 333-0179
Fax (605) 333-0139
GM: Gary Weckworth

Thunder Bay Whiskey Jacks
PO Box 864
Thunder Bay, Ontario P7C 4X7
(807) 344-5225
Fax (807) 343-4611
GM: Joe Easton

Winnipeg Gold Eyes
1430 Maroons Road
Winnipeg, Manitoba R3B 0S1
(204) 982-2273
Fax (204) 982-2274
GM: John Hindle

The Northern League began its
inaugural season in 1993.

BASEBALL

Major League Baseball

350 Park Avenue
New York, NY 10022
(212) 339-7800
Fax (212) 759-8391
Chmn. Exec. Council: Bud Selig
PR: Rich Levin

**Major League Baseball
Players Association**
805 Third Avenue
New York, NY 10022
(212) 826-0808
Exec. Dir.: Donald Fehr

American League

350 Park Ave., NY 10022
New York, 339-7600
Pres: Dr. Bobby Brown
PR: Phyllis Merhige

Baltimore Orioles
333 W. Camden Street
Baltimore, MD 21201
(410) 685-9800
Fax (410) 685-547-6272
GM: Roland Hemond
PR: Rick Vaughn

Boston Red Sox
Fenway Park
Boston, MA 02115
(617) 267-9440
Fax (617) 236-6797
GM: Lou Gorman
PR: Dick Bresciani

California Angels
PO Box 2000
Anaheim, CA 92803
(714) 937-6700
Fax (714) 634-3410
GM: Whitey Herzog
PR: Tim Mead

Chicago White Sox
333 West 35th Street
Chicago, IL 60016
(312) 924-1000
Fax (312) 451-5116
GM: Ron Schueler
PR: Chuck Adams

Cleveland Indians
Indians Park
2401 Ontario Street
Cleveland, OH 44115
(216) 861-1200
Fax (216) 420-4396
GM: John Hart
PR: Bob DiBiasio

Detroit Tigers
Tiger Stadium
Detroit, MI 48216
(313) 962-4000
Fax (313) 962-1128
GM: Jerry Walker
PR: Dan Ewald

Kansas City Royals
PO Box 419969
Kansas City, MO 64141
(816) 921-2200
Fax (816) 921-5775
GM: Herk Robinson
PR: Dean Vogelaar

Milwaukee Brewers
Milwaukee County Stadium
Milwaukee, WI 53214
(414) 933-4114
Fax (414) 933-7323
GM: Sal Bando
PR: Tom Skibash

Minnesota Twins
501 Chicago Ave. South
Minneapolis, MN 55415
(612) 375-1366
Fax (612) 375-7473
GM: Andy MacPhail
PR: Tom Mee

New York Yankees
Yankee Stadium
Bronx, NY 10451
(718) 793-4300
Fax (718) 293-8414
GM: Gene Michael
PR: Arthur Richman

Oakland Athletics
Oakland Alameda County Coliseum
Oakland, CA 94621
(510) 638-4900
Fax (510) 638-4937
GM: Sandy Alderson
PR: Jay Alves

Seattle Mariners
PO Box 4100
Seattle, WA 98104
(206) 628-3555
Fax (206) 628-3340
GM: Woody Woodward
PR: Dave Aust

Texas Rangers
PO Box 90111
Arlington, TX 76004
(817) 273-5222
Fax (817) 273-5206
GM: Tom Grieve
PR: John Blake

Toronto Blue Jays
The Skydome
Toronto, Ontario, Canada M5V 3B3
(416) 341-1000
Fax (416) 341-1250
GM: Pat Gillick
PR: Howie Starkman

National League

350 Park Avenue
New York, NY 10022
(212) 339-7700
President: Leonard Coleman, Jr.

Atlanta Braves
PO Box 4064
Atlanta, GA 30302
(404) 522-7630
Fax (404) 614-1391
GM: John Schuerholz
PR: Jim Schultz

Chicago Cubs
1060 W. Addison Street
Chicago, IL 60613
(312) 404-2827
Fax (312) 404-4129
GM: Larry Himes
PR: Sharon Pannozzo

Cincinnati Reds
100 Riverfront Stadium
Cincinnati, OH 45202
(513) 421-4510
Fax (513) 421-7342
GM: Jim Bowden
PR: John Braude

Colorado Rockies
1700 Broadway, Suite 2100
Denver, CO 80290
(303) 292-0200
Fax (303) 830-8977
GM: Bob Gebhard
PR: Mike Swanson

Florida Marlins
100 N.E. 3rd Avenue, 3rd Fl.
Fort Lauderdale, FL 33301
(305) 779-7070
Fax (305) 356-8123
GM: Dave Dombrowski
PR: Chuck Pool

Houston Astros
PO Box 288
Houston, TX 77001
(713) 799-9500
Fax (713) 799-9512
GM: Bill Wood
PR: Rob Matwick

Los Angeles Dodgers
1000 Elysian Park Ave.
Los Angeles, CA 90012
(213) 224-1500
Fax (213) 224-1269
GM: Fred Claire
PR: Jay Lucas

Montreal Expos
PO Box 500, Station M
Montreal, Quebec H1V 3P2
(514) 253-3434
Fax (514) 253-8282
GM: Dan Duquette
PR: Richard Griffin

New York Mets
Shea Stadium
Flushing, NY 11368
(718) 507-6387
Fax (718) 565-4382
GM: Al Harazin
PR: Jay Horowitz

Philadelphia Phillies
PO Box 7575
Philadelphia, PA 19101
(215) 463-6000
Fax (215) 389-3050
GM: Lee Thomas
PR: Larry Shenk

Pittsburgh Pirates
Three Rivers Stadium
Pittsburgh, PA 15212
(412) 323-5000
Fax (412) 323-5024
GM: Ted Simmons
PR: Rick Cerrone

St. Louis Cardinals
250 Stadium Plaza
St. Louis, MO 63102
(314) 421-3060
Fax (314) 425-0640
GM: Dal Maxvil
PR: Jeff Wehling

San Diego Padres
PO Box 2000
San Diego, CA 92112
(619) 283-4494
Fax (619) 282-8886
GM: Joe McIlvaine
PR: Jim Ferguson

San Francisco Giants
Candlestick Park
San Francisco, CA 94124
(415) 468-3700
Fax (415) 467-0485
GM: Bob Quinn
PR: Bob Rose

MLB Spring Training Camps
American League

Baltimore Orioles
Twin Lakes Park
6700 Clark Road
Sarasota, FL 34241
(813) 923-1996
(Feb 18-March 4)
Huggins-Stengel Field
1320 Fifth Street North
St. Petersburg, FL 33701
(813) 892-5971
(March 5-April 1)

Boston Red Sox
City of Palms Park
2201 Edison Avenue
Fort Myers, FL 33901
(813) 334-4700

California Angels
Tempe Diablo Stadium
2200 West Alameda
Tempe, AZ 85282
(602) 438-4300

Chicago White Sox
1909 North Euclid Avenue
Sarasota, FL 34237
(813) 366-8451

Cleveland Indians
Chain O'Lakes Park
Winter Haven, FL 33880
(813) 291-5803

Detroit Tigers
Tigertown
Box 90187
Lakeland, FL 33804
(813) 686-8075

Kansas City Royals
300 Stadium Way
Davenport, FL 33837
(813) 424-7211

Milwaukee Brewers
P.O. Box 2650
Chandler, AZ 85248
(602) 895-6000

Minnesota Twins
Lee County Sports Complex
14100 Six Mile Cypress Pkwy.
Fort Meyers, FL 33912
(813) 678-4200

New York Yankees
Fort Lauderdale Stadium
5301 N.W. 12th Avenue
Fort Lauderdale, FL 33309
(305) 772-4537

Oakland Athletics
Phoenix Stadium
5999 East Van Buren
Phoenix, AZ 85258
(602) 225-9400

Seattle Mariners
P.O. Box 999
Peoria, AZ 85380-0999
(602) 412-3062

Texas Rangers
P.O. Box 3609
Port Charlotte, FL 33949-3609
(813) 625-9500

Toronto Blue Jays
Box 957
Dunedin, FL 34697
(813) 733-9302

National League

Atlanta Braves
P.O. Box 2619
West Palm Beach, FL 33402-2619
(407) 683-6100

Chicago Cubs
P.O. Box 4066
Mesa, AZ 85201
(602) 461-0061

Cincinnati Reds
P.O. Box 2275
Plant City, FL 33564
(813) 752-1878

Colorado Rockies
Hi Corbett Field
3400 E. Camino Campestre
Tucson, AZ 85726
(602) 327-9467

Florida Marlins
5600 Stadium Parkway
Melbourne, FL 32940
(407) 933-9200

Houston Astros
P.O. Box 422229
Kissimmee, FL 34742-2229
(407) 933-6500

Los Angeles Dodgers
Dodgertown
4001 26th Street
Vero Beach, FL 32961-2887

Montreal Expos
P.O. Box 3566
West Palm Beach, FL 33402
(407) 684-6801

New York Mets
525 N.W. Peacock Blvd.
Port St. Lucie, FL 34986
(407) 871-2100

Philadelphia Phillies
P.O. Box 10336
Clearwater, FL 34617
(813) 441-9941

Pittsburgh Pirates
P.O. Box 1359
Bradenton, FL 34206
(813) 747-3031

St. Louis Cardinals
Al Lang Stadium
180 Second Avenue S.E.
St. Petersburg, FL 33701
(813) 896-4641

San Diego Padres
P.O. Box 4668
Yuma, AZ 85246
(602) 726-6040

San Francisco Giants
Scottsdale Stadium
7402 E. Osborn Road
Scottsdale, AZ 85251
(602) 990-7972

Japanese Baseball

Imperial Tower 7F
1-1-1 Uchisaiwai-cho,
Chiyoda-ku, Tokyo 100, Japan
(03) 3502-0022
Commissioner: Ichiro Yoshikuni

Central League

Asahi Bldg. 3F, 6-6-7 Ginza
Chuo-ku, Tokyo 104 Japan
03-3572-1673
Pres: Hiromori Kawashima

Chunichi Dragons
Chunichi Bldg., 9F, 4-1-1 Sakae
Naka-ku, Nagoya 460, Japan
052 (261) 8811
GM: Hiroo Suzuki

Hanshin Tigers
1-47 Koshien-cho
Nishinomiya-shi, Hyogo-ken 663, Japan
0798-46-1515
GM: Kuniaki Sawada

Hiroshima Toyo Carp
5-25 Moto-machi,
Naka-ku, Hiroshima 730, Japan
0822 (21) 2040
GM: Hirokazu Nozaki

Yakult Swallows
Yakult Bldg., 7F, 1-1-19
Higashi-Shimbashi,
Minato-ku, Tokyo 105, Japan
(03) 3574 0671
GM: Kazuo Soma

Yokohama Bay Stars
Kinoshita Bldg. 7F, 4-43 Masago-cho
Naka-ku, Yokohama 231, Japan
045 (681) C811
GM: Jiro Shibayama

Yomiuri Tokyo Giants
1-3-7 Uchikanda
Chiyoda-ku
Tokyo 101, Japan
03 3295 7711
GM: Jitsuo Hasegawa

Pacific League

6-6-7 Ginza, Asahi Bldg., 9F
Chuo-ku, Tokyo 104, Japan
03 (573) 1551
President: Shintaro Fukushima

Fukuoka Daiei Hawks
Pine Bldg., 6F
1-1-12 Otemon
Chuo-Ku, Fukuoka 810, Japan
092-711-1189
GM: Hisao Nakauchi

Kintetsu Buffaloes
Kintetsu Namba Bldg., 7F
4-1-15 Namba
Chuo-ku, Osaka 542, Japan
(06) 644-5557
GM: Hitomi Yamazaki

Chiba Lotte Marines
WBG Marive West, 25F
2-6 Nakase, Chibashi
Chiba-ken 261-71 Japan
0432-97-2101
GM: Toshio Abe

Nippon Ham Fighters
Roppongi Denki Bldg. 6F
6-1-20 Roppongi,
Minato-ku, Tokyo 106, Japan
03 (403) 9131
GM: Takeshi Kojima

Orix Blue Wave
Kanri Center 2F
Midoridai, Suma-ku
Kobe 654-01, Japan
078-795-1001
GM: Shigeyoshi Ino

Seibu Lions
Seibu Lions Stadium
2135 Kami-Yamaguchi
Tokorozawa-shi, Saitami-ken 359, Japan
0429-24-1155
GM: Nobuhito Shimizo

Korean Professional Baseball

445-6 Yok Sam-Dong
Kangnam-ku, Seoul, Korea
02-557-7887
Sec. Gen.: Lee Yong-il

Chinese Taipei Professional Baseball

No. 51, 8F, Sec. 4
Nanking East Road
Taipei, Taiwan
Republic of China
(02) 752-1006
Pres: P.P. Tang

Men's Senior Baseball

8 Sutter Terrace
Jericho, NY 11753
(516) 931-2615
President: Steven Sigler

Great Central League

Champaign-Urbana Bandits
1817 S. Neil Street
Champaign, IL 61820
(217) 355-2255

Lafayette Leopards
1915 Scott Street
Lafayette, IN 47901
(317) 449-2529

Mason City Bats
202 First Street S.E.
Suite 204
Mason City, IA 50401
(515) 44-HOMER

Minneapolis Millers
2717 Hennepin Avenue S.
Minneapolis, MN 55408
(612) 872-8989

The Great Central League is an independent league which began play in 1994.

Northwoods League

Dubuque Mud Puppies
PO Box 3124
Dubuque, IA 52004
(319) 582-6191

Kenosha Krokers
PO Box 4222
Kenosha, WI 53141
(414) 657-7663

Manitowoc Skunks
PO Box 233
Manitowoc, WI 54221
(414) 682-8810

Rochester Honkers
PO Box 482
Rochester, MN 55903
(507) 281-5908

Wausau Woodchucks
PO Box 2216
Wausau, WI 54403
(715) 845-5055

The Northwoods League is a Summer collegiate league that began its inaugural season in 1994.

Minor League Baseball

National Association of Professional Baseball Leagues

P.O. Box A
St. Petersburg, FL 33703
(813) 822-6937
Fax (813) 821-5819
Pres: Mike Moore
Publicity: Bob Sparks

Class AAA Leagues

American Association

6801 Miami Avenue
Suite 3
Cincinnati, OH 45243
(513) 271-4800
Fax (513) 271-7887
Pres: Branch Rickey

Buffalo Bisons
PO Box 450
Buffalo, NY 14205
(716) 846-2000
Fax (716) 846-2258
GM: Mike Buczkowski

Indianapolis Indians
1501 W. 16th Street
Indianapolis, IN 46202
(317) 632-5371
Fax (317) 269-3541
GM: Max B. Schumacher

Iowa Cubs
350 S.W. First
Des Moines, IA 50309
(515) 243-6111
Fax (515) 243-5151
GM: Sam Bernabe

Louisville Redbirds
PO Box 36407
Louisville, KY 40233
(502) 367-9121
Fax (502) 368-5120
GM: Dale Owens

Nashville Sounds
PO Box 23290
Nashville, TN 37202
(615) 256-5684
GM: Larry Schmittou

New Orleans Zephyrs
PO Box 24672
New Orleans, LA 70184
(504) 282-6777
Fax (504) 282-9821
GM: Jay Cicero

Oklahoma City 89ers
PO Box 75089
Oklahoma City, OK 73147
(405) 946-8989
Fax (405) 942-4198
GM: Dorsena Picknell

Omaha Royals
PO Box 3665
Omaha, NE 68103
(402) 734-2550
Fax (402) 734-7166
GM: Bill Gorman

International League

55 S. High Street, Suite 202
Dublin, OH 43017
(614) 791-9300
Fax (614) 791-9009
Pres: Randy Mobley

Charlotte Knights
PO Box 1207
Fort Mill, SC 29716
(803) 548-8051
Fax (803) 548-8055
GM: Bill Lavelle

Columbus Clippers
1155 W. Mound Street
Columbus, OH 43223
(614) 462-5250
Fax (614) 462-3271
GM: Ken Schnacke

Norfolk Tides
PO Box 12111
Norfolk, VA 23502
(804) 622-2222
Fax (804) 624-9090
GM: Dave Rosenfield

Ottawa Lynx
300 Coventry Road
Ottawa, Ontario KIK 4P5
(613) 747-5969
Fax (613) 747-0003
GM: Howard Darwin

Pawtucket Red Sox
PO Box 2365
Pawtucket, RI 02861
(401) 724-7303
Fax (401) 724-2140
GM: Mike Tamburro

Richmond Braves
PO Box 6667
Richmond, VA 23230
(804) 359-4444
Fax (804) 359-0731
GM: Bruce Baldwin

Rochester Red Wings
500 Norton Street
Rochester, NY 14621
(716) 467-3000
Fax (716) 467-6732
GM: Naomi Silver

Scranton/Wilkes-Barre Red Barons
PO Box 3449
Scranton, PA 18505
(717) 963-6556
Fax (717) 963-6564
GM: Bill Terlecky

Syracuse Chiefs
MacArthur Stadium
Syracuse, NY 13208
(315) 474-7833
Fax (315) 474-2658
GM: Anthony `Tex' Simone

Toledo Mud Hens
PO Box 6212
Toledo, OH 43614
(419) 893-9483
Fax (419) 893-5847
GM: Gene Cook

2345 S. Alma School Rd.
Suite 110
Mesa, AZ 85210
(602) 838-2171
Fax (602) 838-2741
Pres: William S. Cutler

Albuquerque Dukes
P.O. Box 26267
Albuquerque, N.M. 87125
(505) 243-1791
Fax (505) 842-0561
GM: Pat McKernan

Calgary Cannons
P.O. Box 3690, Station B
Calgary, Alberta T2M 4M4
(403) 284-1111
Fax (403) 284-4343
GM: Gary Arthur

Colorado Springs Sky Sox
4385 Tutt Avenue
Colorado Springs, CO 80922
(719) 597-1449
Fax (719) 597-2491
GM: Bob Goughan

Edmonton Trappers
10233 96th Avenue
Edmonton, Alberta T5K 0A5
(403) 429-2934
Fax (403) 426-5640
GM: Mel Kowalchuk

Las Vegas Stars
850 Las Vegas Blvd. North
Las Vegas, NV 89101
(702) 386-7200
Fax (702) 386-7214
GM: Don Logan

Phoenix Firebirds
PO Box 8528
Scottsdale, AZ 85252
(602) 275-0500
Fax (602) 990-8987
GM: Craig Pletenik

Salt Lake City Buzz
PO Box 4108
Salt Lake City, UT 84110
(801) 485-3800
Fax (801) 532-1852
GM: Tammy Felker-White

Tacoma Tigers
P.O. Box 11087
Tacoma, WA 98411
(206) 752-7707
Fax (206) 752-7135
GM: Frank Colarusso

Tucson Toros
P.O. Box 27045
Tucson, AZ 85726
(602) 325-2621
Fax (602) 327-2371
GM: Mike Feder

Vancouver Canadians
4601 Ontario St.
Vancouver, B.C. V5V 3H4
(604) 872-5232
Fax (604) 872-1714
GM: Brent Imlach

Mexican League

Angel Pola 16,
Col. Periodista, C.P. 11220
Mexico, D.F.
(905) 557-1007
Fax (905) 395-2454
Commissioner: Alejo Peralta

Aguascalientes Railroadmen
Venustiano Carranza #122
1st floor, A Int. 1
Aguascalientes, Ags.
(491) 580-33 or 524-79
Presidente: Armando Medina G.

Campeche Pirates
Unidad Deportiva 20 de Nov. Local 4
Campeche, Cam.
(981) 660-71
Presidente: Carlos Ivan Perez Ortiz

Cordoba Coffeegrowers
Calle 15, No. 119, Espacho 4
Cordoba, Veracruz
(271) 278-08
Comm: Jose Luis Vergara

Jalisco Charros
Alfredo Chavero #222, Sector
Hidalgo, Guadalajara, Jal.
(36) 25-65-43
GM: Guillermo Ruiz Becerril

Leon Braves
Blvd. Adolfo Lopez Mateos #1139
Int. 212 Ote., C.P.
37000 Leon, Gto.
(471) 4-97-51 or 6-83-61
GM: Manuel Cortes Conde

Mexico City Reds
Obrero Mundial #410-201
Mexico, D.F.
(5) 543-10-75 and 536-31-46
Presidente: Roberto Mansur Galan

Mexico City Tigers
Tuxpan #45-A 5th Floor, Col. roma
C.P. 06760 Mexico, D.F.
(5) 584-02-16 or 584-0249
Presidente: Alejo Peralta

Monclova Steelers
Avenida Hidalgo #214, Altos, C.P.
25700 Monclova, Coah.
(863) 334-91
Pres: Jorge Williamson Bosques

Monterrey Industrials
Rio Panuco No. 452 Oriente
Col. De Valle
Monterrey, Nuevo Leon
(83) 7862-63
GM: Tomas Herrera

Monterrey Sultans
Calzada Madero #3542 Pte.
Monterrey, N.L.
(83) 48-19-95 or 46-63-06
Presidente: Jose Maiz Garcia

Saltillo Sarape Makers
Lic. Salvador Gonzalex Lobo
No. 893 Altos, C.P. 25000
Saltillo, Coah.
(841) 208-72
Pres: Armando Guadiana Tijerina

San Luis Potosi Cactus Men
Ave. Venustiano Carranza
No. 985-603, San Luis.
(481) 4-16-38 or 4-16-39
Presidente: Juan Abusaid Rios

Tabasco Cattlemen
Ave. Juarez #606 Altos
Villahermosa, Tabasco
(931) 275-00
Presidente: Humberto Tapia

Owls of the Two Laredos
Ave. Obregon #1035, C.P. 88000
Nuevo Laredo, Tamps.
(871) 271-92
Pres: Victor Lozano Rendon

Union Laguna Cotton Pickers
Avenue Juarez #1850 Ote.
Torreon, Coah.
(171) 849-25 or 855-15
Pres: Jorge Duenes Zurita

Yucatan Lions
Calle 17 #96-C
Col. Chuminopolis, C.P. 97158
Merida, Yucatan
(992) 459-45
Pres: Romeo Magana Carrillo

Dominican Summer League
Ave. John F. Kennedy #3
Santo Domingo, Dom. Republic
(809) 565-0714
Fax (809) 566-8645
Presidente: Freddy Jana

Class AA Leagues

Eastern League

PO Box 716
Plainville, CT 06062
(203) 747-9332
Fax (203) 747-9463
Pres: John Levenda

Albany Yankees
HeritagePark
Albany Shaker Road
Albany, NY 12211
(518) 869-9236
Fax (518) 869-9237
GM: George Brzezinski

Binghamton Mets
PO Box 598
Binghamton, NY 13902
(607) 723-6387
Fax (607) 723-7779
GM: R.C. Reuteman

Bowie Bay Sox
PO Box 1661
Bowie, MD 20717
(301) 805-6000
Fax (301) 805-6008
GM: Keith Lupton

Canton-Akron Indians
2501 Allen Avenue S.E.
Canton, OH 44707
(216) 456-5100
Fax (216) 456-5450
GM: Jeff Auman

Harrisburg Senators
PO Box 15757
Harrisburg, PA 17105
(717) 231-4444
Fax (717) 231-4445
GM:Todd Vander Woude

New Britain Red Sox
PO Box 1718
New Britain, CT 06050
(203) 224-8383
Fax (203) 225-6267
GM: Gerald Berthiaume

New Haven Ravens
63 Grove Street
New Haven, CT 06510
(203) 782-1666
Fax (203) 782-1555
GM: Charlie Dowd

Portland Sea Dogs
PO Box 636
Portland, ME 04104
(207) 874-9300
Fax (207) 780-0317
GM: Charlie Eshbach

Reading Phillies
PO Box 15050
Reading, PA 19612
(215) 375-8469
Fax (215) 373-5868
GM: Chuck Domino

Trenton Thunder
210 Riverview Exec. Plaza
Trenton, NJ 08611
(609) 394-8326
Fax (609) 394-9666

Southern League

235 Main Street, Suite 103
Trussville, AL 35173
(205) 655-7062
Fax (205) 655-7512
Pres: Jimmy Bragan

Birmingham Barons
PO Box 360007
Birmingham, AL 35236
(205) 988-3200
Fax (205) 988-9698
Pres: Bill Bill Hardekopf

Carolina Mudcats
PO Drawer 19045
Raleigh, NC 27619
(919) 781-4487
Fax (919) 881-9082
GM: Joe Kremer

Chattanooga Lookouts
PO Box 11002
Chattanooga, TN 37401
(615) 267-2208
Fax (615) 267-4258
GM: Bill Davidson

Greenville Braves
PO Box 16683
Greenville, SC 29606
(803) 299-3456
Fax (803) 277-7369
GM: Steve DeSalvo

Huntsville Stars
PO Box 2769
Huntsville, AL 35804
(205) 882-2562
Fax (205) 880-0801
GM: Don Mincher

Jacksonville Suns
PO Box 4756
Jacksonville, FL 32201
(904) 358-2846
Fax (904) 358-2845
GM: Peter Bragan, Jr.

Knoxville Smokies
633 Jessamine Street
Knoxville, TN 37917
(615) 525-3809
Fax (615) 523-9913
GM: Dan Rajkowski

Memphis Chicks
800 Home Run Lane
Memphis, TN 38104
(901) 272-1687
Fax (901) 278-3354
GM: David Hersh

Nashville Xpress
PO Box 23290
Nashville, TN 37202
(615) 242-4371
Fax (615) 256-5684
GM: Larry Schmittou

Orlando Cubs
287 S. Tampa Avenue
Orlando, FL 32805
(407) 872-7593
Fax (407) 649-1637
GM: Roger Wexelberg

Texas League

2442 Facet Oak
San Antonio, TX 78232
(210) 545-5297
Fax (210) 545-5298
Pres: Tom Kayser

Arkansas Travelers
P.O. Box 5599
Little Rock, AR 72215
(501) 664-1555
Fax (501) 664-1834
GM: Bill Valentine

El Paso Diablos
P.O. Drawer 4797
El Paso, TX 79914
(915) 755-2000
Fax (915) 757-0671
GM: Rick Parr

Jackson Generals
P.O. Box 4209
Jackson, MS 39296
(601) 981-4664
Fax (601) 981-4669
GM: Bill Blackwell

Midland Angels
P.O. Box 51187
Midland, TX 79710-1187
(915) 683-4251
Fax (915) 683-0994
GM: Monty Hoppel

San Antonio Missions
PO Box 28268
San Antonio, TX 78228
(210) 434-9311
Fax (210) 434-9431
GM: Burl Yarbrough

Shreveport Captains
PO Box 3448
Shreveport, LA 71133
(318) 636-5555
Fax (318) 636-5670
GM: Taylor Moore

Tulsa Drillers
P.O. Box 4448
Tulsa, OK 74159
(918) 744-5901
Fax (918) 747-3267
GM: Joe Preseren

Wichita Wranglers
P.O. Box 1420
Wichita, KS 67201
(316) 267-3372
Fax (316) 267-3382
GM: Steve Shaad

Class A

California League

2380 S. Bascom Avenue
Suite 200
Campbell, CA 95008
(408) 369-8038
Fax (408) 369-1409
Pres: Joe Gagliardi

Bakersfield Dodgers
PO Box 10031
Bakersfield, CA 93389
(805) 322-1363
Fax (805) 322-6199
GM: Rick Smith

Central Valley Rockies
PO Box 0048
Visalia, CA 93279
(209) 625-0480
Fax (209) 739-7732
GM: Bruce Bucz

High Desert Mavericks
12000 Stadium Road
Adelanto, CA 92301
(619) 246-6287
Fax (619) 246-3197
GM: Leanne Pagliai

Lake Elsinore Storm
PO Box 535
Lake Elsinore, CA 92531
(909) 245-4487
Fax (909) 245-0305
GM: Kevin Haughian

Modesto A's
PO Box 833
Modesto, CA 95353
(209) 529-7368
Fax (209) 529-7213
GM: Tim Marting

Rancho Cucamonga Quakes
P.O. Box 3538
Rancho Cucamonga, CA 91729
(909) 481-5000
Fax (909) 481-5005
GM: John LeCompte

Riverside Pilots
P.O. Box 56171
Riverside, CA 92517
(909) 276-3352
Fax (909) 276-4954
GM: Jack Patton

San Bernardino Spirit
P.O. Box 30780
San Bernardino, CA 92413
(909) 881-1836
Fax (909) 883-6179
GM: Patrick Brown

San Jose Giants
P.O. Box 21727
San Jose, CA 95151
(408) 297-1435
Fax (408) 297-1453
GM: Mark Wilson

Stockton Ports
P.O. Box 8550
Stockton, CA 95208
(209) 944-5943
Fax (209) 463-4937
GM: Dan Chapman

Carolina League

PO Box 9503
Greensboro, NC 27429
(910) 691-9030
Fax (910) 691-9070
Pres: John Hopkins

Durham Bulls
PO Box 507
Durham, NC 27702
(919) 688-8211
Fax (919) 688-4593
GM: Peter Anlyan

Frederick Keys
PO Box 3169
Frederick, MD 21701
(301) 662-0013
Fax (301) 662-0018
GM: Larry Martin

Kinston Indians
PO Box 3542
Kinston, NC 28501
(910) 527-9111
Fax (910) 527-2328
GM: North Johnson

Lynchburg Red Sox
PO Box 10213
Lynchburg, VA 24506
(804) 528-1144
Fax (804) 846-0768
GM: Paul Sunwall

Prince William Cannons
PO Box 2148
Woodbridge, VA 22193
(703) 590-2311
Fax (703) 590-5716
GM: Patrick Filippone

Salem Buccaneers
PO Box 842
Salem, VA 24153
(703) 389-3333
Fax (703) 389-9710
GM: Sam Lazzaro

Wilmington Blue Rocks
801 S. Madison Street
Wilmington, DE 19801
(302) 888-2015
Fax (302) 888-2032
GM: Chris Kemple

Winston-Salem Spirits
PO Box 4488
Winston-Salem, NC 27105
(910) 759-2233
Fax (910) 759-2042
GM: John Rocco

Florida State League

P.O. Box 349
Daytona Beach, Fl 32115
(904) 252-7479
Fax (904) 252-7495
Pres: Chuck Murphy

Brevard County Manatees
5800 Stadium Parkway
Melbourne, FL 32940
(407) 633-9200
Fax (407) 633-9210
GM: Ken Lehner

Charlotte Rangers
PO Box 3609
Port Charlotte, FL 33949
(813) 625-9500
Fax (813) 624-5168
GM: Tim Murphy

Clearwater Phillies
PO Box 10336
Clearwater, FL 34617
(813) 441-8638
Fax (813) 447-3924
GM: John Timberlake

Daytona Cubs
PO Box 15080
Daytona Beach, FL 32115
(904) 257-3172
Fax (904) 257-3382
GM: Jordan Kobritz

Dunedin Blue Jays
PO Box 957
Dunedin, FL 34697
(813) 733-9302
Fax (813) 734-7661
GM: Gary Rigley

Fort Myers Miracle
14400 Six Mile Cypress Pkwy.
Fort Myers, FL 33912
(813) 768-4281
Fax (813) 768-4211
GM: Mark Schuster

Lakeland Tigers
PO Box 90187
Lakeland, FL 33804
(813) 688-7911
Fax (813) 688-5399
GM: Karl Rogozenski

Osceola Astros
PO Box 422229
Kissimmee, FL 34742
(407) 933-5500
Fax (407) 847-6237
GM: Tim Bawmann

St. Lucie Mets
525 N.W. Peacock Blvd.
Port St. Lucie, FL 34986
(407) 871-2100
Fax (407) 878-9802
GM: Ross Vecchio

St. Petersburg Cardinals
PO Box 12557
St. Petersburg, FL 33733
(813) 822-3384
Fax (813) 95-1556
GM: Tony Flores

Sarasota Red Sox
PO Box 2816
Sarasota, FL 34230
(813) 365-4460
Fax (813) 365-4217
GM: Kevin Cummings

Tampa Yankees
PO Box 290698
Tampa, FL 33687
(813) 632-9855
Fax (813) 979-4752
GM: Chris Zieg

Vero Beach Dodgers
PO Box 2887
Vero Beach, FL 32961
(407) 569-4900
Fax (407) 567-0819
GM: Tom Simmons

West Palm Beach Expos
PO Box 3566
West Palm Beach, FL 33402
(407) 684-6801
Fax (407) 686-0221
GM: Rob Rabenecker

Midwest League

P.O. Box 936
Beloit, WI 53511
(608) 364-1188
Fax (608) 364-1913
Pres: George Spelius

Appleton Foxes
P.O. Box 464
Appleton, WI 54912
(414) 733-4512
Fax (414) 733-8032
GM: Kevin Scotellaro

Beloit Brewers
P.O. Box 855
Beloit, WI 53511
(608) 362-2272
Fax (608) 362-0418
GM: Steve Kretz

Burlington Bees
PO Box 824
Burlington, IA 52601
(319) 754-5705
Fax (319) 754-5882
GM: Ryan Richeal

Cedar Rapids Kernels
P.O. Box 2001
Cedar Rapids, IA 52406
(319) 363-3887
Fax (319) 363-5631
GM: Jack Roeder

Clinton Lumberkings
PO Box 1295
Clinton, IA 52733
(319) 242-0727
Fax (319) 242-1433
GM: Kevin Temperly

Fort Wayne Wizards
4000 Parnell Avenue
Fort Wayne, IN 46805
(219) 423-6400
Fax (219) 423-4611
GM: Mike Tatoian

Kane County Cougars
34W002 Cherry Lane
Geneva, IL 60134
(708) 232-8811
Fax (708) 232-8815
GM: Bill Larsen

Madison Hatters
PO Box 882
Madison, WI 53701
(608) 244-4287
Fax (608) 244-5482
GM: Tom O'Reilly

Peoria Chiefs
1524 W. Nebraska Ave.
Peoria, IL 61604
(309) 688-1622
Fax (309) 686-4516
GM: Greg Ayers

Quad City River Bandits
PO Box 3496
Davenport, IA 52808
(319) 324-2032
Fax (319) 324-3109
GM: Dan Kable

Rockford Royals
PO Box 6748
Rockford, IL 61125
(815) 964-5400
Fax (815) 961-2002
GM: Mike Holmes

South Bend Silver Hawks
PO Box 4218
South Bend, IN 46634
(219) 284-9988
Fax (219) 284-9950
GM: John Tull

Springfield Sultans
1351 N. Grand Avenue
Springfield, IL 62702
(217) 544-7300
Fax (217) 544-7388
GM: Lee Landers

West Michigan Whitecaps
50 Louis N.W.
Grand Rapids, MI 49503
(616) 451-6166
Fax (616) 451-3596
GM: Scott Lane

New York-Penn League

1629 Oneida Street
Utica, NY 13501
(315) 733-8036
Fax (315) 797-7403
Pres: Bob Julian

Auburn Astros
P.O. Box 651
Auburn, NY 13021
(315) 255-2489
Fax (315) 255-1883
GM: Derek Duin

Batavia Clippers
P.O. Box 802
Batavia, NY 14020
(716) 343-7531
Fax (716) 343-9372
GM: Bradley F. Rogers

Elmira Pioneers
P.O. Box 238
Elmira, NY 14902
(607) 734-1811
Fax (607) 734-4975
GM: Clyde Smoll

Hudson Valley Renegades
PO Box 661
Fishkill, NY 12524
(914) 838-0094
Fax (914) 838-0014
GM: Skip Weisman

Jamestown Jammers
7 E. Third Street
Jamestown, NY 14701
(716) 664-3925
Fax (716) 664-7192
GM: Mike Billoni

New Jersey Cardinals
PO Box 117
Augusta, NJ 07822
(201) 579-5000
Fax (201) 579-7502
GM: Tony Torre

Oneonta Yankees
95 River Street
Oneonta, NY 13820
(607) 432-3151
Fax (607) 432-1965
Pres: Sam Nader

Pittsfield Mets
PO Box 328
Pittsfield, MA 01201
(413) 499-6387
Fax (413) 448-6031
GM: Richard J. Murphy

St. Catharines Blue Jays
PO Box 1088
St. Catharines, Ontario L2R 3B0
(416) 641-5297
Fax (416) 641-3007
GM: Ellen H. Charles

Utica Blue Sox
PO Box 751
Utica, NY 13503
(315) 738-0999
Fax (315) 738-6992
GM: Rob Fowler

Vermont Expos
#4 Champlain Mall
Winooski, VT 05404
(802) 655-4200
Fax (802) 864-6830
GM: Chris Corley

Watertown Indians
PO Box 802
Watertown, NY 13601
(315) 788-8747
Fax (315) 788-5949
GM: Jack Tracz

Welland Pirates
PO Box 594
Welland, Ontario L3B 5R3
(416) 735-7634
Fax (416) 735-7114
GM: Brian Sloan

Northwest League

PO Box 848
Eugene, OR 97440
(503) 686-5412
Fax (503) 484-7672
Pres: Bob Richmond
(June-October)

PO Box 4941
Scottsdale, AZ 85261
(602) 483-8224
Fax (602) 443-3450
(permanent office)

Bellingham Mariners
1316 King Street
Bellingham, WA 98226
(206) 671-6347
Fax (206) 647-2254
GM: Jerry Walker

Bend Bucks
PO Box 6603
Bend, OR 97708
(503) 382-8011
Fax (503) 382-8875
GM: Jack Cain

Boise Hawks
5600 N. Glenwood
Boise, ID 83714
(208) 322-5000
Fax (208) 322-7432
GM: John Cunningham

Eugene Emeralds
PO Box 5566
Eugene, OR 97405
(503) 342-5367
Fax (503) 342-6089
GM: Bob Beban

Everett Giants
PO Box 7893
Everett, WA 98201
(206) 258-3673
Fax (206) 258-3675
GM: Melody Tucker

Southern Oregon A's
PO Box 1457
Medford, OR 97501
(503) 770-5364
Fax (503) 772-4466
GM: Fred Herrmann

Spokane Indians
PO Box 4758
Spokane, WA 99202
(509) 535-2922
Fax (509) 534-5368
GM: Andy Billig

Yakima Bears
PO Box 483
Yakima, WA 98907
(509) 457-5151
Fax (509) 457-9909
GM: Bob Romero

South Atlantic League

SOUTH ATLANTIC LEAGUE
P.O. Box 38
Kings Mountain, NC 28086
(704) 739-3466
Fax (704) 739-1974
Pres: John H. Moss

Albany Polecats
P.O. Box 50485
Albany, GA 31705-0009
(912) 435-6444
Fax (912) 435-6618
GM: Scott A. Skadan

Asheville Tourists
P.O. Box 1556
Asheville, NC 28802
(704) 258-0428
Fax (704) 258-0320
GM: Ron McKee

Augusta GreenJackets
PO Box 3746, Hill Sta.
Augusta, GA 30904
(404) 736-7889
Fax (404) 736-1122
GM: Chris Scheuer

Charleston RiverDogs
PO Box 20849
Charleston, SC 29413
(803) 723-7241
Fax (803) 723-2641
GM: Rob Dlugozima

Capital City Bombers
PO Box 7845
Columbia, SC 29202
(803) 256-4110
Fax (803) 256-4338
GM: Bill Shanahan

Columbus Redstixx
PO Box 1886
Columbus, GA 31902
(404) 571-8866
Fax (404) 571-9107
GM: John Dittrich

Fayetteville Generals
PO Box 64939
Fayetteville, NC 28306
(919) 424-6500
Fax (919) 424-4325
GM: Don Moushon

Greensboro Bats
PO Box 22093
Greensboro, NC 27420
(919) 275-1641
Fax (919) 273-7350
GM: John Frye

Hagerstown Suns
PO Box 230
Hagerstown, MD 21741
(301) 791-6266
Fax (301) 791-6066
GM: Bob Miller

Hickory Crawdads
PO Box 1268
Hickory, NC 28603
(704) 322-3000
Fax (704) 322-6137
GM: Marty Steele

Macon Braves
PO Box 4525
Macon, GA 31208
(912) 745-8943
Fax (912) 743-5559
GM: Ed Holtz

Savannah Cardinals
PO Box 3783
Savannah, GA 31414
(912) 351-9150
Fax (912) 352-9722
GM: Richard Sisler, Jr.

Spartanburg Phillies
PO Box 1721
Spartanburg, SC 29304
(803) 585-6279
Fax (803) 582-0877
GM: Fred Palmerino

West Virginia Wheelers
PO Box 4669
Charleston, WV 25304
(304) 925-8222
Fax (304) 344-0083
GM: Heath Brown

Rookies Leagues

Appalachian League

20360 Carson Lane
Bristol, VA 24202
(703) 669-3644
Fax (703) 669-2618
Pres: William Halstead

Bluefield Orioles
P.O. Box 356
Bluefield, WV 24701
(703) 326-1326
Fax (703) 326-1318
GM: George Fanning

Bristol Tigers
P.O. Box 1434
Bristol, VA 24203
(703) 466-8310
Fax (703) 466-2247
Pres: Boyce Cox

Burlington Indians
1450 Graham Street
Burlington, NC 27216
(919) 222-0223
Fax (919) 226-2498
GM: Dean Gyorgy

Danville Braves
PO Box 3637
Danville, VA 24543
(804) 791-3346
Fax (804) 791-3347
GM: Tim Cahill

Elizabethton Twins
136 S. Sycamore
Elizabethton, TN 37643
(615) 543-4395
GM: Bill Crow

Huntington Cubs
PO Box 7005
Huntington, WV 25775
(304) 429-1700
Fax (304) 429-1706
GM: Tom Glick

Johnson City Cardinals
PO Box 1535
Johnson City, TN 37605
(615) 461-4850
Fax (615) 461-4864
GM: Herb ledford

Kingsport Mets
2908 Ashley Street
Kingsport, TN 37664
(615) 246-6464
Fax (615) 245-1935
GM: Janice Archer

Martinsville Phillies
PO Box 3614
Martinsville, VA 24115
(703) 666-2000
Fax (703) 666-2139
GM: Timothy Cahill

Princeton Reds
PO Box 5646
Princeton, WV 24740
(304) 487-2000
Fax (304) 425-6999
GM: Jim Holland

Pioneer League

PO Box 2564
Spokane, WA 99220
(509) 456-7615
Fax (509) 456-1036
Pres: Jim McCurdy

Billings Mustangs
PO Box 1553
Billings, MT 59103
(406) 252-1241
Fax (406) 252-2968
GM: Bob Wilson

Butte Copper Kings
PO Box 186
Butte, MT 59703
(406) 723-8206
Fax (406) 723-3376
GM: Bob Larkins

Great Falls Dodgers
PO Box 1621
Great Falls, MT 59403
(406) 452-5311
Fax (406) 452-5311
GM: Ray Klesh

Helena Brewers
PO Box 4606
Helena, MT 59604
(406) 449-7616
Fax (406) 449-6979
GM: Joe Easton

Idaho Falls Braves
PO Box 2183
Idaho Falls, ID 83403
(208) 522-8366
Fax (208) 522-8363
GM: Kevin Green

Lethbridge Mounties
PO Box 1986
Lethbridge, Alberta T1J 4K5
(403) 327-7975
Fax (403) 327-8085
GM: Matt Ellis

Medicine Hat Blue Jays
PO Box 465
Medicine Hat, Alberta T1A 7G2
(403) 526-0404
Fax (403) 526-4000
GM: Kevin Friesen

Ogden Raptors
2404 Washington Blvd.
Suite 312
Ogden, UT 84401
(801) 393-2400
Fax (801) 393-2473
GM: John Stein

Arizona State League

P.O. Box 4941
Scottsdale, AZ 85261-4941
(602) 483-8224
Fax (602) 991-5766
Pres: Bob Richmond

Gulf Coast League

1503 Clower Creek Dr. #262
Sarasota, FL 34231
(813) 966-6407
Fax (813) 966-6872
Pres: Thomas J. Saffell

Mid-South League
PO Box 578
Booneville, MS 38829
(601) 462-5906
Pres: Richard Grottanelli

Proposed independent league

Winter Leagues

The following is a list of Winter baseball leagues. Many Major and Minor League players participate in these leagues. League schedules usually run from November through February.

Caribbean Baseball Confederation

Israel G. Gonzalez
(perimetral Oeste) 171-A
C.P. 83190
Hermosillo, Sonora, Mexico
(011-52-621) 43562
Fax (011-52-621) 49517
Commissioner: Horacio Lopez Diaz

The Dominican League

Av. de Febreo #218
Edificio Standard Quimica
4th Planta, Apartado Postal 1246
Santo Domingo, Dominican Republic
(809) 567-6371
Fax (809) 567-5720
Pres: Juan Herrerra-Puello

Aguilas Baseball Club
Apartado de Correos 111
Santiago, Dominican Republic
(809) 582-4310
Pres: Ricardo T. Hernandez

Escogido Baseball Club
Apartado 1187
Santiago, Dominican Republic
(809) 565-1910
Fax (809) 562-6699
Pres: Julio Morales

Estrellas Baseball Club
Avenida Independicia #33
San Pedro de Macoris
Dominican Republic
(809) 529-3340
Pres: Julio Morales

Licey Baseball Club
Estadio Quisqueya
Santo Domingo, Dominican Republic
(809) 567-3090
Fax (809) 542-7714
Pres: Domingo E. Pichardo

Calmanes del Sur (San Cristobal)
Apartado Postal 1723
Calle 12 #8
Reparto Julieta
Santo Domingo, Dominican Republic
(809) 566-3157
Pres: Servio Tulio Mancebo

Los Azucareros (La Romana)
Apartado Postal 145
La Romana, Dominican Republic
(809) 556-4955
Pres: Arturo Gil

The Mexican League
Pesqueria #401-R Altes
Edif. Burques
Novojoa, Sonora, Mexico
(52) (642) 2-31-00
Fax (52) 642-27250
Pres: Arturo Leon Lerma

Tijuana Baseball Club
Francisco Cardenas #100-203
Col. Aviacion
Tijuana, B.C.
(011-52-668) 62964
Pres: Jaime Bonilla Valdez

Mexicali Baseball Club
Estadio del Beisbol de la Cd.
Deportiva, Calz. Ex-Aviacion, s/n
Mexicali, B.C.
(011-656) 62695
Pres: Mario Hernandez M.

Hermosillo Baseball Club
Nayarti 130, Local 4
Hermosillo, Sonora, Mexico
Pres: Enrique Mazon

Guaymas Baseball Club
Zerimar Automotriz
Calz. Garcia Lopez y Fresno
Guaymas, Sonora, Mexico
Pres: Ramon Ramirez

Obregon Baseball Club
Yucatan y Nainari #294
Edificio 'c', Dpto. #11
Ed. Obregon, Sonora, Mexico
(011) 641-41156
Pres: Jose Maria Parada

Navojoa Baseball Club
Pesqueira y Matamoros Desp. #8
Novojoa, Sonora, Mexico
(011) 642-21433
Pres: Luis Salido Ibarra

Los Mochis Baseball Club
Guillermo Prieto 130 Nte.
Los Mochis, Sin., Mexico
(011) 681-50045
Pres: Roque Chavez Lopez

Guasave Baseball Club
Obregon #43
Guasave, Sin., Mexico
(011) 687-20000
Pres: Enrique Terminel

Culiacan Baseball Club
Carret. Intern. y Calle Deportiva
Culiacan, Sin., Mexico
(011) 671-28864
Pres: Juan Manuel Ley

Mazatlan Baseball Club
Estadio de Beisbol
Teodor Mariscal s/n
Apartado Postal 488
Mazatlan, Sin., Mexico
(011) 678-33012
Pres: Hermilo Diaz Bringas

Puerto Rican League

Ave. Munoz Rivera
Edif. First Federal
Rio Piedras, PR 00928
(809) 765-6285
Pres: Lcdo. Juan Cancel Rios

Arecibo Baseball Club
Apartado 2506
Arecibo, PR 00613
(809) 878-5200
Pres: Regino Babilonia

San Juan Baseball Club
P.O. Box AV
San Juan, PR 00936
(809) 754-1300
Pres: Ernesto Diaz

Caguas Baseball Club
P.O. Box 8877
Caguas, PR 00626
(809) 744-4343
Pres: Johnny Vasquez

Mayaguez Baseball Club
GPO Box 3786
San Juan, PR 00936
(809) 744-4343
Pres: Luis Gomez, Jr.

Ponce Baseball Club
Apartado 1524
Ponce, PR 00731
(809) 842-6116
Pres: Lcdo. Jose A. Cangiano

Santurce Baseball Club
GPO Box 1144
San Juan, PR 00936
(809) 765-0140
Pres: Lcdo. Reinaldo Paniagua Diez

The Venezuelan League

Avenida Sorbana
Edif. Marta - 2do. Piso, #25
Colinas de Bello Monte
Caracas, Venezuela
Telefax: (011-58-02) 751-0891
Pres: Rafael Marcial Germendia

Caracas Baseball Club
Avenida Francisco de Maranda
Centro Segueros
Piso 4 La Pas, oficina #526
Caracas, Venezuela
011-58 (2) 2380691
Pres: Pablo Moralez Chirinos

Aragua Baseball Club
Estadio Jose Perez Coimenares
Barrio La Democracia
Maracay - Edo.
Aragua, Venezuela
(043) 54-46-32
Pres: Homero Diaz Osuna

LaGuaira Baseball club
Edif. Cada, Avda. Soublette
Piso 1, Oficina #8
La Guaira, Venezuela
(031) 25-5-79
Pres: Pedro Padron Panza

Magallanes Baseball Club
Estadio Jose Bernardo Perez
Valencia - Edo Carabobo
Venezuela
(041) 21-59-44
Pres: Santiago Sanchez

Lara Baseball Club
Av. Rotaria, Estadio Barquisimeto
Barquisimeto - Edo. Lara
Venezuela
(051) 42-45-43
Pres: Adolfo Alvarez

Zulia Baseball Club
Ave. 8 (Santa Rita)
Edifco 'Las Carolinas' Local M-10
Maracaibo, Zulia
Venezuela
(061) 92-03-37
Pres: Lucas Rincon

Australian Baseball League

100 Victoria Street
Potts Point
Sydney, N.S.W.
Australia 2011
(011-61-2) 357-3595
Fax 357-7068
Comm: George Anderson

Adelaide Giants

283 Burbridge Road
Suite 29
Brooklyn, S.A. 5032 Australia
(08) 234-1877
GM: Kingsley Wellington

Brisbane Bandits

20 Duncan St., Suite 319
Fortitude Valley, QLD 4008 Australia
(07) 252-5898
GM: Tom Nicholson

Gold Coast Dolphins

Runaway Bay Marina, Ste. 14
245 Bayview Street
Runaway Bay, QLD 4216 Australia
(07) 577-4091
GM: Gary Coward

Melbourne Bushrangers

10 Cameron Street
Moreland, Victoria 3058 Australia
(03) 384-8299
GM: David White

Melbourne Monarchs

P.O. Box 463
Werst Footscray, Victoria
3012 Australia
(03) 689-3100
GM: Dennis Galimberti

Perth Heat

Level 3, South Shore Centre 83
The Esplanade
South Perth, W.A.
6151 Australia
(09) 474-2199
GM: Don Knapp

Sydney Blues

P.O. Box 249
Baulkham Hills, NSW
2153 Australia
(02) 899-4006
GM: Ian Maurice

Waverly Reds

32 Amelia Street
Wheelers Hill, Victoria
3150 Australia
(03) 560-1475
GM: Tony Peek

Amateur Baseball

The following summer collegiate baseball leagues are sanctioned members of the NCAA, AABC, USBF, NABF, and NBC, governing bodies of amateur baseball. Most leagues operate on a June to August schedule.

Alaska Baseball League

1625 Old Steese Highway
Fairbanks, AK 99701
(907) 452-1991
Comm: Ralph Seekins

Alaska Goldpanners
P.O. Box 71154
Fairbanks, AK 99707
(907) 451-0095
GM: Don Dennis

Anchorage Bucs
P.O. Box 24061
Anchorage, AK 99524
(907) 272-2827

Anchorage Glacier Pilots
P.O. Box 100895
Anchorage, AK 99510
(907) 274-3627
GM: Lou Sinnett

Hawaii Island Movers
P.O. Box 17865
Honolulu, HI 96817
(808) 521-4761
GM: Don Takaki

Kenai Peninsula Oilers
P.O. Box 5008
Kenai, AK 99611
(907) 283-4271
GM: Coral Seymour

Mat-Su Miners
SRD 9480
Palmer, AK 99645
(907) 745-4901
GM: Stan Zaborack

North Pole Nicks
P.O. Box 55681
North Pole, AK 99705
(907) 452-5488
GM: Bud Hollowell

Arizona Summer Collegiate League
3652 W. Marco Polo
Glendale, AZ 85308
(602) 582-8995
Comm: Rick Siebert

Southern California Collegiate league
830 Hilly Field lane
San Bernardino, CA 92407
(909) 887-2041

Alaska Central League

P.O. Box 1332
Kenai, AK 99611
(907) 269-4122
Pres: Jack Slama

Atlantic Collegiate Baseball League

130 Colony Avenue
Park Ridge, NJ 07656
(201) 391-9376
Pres: Bob Pertsas

Brooklyn Clippers
385 Ashland Avenue
Staten Island, NY 10309
(718) 317-1249
GM: Tony Barone

Long Island Nationals
25-06 30th Drive
Long Island City, NY 11102
(718) 728-3015
GM: Eric Lincoln

Nassau Collegians
37-45 89th Street
Jackson Heights, NY 11372
(718) 478-2582
GM: Steve Balsan

New Jersey A's
245 Old Hook Road
Westwood, NJ 07675
(201) 666-1520
GM: Mike Gremaud

New York Generals
25 Woodglen Drive
New City, NY 10956
(914) 634-7384
GM: Mort Meyers

**North Plainfield
Jersey Pilots**
401 Timber Drive
Berkeley Heights, NJ 07922
(201) 464-8042
GM: Ben Smookler

Quakertown Blazers
200 E. Broad Street
Quakertown, PA 18951
(215) 536-5845
GM: C. Robert Roth

Scranton Red Soxx
1224 Monroe Avenue
Dunmore, PA 18512
(717) 346-3446
GM: Bill Howerton

Tri-State League
6520 S.W. 21st Street
Topeka, KS 66615
(913) 272-4164
Pres: Lee Dodson

*This is a semi-pro league
that began its first season
this past Summer. Teams
include Beatrice, NE; I
ndependence, Manhattan,
Salina, Sterling & Topeka, KS.*

Cape Cod Baseball League

P.O. Box 164
South Harwich, MA 02661
(508) 430-7207
Comm: Fred Ebbett

Bourne Braves
42 Tan Bark Road
Marston Hills, MA 02648
(508) 428-0525
GM: Ed Gendron

Brewster White Caps
350 Run Hill Road
Brewster, MA 02631
(508) 896-5665
GM: Barry Souder

Chatham A's
82 Bearberry Lane
Chatham, MA 02659
(508) 452-6620
GM: Jack Hammond

Cotuit Kettleers
P.O. Box 371
Cotuit, MA 02635
(508) 428-2782
GM: Arnold Mycock

Falmouth Commodores
100 Gifford Street
Falmouth, MA 02540
(508) 540-8521
GM: Tom Moran

Harwich Mariners
45 Hiawatha Road
Harnockport, MA 02646
(508) 432-8748
GM: Jim McGonigle

Hyannis Mets
68 Barnacle Road
Yarmouthport, MA 02675
(508) 362-2895
GM: Alan Harrison

Orleans Cardinals
P.O. Box 2200
Orleans, MA 02653
(508) 255-3320
GM: Dave Mullholland

Wareham Gatemen
2482 Cranberry Highway
Wareham, MA 02571
(617) 295-6016
GM: Dick Landis

Yarmouth-Dennis Red Sox
8 Hosking Lane
S. Yarmouth, MA 02664
(508) 394-9466
GM: Jack Martin

Central Illinois Collegiate League
RR #13, Box 369
Bloomington, IL 61704
(309) 828-4429
Commissioner: Mike Woods
Deputy Comm: Tom Lamonica

Champaign County Colts
902 W. Church
Champaign, IL 61821
(217) 384-3080
GM: Bob Auler

Danville Dans
4 Maywood
Danville, IL 61832
(217) 443-3588
GM: Rick Kurth

Decatur Blues
1416 W. Decatur
Decatur, IL 62522
(217) 429-4626
GM: Galen S. Woods

Fairview Heights Mets
5111 West Main
Belleville, IL 62223
(309) 235-0020
GM: Bob Becker

Lincoln Collegiates
P.O. Box 218
Lincoln, IL 62656
(217) 732-8770
GM: Chuck Lindstrom

Springfield Rifles
2048 Cambridge
Springfield, IL 62704
(217) 787-5387
GM: Claude Kracik

Twin City Stars
907 N. School St.
Normal, IL 61761
(309) 452-3317
GM: Duffy Bass

Great Lakes Summer Collegiate League
P.O. Box 1121
Bowling Green, OH 43402
(419) 354-5556
President: Lou Laslo

Bowling Green Breeze
16630 N. Rive Road
Pemberville, OH 43450
(419) 287-4362
GM: Clifford Duncan

Cincinnati Midland Indians
3269 Broadwell St.
Cincinnati, OH 45211
(513) 662-3667
GM: Gary Beck

Columbus All-Americans
50 W. Broad, Suite 2000
Columbus, OH 43215
(614) 221-3151
GM: Jerry Dicuccio

Lima Locos
3700 South Dixie
Lima, OH 45804
(419) 991-3701
GM: Barry Ruben

Muncie Chiefs
7914 W. Key Drive
Muncie, IN 47304
(317) 759-9231
GM: Kyle Reiser

Toledo All-American Coach
5060 Alexis Road
Sylvania, OH 43560
(419) 885-4601
GM: Tom McGuire

Jayhawk League

5 Adams Place
Halstead, KS 67056
(316) 835-2589
Commissioner: Bob Considine

Amarillo Texans
1211 West Tenth
Amarillo, Texas
(806) 379-7755
GM: Mike Moore

Clarinda Iowa A's
225 E. Lincoln
Clarinda, IA 51632
(712) 542-4272
GM: Merle J. Eberly

Elkhart Dusters
PO Box 1117
Elkhart, KS 67950
(316) 697-2137
GM: Jerry Colborn

Hays Larks
1517 Henry
Hays, Kansas 67601
(913) 625-2137
GM: Laverne Schumacher

St. Joseph Cardinals
1108 S. 37th Street
St. Joseph, MO 66106
(816) 279-4487
GM: Chris Blum

Liberal Bee Jays
1033 North Prospect
Liberal, KS 67901
(316) 624-7000
GM: Don Carlile

Nevada Griffons
Route #3
Nevada, Missouri 64772
(417) 667-5760
GM: Darryl Miller

Red Oak Red Sox
902 Reed Street
Red Oak, IA 51566
(712) 623-3511
GM: Larry Greenough

Topeka Capitols
220 S.E. Sixth
Topeka, KS 66603
(913) 276-8201
Pres: Jim Callaway

Wichita Broncos
865 Fabrique
Wichita, KS
(316) 687-2309
GM: J.D. Schneider

Northeast Collegiate Baseball League

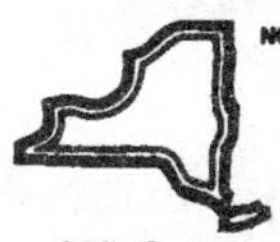

905 Ontario Street
Schenectady, NY 12306
(518) 372-5296
Commissioner: Hank Cuputo

Broome Rangers
P.O. Box 467
Chenango Bridge, NY 13745
(607) 648-5276
GM: Edwin Daub

Cohocton Redwings
P.O. Box 302
Wayland, NY 14572
(716) 728-2951
GM: Jim Burke

Cortland Apples
83 Main Street
Cortland, NY 13045
(607) 753-1334
GM: Donald F. Doloisio

Elmira Horseheads
RD #3, Del. #173A
Elmira, NY 14903
(607) 734-1598
GM: Jeff Manwaring

Little Falls Diamonds
P.O. Box 1022
Little Falls, NY 13365
(315) 823-0497
GM: Neil Baum

Rome Indians
515 E. Bloomfield Road
Rome, NY 13440
(315) 337-7894
GM: Larry Delutis

Schenectady Mohawks
P.O. Box 13145
Albany, NY 12212
(518) 482-7714
GM: Forrest Davis

Syracuse Jr. Chiefs
613 Pond Street
Syracuse, NY 13208
(315) 422-8851
GM: Joseph Antonio

Shenandoah Valley League
P.O. Box 2246
Staunton, VA 24401
(703) 886-1748
President: Dave Biery

Front Royal Cardinals
P.O. Box 1296
Front Royal, VA 22630
(703) 635-2668
GM: Darryl Windham

Harrisonburg Turks
22 Laurel Street
Harrisonburg, VA 22801
(703) 434-5919
GM: Bob Wease

New Market Rebels
P.O. Box 234
New Market, VA 22844
(703) 740-8727
GM: Tom Linski

Staunton Braves
809 Rutherford Street
Staunton, VA 24401
(703) 886-7601
GM: Tom Chrisman

Waynesboro Generals
P.O. Box 243
Waynesboro, VA 22980
(703) 943-4359
GM: Pete Peloso

Winchester Royals
P.O. Box 2485
Winchester, VA 22601
(703) 662-8788
GM: Bill Collins

San Diego Collegiate League
948 Jasmine Court
Carlsbad, CA 92009
Commissioner: Jerry Clements

Unlimited Amateur Baseball

The following leagues are considered Unlimited Amateur (semi-pro) status. Players who are former pros, semi-pros, amateur and collegiates are allowed to play in these leagues without jeapardizing their amateur and professional status. These are non-paying leagues.

National Semi-Pro Baseball Association

P.O. Box 29965
Atlanta, GA 30359
(404) 296-0800
Pres: Donald Valentine

Eastern State Baseball League

3706 Kennedy Blvd.
Jersey City, 07307
(201) 656-7780
Pres: F. Dutch Gesslien

Clifton Indians
956 Broad Street
Newark, NJ 07107
(201) 777-7245
G.M.: Ray Danbrowney

Cory Angels
28 Columia Avenue
Jersey City, NJ 07,307
(201) 656-0698
GM: Jim Bailey

Dumont A.C.
99 E. Revere Dr.
Dumont, NJ 07628
(201) 385-8737
GM: Joe Comastro

Jersey City Rangers
302 Paterson Plank Road
Jersey City, NJ 07307
(201) 798-6576
GM: Jim Gabriele

Jersey City Trojans
2767 Kennedy Blvd.
Jersey City, NJ 07306
(201) 432-6684
GM: Tony Carlucci

Montclair Eagles
139 High Street
Montclair, NJ 07042
(201) 744-8584
GM: Rich Walker

Newark Sharks
238 North IIth Street
Newark, NJ 07107
(201) 481-6189
GM: Charlie Strickland

Summit Anchors
3706 Kennedy Blvd.
Jersey City, NJ 07307
(201) 656-7780
GM: F. Dutch Gesslein

Metropolitan Baseball League

577 Pine Avenue
Saddle Brook, NJ 07662
(201) 791-9265
Commissioner: Bruce McFarlane

American Division

Hackensack Troasts
301 Euclid Avenue
Hackensack, NJ 07602
(201) 342-3679
GM: Dennis Mamatz

Little Ferry Giants
136 Brinkerhoff St.
Ridgefield Park, NJ 07660
(201) 641-3974
GM: Joe Stauffer

Moonachie Braves
464 Liberty Street #309
Little Ferry, NJ 07643
(201) 641-0454
GM: Steve Dembrowski

Saddle Brook Colonials
67 Strathmore Terrace
Saddle Brook, NJ 07662
(201) 797-0365
GM: Art Vander Sande

Teaneck Merchants
106 Chestnut Street
Emerson, NJ 07630
(201) 265-6208
GM: Jon Vatcher

Waldwick Senators
7 Douglas St.
Waldwick, NJ 07463
(201) 445-1985
G M.: Dave Anderson

National Division

Clifton AAMCO Baseball
156 Poplar Avenue
Hackensack, NJ 07602
(201) 488-5438
John Celentano

Clifton Phillies
O-68 Blue Hill Ave.
Fair Lawn, NJ 07410
(201) 796-6699
GM: Bob Potts

Montclair Red Hawks
80 Morningside Rd.
Verona, NJ 07044
(201) 239-3647
GM: Norm Schoenig

Paterson Cardinals
6 Stevenson Lane
Upper Saddle River, NJ 07458
(201) 825-1290
GM: Paul Manganelli

Verona Express
12 Cliff Street
Verona, NJ 07044
(201) 239-2581
GM: Fred Hill

Wayne Athletics
55 Hillside Terrace
Wayne, NJ 07470
(201) 694-8962
G M.: Russ Pudue

Northern Baseball League of Vermont
Box 424
Saxtons River, VT 05154
(802) 869-2020
Pres: Dave Moore

Bennington Generals
115 River Street
Bennington, VT 05201
GM: Bob Long

Battleboro Maples
Box 115
Battleboro, VT 05301
GM: Frank Marach

Burlington A's
397 Saint Paul Street
Burlington, VT 05401
GM: Kevin Mitchell

Hanover Tigers
RR #1, Box 301
Hartland, VT 05048
GM: Larry Fortier

Saxtons River Pirates
Box 424
Saxtons River, VT 05154
GM: Dave Moore

Springfield Blue Sox
RR #1, Box 245
Perkinsville, VT 05156
GM: Dale Whitney

Walpole Blue Jays
Route 123
Drewsville, NH 03604
GM: Rick Prentiss

Canadian Baseball

The following are Canadian Senior and Junior baseball leagues that are similar in status to the U.S. "Unlimited Amateur" divisions.

Eastern Ontario League

459 Murray Street
Peterborough, Ontario
Canada K9H 2T7
(705) 742-0635
Pres: Doug Lustic

Kootenay International Senior Baseball League

P.O. Box 1214
Grand Forks, B.C. V0H 1H0
(604) 442-2238
Pres: Larry Seminoff

Grand Forks Slag Dusters
P.O. Box 404
Greenwood, B.C. V0H 1J0
(604) 445-6390
GM: Dave Clemmons

Kettle Falls Bolts
P.O. Box 61
Kettle Falls, WA 99141
(509) 738-2106
GM: Gary Bolt

Trail Cardinals
45 Hazlewood Drive
Trail, B.C. V1R 1E8
(604) 368-6640
GM: Darrell St. Denis

Trail Orioles
P.O. Box 465
Montrose, B.C. V0G 1P0
(604) 367-6286
GM: Lou Cicchetti

Labatt's Major Baseball League

Harwood, Ontario K0K 2H0
(416) 342-3680
Pres: John Tapscott

Black Rainbow Challenge
30 Elm Drive East #906
Mississauga, Ontario L5A 4C3
(416) 896-1521
GM: Phil Edwards

East York Quinns
40 Eastlea Crescent
Agincourt, Ontario M1T 3A6
(416) 299-3972
GM: Alf Payne

Etobicoke Indians
2045 Russett Road
Mississauga, Ontario L4Y 1B8
(416) 848-0268
GM: Bill Thompson

Leaside Hurricanes
101 King Edward Avenue
Toronto, Ontario M5C 5J7
(416) 429-7361
GM: Jim Eliopoulos

Newmarket Hawks
16 Blackstone Court
Holland Landine
Ontario L0G 1H0
(416) 898-6171
GM: Scott Rettie

North York Blues
122 Trinnel Blvd.
Scarborough, Ontario M1L 1S7
(416) 265-0899
GM: Larry Tearun

Scarborough Majors
43 Winstanly Crescent
Scarborough, Ontario M1B 1N3
(416) 286-6721
GM: Sid Barber

Major Inter-County Baseball League
640 Westmount Road, West
Kitchener, Ontario N2M 1R8
(519) 742-6817
Lorne Hamel

Brantford Red Sox
7 Candlewood Drive
Brantford, Ontario N3R 5Z9
(519) 752-9271
GM: Walter Gretzky

Guelph Royals
Box 964
Guelph, Ontario N1H 6N1
(519) 822-8511
GM: David E. Hastings

Hamilton Cardinals
736 Beach Blvd.
Hamilton, Ontario L8H 6Y8
(416) 549-5964
GM: Ralph Stewart

Kitchener Panthers
18 Roehampton Court
Kitchener, Ontario N2A 3L1
(519) 748-9320
GM: Max Rausch

London Majors
52 Boullee Street
London, Ontario N5Y 1T6
(519) 659-3927
GM: Arden Eddie

Niagara Falls Mariners
5034 Victoria Avenue
Niagara Falls, Ontario L2E 4E1
(416) 356-3902
GM: Bob Lavelle

St. Thomas Elgins
P.O. Box 134
St. Thomas, Ontario N5P 3T7
(519) 631-7225
GM: Bill Wilkinson

Stratford Hillers
187 Ontario Street
Stratford, Ontario N5A 3H3
(519) 273-4145
GM: Dennis Schooley

Toronto Maple Leafs Baseball Club
42 Chestnut Hills Parkway
Islington, Ontario M9A 3P6
(416) 483-2111
GM: Jack Dominico

Waterloo Tigers
102B Northlake Place
Waterloo, Ontario N2V 1B1
(519) 746-5068
GM: Fred Kursikowski

New Brunswick Senior Baseball League
70 Alma Street #11
Moncton, N.B. E1C 4Y4
(506) 854-0656
GM: G.J. (Greg) Yeomans

Chatham Ironmen
27 Center Steet
Chatham, N.B. E1N 1K4
GM: Mike Noel

Fredericton Schooners
386 Queen Street
Fredericton, N.B. E3B 1B2
(506) 472-3217
David Saunders

Grannans LaBatts Blue Jays
259 Gault Road
Saint John, N.B. E2M 5H1
GM: David O'Toole

Moncton Mets
P.O. Box 862
Moncton, N.B. E1C 8N6
GM: Bob Scott

New Brunswick Junior Baseball League
305 Inglewood Drive
Grand Bay, N.B. E0G 1W0
(506) 738-8713
Pres: Bill James

Bathurst Thunderbirds
1170 Rocklane Drive
Bathurst, N.B. E2A 3T9
(506) 546-3834
Mike Brophy

Chatham Jr. Ironmen
P.O. Box 284
Chatham, N.B. E1N 3A6
(506) 773-6796
Mike Bowes

Fredericton Vikings
8 Downing Street
Fredericton, N.B. E3A 4M6
(506) 472-3656
Billy Saunders

Moncton Cubs
175 Dominion Street
Moncton, N.B. E1C 6H2
(506) 382-1058
Rene LeBlanc

Newcastle Cardinals
P.O. Box 402
Douglastown, N.B. E0C 1H0
(506) 773-6619
Robert Stewart

Riverview Sprites
7 Ivan Court #29
Moncton, N.B. E1C 8T3
(506) 384-9638
Kevin Lewis

Saint John Dodgers
108 Boyaner Cres.
Saint John, N.B. E2J 4C7
(506) 696-6988
Harry Stephenson

Saint John Pepsis
820 Harding Street
Saint John, N.B. E2M 3M6
(506) 672-4008
Ian Webster

Amateur Leagues

The following is a listing of selected amateur baseball leagues in the United States. These leagues represent semi-pro baseball, unlimited amateur, etc.

Adray Baseball League
285 Snow Court
Dearbourn, MI 48124
(313) 274-8700

Industrial Baseball League
8757 Georgia Ave., Ninth Floor
Silver Spring, MD 20910
Pres: Duck J. Lee

Greater Illinois Baseball League
6206 N. Hoyne Ave., 3C
Chicago, IL 60659
(312) 465-8333
Commissioner: Marcey Ruiz

Bluegrass Baseball League
3125 Chelsa Drive
Lexington, KY 40503
(606) 223-5497
Pres: Ronald McLeod

Buckeye Baseball League
610 Mitchell East
Cincinnati, OH 45217
(513) 571-1284
Pres: James H. Gruenwald

Bronxborough Baseball League
967 Neill Avenue
Bronx, NY 10462
(212) 892-5315
Pres: Bruno Franco

Central Ohio Baseball League
2711 Ridge Road
Zanesville, OH 43701
(614) 453-9663
Pres: Moe Carpenter

Colonial Baseball League
446 Pinebrook Blvd.
New Rochelle, NY 10804
(201) 778-7978
Pres: Dick Caswell

Columbiana County Baseball League
2457 Woodbine Avenue
East Leverpool, OH 43920
(216) 385-0726
Pres: Gary Daugherty

Credit Union Baseball League
12186 Queens Brigade Drive
Fairfax, VA 22030
Pres: Tony Johnson

Cuyahoga County Baseball League
12269 Sprague Road
North Royalton, OH 44133
(216) 845-5468
Pres: Frank Rozum

Cullman County Baseball League
Route 2, Box 144
Falkville, AL 35622
(205) 462-3697
Pres: Phillip Hill

Detroit AABC Baseball League
4010 14th Street
Ecorse, MI 48229
(313) 383-4767
Pres: Robert Armstrong

Garden State Baseball League
99 Northgate Village
Burlington, NJ 08016
(609) 386-7687
Pres: Ken Stephon

Illinois Suburban Baseball League
99 Northgate Village
Burlington, NJ 08016
(609) 386-7687
Pres: Ken Stephon

Illinois Suburban Baseball League
6700 S. Brainard #421
Countryside, IL 60525
(312) 579-9440
Dir: Al Oremus

Lake County Baseball League
1651 Mentor #3406
Painesville, OH 44077
(216) 357-6389
Pres: F. Robert Faile

Long Island Baseball League
P.O. Box 714
Garden City, NY 11530
(516) 485-6200
Pres: Philip O'Shea

Maryland State Baseball Association
12406 Keynote Lane
Bowie, MD 20715
(301) 468-9953
Commissioner: Charles Blackburn

Metro Suburban Baseball League
1014 N. Alexander
Royal Oak, MI 48067
(313) 546-2047
Pres: Joe Busto

Middle Georgia Baseball League
110 McLean Drive
Warner Robins, GA 31093
(912) 862-3865
Dir: Charles Stevens

Mohawk Hudson Baseball League
131 Main Street
Saugerties, NY 12477
(914) 647-5480
Commissioner: Jack Keeley

Mustang Baseball League
P.O. Box 29965
Atlanta, GA 30359
(404) 455-9731
Dir: Donald Valentine

Northern Michigan Baseball League
3763 Country Club Blvd.
Petoskey, MI 49770
(616) 347-2023
Dir: Bill Hewtitt

Northwest Suburban Baseball League
840 Maple Avenue
Downers Grove, IL 60515
(312) 666-1855
Pres: Bob Kurzka

Peach Baseball League
2612 Oak Shadow Lane
Atlanta, GA 30345
(404) 633-3653
Dir: Gary Staab

Queens Baseball Alliance
41-08 43rd Street
Sunnyside, NY 11104
(212) 784-4160
Pres: William Penney

Richmond County Federal Baseball League
2750 Amboy Street
Staten Island, NY 10306
(718) 351-9233
Pres: Patrick Maglio

San Diego Collegiate League
948 Jasmine Court
Carlsbad, CA 92008
Commissioner: Jerry Clements

Southern Louisiana Baseball League
Route 2, Box 342
Iberville, LA 70746
(504) 642-5797
Dir: Bill Powell

**Suffolk County
Baseball League**
1130 14th Street
West Babylon, NY 11704
(516) 888-0094
Dir: Joe Pepitone

Tri-County Baseball League
7661 View Place Drive
Cincinnati, OH 45224
(513) 771-1818
Pres: Robert Anderson

Tri State League
P.O. Box 519
Dalton, GA 30720
(404) 278-1151
Pres: David Erby

Western International League
7205 Wright Avenue, S.W.
Seattle, WA 98136
(206) 587-0277
Dir: Gary Thomson

International Tournaments

The following two international tournaments are
independent of the AABC, NABF, and NBC
tournaments.

**Grand Forks International
Labor Day Tournament**
P.O. Box 1214
Grand Forks, B.C.
Canada V0H 1H0
(604) 442-2238
Dir: Larry Seminoff
(Largest international
semi-pro tournament in Canada)

**United States Open Amateur
Baseball Tournament**
P.O. Box 971
Minden, NV 92413
(702) 782-4899
(800) 477-OPEN
Ex. Dir: Keith D. Lowe

Listed below are the provincial addresses for Baseball
Canada. All baseball in Canada is of amateur status.
There are no professional leagues except for a few
teams that are members of the U.S. professional and
minor leagues.

Baseball Canada

1600 James Naismith Drive
Goucester, Ontario
Canada K1B 5N4
(613) 748-5606

Alberta Baseball
14904-121A Avenue
Edmonton, Alberta T5V 1A3
Jay Dew

British Columbia Baseball
1200 Hornby Street
Vancouver, B.C. V6Z 2E2
(604) 687-3333
Wayne Norton

Manitoba Baseball
1700 Ellice Avenue
Winnipeg, Manitoba R3H 0B1
(204) 786-5641
Guy Constant

New Brunswick Baseball
451 Charlotte Street
Fredericton, N.B. E3B 1L9
(506) 454-7283

Newfoundland Baseball
Provincial Recreation Center
St. John's, Newfoundland A1B 5T7
(709) 368-2819
Ken Dawe

The following amateur, international, and professional baseball organizations promote the goodwill and excellence of baseball throughout the world.

Nova Scotia Baseball
P.O. Box 3010 South
Halifax, N.S. B3J 3G6
(902) 423-3859
Ron Jefferson

Ontario Baseball
Box 213
Fresherton, Ontario N0C 1E0
(519) 924-2574
Ron Pegg

Prince Edward Island Baseball
RR #5
Charlottetown, P.E.I. C1A 7J8
(902) 569-2038
James Koughan

Quebec Baseball
4545 Pierre Du Coubertin
Montreal, Quebec H1V 3R2
(514) 252-3000
Leonard Pelland

Saskatchewan Baseball
2205 Victoria Avenue
Regina, Sask. S4P 0S4
(306) 522-3651
Ron Knaus

B.C. Senior Baseball Association
P.O. Box 1214
Grand Forks, G.C. V0H 1H0
(604) 442-2238
Commissioner: Larry Seminoff

International Baseball Association
201 S. Capitol Avenue, Suite 490
Indianapolis, IN 46225
(317) 237-5757
Fax (317) 237-5758
Pres: Dr. Robert Smith
Pres. Telephone: (618) 664-1840

All American Baseball Association

340 Walker Drive
Zanesville, OH 43701
(614) 453-7349
Pres: Dino Zarrella

American Amateur Baseball Congress
P.O. Box 467
118-19 Redfield Plaza
Marshall, MI 49068
(616) 781-2002
Pres: Joe Cooper

American Legion Baseball
National Americanism Commission
P.O. Box 1055
Indianapolis, IN 46206
(317) 635-8411

Association of Professional Baseball
Players of America
12062 Valley View Street Suite 211
Garden Grove, CA 92645
(714) 892-9900
Pres: John McHale

Babe Ruth Baseball
1770 Brunswick Avenue
P.O. Box 5000
Trenton, NJ 08638
(609) 695-1434
Fax (609) 695-2505
Pres: Ronald Tellefsen

**Baseball Writers Assoc.
of America**
36 Brookfield Road
Fort Salonga, NY 11768
(516) 757-0562
Pres: Phil Pepe

Baseball Chapel
P.O. Box 300
Bloomingdale, NJ 07403
(201) 838-8111
Pres: Bobby Richardson

Baseball Statistics Bureau
Elias Sports Bureau
500 Fifth Avenue
New York, NY 10036
(212) 869-1530

Howe Sportsdata International
Boston Fish Pier
West Bldg. 2, Suite 306
Boston, MA 02210
(617) 269-0304

**Continental Amateur Baseball
Association**
82 University Street
Westerville, OH 43081
(614) 882-1361
Pres: Roger Tremaine

Baseball Canada
1600 James Naismith Drive
Goucester, Ontario
Canada K1B 5N4
(613) 748-5606

Little League Baseball, Inc.
P.O. Box 3485
Williamsport, PA 17701
(717) 326-1921
Pres: Dr. Creighton Hale

**Major League Baseball
Players Association**
805 Third Avenue
New York, NY 10022
(212) 826-0808
Ex. Dir: Donald Fehr

**Major League Baseball
Player Relations**
350 Park Avenue
New York, NY 10022
(212) 371-2211
Ex. Dir: Barry Rona

**Major League Baseball
Productions**
1212 Avenue of the Americas
New York, NY 10036
(212) 921-8100
Pres: James Holland

**Major League Baseball Umpire
Development**
P.O. Box A
St. Petersburg, FL 33731
(813) 823-1286
Pres: Edwin Lawrence

Major League Scouting Bureau
23712 Birtcher Drive, Suite A
El Toro, CA 92630
(714) 458-7600
Pres: Don Pries

**Major League Baseball Umpires
Association**
3 Girard Plaza, Suite 2106
Philadelphia, PA 19102
(215) 568-7273

**National Association of
Professional Baseball Leagues**
P.O. Box A
St. Petersburg, FL 33731
(813) 822-6937

**American Baseball Coaches
Association**
P.O. Box 3545
Omaha, NE 68103
(402) 733-0374
Pres: Jerry Miles

National Amateur Baseball Federation
12406 Keynote Lane
Bowie, MD 20715
(301) 262-0770
Pres: Robert Frank

National Baseball
Hall of Fame
Box 590
Cooperstown, NY 13326
(607) 547-9988
Pres: Edward Stack

National Baseball Congress
P.O. Box 1420
Wichita, KS 67201
(316) 267-3372
Pres: Bob Rich, Jr.

National Semi-Pro Baseball
Association
Box 29965
Atlanta, GA 30359
(404) 296-0800
Pres: Donald Valentine

Pony Baseball, Inc.
P.O. Box 225
Washington, PA 15301
(412) 225-1060
Pres: Roy Gillispie

Society of American Baseball
Research
P.O. Box 93183
Cleveland, OH 44101
(216) 575-0500
Ex. Dir: Morris Eckhouse

United States Baseball
Federation
2160 Greenwood Avenue
Trenton, NJ 08609
(609) 586-2381
Pres: Mark Marquess

Caribbean Baseball
Confederation
171-A, C.P. 83190
Hermosillo, Sonora, Mexico
(52-621) 4-35-62

U.S. Open Baseball
P.O. Box 971
Minden, NV 89423
(702) 782-4899
Ex. Dir: Keith D. Lowe

Baseball Publications

The following is a list of publications that are oriented towards the sport of baseball.

**USA Today Baseball
Weekly**
1000 Wilson Blvd.
Arlington, VA 22229
(703) 276-3400

Baseball America's Publications
P.O. Box 2089
Durham, NC 27702
(800) 845-2726

Baseball News
P.O. Box A
St. Petersburg, FL 33731
(813) 823-4050

Baseball Quarterly Reviews
P.O. Box 9343
Schenectady, NY 12309

Collegiate Baseball
P.O. Box 50566
Tucson, AZ 85703
(602) 623-7495

Baseball Cards
Baseball Card News
700 E. State Street
Iola, WI 54990
(715) 445-2214

Baseball Marketplace
P.O. Box 1417
Princeton, NJ 08542
(609) 921-8599

Old Tyme Baseball News
P.O. Box 833
Petoskey, MI 49770
(616) 348-3982

SABR Bulletin
P.O. Box 93183
Cleveland, OH 44101
(216) 575-0500

Sports All Stars Baseball
699 Madison Avenue
New York, NY 10021
(212) 371-8500

**Street & Smith's Baseball
Yearbook**
304 E. 45th Street
New York, NY 10017
(212) 880-8698

Baseball Digest
990 Grove Street
Evanston, IL 60201
(312) 941-6440

World Baseball Magazine
IBA
Pan American Plaza, Suite 490
Indianapolis, IN 46225
(317) 237-5757

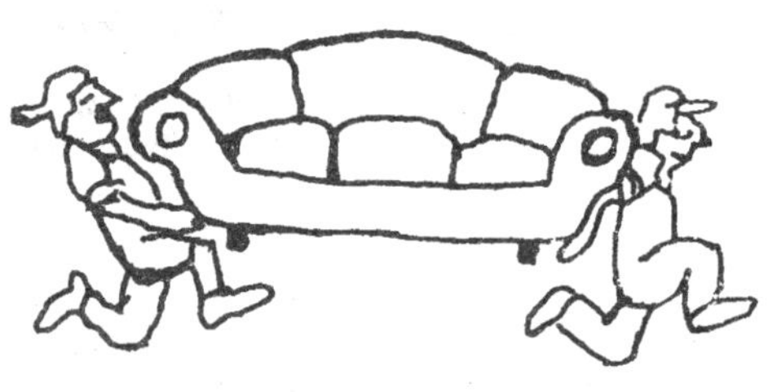

MOVING???

BE SURE TO SUPPLY
THE AUTHOR WITH
YOUR **NEW** ADDRESS!

Ed Kobak, Jr.
Global Sports Productions, Ltd.
1223 Broadway, Suite 102
Santa Monica, CA 90404
(310) 454-9480

Basketball

National Basketball Association

Olympic Tower
645 Fifth Avenue
New York, NY 10022
(212) 826-7000
Fax (212) 826-0579
Comm: David Stern
PR: Brian McIntyre

NBA Entertainment, Inc.
38 East 32nd Street
New York, NY 10016
(212) 532-6223
VP: Ed Desser

NBA Properties, Inc.
Olympic Tower
645 Fifth Avenue
New York, NY 10022
(212) 826-7000
Pres: Rick Welts

Atlanta Hawks
One CNN Center
South Tower, Suite 405
Atlanta, GA 30303
(404) 827-3800
GM: Pete Babcock
PR: Arthur Triche

Boston Celtics
151 Merrimac Street
Boston, MA 02114
(617) 523-6050
GM: Jan Volk
PR: Jeff Twiss

Charlotte Hornets
Hive Drive
Charlotte, NC 28217
(704) 357-0252
GM: Dave Twardzik
PR: Harold Kaufman

Chicago Bulls
One Magnificent Mile
980 N. Michigan Avenue
Suite 1600
Chicago, IL 60611
(312) 943-5800
GM: Jerry Krause
PR: Tim Hallam

Cleveland Cavaliers
PO Box 5000
Richfield, OH 44286
(216) 659-9100
GM: Wayne Embry
PR: Bob Price

Dallas Mavericks
Reunion Arena
777 Sports Street
Dallas, TX 75207
(214) 748-1801
GM: Norm Sonju
PR: Kevin Sullivan

Denver Nuggets
1635 Clay Street
Denver, CO 80204
(303) 893-6700
GM: Bernie Bickerstaff
PR: Jay Clark

Detroit Pistons
The Palace
Two Championship Drive
Auburn Hills, MI 48057
(810) 377-0100
GM: Bill McKinney
PR: Matt Dobek

Golden State Warriors
Oakland Coliseum Arena
Nimitz Fwy. & Hegenberger Rd.
Oakland, CA 94621
(510) 638-6300
GM: Don Nelson
PR: Julie Marvel

Houston Rockets
PO Box 27349
Houston, TX 77277
(713) 627-0600
GM: Todd Leiweke
PR: Jay Goldberg

Indiana Pacers
300 E. Market Street
Indianapolis, IN 46204
(317) 263-2100
GM: Don Walsh
PR: Dale Ratermann

Los Angeles Clippers
3939 S. Figueroa
Los Angeles, CA 90037
(213) 748-8000
GM: Elgin Baylor
PR: Joe Safety

Los Angeles Lakers
PO Box 10
Inglewood, CA 90306
(310) 419-3100
GM: Jerry West
PR: John Black

Miami Heat
Miami Arena
Miami, FL 33136
(305) 577-4328
GM: Lewis Schaffel
PR: Mark Pray

Milwaukee Bucks
1001 N. Fourth Street
Milwaukee, WI 53203
(414) 227-0500
GM: John Steinmiller
PR: Bill King

Minnesota Timberwolves
Target Center
600 First Avenue N.
Minneapolis, MN 55403
(612) 673-1600
GM: Jack McCloskey
PR: Kent Wipf

New Jersey Nets
Meadowlands Arena
East Rutherford, NJ 07073
(201) 935-8888
GM: Willis Reed
PR: John Mertz

New York Knickerbockers
Four Pennsylvania Plaza
New York, NY 1001
(212) 563-8000
GM: Ernie Grunfeld
PR: John Cirillo

Orlando Magic
Orlando Arena
One Magic Place
Orlando, FL 32801
(407) 649-3200
GM: Pat Williams
PR: Alex Martins

Philadelphia 76ers
Veterans Stadium
PO Box 25040
Philadelphia, PA 19147
(215) 339-7600
GM: Jim Lynam
PR: Joe Favorito

Phoenix Suns
201 E. Jefferson
Phoenix, AZ 85004
(602) 379-7900
GM: Jerry Colangelo
PR: Julie Fie

Portland Trail Blazers
700 N.E. Multnomah St.
Lloyd Building, Suite 950
Portland, OR 97232
(503) 234-9291
GM: Bob Whitsitt
PR: John Lashway

Sacramento Kings
One Sports Parkway
Sacramento, CA 95834
(916) 928-0000
GM: Jerry Reynolds
PR: Travis Stanley

San Antonio Spurs
600 E. Market, Suite 102
San Antonio, TX 78205
(210) 554-7787
GM: Bob Bass
PR: Dave Senko

Seattle Supersonics
190 Queen Anne Ave. N.
Suite 200
Seattle, WA 98109
(206) 281-5800
GM: Wally Walker
PR: Cheri White

Utah Jazz
Delta Center
301 W. South Temple
Salt Lake City, UT 84101
(801) 329-2500
GM: Tim Howells
PR: Kim Turner

Washington Bullets
US Air Arena
One Harry S. Truman Drive
Landover, MD 20785
(301) 773-2255
GM: John Nash
PR: Matt Williams

Continental Basketball Association

701 Market Street
St. Louis, MO 63101
(314) 621-7222
Fax (314) 621-1202
Comm: Mark Lamping
PR: Brett Meister

Chicago Rockers
101 W. Grand
Suite 600
Chicago, Il 60610
(312) 755-1300
Fax (312) 755-0336
GM: Jeff Schwarz

Fort Wayne Fury
PO Box 11489
Fort Wayne, IN 46858
(219) 424-6233
Fax (219) 424-3392
GM: Art Saltsberg

Grand Rapids Mackers
820 Monroe N.W., Suite 222
Grand Rapids, MI 49503
(616) 458-7788
Fax (616) 458-2123
GM: Mark Kimball

Harrisburg Hammerheads
119 Strawberry Square Mall
Suite 133
Harrisburg, PA 17101
(717) 233-7777
Fax (717) 238-1442
GM: Dick Barnett

Hartford Hellcats
One Civic Center Plaza
Hartford, CT 06103
(203) 947-6200
Fax (203) 947-6205
Pres: Michael Kerski

Mexico Aztecas
OCESA
Av. Rio Churubusco y Aril
Mexico 08400, Mexico
525-237-9999
Fax 525-649-1653
Pres: Doug Logan

Oklahoma City Cavalry
100 W. Sheridan
Oklahoma City, OK 73102
(405) 232-3865
Fax (405) 232-3866
GM: Chip Land

Omaha Racers
6300 Shirley Street
Omaha, NE 68106
(402) 551-5151
Fax (402) 551-1008
GM: Mike Thibault

Pittsburgh Piranhas
2000 Quicksilver Road
Midway, PA 15060
(412) 796-1825
Fax (412) 796-1808
GM: Robert Murphy, Jr.

Quad City Thunder
329 18th Street
Rock Island, IL 61201
(309) 788-2255
Fax (309) 788-2335
GM: Ed DeLong

Rapid City Thrillers
444 Mt. Rushmore Rd. N.
Rapid City, SD 57701
(605) 342-2255
Fax (605) 342-8024
GM: Eric Musselman

Rockford Lightning
404 Elm Street
Rockford, IL 61101
(815) 968-5666
Fax (815) 968-4144
GM: Tom Maloney

Shreveport Crawdads
American Tower
401 Market St., Suite 530
Shreveport, LA 71101
(318) 425-7526
Fax (318) 221-3865
GM: Richard Coffey

Sioux Falls Sky Force
330 N. Main Avenue
Suite 101
Sioux Falls, SD 57102
(605) 332-0605
Fax (605) 332-2305
GM: Thomas Walsh, Sr.

Tri-City Chinook
7100 W. Quinault Ave.
Kennewick, WA 99336
(509) 783-5000
Fax (509) 783-3047
GM: Mike Lundgren

Yakima Sun Kings
PO Box 2626
Yakima, WA 98907
(509) 248-1222
Fax (509) 248-1537
GM: Brooks Ellison

Women's Basketball Association
4011 N. Bennington
Suite 101
Kansas City, MO 64117
(816) 452-6850
Director: Lightning Mitchell
Pres: Debbie Summers

The WBA will be entering its third season in the Summer of '95.

FAST BREAK

National Basketball League
177 McDermot Avenue E.
Suite 200
Winnipeg, Manitoba R3B 0S1
(204) 942-6247
Fax (204) 942-6279
Pres: Sam Katz
Comm: Tom Nissalke

The NBL, which absorbed the remaining Canadian WBL clubs, disbanded in July 1994.

United States Basketball League

46 Quirk Road
Milford, CT 06460
(203) 877-9508
Fax (203) 878-8109
Comm.: Daniel Meisenheimer, III
Media: Stephen Kirck

Atlanta Trojans
PO Box 490746
College Park, GA 30349
(404) 761-6572
Fax (404) 762-6716
GM: Al Outlaw

Connecticut Skyhawks
PO Box 3156
Milford, CT 06460
(203) 874-2055
Fax (203) 878-5123
GM: Terry Munk

Jacksonville Hooters
6999-2 Merrill Road
Jacksonville, FL 32211
(904) 350-1634
Pres: Artis Gilmore

Long Island Surf
103 Godfrey Lane
Huntington, NY 11743
(516) 754-4012
Fax (516) 754-4012
GM: Ed Krinsky

Memphis Fire
3355 Poplar Avenue
Suite 188
Memphis, TN 38111
(901) 323-2272
Fax (901) 323-3042
GM: Jeff Walker

Miami Tropics
7220 N.W. 36th Street
Suite 610
Miami, FL 33166
(305) 591-1030
Pres: John Lucas

Mississippi Coast Gamblers
625 Courthouse Rd, Suite 100
Gulfport, MS 39507
(601) 896-9760
Fax (601) 896-9841
Pres: T.L. Phillips

Palm Beach Stingrays
1639 Forum Place, Suite 4
West Palm Beach, FL 33401
(407) 688-9814
Fax (407) 688-9815
GM: Joe Ceravolo

Westchester Stallions
273 Central Avenue
White Plains, NY 10606
(914) 946-7735
Fax (914) 684-5898
Pres: Joe Abergel

Atlantic Basketball Association

12 N. Third Street
Easton, PA 18042
(215) 252-4170
Fax (215) 252-7607
Pres: George Daniel

Allentown Jets

PO Box 663
Allentown, PA 18105
(215) 439-8855
Fax (215) 439-8801
GM: David Ziegenfuss

Delaware Blue Bombers

PO Box 12727
Wilmington, DE 19850
(302) 426-9334
Fax (302) 426-9335
GM: R. Scott Barker

Frederick Flyers

PO Box 1859
Frederick, MD 21702
(301) 694-8549
Fax (301) 662-2376
GM: John W. Balch

Hazeleton Hawks

327 St. James Avenue
Phillipsburg, NJ 08865
(908) 454-1204
GM: Dave Ungerer

Pottsville Stingers

101 N. Centre Street
6th Floor
Pottsville, PA 17901
(717) 622-4483
Fax (717) 622-0259
GM: John Flanigan

Scranton Miners

12 N. Third Street
Easton, PA 18042
(215) 252-7050
Fax (215) 252-7607
GM: Terry Wilcox

Organizations

Canadian Amateur Basketball Association
1600 James Naismith Drive
Gloucester, Ontario
Canada KIB 5N4
(613) 746-0060

National Pro-Am City League Association
575 Madison Avenue
Suite 1006
New York, NY 10022
(212) 605-0260
Director: Cecil Watkins

USA Basketball
1750 East Boulder Street
Colorado Springs, CO 80909
(719) 632-7687
Fax (719) 632-3227
Exec. Dir: Bill Wall

Athletes In Action
9815 Mason-Montgomery Road
Mason, OH 45040
(513) 459-9597
Fax (513) 459-9690
Director: Scott Opplinger
Publicity: Lillie Nye

All American Red Heads
P.O. Box 100
Caraway, AR 72419
(501) 482-3922
Pres: Orwell Moore
Touring Women's Team

Harlem Globetrotters
6121 Santa Monica Blvd.
Hollywood, CA 90038
(213) 461-5400
Pres: Terry Hairston

Harlem Wizards Basketball Club
P.O. Box 7374
North Bergen, NJ 07047
(201) 854-6365
Touring pro team

The Fabulous Magicians
P.O. Box 9246
Tulsa, OK 74157
(918) 445-4612
Pres: Marque Haynes

NBA Players Association
1775 Broadway, Suite 2401
New York, NY 10019
(212) 333-7510
Ex. Dir: Charles Grantham

NBA Properties, Inc.
645 Fifth Avenue
New York, NY 10022
(212) 826-7000
Fax (212) 826-0579

Publications

Basketball Digest
990 Grove Street
Evanston, IL 60201
(312) 941-6440

Basketball Weekly
17820 E. Warren Avenue
Detroit, MI 48224
(313) 881-9554

California Basketball
1801 S. Catalina Avenue
Suite 301
Redondo Beach, CA 90277
(213) 375-9860
Editor: David Raatz

Eastern Basketball Magazine
7 May Court
West Hempstead, NY 11552
(516) 483-9495

English Basketball Monthly
12 Rumford Place
Liverpool L39 DG
England

Hoop
600 Third Avenue
New York, NY 10016
(212) 697-1460

International Basketball
320 East 23rd Street #9C
New York, NY 10010
(212) 533-6099

Midwest Basketball News
P.O. Box 21393
Columbus, OH 43221
(614) 486-8747

NBA Today
437 Madison Avenue
New York, NY 10022
(212) 826-7000

Football

National Football League

410 Park Avenue
New York, NY 10022
(212) 758 1500
FAX: (212) 826-3454
Commissioner: Paul Tagliabue
Public Relations: Jim Heffernan

American Football Conference

Buffalo Bills
One Bills Drive
Orchard Park, New York 14127
(716) 648-1800
GM: Bill Polian
PR: Denny Lynch

Cincinnati Bengals
200 Riverfront Stadium
Cincinnati, Ohio 45202
(513) 621-3550
GM: Paul Brown
PR: Al Heim

Cleveland Browns
Cleveland Stadium
Cleveland, Ohio
(216) 696-5555
Pres: Art Modell
PR: Kevin Byrne

Denver Broncos
13655 E. Dove Valley Pkwy.
Englewood, CO 80112
(303) 649-9000
GM: John Beake
PR: Jim Saccomano

Houston Oilers
6910 Fannin Street
Houston, Texas 77030
(713) 797-9111
GM: Mike Holovak
PR: Chip Namias

Indianapolis Colts
P.O. Box 24100
Indianapolis, IN 46253
(317) 297-2658
GM: James Irsay
PR: Craig Kelley

Kansas City Chiefs
One Arrowhead Drive
Kansas City, MO 64129
(816) 924-9300
Pres: Carl Peterson
PR: Bob Moore

Los Angeles Raiders
332 Center Street
El Segundo, CA 90245
(310) 322-3451
Pres: Al Davis
PR: Al LoCasale

Miami Dolphins
Joe Robbie Stadium
2269 NW 199th St.
Miami, FL 33056
(305) 620-5000
GM: Eddie Jones
PR: Harvey Greene

New England Patriots
Foxboro Stadium - Route 1
Foxboro, MA 02035
(508) 543-7911
GM: Sam Jankovich
PR: Dave Wintergrass

New York Jets
1000 Fulton Avenue
Hempstead, NY 11550
(516) 538-7200
GM: Dick Steinberg
PR: Frank Ramos

Pittsburgh Steelers
Three Rivers Stadium
300 Stadium Circle
Pittsburgh, PA 15212
(412) 323-1200
Pres: Dan Rooney
PR: Dan Edwards

San Diego Chargers
San Diego-Jack Murphy Stadium
9449 Friars Road
San Diego, California 92120
(619) 280-2111
GM: Bobby Beathard
PR: Bill Johnston

Seattle Seahawks
11220 N.E. 53rd Street
Kirkland, WA 98033
(206) 827-9777
GM: Tom Flores
PR: Gary Wright

National Football Conference

Arizona Cardinals
8701 South Hardy
Phoenix, AZ 85284
(602) 379-0101
Fax (602) 379-1819
GM: Larry Wilson
PR: Paul Jensen

Atlanta Falcons
Suwanee Road at I-85
Suwanee, GA 30174
(404) 945-1111
Pres: Rankin Smith, Jr.
PR: Charley Taylor

Chicago Bears
Halas Hall
250 N. Washington Road
Lake Forest, IL 60045
(708) 295-6600
Pres: Mike McCaskey
PR: Bryan Harlan

Dallas Cowboys
Cowboys Center
1 Cowboys Parkway
Irving, TX 75063-4727
(214) 556-9900
Pres: Jerry Jones
PR: Rich Dalrymple

Detroit Lions
1200 Featherstone Road
Pontiac, MI 48057
(313) 335-4131
GM: Chuck Schmidt
PR: Bill Keenist

Green Bay Packers
1265 Lombardi Avenue
Green Bay, WI 54307
(414) 496-5700
GM: Tom Braatz
PR: Lee Remmel

Los Angeles Rams
2327 W. Lincoln Avenue
Anaheim, CA 92801
(714) 535-7267
Pres: Georgia Frontiere
PR: John Oswald

Minnesota Vikings
9520 Viking Drive
Eden Prairie, MN 55344
(612) 828-6500
Pres: John Skoglund
PR: Merrill Swanson

New Orleans Saints
6928 Saints Avenue
Metairie, LA 70003
(504) 522-1500
GM: Jim Finks
PR: Greg Suit

New York Giants
Giants Stadium
East Rutherford, NJ 07073
(201) 935-8111
GM: George Young
PR: Ed Croke

Philadelphia Eagles
Broad Street & Pattison Avenue
Philadelphia, PA 19148
(215) 463-2500
Pres: Norman Braman
PR: Ron Howard

San Francisco 49ers
4949 Centennial Blvd.
Santa Clara, CA 95054-1229
(408) 562-4949
GM: John McVay
PR: Jerry Walker

Tampa Bay Buccaneers
One Buccaneer Place
Tampa, FL 33607
(813) 870-2700
Pres: Hugh Culverhouse
PR: Rick Odioso

Washington Redskins
P.O. Box 17247
Dulles International Airport
Washington, D.C. 20041
(703) 471-9100
GM: Charles Casserly
PR: Charlie Dayton

Will begin play in 1995

Carolina Panthers
227 West Trade Street
Suite 1600
Charlotte, NC 28202
(704) 358-7000
Fax (704) 358-0764
GM: Bill Polian

Jacksonville Jaguars
One Stadium Place
Jacksonville, FL 32202
(904) 633-6000
Fax (904) 633-6050
Pres: David Seldon

Canadian Football League

110 Eglinton Ave., 5th Floor
Toronto, Ontario
Canada M4R 1A3
(416) 322-9650
Fax (416) 322-9651
Commissioner: Larry W. Smith
P.R.: Diane Mihalek

British Columbia Lions
10605 135th Street
Surrey, B.C. V3T 4C8
(604) 583-7747
Fax (604) 583-7882
G.M.: Eric Tillman
P.R.: Roger Kelly

Calgary Stampeders
1817 Crowchild Trail, N.W.
McMahon Stadium
Calgary, Alberta
Canada T2M 4R6
(403) 289-0205
Fax (403) 289-7850
GM: Norman Kwong
PR: Kevin Gallant

Edmonton Eskimos
9023-111 Avenue
Edmonton, Alberta T5B 0C3
(403) 429-2821
Fax (403) 429-3452
GM: Hugh Campbell
PR: Allan Watt

Hamilton Tiger-Cats
P.O. Box 172
Hamilton, Ontario
Canada L8N 3A2
(416) 547-2418
Fax (416) 549-6610
GM: Joe Zuger
PR: Chris Dowhun

Ottawa Rough Riders
Lansdowne Park
Ottawa, Ontario
Canada K1S 3W7
(613) 563-4551
Fax (613) 563-0391
Pres: Hap Nicholds
PR: Sal DeMeo

Sacramento Gold Miners
14670 Cantova Way
Rancho Murieta, CA 95683
(916) 354-1000
Fax (916) 354-3244
G.M.: Tom Huiskens
P.R.: Tim McDowd

Saskatchewan Roughriders
2940 10th Avenue
P.O. Box 1277
Regina, Saskatchewan
Canada S4P 3B8
(306) 569-2323
Fax (306) 359-0809
GM: Al Ford
PR: Jim Dorash

Toronto Argonauts
Skydome-Gate 7
One Blue Jays Way
PO Box 188, Sta. C
Toronto, Ontario M6J 3M9
(416) 595-9600
Fax (416) 595-0797
GM: Bob O' Billovich
PR: Mike Cosentino

Winnipeg Blue Bombers
1465 Maroons Road
Winnipeg, Manitoba R3G 0L6
(204) 784-2583
Fax (204) 783-5222
GM: Cal Murphy
PR: Kevin O'Donovan

Expansion Teams

Baltimore CFL Colts
Memorial Stadium
1000 E. 33rd Street
Baltimore, MD 21218
(410) 554-1010
Fax (410) 554-1015
President: Jim Speros
PR: Mike Gathagan

Las Vegas Posse
6900 W. Cliff Drive
Suite 500
Las Vegas, NV 89128
(702) 242-4200
Fax (702) 242-5355
President: Nick Mileti
PR: Lee Meade

Shreveport Pirates
N.O. Thomas Plaza
505 Travis St., Suite 602
Shreveport, LA 71101
(318) 222-3000
Fax (318) 222-4271
Pres.:Lonie Glieberman
PR: Missy Parker-Setters

The Arena Indoor Football League began operation 1987

2200 E. Devon, Suite 247
Des Plaines, IL 60018
(708) 390-7400
Fax (708) 297-0998
Pres: Joseph J. O'Hara
Media: Kim Clements

Charlotte Rage
5601-77 Center Drive
Suite 250
Charlotte, NC 28217
(704) 527-RAGE
Fax (704) 527-9737
GM: Galen Hall

Cleveland Thunderbolts
981 Keynote Circle, Suite 9
Cleveland, OH 44131
(216) 351-BOLT
Fax (216) 351-7322
GM: Jeff Kuczek

Fort Worth Cavalry
904 Houston Street
Fort Worth, TX 76102
(817) 338-0101
Fax (817) 336-4800
Pres: Peter "Woody" Kern

Las Vegas Sting
105 E. Reno, Suite 4
Las Vegas, NV 89119
(702) 739-PROS
Fax (702) 739-1475
Pres: Bill MacFarland

Massachusetts Marauders
The Centrum
50 Foster Street
Worcester, MA 01608
(508) 755-6800
Fax (508) 754-9972
GM: Gordon Kaye

Miami Hooters
2977 McFarlane Rd.
Coconut Grove, FL 33133
(305) 461-8665
Fax (305) 461-8645
GM: Bob Hewko

Milwaukee Mustangs
1020 N. Broadway, Suite 200
Milwaukee, WI 53202
(414) 272-3500
Fax (414) 272-3891
Pres: Andrew Vallozzi

Orlando Predators
20 N. Orange Avenue
Orlando, FL 32801
(407) 648-4444
Fax (407) 648-8101
GM: L. Eric Leins

Tampa Bay Storm
Thunderdome
One Stadium Drive
St. Petersburg, FL 33705
(813) 894-2894
Fax (813) 822-1897
GM: Larry Kuharich

Minor League Football

American Football Association
P.O. Box 1058
Bensenville, IL 60106
(708) 833-0824
Fax: (708) 238-8875
Exec. Director: Ron Real

*The AFA is the national
association for semi-pro
football.*

**America's Football League
of Florida**
7009 N. Center Drive
Tampa, FL 33604
(813) 985-7222
Commissioner: John Mays

Carolina Football League
P.O. Box 1177
Davidson, NC 28036
(704) 896-0023
Commissioner: Jim Brannon

Chicagoland Football League
1709 N. Indiana
Griffith, IN 46319
(219) 923-4443
Commissioner: Lou Ince

**Continental Football League
of America**
2315 Richmond
Suite 215
Texarkana, TX 75503
(903) 832-1236
Commissioner: Jim Chambers

Eastern Football League
55 Brookside
Winchester, MA 01890
(617) 729-4840
Commissioner: George Murphy

Empire Football League
53 James Street
Hudson, NY 12534
(519) 828-1107
Commissioner: Gary Shaver

Mason-Dixon Football League
8729 Sheridan Farms Court
Suite 200
Springfield, VA 22152
(703) 866-7765
Commissioner: Vic Lent

Michigan Football League
12450 Airport Road
Dewitt, MI 48820
(517) 321-6954
Comm: Joe Costello

Mid-Atlantic Football League
4448 Strahle Street
Philadelphia, PA 19136
(215) 331-1074
Pres.: Frank kosman

Mid-Continental Football League
7134 Bletch Court
Cleveland, OH 44125
(216) 341-5962
PR: Dick Suess

Mid-Eastern Football Conference
One World Trade Center
Suite 3327
New York, NY 10048
Comm: Lou Policastro

Midwest Football League
900 W. Jackson, Suite 5W
Chicago, IL 60607
(312) 726-4709
Commissioner: Jerry Kurz

Northwest Football League
P.O. Box 1001, Suite 49
Arlington, WA 93223
(206) 435-8538
Commissioner: Richard Fleck

Pacific Football League
25881 Coriander
Moreno Valley, CA 92388
(909) 924-1909
Commissioner: John Musso

Pro Style Football League
c/o World Hotel Express
4405 Beltwood Pkwy.
Dallas, TX 75244
(214)991-5482
Commissioner: John Lovelace

Southern Football League
1204-H Ashborough Terrace
Marietta, GA 30067
(404) 425-4121
Commissioner: Dave Lowe

Texas Football League
9917 Champa Street
Dallas, TX 75218
(214) 394-2063
Commissioner: W.O. Gunstanson

Minor League Football Alliance
1317 Yout Street
Racine, WI 53402
(414) 633-2555
Comm: Mark Eickhorst

Great Atlantic Football League
695 Cumberland
Chambersburg, PA 17201
(717) 263-5987
Commissioner: Jim Bard

U.S. Flag-Touch League

7709 Ohio Street
Mentor, OH 44060
(216) 974-8735
Exec. Dir: Mike Cihon

The USFTL is the national association for amateur flag-touch football.

Football Canada

Canadian Amateur Football Association

1600 James Naismith Drive
Gloucester, Ontario
Canada K1B 5N4
(613) 748-5636
Pres: Scott Spurgeon

Canadian Junior Football League

32 St. Elmo Road
Winnipeg, Manitoba R2M 3H3
204) 256-2522
FAX: (204) 985-4028
Comm: Peter Sawchuk
The CJFL is the development system to the CFL.

Canadian Junior Football League

B.C. Junior Football Association
#104-5955 Yew Street
Vancouver, B.C., Canada V6M 3Y7
(604) 681-1182
Pres.: Duke DeWest

Manitoba Junior Football Conference
7 Lomond Blvd.
Winnipeg, Manitoba, Canada R2J 1Y1
(204) 254-3160
Pres.: Ed Aplin

Ontario Football Conference
2737 Ulster crescent
Ottawa, Ontario, Canada K1V 8J5
(613) 731-6467
Pres.: Bob Mahlitz

Prairie Junior Football Conference
c/o McDougall, Ready
700-2010 11th Avenue
Regina, Saskatchewan, Canada S4P 0J
(306) 757-1641
Pres.: Bob Miller

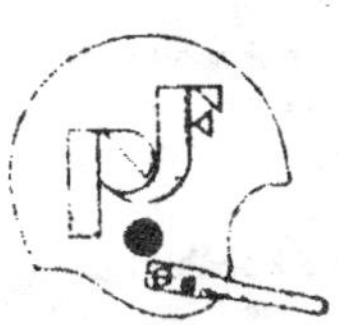

Quebec Major Junior Football League
46 Labrador Street
Kirkland, Quebec, Canada H9J 3W8
(514) 343-3671
Pres.: Glenn Keeble

Publications

**Athalon's Pro & College
Football Publications**
220 25th Avenue North
Nashville, TN 37203
(615) 297-7581
(800) 251-1201

Coffin Corner
12870 Route 30
N. Huntingdon, PA 15642
(412) 863-6345

**College & Pro Football News/
Football Action**
18 Industrial Park Drive
Port Washington, NY 11050
(516) 484-3300

Football Digest
990 Grove Street
Evanston, IL 60201
(708) 491-6440

The Football News
17820 E. Warren Avenue
Detroit, MI 48224
(313) 881-9554

**Petersen's Pro Football
Annual**
8490 Sunset Blvd.
Los Angeles, CA 90069
(213) 657-5100

Pro Football Weekly
666 Dundee Road
Suite 1101
Northbrook, IL 60062
(708) 272-1237

**Street & Smith College
& Pro Football Yearbooks**
304 East 45th Street
New York, NY 10017
(212) 880-8698

Hockey

National Hockey League

1251 Avenue of the Americas
New York, NY 10020
(212) 789-2000
Fax (212) 789-2020
Pres: Gary Bettman

Anaheim Mighty Ducks
Arrowhead Pond
2695 Katella Avenue
Anaheim, CA 92806
(714) 704-2700
Fax (714) 704-2753
GM: Jack Ferriera
PR: Bill Robertson

Boston Bruins
Boston Garden
150 Causeway Street
Boston, MA 02114
(617) 227-3206
Fax (617) 523-7184
GM: Harry Sinden
PR: Heidi Holland

Buffalo Sabres
Memorial Auditorium
Buffalo, NY 14202
(716) 856-7300
Fax (716) 856-7352
GM: John Muckler
PR: Steve Rossi

Calgary Flames
Olympic Saddledome
PO Box 1540, Station M
Calgary, Alberta T2P 3B9
(403) 261-0475
Fax (403) 261-0470
GM: Doug Risenbrough
PR: Rick Skaggs

Chicago Blackhawks
1901 W. Madison Street
Chicago, IL 60612
(312) 733-5300
Fax (312) 733-5356
GM: Robert Pulford
PR: Jim DeMaria

Dallas Stars
901 Main Street
Suite 2301
Dallas, TX 75202
(214) 712-2890
Fax (214) 712-2800
GM: Bob Gainey
PR: Larry Kelly

Detroit Red Wings
Joe Louis Sports Arena
600 Civic Center Drive
Detroit, MI 48226
(313) 567-3900
Fax (313) 567-0296
GM: Bryan Murray
PR: Bill Jamieson

Edmonton Oilers
Northlands Coliseum
Edmonton, Alberta T5B 4M9
(403) 474-8561
Fax (403) 471-2171
GM: Glen Sather
PR: Bill Tuele

Florida Panthers
100 N.E. Third Avenue
10th Floor
Fort Lauderdale, FL 33301
(305) 768-1900
Fax (305) 768-1920
GM: Bill Torrey
PR: Greg Bouris

Hartford Whalers
242 Trumbull Street
Hartford, CT 06103
(203) 728-3366
Fax (203) 522-7707
GM: Jim Rutherford
PR: Mark Mancini

Los Angeles Kings
The Forum
PO Box 10
Inglewood, CA 90306
(310) 419-3160
Fax (310) 673-8927
GM: Nick Beverly
PR: Sue Carpenter

Montreal Canadiens
Montreal Forum
2313 St. Catherine St Ouest
Montreal, Quebec H3H 1N2
(514) 932-2582
Fax (514) 989-2890
GM: Serge Savard
PR: Donald Beauchamp

New Jersey Devils
Byrne Meadowlands Arena
PO Box 504
East Rutherford, NJ 07073
(201) 935-6050
Fax (201) 935-2127
GM: Lou Lamoriello
PR: Dave Freed

New York Islanders
Nassau Veterans Memorial Coliseum
Uniondale, NY 11553
(516) 794-4100
Fax (516) 794-8083
GM: Don Maloney
PR: Ginger Killian

New York Rangers
Madison Square Gardens
4 Pennsylvania Plaza
New York, NY 10001
(212) 465-6000
Fax (212) 465-6494
GM: Neil Smith
PR: Barry Watkins

Ottawa Senators
301 Moodie Drive
Suite 200
Nepean, Ontario K2H 9C4
(613) 726-0540
Fax (613) 726-1419
GM: Randy Sexton
PR: Laurent Benoit

Philadelphia Flyers
The Spectrum
Pattison Place
Philadelphia, PA 19148
(215) 465-4500
Fax (215) 389-9403
Pres: Bobby Clarke
PR: Mark Piazza

Pittsburgh Penguins
Civic Arena
Pittsburgh, PA 15219
(412) 642-1800
Fax (412) 642-1925
GM: Craig Patrick
PR: Cindy Himes

Quebec Nordiques
Colisee de Quebec
2205 Ave. du Colisee
Quebec, Quebec GIL 4W7
(418) 529-8441
Fax (418) 529-1052
GM: Pierre Page
PR: Jean Martineau

St. Louis Blues
St. Louis Arena
5700 Oakland Avenue
St. Louis, MO 63110
(314) 781-5300
Fax (314) 645-1340
GM: Mike Keenan
PR: Susie Mathieu

San Jose Sharks
525 W. Santa Clara St.
San Jose, CA 95113
(408) 287-7070
Fax (408) 999-5797
GM: Dean Lombardi
PR: Tim Bryant

Tampa Bay Lightning
501 E. Kennedy Blvd.
Suite 175
Tampa, FL 33602
(813) 229-2658
Fax (813) 229-3350
GM: Phil Esposito
PR: Gerry Helper

Toronto Maple Leafs
Maple Leaf Gardens
60 Carlton Street
Toronto, Ontario M5B 1L1
(416) 977-1641
Fax (416) 977-5364
GM: Cliff Fletcher
PR: Bob Stellick

Vancouver Canucks
100 N. Renfrew Street
Vancouver, B.C. V5K 3N7
(604) 254-5141
Fax (604) 251-5123
GM: Pat Quinn
PR: Steve Tambellini

Washington Capitals
One Harry S. Truman Drive
Landover, MD 20785
(301) 386-7000
Fax (301) 386-7082
GM: David Poile
PR: Ed Quinlan

Winnipeg Jets
15-1430 Maroons Road
Winnipeg, Manitoba R3G 0L5
(204) 783-5387
Fax (204) 788-4668
GM: Mike Smith
PR: Mike O'Hearn

Minor League Hockey

American Hockey League

425 Union Street
West Springfield, MA 01089
(413) 781-2030
Fax (413) 733-4767
Commissioner: Dave Andrews

Adirondack Red Wings
1 Civic Center Plaza
Glens Falls, NY 12801
(518) 798-0366
Fax (518) 798-0816
GM: Ken Holland

Albany River Rats
51 S. Pearl Street
Albany, NY 12207
(518) 487-2244
Fax (518) 487-2248
Pres: Doug Burch

Binghamton Rangers
1 Stuart Street
Binghamton, NY 13901
(607) 723-8937
Fax (607) 724-6892
GM: Tom Mitchell

Cape Breton Oilers
PO Box 1510
Sydney, Nova Scotia BIT 6R7
(902) 562-0780
Fax (902) 562-1806
GM: Dave Andrews

Cornwall Aces
100 Water Street
Cornwall, Ontario K6H 6G4
(613) 937-4132
Fax (613) 937-2695
GM: Jacques Martin

Fredericton Canadiens
PO Box HABS
Fredericton, New Brunswick E3B 4Y2
(506) 459-4227
Fax (506) 859-4250
GM: Wayne Gamble

Hershey Bears
PO Box 866
Hershey, PA 17033
(717) 534-3380
Fax (717) 534-3383
GM: Jay Feaster

Portland Pirates
1 Civic Center Square
Portland, ME 04101
(207) 828-4665
Fax (207) 773-3278
GM: Godfrey Wood

Prince Edward Island Senators
PO Box 22093
Charlottetown, P.E.I., C1A 9J2
(902) 566-5450
Fax (902) 566-5170
GM: Gary Thompson

Providence Bruins
1 LaSalle Square
Providence, RI 02903
(401) 273-5000
Fax (401) 273-5004
GM: Ed Anderson

Rochester Americans
100 Exchange Street
Rochester, NY 14614
(716) 454-5335
Fax (716) 454-3954
GM: Joe Baumann

Saint John Flames
PO Box 4040, Station B
Saint John, New Brunswick E2M 5E6
(506) 635-2637
Fax (506) 633-4625
GM: Gord Thorn

St. John's Maple Leafs
6 Logy Bay Road
St. John's, Newfoundland A1A 1J3
(709) 726-1010
Fax (709) 726-1511
GM: Glenn Stanford

Springfield Falcons
PO Box 3190
Springfield, MA 01101
(413) 739-3344
Fax (413) 739-3389
Pres: Bruce Landon

Syracuse Crunch
800 State Street
Syracuse, NY 13202
(315) 473-4444
Fax (315) 473-4449
GM: David Gregory

Worcester Icecats
33 Waldo Street
Worcester, MA 01608
(508) 798-5400
Fax (508) 799-5267
GM: Jim Roberts

International Hockey League

505 N. Woodward Avenue
Suite 1500
Bloomfield, MI 48304
(810) 258-0580
Fax (810) 540-0884
Comm: Robert P. Ufer
PR: Tim Bryant

Hockey Operations

3850 Priority Way S. Dr.
Suite 100
Indianapolis, IN 46240
(317) 573-3888
Fax (317) 573-3880

Atlanta Knights
100 Techwood Drive
Atlanta, GA 30303
(404) 525-5800
Fax (404) 525-0044
GM: Joe Bucchino

Chicago Wolves
10550 Lunt Avenue
Rosemont, IL 60018
(708) 390-0404
Fax (708) 390-9792
GM: Grant Mulvey

Cincinnati Cyclones
2250 Seymour Ave.
Cincinnati, OH 45212
(513) 531-7825
Fax (513) 531-0209
GM: Doug Kirchhofer

Cleveland Lumberjacks
504 Superior Ave., N.E.
Cleveland, OH 44114
(216) 696-0909
Fax (216) 696-3909
GM: Larry Gordon

Denver Grizzlies
1635 Clay Street
Denver, CO 80204
(303) 592-7825
Fax (303) 592-7171
GM: Butch Goring

Detroit Vipers
2 Championship Drive
Auburn Hills, MI 48326
(810) 377-0861
Fax (810) 377-2695
GM: Rick Dudley

Fort Wayne Komets
4000 Parnell Avenue
Fort Wayne, IN 46805
(219) 483-0011
Fax (219) 483-3899
GM: David Franke

Houston Aeros
PO Box 271469
Houston, TX 77277
(713) 621-2842
Fax (713) 627-0397
GM: Steve Patterson

Indianapolis Ice
1202 E. 38th Street
Indianapolis, IN 46205
(317) 924-1234
Fax (317) 924-1248
GM: Ray Compton

Kalamazoo Wings
3620 Van Rick Drive
Kalamazoo, MI 49002
(616) 349-9772
Fax (616) 345-6584
GM: Bill inglis

Kansas City Blades
1800 Genessee
Kansas City, MO 64102
(816) 842-5233
Fax (816) 842-5610
GM: Doug Soetaert

Las Vegas Thunder
PO Box 70065
Las Vegas, NV 89170
(702) 798-7825
Fax (702) 798-9464
GM: Bob Strumm

Milwaukee Admirals
1001 N. Fourth Street
Milwaukee, WI 53203
(414) 227-0550
Fax (414) 227-0568
GM: Phil Wittliff

Minnesota Moose
28 West 6th Street
St. Paul, MN 55102
(612) 292-3333
Fax (612) 221-0292
GM: Ron Minegar

Peoria Rivermen
201 S.W. Jefferson
Peoria, IL 61602
(309) 676-1040
Fax (309) 676-2488
GM: Denis Cyr

Phoenix Roadrunners
1826 W. McDowell Road
Phoenix, AZ 85007
(602) 340-0001
Fax (602) 340-0041
GM: Adam Keller

San Diego Gulls
3780 Hancock Street, Suite G
San Diego, CA 92110
(619) 688-1800
Fax (602) 688-1808
GM: Don Waddell

*The IHL announced expansion
into six european cities for the
`95-6 season. Teams were not
announced.*

East Coast Hockey League

AA 520, Mart Office Bldg.
800 Briar Creek Road
Charlotte, NC 28205
(704) 358-3658
Fax (704) 358-3560
Comm: Pat Kelly
PR: Doug Price

Birmingham Bulls
PO Box 1506
Birmingham, AL 35201
(205) 458-8833
Fax (205) 458-8489
GM: Art Clarkson

Charlotte Checkers
2700 E. Independence Blvd.
Charlotte, NC 28205
(704) 342-4423
Fax (704) 377-4595
GM: Carl Scheer

Columbus Chill
7001 Dublin Park Drive
Dublin, OH 43017
(614) 791-9999
Fax (614) 791-9302
GM: David Paitson

Dayton Bombers
PO Box 5952
Dayton, OH 45405
(513) 277-3765
Fax (513) 278-3077
GM: Arnold Johnson

Erie Panthers
PO Box 6116
Erie, PA 16512
(814) 455-3936
Fax (814) 456-8287
GM: Ron Hansis

Greensboro Monarchs
PO Box 5447
Greensboro, NC 27435
(919) 852-6170
Fax (919) 852-6259
GM: Jeff Brubaker

Hampton Roads Admirals
PO Box 299
Norfolk, VA 23501
(804) 640-1212
Fax (804) 640-8447
GM: John Brophy

Huntington Blizzard
763 Third Avenue
Huntington, WV 25701
(304) 697-7825
Fax (304) 697-7832
GM: Bob Henry

Johnstown Chiefs
326 Napoleon Street
Johnstown, PA 15901
(814) 539-1799
Fax (814) 536-1316
GM: Eddie Johnstone

Knoxville Cherokees
500 E. Church Street
Knoxville, TN 37915
(615) 546-6707
Fax (615) 546-5521
GM: Tim Bernal

Nashville Knights
417 4th Avenue N.
Nashville, TN 37201
(615) 255-7825
Fax (615) 255-0024
GM: Greg Lutz

Raleigh IceCaps
PO Box 33219
Raleigh, NC 27636
(919) 755-1427
Fax (919) 755-0899
GM: Pete Bock

Richmond Renegades
601 E. Leigh Street
Richmond, VA 23219
(804) 643-7825
Fax (804) 649-0651
GM: Craig Laughlin

Roanoke Express
4502 Starkey Road S.W.
Suite 211
Roanoke, VA 24014
(703) 989-4625
Fax (703) 989-8681
GM: Pierre Paiement

South Carolina Stingrays
5001 Coliseum Drive
North Charleston, SC 29418
(803) 744-2248
Fax (803) 744-2898
GM: Frank Milne

Tallahassee Tiger Sharks
505 W. Pensacola Street
Tallahassee, FL 32302
(904) 224-7700
Fax (904) 224-6300
GM: Tim Mouser

Toledo Storm
One Main Street
Toledo, OH 43605
(419) 691-0200
Fax (419) 698-8998
GM: Barry Soskin

Wheeling Thunderbirds
PO Box 6563
Wheeling, WV 26003
(304) 234-4625
Fax (304) 233-4846
GM: Larry Kish

PO Box 45
Copetown, Ontario LOR IJ0
(905) 627-2096
Fax (905) 627-2097
Comm: Bob Myers
PR: Gord Stellick

Brantford Smoke
69-79 Market Street S.
Brantford, Ontario N3T 5R7
(519) 751-9467
Fax (519) 751-2366
GM: Rod Davidson

Detroit Falcons
34400 Utica Road
Fraser, MI 48026
(810) 294-2488
Fax (810) 294-2358
GM: Mostafa Afr

Flint Generals
3501 Lapeer Road
Flint, MI 48503
(313) 742-9422
Fax (313) 742-5892
GM: Peter Horachek

London Blues
1408 Wellington Road S.
London, Ontario N6E 2Z5
(519) 681-0800
Fax (519) 681-7291
GM: Doug Tarry, Jr.

Muskegon Fury
470 W. Western Avenue
Muskegon, MI 49440
(616) 726-5058
Fax (616) 728-0428
GM: Tony Lisman

Saginaw Gears
400 Johnson Street
Saginaw, MI 48607
(517) 752-4200
Fax (517) 752-1960
GM: Tom Barrett

Thunder Bay Senators
901 Miles Street E.
Thunder Bay, Ontario P7C 1J9
(807) 623-7121
Fax (807) 622-3306
GM: Gary Cook

Utica Bulldogs
400 Oriskany Street W.
Utica, NY 13502
(315) 734-8483
Fax (315) 734-8486
GM: Jeff Croop

Canada Junior Hockey

The following three leagues are Canadian Major Junior
Hockey Leagues, part of the Canadian junior hockey
system. The NHL drafts from these leagues as well as
the U.S. colleges, high schools, and foreign players.
The three leagues play for the MemorialCup, Canada's
championship for junior hockey supremacy.

Canadian Amateur Hockey Association

1600 James Naismith Drive
Gloucester, Ontario
Canada K1B 5N4
(613) 748-5613
Fax (613) 748-5709
Pres: Murray Costello

Ontario Hockey League

305 Milner Ave., Suite 208
Scarborough, Ontario M1B 3V4
(416) 299-8700
Fax (416) 299-8787
Comm: David Branch
PR: Herb Morrell

Belleville Bulls
265 Cannifton Road
Belleville, Ontario K8N 4V8
(613) 966-8338
Fax (613) 966-8761
GM: Larry Mavety

Detroit Jr. Red Wings
P.O. Box 9080
Farmington Hills, MI 48333
(313) 737-7373
Fax (313) 737-2718
GM: Jim Rutherford

Guelph Storm
P.O. Box 158
Guelph, Ontario NIJ 6J8
(519) 837-9690
Fax (519) 837-9692
GM: Mike Kelly

Kingston Frontenacs
P.O. Box 665
Kingston, Ontario K7L 4X1
(613) 542-4042
Fax (613) 542-2834
GM: Wren Blair

Kitchener Rangers
PO Box 43013
Kitchener, Ontario N2H 6S9
(519) 576-3700
Fax (519) 576-7571
GM: Joe McDonnell

London Knights
London Gardens
1408 Wellington Road S.
London, Ontario N6E 2Z5
(519) 681-0800
Fax (519) 668-7291
GM: Gary Agnew

Newmarket Royals
Upper Canada Postal Outlet
PO Box 21559
Newmarket, Ontario L3Y 8JI
(905) 830-6721
Fax (905) 830-6727
GM: Don Boyd

Niagara Falls Thunder
5145 Centre Street
Niagara Falls, Ontario L2G 3P3
(416) 374-8100
Fax (416) 374-0866
GM: George Burnett

North Bay Centennials
100 Chippewa Street
North Bay, Ontario P1B 6G2
(705) 474-4022
Fax (705) 474-6956
GM: Bert Templeton

Oshawa Generals
99 Thornton Rd. S.
Oshawa, Ontario L1J 5Y1
(416) 433-0900
Fax (416) 433-0868
GM: Wayne Daniels

Ottawa 67's
Ottawa Civic Centre
Lansdowne Park
Ottawa, Ontario K1S 3W7
(613) 232-6767
Fax (613) 232-5582
GM: Brian Kilrea

Owen Sound Platers
P.O. Box 1420
1900 3rd Ave. East
Owen Sound, Ontario N4K 6T5
(519) 371-7452
Fax (519) 371-7990
GM: Rob Holody

Peterborough Petes
5 Lansdowne Street W.
Peterborough, Ontario K9J 1Y4
(705) 743-3681
Fax (705) 743-5497
GM: Dick Todd

Sault Ste. Marie Greyhounds
269 Queen Street East
Sault Ste. Marie, Ontario P6A 1Y9
(705) 253-5976
Fax (705) 945-9458
GM: Sherwood Bassin

Sudbury Wolves
240 Elgin Street S.
Sudbury, Ontario P3E 3N6
(705) 675-3941
Fax (705) 675-7951
GM: Sam McMaster

Windsor Spitfires
334 Wyandotte St. E.
Windsor, Ontario N9A 3H6
(519) 254-9256
Fax (519) 254-9257
GM: Wayne Maxner

Quebec Major Junior Hockey League

255 boul. Roland-Therien
Bureau 101
Longueuil, Quebec
Canada J4H 4A6
(514) 442-3590
Fax (514) 442-3593
Pres: Gilles Courteau

Beauport Harfangs
655 Blvd. des Chutes
Beauport, Quebec G1E 2B6
(418) 666-5603
Fax (418) 666-1504
GM: Rene Young

Chicoutimi Sagueneens
Case Postale 323
Chicoutimi, Quebec G7H 5C2
(418) 549-9489
Fax (418) 549-1645
GM: Andre Girard

Drummondville Voltigeurs
300, rue Cockburn
Drummondville, Quebec J2C 4L6
(819) 477-9400
GM: Jean Hamel

Granby Bisons
601, rue Leon-Harmel
Granby, Quebec J2G 3G6
(514) 378-1363
GM: Rene Constantin

Hull Olympiques
Case Postale 251
Succursale A
Hull, Quebec J8Y 6M8
(819) 777-0661
Fax (819) 777-6933
GM: Charles Henry

Laval Titans
1110, Avenue Desnoyers
Laval, Quebec H7C 1Y5
(514) 661-4210
Fax (514) 661-1684
GM: George Morissette

St. Hyacinthe Lasers
C.P. 181, 900 rue Turcot
St. Hyacinthe, Quebec J2S 7B4
(514) 771-4800
Fax (514) 771-6679
GM: Gaetan Pion

St. Jean Lynx
965 rue Choquette
St. Jean-Sur-Richelieu,
Quebec J3A 1P4
(514) 348-0914
GM: George Marien

Shawinigan Cataractes
855, Avenue Broadway
Shawinigan, Quebec G9N 8B8
(819) 537-5126
Fax (819) 537-3538
GM: Jacques Dube

Sherbrooke Faucons
360 rue Parc
Sherbrooke, Quebec J1E 2J9
(819) 346-8789
Fax (819) 346-6505
Mkt: Charles Lamoureux

Foreurs de Val D`Or
810 de la 6e Avenue
Val D`Or, Quebec J6P 1B4
(819) 825-0093
Fax (819) 824-7602
Mkt: Yvons Rioux

College Francais de Verdun HC
4110 boul. Lasalle
Verdun, Quebec H4G 2A5
(514) 761-4705
Fax (514) 761-7776
Mkt: Pierre Leduc

Victoriaville Tigres
400 Est. Blvd. Jutras
Victoriaville, Quebec G6P 7W7
(819) 752-6353
Fax (819) 758-1441
GM: Michel Cormier

Western Hockey League

10333 Southport Road, S.W.
Suite 521
Calgary, Alberta, Canada T2W 3X6
(403) 253-8113
Fax (403) 258-1455
Pres: Ed Chynoweth

Brandon Wheat Kings
#2, 1175-18 Street
Brandon, Manitoba R7A 7C5
(204) 726-3535
Fax (204) 726-3540
GM: Kelly McCrimmon

Kamloops Blazers
300 Lorne Street
Kamloops, B.C. V2C 1W1
(604) 828-1144
Fax (604) 828-7822
GM: Bob Brown

Lethbridge Hurricanes
P.O. Box 2143
Lethbridge, AB. T1J 4K7
(403) 328-1986
Fax (403) 329-1622
GM: Bob Bartlett

Medicine Hat Tigers
Box 507
Medicine Hat, Alberta T1A 7G2
(403) 526-2666
Fax (403) 526-3072
GM: Jack Shupe

Moose Jaw Warriors
P.O. Box 74
Moose Jaw, Saskatchewan S6H 4N7
(306) 694-5711
Fax (306) 692-7833
GM: Greg Kvisle

Portland Winter Hawks
P.O. Box 3009
Portland, OR 97208
(503) 238-6366
Fax (503) 238-7629
GM: Brian Shaw

Prince Albert Raiders
P.O. Box 351
Prince Albert, Saskatchewan S6V 5R7
(306) 764-5348
Fax (306) 764-5454
GM: Dale Engel

Red Deer Rebels
PO Bag 5020
Red Deer, Alberta T4N 6A1
(403) 341-6000
Fax (403) 341-6009
GM: Wayne Simpson

Regina Pats
Box 104
Regina, Saskatchewan S4P 2Z5
(306) 522-5604
Fax (306) 569-1021
GM: Bill Hicke

Saskatoon Blades
R.R. #4, G.B. 256
Saskatoon, Saskatchewan S7K 3J7
(306) 975-8844
Fax (306) 934-1097
GM: Daryl Lubiniecki

Seattle Thunderbirds
P.O. Box 19391
Seattle, WA 98109
(206) 728-9121
Fax (206) 728-0169
GM: Peter Anholt

Spokane Chiefs
P.O. Box 5371
Spokane, WA 99205
(509) 328-0450
Fax (509) 328-7608
GM: Tim Speltz

Swift Current Broncos
P.O. Box 2345
Swift Current, Saskatchewan S9H 4X6
(306) 773-1509
Fax (306) 773-5406
GM: Graham James

Tacoma Rockets
222 E. 26th Street
Suite 104
Tacoma, WA 98421
(206) 627-3653
Fax (206) 627-8575
GM: Bruce Hamilton

Tri-City Americans
Tri-City Coliseum
7100 West Quinault
Kennewick, WA 99336
(509) 736-0606
Fax (509) 783-4591
GM: Ron Toigo

Victoria Cougars
632, 345 Quebec Street
Victoria, B.C. V8V 1W4
(604) 385-5611
Fax (604) 385-3157
GM: Rick Brodsky

Canadian Hockey League

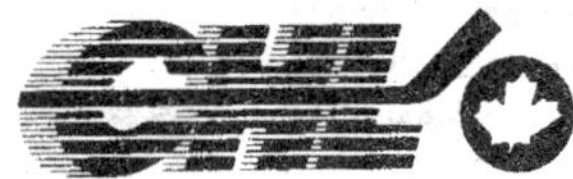

305 Milner Avenue
Suite 208
Scarborough, Ontario M1B 3V4
(416) 298-3523
Fax (416) 298-3187
Pres: Ed Cynoweth
PR: Jim Price

The CHL governs the three Canadian Major Jr. hockey leagues of Ontario, Quebec, and WHL.

USA Hockey

2997 Broadmoor Valley Road
Colorado Springs, CO 80906
(719) 576-4990
Fax (719) 577-5700

The USHL & North American Leagues are Junior A Calibre.

United States Hockey League

P.O. Box 3644
Sioux City, IA 51102
(712) 258-1525
Stat: John Cowley
PR: Steve McCall
(319) 232-3489

Des Moines Buccaneers
P.O. Box 3642
Des Moines, IA 50322
(515) 278-9757
GM: Bob Ferguson

Dubuque Fighting Saints
P.O. Box 265
Dubuque, IA 52001
(319) 589-4353
GM: Cary Eades

Madison Capitols
6000 Gisholt Drive
Madison, WI 53713
(608) 221-0991
GM: Kevin McCaffrey

North Iowa Huskies
P.O. Box 1713
Mason City, IA 50401
(515) 424-3856
GM: P.K. O'Handley

Omaha Lancers
5015 Underwood Ave.
Omaha, NE 68132
(402) 556-7825
GM: Dave Morinville

Rochester Mustangs
P.O. Box 5872
Rochester, MN 55903
(507) 282-3301
GM: Mark Kaufman

St. Paul Vulcans
3415 University Ave.
St. Paul, MN 55114
(612) 642-4662
GM: Mike Guentzel

Sioux City Musketeers
P.O. Box 3313
Sioux City, IA 51102
(712) 252-2116
GM: David Lohrei

Thunder Bay Flyers
P.O. Box 2301
Thunder Bay, Ontario P7B 5E8
(807) 625-3320
GM: Dave Siciliano

Waterloo Black Hawks
P.O. Box 2222
Waterloo, IA 50704
(319) 232-3444
GM: Rob Grillo

North American Junior Hockey League

4051 Circle Drive
West Bloomfield, MI 48323
(313) 363-2554
Pres: Hugh Melvin

Junior B Hockey

Northeastern Junior Hockey League

15 Hinkleyville Road
Spencerport, NY 14559
(716) 352-1521
Pres: William K. Smith

New England Junior Hockey League

Springfield Olympics
Enfield Twin Rinks
One Prior Road
Enfield, CT 06082
(203) 745-5588
Pres: Gary Dineen
Springfield plays an independent
schedule but is part of the NEJHL.

The Metropolitan Association
(201) 748-2893
Pres: Dick Foster

Includes Jr. B. clubs in N.Y., Long Island, N.J. & D.C.
area.

Atlantic Hockey League
3 Pendleton Drive
Cherry Hill, N.J. 08003
(609) 424-8343
Pres: Joan Scofield

Delaware Valley Hockey League
P.O. Box 178
Willow Grove, PA 19090
(215) 659-4253
Pres: Ed Fino

Minnesota Jr. B. Hockey League
(612) 421-7325
Pres: Pat Cleath
Has clubs in Duluth, Roseville,
Anoka, and Hopkins.

USA Hockey Junior Council
500 Waterloo Building
Waterloo, IA 50701
(319) 291-7202
Chairman: Dave Tyler

Canadian Junior Hock

The following is a list of Canadian Jr. A. hockey
leagues. Players from these leagues are drafted by the
Major Junior Leagues. Junior A leagues compete for
the Centennial Cup.

Alberta Junior Hockey League

9914-96A Avenue
Fort Saskatchewan, Alberta T8L 1P6
(403) 992-0466
Pres: Dave Cranston

Bonnyville Pontiacs
#26, 4718-50 Avenue
Bonnyville, Alberta T9N 1A2
(403) 826-2893
GM: Kris Barnes

Calgary Canucks
P.O. Box 3039, Sta. B
Calgary, Alberta T2M 4L6
(403) 272-7211
GM: Morley Bengert

Calgary Royals
6420-6A St. S.E.
Calgary, Alberta T2H 2B7
(403) 255-8387
Pres: Don MacCallum

Fort McMurray Oil Barons
P.O. Box 5689
Fort McMurray, Alberta T9H 4V9
(403) 743-5509
Pres: Brian Blackburn

Fort Saskatchewan Traders
P.O. Box 3333
Fort Saskatchewan, Alberta T8L 2T3
(403) 998-7170
Pres: Stephen Bluett

Lloydminster Blazers
P.O. Box 1122
Lloydminster, Sask. S9V 1E9
(403) 875-1980
Pres: Bill Kondro

Olds Grizzlys
Box 2859
Olds, Alberta T0M 1P0
(403) 556-2600
Pres: Dan Wourms

St. Albert Saints
P.O. Box 91
St. Albert, Alberta T8N 1E0
(403) 459-6052
Dr. Max Plageman

Sherwood Park Crusaders
Box 3108
Sherwood Park, Alberta T8A 2A6
(403) 431-1143
Pres: Bob Green

AJHL Publicity
P.O. Box 592
Crossfield, Alberta T0M 0S0
(403) 946-4240
Fax (403) 337-3460
PR: Dave Cuming

B.C. Junior Hockey League
16235 Beach Rd., R.R. #7
Surrey, B.C. V4B 5A8
(604) 538-8506
Fax (604) 538-8531
Pres: Ron Boileau

Bellingham Ice Hawks
1801 W. Bakerview Rd.
Bellingham, WA 98226
(206) 676-8090
GM: Don Steinke

Chilliwack Chiefs
9291 Corbould Street
Chilliwack, B.C. V2P 4A6
(604) 795-7300
Pres: Orland Kurtenbach

Kelowna Spartans
P.O. Box 1605, Station A
Kelowna, B.C. V1Y 7N3
(604) 763-9009
Pres: Don Haakstad

Merritt Centennials
P.O. Box 1730
Merritt, B.C. V0K 2B0
(604) 378-5778
Pres: Brian Barrett

Nanaimo Clippers
P.O. Box 605, Station A
Nanaino, B.C. V9R 5L9
(604) 754-2361
Pres: Cliff McNabb

Penticton Panthers
399 Power Street
Penticton, B.C. V2A 7K9
(604) 493-4312
Pres: Mark Wagstaff

Powell River Paper Kings
P.O. Box 342
Powell River, B.C. V8A 5C2
(604) 485-6525
Pres: Joe Mastordonato

Surrey Eagles
15239 N. Bluff Road
Surrey, B.C. V4A 1R6
(604) 531-4625
GM: Colin Campbell

Vernon Lakers
920 Waddington Drive
Vernon, B.C. V1T 8T3
(604) 549-5113
Pres: Mel Lis

Cowichan Valley Capitals
2687 James Street
Duncan, B.C. V9L 2X5
(604) 748-9930
Pres: Ron Smith

The Central Junior League has been in existence for over 25 years. The CHJL has sent such players as Steve Yzerman, Rod Shutt, Larry Robinson, and Billy Smith on to the NHL.

Central Junior Hockey League

91 Country Lane
Kanata, Ontario K2L 1J4
(613) 836-2367
Pres: Don Brown

Brockville Braves
P.O. Box 254
Brockville, Ontario K6V 5V5
(613) 342-7881
Pres: Mac MacLean

Gloucester Rangers
Earl Armstrong Arena
2020 Ogilvie Road
Gloucester, Ontario K1J 7N8
(613) 749-3532
Pres: Bill Dewsnap

Hawkesbury Hawks
P.O. Box 514
Hawkesbury, Ontario K6A 2Y2
(613) 632-2257
Pres: Ray Reneud

Kanata Valley Lasers
10 McKitrick Drive
Kanata, Ontario K2L 1M7
(613) 831-0445
Pres: James Mulligan

Massena Turbines
P.O. Box 5002
Massena, NY 13662
(315) 760-9799
Pres: Jim Kelley

Nepean Raiders
P.O. Box 5695, Station F
Ottawa, Ontario K2C 3M1
(613) 820-0822
Pres: Jeff MacLean

Ottawa Senators
523 Sirois Avenue
Ottawa, Ontario K1K 1H3
(613) 749-2505
Pres: Maurice Laurin

Pembroke Lumber Kings
P.O. Box 92
Pembroke, Ontario K8A 6X1
(613) 687-5406
Pres: James Farelli

Smiths Falls Bears
P.O. Box 1046
Smiths Falls, Ontario K7A 5A5
(613) 283-3131
Pres: Brian Kirby

Manitoba Junior Hockey League

516 Hargrave Street
Winnipeg, Manitoba R3A 0X8
(204) 942-2456
Commissioner: Gary W. Cribbs

Dauphin Kings
Box 134
Dauphin, Manitoba R7N 2T9
(204) 638-8968
Pres: I.B. Petersen

Kildonan North Stars
38 Pilgrim Avenue
Winnipeg, Manitoba R2M 0L3
(204) 943-5700
Pres: Carey Chartier

Portage & District Terriers
Box 33
Portage La Prairie, Manitoba R1N 3B2
(204) 857-7380
Pres: Cameron Allison

St. Boniface Saints
123 Edgewater Drive
Winnipeg, Manitoba R2J 2V4
(204) 256-2092
Pres: Ralph Borger

St. James Canadians
81 Amarynth Crescent
Winnipeg, Manitoba R2Y 0C3
(204) 888-3042
Pres: J.M. Gilhooly

Selkirk Steelers
Box 161
Selkirk, Manitoba R1A 2B2
(204) 785-2900
Pres: Dennis Stewart

Southeast Thunderbirds
201-511 Ellice Avenue
Winnipeg, Manitoba R3P 1B6
(204) 254-0296

Winkler Flyers
Box 3000
Winkler, Manitoba R0G 2X0
(204) 325-8239
Pres: Ken Loewen

Winnipeg South Blues
112-138 Portsmouth Road
Winnipeg, Manitoba R3P 1B6
(204) 895-0325
Pres: Rod Docker

Maritime Junior Hockey League
PO Box 1312
Dartmouth, Nova Scotia B2Y 4B9
(902) 464-4257
Fax (902) 461-1900
Vice Pres: Terry Seifried

Amherst Ramblers
RR #2
Tindish Bridge, N.S. B4H 3X9
(902) 661-8053
PR: Larry Rhindress

Antigonish Bulldogs
RR #5 (West River)
Antigonish, NS B2G 2L3
(902) 863-2897
Vice Pres: Bill Fraser

Charlottetown Jr. Abbies
8 Aberdeen Drive
East Royalty, P.E.I. CIC IH8
(902) 629-1705
GM: Jim Kennedy

Cole Harbour Colts
23 Clearview Street
Dartmouth, N.S. B3A 2M8
(902) 469-2331
PR: David Graham

Halifax Exports
117 Flamingo Drive
Halifax, N.S. B3M 1T5
(902) 443-4015
GM: Ralph Matheson

Moncton Beavers
22 Bessborough Avenue
Moncton, N.B. EIE 1P2
(902) 855-2507
Pres: Bob Taylor

Summerside Capitals
148 Brennan Avenue
Summerside, P.E.I. CIN 2K7
(902) 436-6664
Pres: Clair Sudsbury

The Peace Cariboo League operates in northern B.C. about 8 hours North of Vancouver. The Peace Cariboo League has been in existence for nearly 14 years.

Peace Cariboo Hockey League
906 - 550 Victoria Street
Prince George, B.C. V2L 2K1
(604) 562-6159
Fax (604) 563-1695
Pres: Neil Fowlie

Fort St. John Huskies
Box 6483
Fort St. John, B.C. V1J 4H9
Fax: (604) 785-0242
GM: Pat Hall

Prince George Spruce Kings
P.O. Box 2174
Prince George, B.C. V2N 2J6
(604) 564-1747
GM: Bryan Mix

Quesnel Millionaires
P.O. Box 4478
Quesnel, B.C. V2J 3J4
Fax: (604) 992-2552
GM: Jess Armstrong

Williams Lake Mustangs
Box 4368
Williams Lake, B.C. V2G 2V4
(604) 392-5632
GM: Doug Beaman

Prince Edward Island Junior A Hockey League
6 Waverly Court
Charlottetown, P.E.I.
Canada C1H 3C3
Pres: Tony Hansen

Saskatchewan Junior Hockey League

152 MacDougal Crescent
Regina, Saskatchewan S4S 5M7
(306) 586-2615
Fax: (306) 585-0005
Pres: Wayne M. Kartusch

Estevan Bruins
P.O. Box 146
Estevan, Saskatchewan S4A 2A2
(306) 634-7730
GM: Bill Shinske

Flin Flon Bombers
P.O. Box 762
Flin Flon, Manitoba R8A 1N6
(204) 687-4404
GM: John Kuzub

Humbolt Broncos
P.O. Box 1414
Humbolt, Sask. S0K 2A0
(306) 682-4302
GM: Dave Guilbault

Melfort Mustangs
P.O. Box 3640
Melfort, Sask. S0E 1A0
(306) 752-2799
GM: Len Strandberg

Melville Millionaires
P.0 Box 2197
Melville, Sask. S0A 2P0
(306) 728-2363
GM: Don Rathgeber

Minot Americans
P.O. Box 1796
Minot, ND 58702
(701) 852-8663
GM: Jack Kleven

Nipawin Junior Hawks
P.O. Box 2678
Nipawin, Sask. S0E 1E0
(306) 862-4878
GM: Neil Little

North Battleford North Stars
P.O. Box 1247
North Battleford, Sask. S9A 3K2
(306) 446-0166
GM: Leo McDonnald

Notre Dame Hounds
P.O. Box 220
Wilcox, Sask. S0G 5E0
(306) 732-2080
GM: David Kenney

Lebret Eagles
PO Box 1
Leberet, Sask. S0G 2Y0
(306) 332-2140
Pres: Noel Starblanket

Weyburn Red Wings
P.0 Box 1112
Weyburn, Sask. S4H 2L3
(306) 842-2212
GM: Dwight McMillan

Yorkton Terriers
P.O. Box 277
Yorkton, Sask. S3N 2V7
(306) 783-4077
GM: Dennis Polonich

Kindersley Klippers
PO Box 2398
Kindersley, Sask. S0L 1S0
(306) 463-2927
Pres: Bruce Adams

New Brunswick Junior Hockey League

Moncton Junior Hawks
125 Brentwood Drive
Moncton, New Brunswick E1E 1N1
(506) 857-8309
GM: Joseph Robinson

Richibudo Voyageurs
P.O. Box 211
St. Louis Kent Co., N.B. E0A 2M0
(506) 743-2462
GM: Roger Brun

St. John Stingers
256 Lakeside Drive
St. John, New Brunswick E2N 1H9
(506) 652-2803

New Foundland Junior Hockey League
P.O. Box 176
Grand Falls, Nfld. A2A 2J4
(709) 489-5512
Sec: Harold Hillier

Avalon Capitals
23 Limerick Place
St. John's, Nfld. A1B 2H2
GM: Lance Reid

Bay Arena Rovers
Bay Roberts, Nfld. A0A 1G0
GM: Dennis Brown

Celtics Jr. Hockey Club
P.O. Box 2632, Station A
St. John's, Nfld. A1C 6K1
GM: Les Thoms

Clarenville Caribous
P.O. Box 423
Clarenville, Nfld. A0E 1J0
GM: Derek Barbour

St. John's Jr. 50's
5 Vancouver Street
St. John's, Nfld. A1A 2R5
GM: Bob McLellan

Mount Pearl Blades
P.O. Box 504
Mount Pearl, Nfld.   A1N 2W4
GM: Ralph Neil

Quebec Junior A Hockey League

6408 Beaucourt
Montreal, Quebec H1G 2G4
(514) 326-6417
Pres: Yvon La Fortune

Chateauguay Elites
127 rue Chapais
Chateauguay, Quebec J6K 1K5
(514) 691-8667
Pres: Andrew Gledhill

Hochelaga Junes Sportifs
3760 Marcil
Montreal, Quebec H4A 2Z4
(514) 489-5039
Pres: Pierre Robin

LaSalle Cyclones
714, 44e Avenue
LaSalle, Quebec H8P 2T6
(514) 364-9363
Pres: Andre Trudeau

Laval Jr. Titans
8265, 15ieme Avenue
Laval, Quebec H7A 1B3
(514) 665-0706
Pres: Louis Kozel

Longueuil Sieurs
3110 Routhier
Longueuil, Quebec J4L 3N5
(514) 670-4270
Pres: Serge Sevigny

Montreal Athletiques
10135 rue Fabre
Montreal, Quebec H2C 3E1
(514) 389-8190
Pres: Roland Menard

Pierrefonds Lions
12487 St. Louis
Pierrefonds, Quebec H8Z 1A3
(514) 684-3795
Pres: Peter Simpson

Repentigny Olympiques
61 rue Bellefeuille
Repentigny, Quebec J6A 5G4
(514) 581-3336
Pres: Andre Boucher

St. Antoine Rapidos
2707 lere rue
St. Sophie, Quebec J0R 1S0
(514) 436-1496
Pres: Claude Delage

St. Hyacinthe Toros
4720 Boul. Laurier
St. Hyacinthe, Quebec J2S 3V2
(514) 773-9642
Pres: Claude Lemieux

St. Leonard Express
1197 rue Ovide Clermont
Montreal-nord, Quebec H1G 3Z4
(514) 322-1364
Pres: Ronald St. Jean

Ontario Junior Hockey League

P.O. Box 2
Belmont, Ontario N0L 1B0
(519) 644-0190
Chmn: Don Yeck
The OHA Junior A League has not operated since the 1987-88 season.

The following are Junior B leagues in Canada.

Pacific Coast Amateur Hockey League

215-10138 136th A Street
Surrey, B.C.
Canada V3T 4G2
(604) 858-3565
Pres: Edith Michael

West Coast Junior B
Hockey League
6171 Skaha Crescent
Richmond, B.C.
Canada V7C 2R3
(604) 277-1348
Pres: Tom Shaw

Kootenay Junior B
Hockey League
Box 1068
Fruitvale, B.C.
Canada V0G 1L0
(604) 367-6502
Pres: Vince Morelli

Mainland Junior B
Hockey League
6475 Berlin Street
Halifax, Nova Scotia
Canada B3L 1T7
(902) 454-5365
Comm: Gordon Cluett

Midwestern Junior B
Hockey League
39 Hillsborough Crescent
Kitchener, Ontario N2G 1J5
(519) 741-2277
Chmn: Lloyd Parkhouse

Western Junior B
Hockey League
P.O. Box 2
Belmont, Ontario N0L 1B0
(519) 644-0190
Pres: Don Yeck

Golden Horseshoe Junior B
Hockey League
1548 Warland Road
Oakville, Ontario L6L 1N5
(416) 827-1017
Chmn: Bob MacKinnon

Central Junior B
Hockey League
177 Steeles Avenue E.
North York, Ontario M2M 3Y6
(416) 225-3987
Chmn: Al Morris

Metro Junior B
Hockey League
P.O. Box 595
Port Perry, Ontario L0B 1N0
(416) 985-7295

Ligue de Hockey de
Junior AA
44, rue St. Laurent
Windsor, Quebec J1S 1N0
(819) 826-5684
Pres: Real Veilleux

Ligue Circuit Ultramar
Junior AA
2355 rue Laliberte
Jonquiere, Quebec G7X 5W7
(418) 343-3017
Pres: Marcel Maltais

Great Lakes Junior C
Hockey League
126 Cedar Crescent
Sarnia, Ontario N7T 4J5
(519) 332-2220
Conv: Bob Williamson

Western Junior C
Hockey League
P.O. Box 712
Port Elgin, Ontario N0M 2C0
(519) 332-2510
Chmn: Gordon Gottscheu

Mid-Ontario Junior C
Hockey League
108 Walton Drive
Aurora, Ontario L4G 3K4
(416) 475-4417
Chmn: Gary Moroney

**Central Junior C
Hockey League**
12 Trent Street N.
Frankford, Ontario K0K 2C0
(613) 398-6200
Chmn: Wayne Tod

**Western Junior D
Hockey League**
P.O. Box 2
Belmont, Ontario N0L 1B0
(519) 644-0190
Chmn: Don Yeck

**Southern Counties Junior D
Hockey League**
139 Main Street S.
Belmont, Ontario N0L 1B0
(519) 644-0525
Conv: Wayne Smith

Canadian Senior Hockey

Monashee AA Senior Hockey League
#200 3103A 31st Avenue
Vernon, B.C. V1T 2G9
(604) 542-1521
Pres: Dick Henderson

Ashcroft Warriors
Box 440
Ashcroft, B.C. V0K 1A0
(604) 453-9154
GM: Cliff Kirkpatrick

Penticton Silver Bullets
215 Windsor Avenue
Penticton, B.C. V2A 2K3
(604) 493-0442
GM: Don McCall

Revelstoke Merchants
1573 Mountain View
Revelstoke, B.C. Canada
(604) 837-3749
GM: John Kehler

Sicamous Eagles
813 Kappel Street
Sicamous, B.C. Canada
(604) 836-3157
GM: Wayne March

Vernon Vikings
#310 3201 30th Avenue
Vernon, B.C. V1T 1W8
(604) 542-5872
GM: Art Brochu

Nova Scotia Senior Hockey League
187 Caldwell Road
Cole Harbour, Nova Scotia
Canada B2V 1J5
(902) 462-8875
Pres: Frank O'Brien

Canadian Amateur Hock Association
1600 James Naismith Drive
Gloucester, Ont. K1L 8H9
(613) 748-5613
Fax (613) 748-5709
Pres: Murray Costello

CAHA Provincial Association:

Alberta AHA
1-7875 48th Avenue
Red Deer, Alberta T4P 2K1
(403) 342-6777
Ex. Dir: Ken Craig

British Columbia AHA
1551 Broadmead Avenue
Victoria, B.C. V8P 2V1
(604) 477-9551
Ex. Dir: Don Freer

Manitoba AHA
200 Main Street
Winnipeg, Manitoba R3C 4M2
(204) 985-4240
Ex. Dir: George Allard

New Brunswick AHA
390 King Street, Suite 312
Fredericton, New Brunswick
Canada E3B 4Z9
(506) 453-0089
Ex. Dir: Bob White

Newfoundland AHA
15A High Street, Box 176
Grand Falls, Newfoundland A2A 2J4
(709) 489-5512
Exec. Dir: Harold Hillier

Northern Ontario AHA
800 Ferguson Street
North Bay, Ontario P1B 1X9
(705) 474-8851
Exec. Dir: Betty Blair

Nova Scotia AHA
Box 3010 South
5516 Spring Garden Road
Halifax, Nova Scotia B3J 2G6
(902) 420-1550
Exec. Dir: Mrs. Pat MacDougall

Ontario Hockey Association
1425 Bishop Street, Unit 6
Cambridge, Ontario N1R 6J9
(519) 622-2402
Pres: Brent Ladds

Ottawa & District AHA
1891 Merivale Road
Nepean, Ontario K2G 1E5
(613) 224-7686
Exec. Dir: Heidi Sprung

Prince Edward Island AHA
89 Upper Prince Street
Charlottetown, P.E.I. C1A 4S6
(902) 892-2849
Exec. Dir: Jack Kane

Quebec Ice Hockey Federation
4545 Pierre de Coubertin
Box 1000, Station M
Montreal, Quebec H1V 3R2
(514) 252-3081
Exec. Dir.: Guy Blondeau

Saskatchewan AHA
2931 Park Street
Box 883
Regina, Saskatchewan S4P 3B1
(306) 789-5101
Exec. Dir: Raymond Rambow

Thunder Bay AHA
415 E. Victoria Avenue
Thunder Bay, Ontario P7C 1A6
(807) 622-0981
Exec. Dir: Joe Ward

The following are Senior Leagues and organizations throughout the U.S. Senior Leagues are allowed to carry semi-pro, amateur and former professional players on their rosters.

Badger State Hockey League

165 East 10th Street
Fond du Lac, WI 54935
(414) 923-4535
Pres: Don Kohlman

DePere Deacons
2623 Oakwood Drive
Green Bay, WI 54304
(414) 499-7478
GM: Carl Magnuson

Eagle River Falcons
1432 Woodland Lane
Eagle River, WI 54521
(715) 479-6215
GM: Dennis Carter

Fond du Lac Bears
165 East 10th Street
Fond du Lac, WI 54935
(414) 923-4535
GM: Don Kohlman

Kenosha Komets
7810 Sheridan Road
Kenosha, WI 53143
(414) 652-5454
GM: Jerry Simonsen

Mosinee Paper Makers
766 Landfried
Mosinee, WI 54455
(715) 693-2383
GM: John Berkhahn

Wausau Cyclones
1932 Emerson Street
Wausau, WI 54401
(715) 845-2054
GM: Myron Schael

Minnesota Senior Hockey
Mr. John Carter
Rosseau, MN 56751
(218) 463-1139

Warroad Lakers
Memorial Arena
Warroad, MN 56763
(218) 386-1477
Pres: Cal Marvin

Illinois Senior Hockey League

928 S. Summit
Villa Park, IL 60188
(312) 834-0529
Pres: Ed Howe

USA Hockey Senior Council
165 E. Tenth Street
Fond du Lac, WI 54935
(419) 923-4535
Chairman: Don Kohlman
USA Hockey (AHAUS) governs
amateur hockey in the U.S.

Hockey Publications

American Hockey Magazine
2997 Broadmoor Valley Road
Colorado Springs, CO 80906
(719) 576-4990
Editor: Michael Schroeder

Eishockey Magazine
WIBA - DRUCK
Haunstetter Strasse 26
8900 Augsburg, Germany

The European Hockey Report
12275 Cote de Liesse Road
Dorval, Quebec
Canada H4P 1B4
(514) 631-4266

Hockey Digest
990 Grove Street
Evanston, IL 60201
(312) 941-6440

The Hockey News
85 Scarsdale Road, Suite 100
Don Mills, Ontario M3B 2R2
(416) 445-5702
(800) 268-7793

Hockey Pictorial
85 Scarsdale Road, Suite 100
Don Mills, Ontario M3B 2R2
(416) 445-5702
(800) 268-7793

Let's Play Hockey
8100 26th Avenue South
Suite 110
Bloomington, MN 55425
(612) 854-4299
Editor: Dave Wright

Midland Hockey Review
P.O. Box 34334
Omaha, NE 68134
Editor: Gary Kuti

Oldtimers' Hockey News
Box 951
640 Christopher Road
Peterborough, Ontario K9J 7A5
Publisher: Dave Tatham

Hockey Ink
3514 Stellhorn Road
Suite A
Fort Wayne, IN 46815
(219) 486-PUCK
Editor: Gerald Mommer

Central Hockey League

5840 S. Memorial Drive
Suite 302
Tulsa, OK 74145
(918) 664-8881
Fax (918) 664-2215
Pres: Ray Miron
PR: Jason Rothwell

Dallas Freeze

2700 Stemmons Freeway
Suite 402 Tower East
Dallas, TX 75207
(214) 631-7825
Fax (214) 631-8090
GM: Tom Koch

Fort Worth Fire

910 Houston Street
Suite 400
Fort Worth, TX 76102
(817) 336-1992
Fax (817) 336-1997
GM: George Branum

Memphis RiverKings

Mid-South Coliseum
The Fairgrounds
Memphis, TN 38104
(901) 278-9009
Fax (901) 274-3209
GM: Jim Riggs

Oklahoma City Blazers

Sheraton-Century Mall
100 W. Main, Suite 172
Oklahoma City, OK 73102
(405) 235-7825
Fax (405) 272-9875
GM: Brad Lund

San Antonio Iguanas

110 Broadway, Suite 25
San Antonio, TX 78205
(210) 227-4449
Fax (210) 227-4484
GM: Jim Goodman

Tulsa Oilers

4528 S. Sheridan Road
Suite 212
Tulsa, OK 74145
(918) 663-5888
Fax (918) 663-5977
GM: Jeff D. Lund

Wichita Thunder

410-A N. St. Francis
Wichita, KS 67202
(316) 264-4625
Fax (316) 264-3037
GM: Bill Shuck

Sunshine Hockey League

700 W. Lemon Street
PO Box 1808
Lakeland, FL 33802
(813) 499-8112
Comm: Bill Friday

Daytona Beach Sun Devils

222 S. Peninsula Drive
Daytona Beach, CA 32118
(904) 257-6264
Fax (904) 257-2217
GM: Dominique DeLannoy

Jacksonville Bullets

15721 Northside Drive
Jacksonville, FL 32218
(904) 399-3223
Fax (904) 396-6768
GM: Bob Sabourin

Lakeland Ice Warriors

700 West Lemon Street
PO Box 1808
Lakeland, FL 33802
(813) 499-8112
Fax (813) 499-8114
GM: David Groulx

West Palm Beach Blaze

1610 Palm Beach Lakes Blvd.
West Palm Beach, FL 33401
(407) 640-9544
Fax (407) 686-4713
GM: Bill Nyrop

Frontier Junior Hockey League

PO Box 1526
Vail, CO 81658
(303) 476-4071
Pres: Stuart Borne

Lacrosse

International Lacrosse Federation
16 Deans Wood Close
Wantirna South
3152 Victoria, Australia
(03) 801-1575
Sec. Treas.: George Tillotson
ILF Vice President:
P.O. Box 1149
Piscataway, NJ 08854
(201) 463-7869
VP: Tom Hayes

The Lacrosse Foundation
Newton H. White Jr.
Athletic Center
Homewood
Baltimore, MD 21218
(301) 235-6882

Major Indoor
Lacrosse League

2310 W. 75th Street
Prairie Village, KS 66208
(913) 384-8960
Fax (913) 384-8961
Pres.: Chris Fritz
VP: Russ Cline
PR: Leigh Collins

The MILL is the only professional league
in North America. Pro Indoor Lacrosse is
discovering a rebirth where its
predecessors, the NALA, NLL, and the
outdoor ALL failed in the past.

Baltimore Thunder
Baltimore Arena
Baltimore, MD 21201
(301) 347-2020
GM: G. Darrell Russell

Boston Blazers
Boston Garden
150 Causeway Street
Boston, MA 02114
(401) 863-2277
GM: Peter Lasagna

Buffalo Bandits
Memorial Auditorium
140 Main Street
Buffalo, NY 14202
(716) 856-7300
GM: John Mouradian

Detroit Turbos
Joe Louis Arena
Detroit, MI 48226
(313) 567-6000
GM: Tom Wright

New York Saints
Veterans Memorial Coliseum
Uniondale, NY 11553
(516) 794-9300
GM: Tom Flately

Philadelphia Wings
The Spectrum
Philadelphia, PA 19148
(215) 336-3600
GM: Michael French

Pittsburgh Bulls
Civic Arena
Pittsburgh, PA 15219
(412) 642-1800
GM: Ernest Lichtfuss

**U.S. Club Lacrosse
Assocation**
2800 Whitney Avenue
Baltimore, MD 21215
(301) 235-8532

The following leagues are amateur status, mainly representing Canada where Lacrosse is considered the national sport. Most lacrosse played in Canada is indoor box lacrosse.

Can-Am Lacrosse League
411 Bloomingdale
Akron, NY 14001
(716) 542-4116
Pres: Marty Ground

Canadian Lacrosse Association

1600 James Naismith Drive
Gloucester, Ontario
Canada K1B 5N4
(613) 748-5641
Fax (613) 748-5706
Dir: Michael Lachapelle

Provincial Lacrosse Associations

Alberta Lacrosse Assocation
Percy Page Centre
11759 Groat Road
Edmonton, Alberta T5M 3K6
(403) 453-8676
Coordinator: Warren Renden

British Columbia Lacrosse Association
6362 Fraser Street
Vancouver, B.C. V5W 3A4
(604) 324-2114
Pres: George Goodrich

Manitoba Lacrosse Association
1700 Ellice Avenue
Winnipeg, Manitoba R3H 0B1
(204) 985-4000
Exec. Dir: Rick Brownlee

New Brunswick Lacrosse Federation
6 Elizabeth Court
Saint John, N.B. E2K 3B6
(506) 657-6733
Exec. Dir: Ken Crossman

Newfoundland Lacrosse Federation
6 Albany Street
St. John's, Newfoundland A1E 3C5
(709) 579-5823
Pres: Charlie Decker

Nova Scotia Lacrosse Association
P.O. Box 3010 South
Halifax, Nova Scotia B3J 3G6
(902) 420-8880
Pres: Bill Manley

Ontario Lacrosse Association
1220 Sheppard Avenue East
Willowdale, Ontario M2K 2X1
(416) 495-4230
Fax (416) 495-4228
Exec. Dir: Stan Cockerton

Prince Edward Island
Lacrosse Association
96 Prince Street
Charlottetown, P.E.I.
Pres: A.L. Saunders

Quebec Lacrosse Association
4545 Pierre-de-Coubertin
C.P. 1000, Station M
Montreal, Quebec H1V 3R2
(514) 252-3058
Tech. Dir: Pierre Filion

Saskatchewan Lacrosse Association
1879 Lorne Street
Regina, Saskatchewan S4P 2L7
(306) 780-9200
Exec. Dir: Shelley Clubb-Platten

OLA Major Series
R.R. No. 2
Whitby, Ontario L1N 5R5
(416) 668-8423
Comm: Mike Gray

Brampton Excelsiors
231 Elizabeth Street South
Brampton, Ontario L6Y 1S2
(416) 451-5572
GM: Everett Coates

Brooklin Redmen
974 Palm Court
Oshawa, Ontario L1H 2H3
(416) 436-7717
GM: Bob Duignan

Peterborough Quakers
1155 Milburn Street
Peterborough, Ontario K9H 6P1
(705) 743-5080
GM: Clarke Scholey

OLA Senior Series
803 Fifth Avenue A East
Owen Sound, Ontario N4K 2S9
(519) 376-8656
Comm: Cy Lemon

Fergus Thistles
Box 71
289 St. Patrick Street E.
Fergus, Ontario N1M 1M5
(519) 843-5135
GM: Mac Mason

Orangeville Northmen
48 Meadow Drive
Orangeville, Ontario L9W 3Z1
(519) 941-9731
GM: Shane Sanderson

Owen Sound North Stars
792 23rd Street
Owen Sound, Ontario N4K 4H3
(519) 371-0207
GM: Rick Fernall

Onario Junior A Series
39 Dorchester Drive
Bramalea, Ontario L6T 3C8
(416) 793-1083
Comm: Dean McLeod

Bay Area Bengals
2060 Brant Street #6
Burlington, Ontario L7P 3A6
(416) 332-1119
GM: Joe Walsh

Brampton Excelsiors
62 Foster Court
Brampton, Ontario L6V 3M8
(416) 451-9207
GM: Mike Cassidy

Mississauga Tomahawks
1073 West Avenue
Mississauga, Ontario L5E 1W1
(416) 278-9675
GM: Jack Wilson

Peterborough Maulers
1005 Albany Court
Peterborough, Ontario K9J 1J3
(705) 745-6730
GM: Lee Vitarelli

St. Catharines Athletics
75 Richelieu Drive
St. Catharines, Ontario L2M 2C3
(416) 646-1824
GM: Jim Brady

Sarnia Keelan Pacers
624 Bristol Street
Sarnia, Ontario N7S 5E1
(519) 332-1004
GM: Ron Pask

Six Nations Arrows
RR #1
Wilsonville, Ontario N0E 1Z0
(519) 445-2603
GM: Cliff Whitlow

Whitby Warriors
111 Meadow Crescent
Whitby, Ontario L1N 3J5
(416) 728-3079
GM: Al Garrard

Ontario Junior B Series
608 Arbor Road
Port Credit, Ontario L5G 2J9
(416) 278-7346
Comm: Al Baxter

Brampton Excelsiors
14 Lynwood Court
Bramalea, Ontario L6V 2X4
(416) 453-9373
GM: Tom Valade

Elora Mohawks
674 Kitchener Ave.
Fergus, Ontario N1M 1N4
(519) 843-3552
GM: John Rutherford

Gloucester Griffins
157 Rachel Avenue
Ottawa, Ontario K1H 6C5
(613) 737-3476
GM: Dave Smith

Huntsville Hawks
Box 177, R.R. #1
Huntsville, Ontario P0A 1K0
(705) 789-9382
GM: Larry French

Kitchener Waterloo Braves
50 Katherine Crescent
Kitchener, Ontario N2M 2K1
(519) 578-7899
GM: Lawrie Hallman

Niagra Spartan Warriors
264 Grantham Avenue #408
St. Catharines, Ontario L2M 4Z7
(416) 937-7244
GM: Rob Roy

Orangeville Junior Northmen
6 Park Lane
Orangeville, Ontario L9W 3Z2
(519) 941-3937
GM: Bob Cievely

Owen Sound Signmen
617 Ninth Street E.
Owen Sound, Ontario N4K 1P8
(519) 376-1236
GM: Calvin Grimoldby

Peterborough Stags
431 George Street S.
Peterborough, Ontario K9J 3E2
(705) 745-4612
GM: Peter B. Duffus

Scarborough Saints
51 Wyndcliff Crescent
North York, Ontario M4A 2J9
(416) 759-5037
GM: Aubrey Wilkinson

Ontario Senior Field Lacrosse League
337 Linden Street
Oshawa, Ontario L1H 6R2
(416) 571-1980
Director: Paul MacDonald

Ontario Junior Field Lacrosse
871 Niagara Street
Welland, Ontario L3C 1M4
(416) 734-7833
Director: Dave Vernon

Ontario Women's Field Lacrosse
246 Monarch Park Drive
Toronto, Ontario M4J 4S3
(416) 465-8328
Director: Joanne Stanga

British Columbia Lacrosse
Western Lacrosse Association
3958 Parker Street
Burnaby, B.C. V5C 3B6
(604) 294-2274
Comm: Sohen Gill

Coquitlam Adanacs
c/o School of Kinesiology
Simon Fraser University
Burbany, B.C. V5A 1S6
(604) 687-1985
GM: Don Hedges

New Westminster Salmonbellies
424 Glenbrook Drive
New Westminster, B.C. V3L 5J3
(604) 522-7378
GM: K.C. Cook

Richmond Outlaws
12640 Old Yale Road
Surrey, B.C. V3V 3Y2
(604) 584-5853
GM: Wayne Clark

Vancouver Burrards
812 Baker Drive
Coquitlam, B.C. V3J 6W7
(604) 469-0055
GM: Wally Donaldson

Victoria Pay Less
No. 101 - 3930 Shelbourne Street
Victoria, B.C. V8P 5P6
(604) 383-5457
GM: Ron Simpson

West Coast Senior Lacrosse League

Lacrosse League
930 Lillooet Street
Vancouver, B.C. V5K 4H2
(604) 254-7663
Comm: Tony Halters

Burnaby Lakers
6554 Kitchener Street
Burnaby, B.C. V5B 2J6
(604) 291-0564
GM: Dave Taylor

Ladner Pioneers
2375 East 37th Avenue
Vancouver, B.C. V5R 2T5
(604) 435-7534
GM: Mickey Meslo

Nanaimo Timbermen
160 June Avenue
Nanaimo, B.C. V9S 4R7
(604) 754-7334
GM: Irene Morrison

North Shore Indians
319 West 5th Street
North Vancouver, B.C. V7M 1K2
(604) 986-0244
GM: Lance Baker

Port Coquitlam Warriors
340 Simpson Street
New Westminister, B.C. U3L 3J9
(604) 525-3587
GM: Doug Sato

Surrey Rebels
124 Glover Avenue
New Westminster, B.C. V3L 2A6
(604) 521-8523
GM: Maurice McIntyre

West Coast Junior Lacrosse League

Lacrosse League
8083 - 112A Street
Delta, B.C. V4C 4Y7
(604) 591-3793
Comm: Frazer MacDonald

Burnaby Cablevision
1244 Cliff Avenue
Burnaby, B.C.
(604) 420-2695
GM: Jack Crosby

Delta Islanders
5603 Dove Place
Ladner, B.C. V4K 3R2
(604) 946-7129
GM: Max Scabar

Langley Knights
71 Wagonwheel Crescent
Langley, B.C. V3A &n6
(604) 534-7281
GM: Ed Chick

Nanaimo Lacrosse Club
3494 Meadow Lane Road
Nanaimo, B.C. V9T 3G1
(604) 758-2224
GM: Ron Busche

Port Coquitlam Lacrosse Club
2193 Hawthorne Avenue
Port Coquitlam, B.C. V3C 1W2
(604) 941-2739
GM: Garry Grant

Port Moody Lacrosse Club
No. 112 - 2010 St. Johns Street
Port Moody, B.C. V9T 3G1
(604) 939-8164
GM: Ken Clark

South Vancouver Killarney
1286 East 60th Avenue
Vancouver, B.C. V5X 2A7
(604) 327-0514
GM: Bob Orr

B.C. Junior A Lacrosse League
7343 - 11th Avenue
Burnaby, B.C. V3N 2N2
(604) 526-8363
Comm: Murray Lehman

Burnaby Cablevision
1244 Cliff Avenue
Burnaby, B.C. V5A 2J7
(604) 420-2695
GM: Jack Crosby

Coquitlam Adanacs
1836 Windermere Avenue
Port Coquitlam, B.C.
(604) 942-6872
GM: Ted Fridge

Esquimalt Legion
3982 Bel Nor Place
Victoria, B.C.
(604) 477-5495
GM: Fred Wooster

New Westminister Salmonbellies
1728 Dublin Street
New Westminister, B.C.
(604) 522-2660
GM: John Van Os

Richmond Outlaws
10500 Palmberg Road
Richmond, B.C. V6W 1C6
(604) 277-0391
GM: Fred Aspin

Surrey Rebels
12780 - 20A Avenue
White Rock, B.C. V4A 7R6
(604) 538-3540
GM: Pat O'Brien

B.C. Intermediate A Lacrosse League
7432 Dorchester Drive
Burnaby, B.C. V5A 3J6
(604) 420-7478
Comm: Walt Matiash

Soccer

1994 World Cup
USA Committee
2029 Century Park East
Suite 400
Los Angeles, CA 90067
(310) 552-1994
Fax (310) 552-1840
Chmn: Alan Rothenberg
CEO: Charles G. Cale
COO: Scott P. Letellier

Confederation of North & Central American and Caribbean Football (CONCACAF)
717 Fifth Avenue, 13th Floor
New York, NY 10022
(212) 308-0044
Fax (212) 308-1851
Pres: Jack A. Warner (Trin & Tob)
VP: Jim Fleming (Canada)
Sec/Treas: Chuck Blazer (USA)

The following is a list of the top professional indoor and outdoor leagues as well as the top amateur leagues representing North America.

Since the demise of the NASL in the mid-80's, there has not been a major professional outdoor soccer league in North America.

Major League Soccer
2049 Century Park East
Suite 4390
Los Angeles, CA 90067
(310) MLS-KICK
Pres: Alan Rothenberg

MLS is a proposed Division I Outdoor Pro league scheduled to begin play in 1995.

National Professional Soccer League
229 Third Street N.W.
Canton, OH 44702
(216) 455-4625
Fax (216) 455-3885
Comm: Steve M. Paxos
Operations: Paul Luchowski

Baltimore Spirit
201 W. Baltimore Street
Baltimore, MD 21201
(410) 625-2320
Fax (410) 625-2553
GM: Kenny Cooper
PR: Drew Forrester

Buffalo Blizzard
140 Main Street
Buffalo, NY 14202
(716) 856-2500
Fax (716) 852-3749
GM: Tim May
PR: Sean McCrossan

Canton Invaders
1101 Market Avenue N.
Canton, OH 44702
(216) 455-6060
Fax (216) 455-9000
GM: Andy Smiles
PR: Bob Bishop

Chicago Power
10850 Laraway Road
Frankfort, IL 60423
(708) 299-9000
Fax (815) 469-2469
GM: Peter Wilt
PR: Steve Davidson

Cleveland Crunch
34200 Solon Road
Solon, OH 44139
(216) 349-2090
Fax (216) 349-0653
GM: Al Miller
PR: Chuck Murr

Dayton Dynamo
10561 Success Lane
Miamisburg, OH 45342
(513) 885-9551
Fax (513) 885-3966
GM: Mike Donahue
PR: Paul Moses

Detroit Rockers
600 Civic Center Drive
Detroit, MI 48226
(313) 396-7574
Fax (313) 396-7998
GM: Stu Mayer
PR: Ian Parratt

Harrisburg Heat
PO Box 60123
Harrisburg, PA 17106
(717) 652-4328
Fax (717) 233-8297
GM: Patrick Flynn
PR: Gregg Cook

Kansas City Attack
1800 Genessee
Kansas City, MO 64102
(816) 474-2255
Fax (816) 474-8730
GM: Dennis Shaw
PR: Tyler Cundith

Milwaukee Wave
6310 N. Port Washington Rd.
Milwaukee, WI 53217
(414) 962-9283
Fax (414) 962-4837
GM: Mike Bazelon
PR: Jim Harwood

St. Louis Ambush
5700 Oakland Avenue
St. Louis, MO 63110
(314) 647-1001
Fax (314) 647-1002
GM: Ed Gettemeier
PR: Jack Lynch

Wichita Wings
319 S. Broadway
Wichita, KS 67202
(316) 262-3545
Fax (316) 263-8531
GM: Roy Turner
PR: Dave Phillips

The NPSL is an indoor pro league.

Canadian National Soccer League

1980 Sherbrooke Street Ouest
Montreal, Quebec, Canada H3H 1E8

*The Canadian Soccer League
may return for a 1994 or 1995
Summer outdoor season.*

American Professional Soccer League

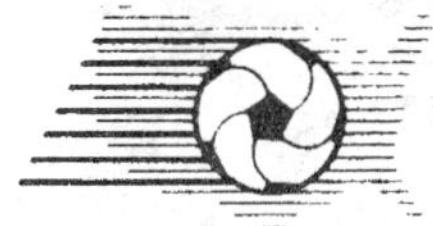

3702 Pender Drive, Suite 210
Fairfax, VA 22030
(703) 273-PROS
Fax (703) 273-9267
Comm: Wm. De La Pena

APSL Media Relations
1120 Connecticut Ave., N.W.
Suite 920
Washington, DC 20001
(202) 296-APSL
Fax (202) 296-6341
PR: Kerry Lynn Bohen
      Steve Winter

Colorado Foxes
6735 Stroh Road
Parker, CO 80134
(303) 840-1111
Fax (303) 840-1238
GM: Robert Healy
PR: Troy Fitz-Gerald

Fort Lauderdale Strikers
5301 N.W. 12th Avenue
Fort Lauderdale, FL 33309
(305) 771-5677
Fax (305) 491-3702
Pres.: Amancio V. Suarez
P.R.: Mike Hoffman

Houston Force
1823 Bissonette
Houston, TX 77005
(713) 523-9856
GM: Rick Clapp

Los Angeles Salsa
PO Box 6220
Fullerton, CA 92634
(714) 547-2572
Fax (714) 870-7070
Pres: William De La Pena
GM: David Bolton

Montreal Impact
8000 Langeller
Suite 104
St. Leonard, Quebec HIP 3K2
(514) 328-3668
Fax (514) 328-1287
Pres.: Joey Saputo
P.R.: Stephane Banfi

Seattle Sounders
1560 140th Ave., N.E.
Suite 200
Bellevue, WA 98005
(206) 622-3415
Fax (206) 643-3515
GM: Stephen Brezniak

Toronto Rockets
7135 Islington Ave., 2nd Fl.
Woodbridge, Ontario L4L 1V9
(905) 856-5511
Fax (905) 856-5522
GM: Frank Arcuri

Vancouver 86ers
1126 Douglas Road
Burnaby, B.C. V5C 4Z6
(604) 299-0086
Fax (604) 299-1886
Pres: Milan Ilich
PR: Ian Michaud

Continental Indoor Soccer League

16027 Ventura Blvd.
Suite 605
Encino, CA 91436
(818) 906-7627
Fax (818) 906-7693
Comm.: Ron Weinstein
P.R.: Dan Courtemanche
    Kristina Mohns

Anaheim Splash
2695 E. Katella Ave.
Anaheim, CA 92806
(714) 704-2400
Fax (714) 704-2443
GM: Tim Ryan

Arizona Sandsharks
201 E. Jefferson Street
Phoenix, AZ 85004
(602) 514-8300
Fax (602) 265-9359
Pres.: Jerry Colangelo
P.R.: Jeff Munn

Charlotte Vipers
2700 Independence Blvd.
Charlotte, NC 28205
(704) 343-2475
Fax (704) 377-4595
GM: Carl Scheer
PR: Brian Laing

Dallas Sidekicks
Reunion Arena
777 Sports Street
Dallas, TX 75207
(214) 653-0200
Fax (214) 748-0510
G.M.: Norm Sonju
P.R.: Kevin Sullivan

Detroit Neon
Two Championship Dr.
Auburn Hills, MI 48326
(313) 377-0100
Fax (313) 377-0981
Pres: William Davidson
PR: Bill Whitten

Houston Hotshots
1400 Post Oak Blvd.
Houston, TX 77056
(713) HOT-5100
Fax (713) 840-0925
GM: Carole Johnston
PR: Darrell Rogers

Las Vegas Dust Devils
105 E. Reno, Suite 4
Las Vegas, NV 89119
(702) 739-7767
Fax (702) 739-1475
GM: Bill MacFarland
PR: Rick Kaufman

Monterrey La Raza
Vasconcelos 715-A
Entre Genaro Garza y Narango
Garza Garcia, Nuevo Leon C.P.
66230 MEXICO
011 52 83 38 5669
Fax 011 52 83 36 4728
G.M.: Miguel Angel Garza
P.R.: Antonio Portilla

Pittsburgh Stingers
Civic Arena, Gate 9
Pittsburgh, PA 15219
(412) 642-1800
Fax (412) 642-1859
GM: Jeff Barrett
PR: Steve Bovino

Portland Pride
320 S.W. Stark
Suite 206
Portland, OR 97204
(800) 788-2378
Fax (503) 222-4939
Pres.: Brian Parrott
P.R.: Joe Schafbuch

Sacramento Knights
One Sports Parkway
Sacramento, CA 95834
(916) 928-0000
Fax (916) 928-6919
GM: Hubert Rotteveel
PR: Troy Hansen

San Diego Sockers
3942 Hancock Street
San Diego, CA 92110
(619) 224-4625
Fax (619) 222-9020
GM: Tim Latta
PR: Jim Moorhouse

San Jose Grizzlies
525 W. Santa Clara St.
San Jose, CA 95113
(408) 971-7627
Fax (408) 999-5855
GM: Art Savage
PR: Tim Bryant

Washington Warthogs
1 Harry S. Truman Dr.
Landover, MD 20785
(301) 499-6300
Fax (301) 499-3329
Pres: Barry Silberman
PR: Nancy Yasharoff

The following leag
amateur status.

United States Interreg
Soccer League

4322 N. Beltline Road
Suite B-205
Irving, TX 75038
(214) 570-7575
Fax (214) 257-1493
Comm: Francisco Marcos
PR: Mike Agnew

*The USISL is both a professi
division 3 and an amateur lea
The USISL plays both an ind
and outdoor schedule and ha
teams coast to coast.*

Prospective Leagues

**Federation of Clubs of
the United States, Inc. (FOCUS)**
P.O. Box 022220
Brooklyn, NY 11202-0047
Chmn.: Robert Wilson

World Soccer League
P.O. Box 501760
Indianapolis, IN 46250-1760
(317) 876-1WSL
Pres.: Richard Campbell
Oper.: John Mitchell

Canadian Soccer

Canadian Soccer Association
1600 James Naismith Drive
Gloucester, Ontario K1B 5N4
(613) 748-5667
Fax (613) 745-1938
Director: Kevan Pipe

Canadian National Team
6255 McKay Avenue
Burnaby, B.C. V5H 2W7
(604) 438-9811
Director: Les Wilson

National Soccer League-Ontario
901 Lawrence Avenue
Toronto, Ontario M6A 1C3
(416) 781-9327
Comm.: Rocco Lo Franco

Heartland Soccer League
11939 Red Lion Drive
St. Louis, MO 63033
(314) 553-2178
Comm.: Bob Reid

Lone Star Soccer Alliance
Box 82-489
12600 Bissonnet
Houston, TX 77099
(713) 541-2061
Comm: Jim Walker

Maritime Soccer League
106 Westview Street
Fredericton, New Brunswick
Canada E3A 1W9
Exec. Dir.: Doreen Thompson

Canadian Minisoccer Federation
660 Lambert Street
Nanaimo, B.C. V9R 3N8
Director: Jose Carlos Mateus

Canadian Indoor Soccer League
192 Riverview Avenue
Woodbridge, Ontario L4L 2L6
(416) 851-5050
Exec. Dir.: Tony Ciamarra

Nova Scotia Soccer League
5516 Spring Garden Road
P.O. Box 3010 South
Halifax, Nova Scotia B3J 3G6
(902) 425-5450
Comm.: George Athanasiou

Provincial Associations

Alberta Soccer Association
11759 Groat Road
Edmonton, Alberta T5M 3K6
(403) 453-8511
Director: Gary Sampley

B.C. Soccer Association
6255 McKay Avenue
Burnaby, B.C. V5H 2W7
(604) 430-6401
Sec.: Alex Kemp

Manitoba Soccer Association
1700 Ellice Avenue
Winnipeg, Manitoba R3H 0B1
(204) 985-4139
Director: Dave Kerr

Soccer New Brunswick
106 Westview Street
Fredericton, New Brunswick
Canada E3A 1W9
(506) 472-7748
Exec. Dir.: Doreen Thompson

Newfoundland Soccer Association
P.O. Box 9064
St. John's, Nfdlnd. A1A 2X3
(709) 576-4932
Exec. Dir.: Wayne Bolt

Northwest Territories Soccer Association
c/o Sam Hearne High School
Bag No. 3
Inuvik, NWT X0E 0T0
(403) 979-4193
Pres. Kelly Reid

Soccer Nova Scotia
P.O. Box 3010 South
Halifax, N.S. B3J 3G6
(902) 425-5457
Exec. Dir.: George Athanasiou

Ontario Soccer Association
1220 Sheppard Avenue East
Willowdale, Ontario M2K 2X1
(416) 495-4250
Exec. Dir.: Brian Avey

Prince Edward Island Soccer Association
69 Trafalgar Street
Charlottetown, PEI C1A 3Z4
(902) 892-7883
Pres.: Tom Wallis

Federation Quebecoise de Soccer-Football
4545 Pierre-de-Coubertin
Montreal, Quebec H1V 3R2
(514) 252-3070
Exec. Dir.: Michel Cardinal

Saskatchewan Soccer Association
1870 Lorne Street
Regina, Sask. S4P 2L7
(306) 780-9224

Organizations

United States Soccer Federation
1801-1811 S. Prairie
Chicago, IL 60616
(312) 808-1300
Fax (312) 808-1301
Exec. Dir: Hank Steinbrecher

FIFA Women's Football Assn.
37 Sussex Road
Ickenham, Middlesex, UB10 8PN
England
(011) 08956-39893

**National Soccer Coaches
Association of America**
RD #5, Box 5074
Stroudsburg, PA 18360
(717) 421-8270
Exec. Dir.: John McKeon

**American Youth Soccer
Organization**
5403 W. 138th Street
Hawthorne, CA 90250
(213) 643-6455
(800) 421-5700 (outside CA)

**Intercollegiate Soccer
Assn. of America (ISAA)**
1821 Sunny Street
St. Louis, MO 63122
(314) 349-1967
Exec. Dir.: Bob Albus

**National Intercollegiate
Soccer Officials Association**
541 Woodview Drive
Longwood, FL 32779
(407) 862-3305
Exec. Dir.: Dr. Raymond Bernabei

**Soccer Industry Council
of America**
200 Castlewood Drive
North Palm Beach, FL 33406
(407) 832-5616

**United States Youth
Soccer Association**
2050 N. Plano Road
Suite 100
Richardson, TX 75082
(800) 4-SOCCER

**National Soccer
Coaches Association**
4220 Shawnee Mission Pkwy.
Suite 105-B
Fairway, KS 66205
(913) 362-1747
Exec. Dir: Jim Sheldon

National Soccer Hall of Fame
5-11 Ford Avenue
Oneonta, NY 13820
(607) 432-3351

Publications

Soccer America
PO Box 23704
Oakland, CA 94623
(510) 528-5000

Soccer Digest
990 Grove Street
Evanston, IL 60201
(708) 941-6440

Soccer International
P.O. Box 246
Artesia, CA 90702-0246
(213) 860-2831
(800) 448-3242

Soccer Match
P.O. Box 39A-27
Los Angeles, CA 90039
(818) 242-9970

World Soccer Magazine
Central House
27 Park Street
Croydon CR0 1YD,
England
(011) 081-686 9777 (Subs)
(011) 071-261 5737 (Editorial)

World Team Tennis

445 N. Wells Street
Suite 404
Chicago, IL 60610
(312) 245-5300
Fax (312) 245-5321
Pres./CEO: Billie Jean King
Publicity: Mike Shapiro

Atlanta Thunder
1720 Peachtree Street
Suite 1022
Atlanta, GA 30309
(404) 881-8811
Fax (404) 881-9327
G.M.: Ken Small,Jr.

Charlotte Express
1337 Hundred Oaks Dr.,
Suite EE
Charlotte, NC 28217
(704) 525-5678
Fax (704) 529-1362
GM: Jeff Ryan

Florida Twist
5500 34th St. W.
Bradenton, FL 34210
(813) 739-8326
Fax (813) 927-2138
GM: Don Lang

Idaho Sneakers
290 Bobwhite Court
Suite 300
Boise, ID 83706
(208) 383-0080
Fax (208) 383-0194
GM: Jim Frye

Kansas City Explorers
PO Box 1521
Mission, KS 66222
(913) 362-9944
Fax (913) 362-9953
GM: Tom Rieger

New Jersey Stars
PO Box 669
Madison, NJ 07940
(201) 377-5171
Fax (201) 377-6130
GM: Becky Vuksta

Newport Beach Dukes
2200 Park Newport, Ste. 303
Newport Beach, CA 92660
(714) 644-5800
Fax (714) 644-1666
GM: Fred Lieberman

Phoenix Smash
201 E. Jefferson
Phoenix, AZ 85012
(602) 379-7900
Fax (602) 379-7990
GM: Bryan Colangelo

Sacramento Capitals
7919 Folsom, Suite 150
Sacramento, CA 95826
(916) 386-8898
Fax (916) 381-0268
GM: Beverly Kindrick

St. Louis Aces
7912 Bonhomme Ave.
Suite 106
St. Louis, MO 63105
(314) 726-ACES
Fax (314) 726-2362
GM: Jack Levitt

San Antonio Racquets
105 S. St. Mary's Street
Suite 1918
San Antonio, TX 78205
(210) 225-0006
Fax (210) 225-0036

Wichita Advantage
2250 N. Rock Road
Suite 118-216
Wichita, KS 67206
(316) 634-2202
Fax (316) 634-2204

Organizations

Association of Tennis Professionals
200 Tournament Players Road
Ponte Vedra Beach, FL 32082
(904) 285-8000

American Tennis Industry Federation
200 Castlewood Drive
North Palm Beach, FL 33408
(407) 848-1026

International Tennis Hall of Fame and Museum
194 Bellevue Avenue
Newport, RI 02840
(401) 849-3990

International Tennis Federation
Palliser Road, Barons Court
London W14 9EN, England
44.1-381 8060

Men's Pro Tennis Council
437 Madison Avenue
New York, NY 10022
(212) 838-8450

Nabisco Grand Prix Tennis
625 Madison Avenue
New York, NY 10022
(212) 418-6990

U.S. Professional Tennis Association
P.O. Box 7077
Wesley Chapel, FL 34249
(813) 973-3777

U.S. Tennis Association
1212 Avenue of the Americas
New York, NY 10036
(212) 302-3322

Volvo Tennis
850 Third Avenue
New York, NY 10022
(212) 888-5240

Women's International Tennis Association
2665 South Bayshore Drive
Suite 1002
Miami, FL 33133
(305) 856-4030

World Championship Tennis
2340 Thanksgiving Tower
Dallas, TX 75201
(214) 969-5554

Women's International Professional Tennis Council
100 Park Avenue
New York, NY 10017
(212) 878-2250

Women's Tennis Association
133 First Street, N.E.
St. Petersburg, FL 33701
(813) 895-5000

Paddle Sports

U.S. Paddle Tennis Association
P.O. Box 30
Culver City, CA 90232
(213) 856-6367

North American Paddlesports Association
715 Boylston Street,
Fourth Floor
Boston, MA 02116
(617) 266-6800

Tennis Publications

Tennis
5520 Park Avenue
Trumbull, CT 06611
(203) 373-7000

Tennis USA
3 Park Avenue
New York, NY 10016
(212) 340-9200

International Tennis News
200 Tournament Players Rd.
Ponte Vedra, FL 32082
(904) 285-8000

Pro Tennis News
2340 Thanksgiving Tower
Dallas, TX 75201
(214) 969-5554

Bob Larson's Tennis Newswire
P.O. Box 2186
Minneapolis, MN 55402
(612) 884-8637

*RHI marks the return of
Dennis Murphy, since the
days of the WFL and WHA.*

Roller Hockey International
5182 Katella Avenue
Suite 106
Los Alamitos, CA 90720
(310) 430-2423
Fax (310) 431-2928
Pres.: Dennis Murphy
Media: Nanci King

Anaheim Bullfrogs
1725 S. Douglas, Suite D
Anaheim, CA 92806
(714) 939-7663
Fax (714) 939-7643
GM: Bob Elder

Atlanta Fire Ants
100 Techwood Drive
Atlanta, GA 30303
(404) 681-2100
Fax (404) 525-0044
GM: Joe Bucchino

Buffalo Stampede
5820 Main Street
Suite 602
Williamsville, NY 14221
(716) 633-3232
Fax (716) 633-4252
GM: Chris Potenza

Calgary Rad'z
1001 Barlow Trail S.E.
Calgary, Alberta T2E 6S2
(403) 569-7230
Fax (403) 272-3090
GM: Glen Gretsky

Chicago Cheetahs
472 N. Milwaukee, 2nd Fl.
Chicago, IL 60610
(312) 433-0180
Fax (312) 433-0184
GM: Red Rush

Edmonton Sled Dogs
830 Terrace Plaza
4445 Calgary Trail S.
Edmonton, Alberta T6H 5R7
(403) 434-6208
Fax (403) 437-2037
GM: Alan Howat

Florida Hammerheads
PO Box 1948
Hallandale, FL 33008
(305) 672-6662
Fax (305) 531-4572
GM: Karen Kielt

Las Vegas Flash
1500 E. Tropicana
Suite 110
Las Vegas, NV 89119
(702) 262-9795
Fax (702) 736-9192
GM: Bob Lawson

Los Angeles Blades
3900 W. Manchester
Inglewood, CA 90305
(310) 419-3263
GM: Jeannie Buss

Minnesota Arctic Blast
PO Box 357
Minneapolis, MN 55540
(612) 376-2806
Fax (612) 376-2824
GM: Peter Jockety

Montreal Roadrunners
3221 Autoroad, 440 W. Rm 210
Chomedey, Laval, PQ, H7P 5P2
(514) 686-9229
Fax (514) 686-8036
GM: Yvan Cournoyer

New England Stingers
1 Civic Center Square
Portland, ME 04101
(207) 828-4665
Fax (207) 773-3278
GM: Godfrey Wood

NJ Rockin' Rollers
55 Horsehill Road
Cedar Knolls, NJ 07927
(201) 538-6012
Fax (201) 538-3060
GM: Nick Fotiu

Oakland Skates
7000 Coliseum Way
Oakland, CA 94621
(510) 283-7655
Fax (510) 283-2902
GM: Bill Glazier

Philadelphia Bulldogs
120 E. Ninth Ave., Suite 3
Runnemede, NJ 08078
(609) 939-6633
Fax (609) 939-9628
GM: Dave Schultz

Phoenix Cobras
1826 W. McDowell
Phoenix, AZ 85055
(602) 256-2722
Fax (602) 256-2640
GM: Madeline Simon

Pittsburgh Phantoms
Civic Arena, Gate 9
Pittsburgh, PA 15219
(412) 642-1800
Fax (412) 642-1859
GM: Jeff Barrett

Portland Rage
825 N.E. 20th, Suite 300
Portland, OR 97232
(503) 236-RAGE
Fax (503) 231-6311
GM: Bill Conyard

Sacramento River Rats
150 B South Auburn St.
Grass Valley, CA 95945
(916) 928-0407
Fax (916) 272-7858
GM: John Murphy

St. Louis Vipers
5700 Oakland
St. Louis, MO 63110
(314) 647-5050
Fax (314) 647-1957
GM: Bernie Federko

San Diego Barracudas
3500 Sports Arena Blvd.
San Diego, CA 92110
(619) 688-1800
Fax (619) 688-1808
GM: Robbie Nichols

San Jose Rhinos
99 Almaden Blvd., Suite 555
San Jose, CA 95113
(408) 287-4442
Fax (408) 287-3653
GM: Brad Porteus

Tampa Bay Tritons
4100 W. Kennedy Blvd.
Suite 116
Tampa, FL 33607
(813) 876-7655
Fax (813) 288-9689
GM: Aldo Esposito

Vancouver VooDoo
PO Box 69020
Vancouver, B.C. V5K 4W3
(604) 253-3011
Fax (604) 253-1303
GM: Tiger Williams

Volleyball

Federation of International Volleyball (FIVB)
Avenue de la Gare 12
1001 Lausanne, Switzerland
(011) 41.21 208 932
Fax (011) 41.21 208 865

United States Volleyball Association
3595 East Fountain Blvd.
Colorado Springs, CO 80910
(719) 637-8300

Canadian Volleyball Association
1600 James Naismith Drive
Gloucester, Ontario K1B 5N4
(613) 748-5681

Association of Volleyball Professionals (AVP)
740 West 190th Street
Gardena, CA 90247
(310) 324-9311
Scores (310) 645-7000

Professional Beach Volleyball Tour
1715 14th Street
Santa Monica, CA 90405
(310) 452-5056
Director: Jack Butefish

Team Cup Volleyball
Great Western Forum
P.O. Box 10
Inglewood, CA 90306
(310) 419-3257
Exec. Dir.: Michael O'Hara

California Beach Volleyball Association
P.O. Box 5246
Carson, CA 90744
(310) 635-6666

U.S. National Team
4510 Executive Drive
Plaza 1
San Diego, CA 92121
(619) 625-8200

FOVA
P.O. Box 2987
Costa Mesa, CA 92626
(714) 646-6010

USA Pro Beach Volleyball
P.O. Box 57
Huntington Beach, CA 92648
(714) 536-4900

Volleyball Hall of Fame
444 Dwight Street
P.O. Box 1895
Holyoke, MA 01040
(413) 536-5770

National Volleyball Association
1001 Mission Street
South Pasadena, CA 91030
(800) NVA-NVA0
PR: (800) 5 SPIKER

New Indoor Pro Co-ed league.

Teams are:
Las Vegas Vipers
Sacramento Stars
San Bernardino Jazz
San Diego Spikers
San Jose Storm

Women's Pro Volleyball Association
1730 Oak Street
Santa Monica, CA 90405
(310) 392-4210
GM: Nancy Lengel

Volleyball Publications

Volleyball Monthly
P.O. Box 3137
San Luis Obispo, CA 93403
(805) 541-2294
(800) 443-0100

Volleyball USA
3595 E. Fountain Blvd.
Colorado Springs, CO 80910
(719) 637-8300

Volley World
12 Ave. de la Gare
1001, Lausanne, Switzerland
(001) 41.21 208 932

Cricket

**International Cricket
Council (ICC)**
Lord's Cricket Ground
St. John's Wood
London, NW8 8QN, England
Sec.: OBE Lt. Col. J.R. Stephenson
(011) 289 1611

**United States Cricket
Association**
2361 Hickory Road
Plymouth Meeting, PA 19462
(215) 825-2356
Pres.: N. Khan

Canadian Cricket Assn.
2041 W. 63rd Avenue
Vancouver, B.C. V6P 2J2
(604) 266-4111
(604) 261-7758
Pres.: Jack Kyle

Polo

**United States Polo
Association**
120 Mill Street
Lexington, KY 40507
(606) 255-0593

U.S. Arena Polo League
Los Angeles Equestrian Center
480 Riverside Drive at Main
Burbank, CA 91503
(818) 840-9063

National Museum of Polo
4059 Iron Works Pike
Lexington, KY 405ll
(606) 281-6285

Pro Cycling

National Cycle League
532 La Guardia Place
Suite 162
New York, NY 10012
(212) 871-7472
Fax (212) 260-7424
Comm: Pete O'Neil

Amsterdam Flying Dutchmen
Walstro 24
3831 WX Leusden,
The Netherlands
011 (31) 33.94.6261
GM: Rene Lith

Houston Outlaws
4400 Memorial Drive
Suite 3098
Houston, TX 77007
(713) 869-2718
GM: Jack Gott

London Lancers
22B Prince of Wales Mansions
Prince of Wales Drive
Battersea, SW11, England
011 (44) 71.498.8645
GM: Sarah Fulkerson

Los Angeles Wings
11245 Van Owen Street
North Hollywood, CA 91605
(818) 506-5656
GM: Bill Blake

Miami Wave
3850 Hollywood Blvd.
Suite 300
Hollywood, FL 33021
(305) 987-8530
Pres: Mike Sadovnick

Forza Milano
Viale Monte Nero, 50
Milano, Italia 20135
011 (39) 2.599.01988
Pres: Cosimo Racco

New York Ghost Riders
532 LaGuardia Place
Suite 162
New York, NY 10012
(212) 984-9522
GM: Owen Singleton

Pittsburgh Power
800 Vinial Street
Suite 311
Pittsburgh, PA 15212
(412) 322-5252
Pres: Franco Harris

Portland Thunder
600 Mayor Building
1120 S.W. Morrison, Ste 600
Portland, OR 97205
(503) 243-2055
Pres: John Billington

San Diego Zoom
8360 Claremont Mesa Blvd.
Suite 104
San Diego, CA 92111
(619) 277-3377
Pres: Kathy Kass

Tulsa Cyclones
1401 S. Cheyenne
Tulsa, OK 74119
(918) 582-8326
Pres: Lonny Davis

Miscellaneous Sport-by-Sport Listings

Bowling Organizations

**American Blind Bowling
Association**
67 Bame Avenue
Buffalo, NY 14215
(716) 836-1472

American Bowling Congress
5301 S. 76th Street
Greendale, WI 53129
(414) 421-6400

**American Wheelchair
Bowling Association**
Larkspur Lane
Menomonee Falls, WI 53051
(414) 781-6876

Ladies Pro Bowler's Tour
7171 Cherryvale Blvd.
Rockford, IL 61112
(815) 332-5657

National Bowling Association
377 Park Avenue South
New York, NY 10016
(212) 689-8308

**National Deaf Bowling
Association**
9244 E. Mansfield Avenue
Denver, CO 80237
(303) 771-9018

**National Duckpin
Bowling Congress**
Fairview Avenue
Linthicum, MD 21090

**Professional Bowlers
Association (PBA)**
1720 Merriman Road
Akron, OH 44313
(216) 836-5568

**Women's International
Bowling Congress**
5301 S. 76th Street
Greendale, WI 53129
(414) 421-9000

**Young American
Bowling Alliance**
5301 S. 76th Street
Greendale, WI 53129
(414) 421-4700

Boxing Organizations

Boxing Canada
1600 James Naismith Drive
Gloucester, Ontario KIB 5N4
(613) 748-5611

**Golden Gloves Association
of America**
8801 Princess Jeanne N.E.
Albuquerque, NM 87112
(505) 888-1176

**International Boxing
Federation (IBF)**
134 Evergreen Place
Ninth Floor
East Orange, NJ 07018
(201) 414-0300

**International Boxing
Writer's Association**
Box 1610
Millwood, NY 10546

**North American
Boxing Federation**
2770 S. Maryland Pkwy.
Suite 314
Las Vegas, NV 89109
(702) 486-6447

**U.S. Amateur Boxing
Federation**
1750 E. Boulder Street
Colorado Springs, CO 80909
(719) 578-4506

**United States Boxing
Association**
134 Evergreen Place
9th Floor
East Orange, NJ 07018
(201) 414-0300

World Boxing Association
Centro Comercial Ciudad Turmero
Local No. 21, piso no. 2
Calle Petion Cruce Con Urdaneta
Tumero , 2115 Estado Aragua, Venezuela
(58) 44 61 645
Pres.: Gilbert Mendoza

World Boxing Council
Genova 33, Desp. 503
Col. Juarez
Cuahtemoc, 0660
Mexico D.F., Mexico
525 533 6546
Pres: Jose Sulaiman

World Boxing Organization
328 Minorca Avenue
Coral Gables, FL 33135
(305) 446-7674
Pres: Ed Levin

Arizona Boxing Commission
1645 W. Jefferson
Suite 212
Phoenix, AZ 85007
(602) 542-1417

**North American Boxing Federation
Nevada Boxing Commission**
2770 S. Maryland Pkwy, Suite 314
Las Vegas, NV 89109
(702) 486-6447

Cycling Organizations

American Bicycle Association
P.O. Box 718
Chandler, AZ 85226
(602) 961-1903

**American Bicycle League
of America**
924 Cherry Street
San Carlos, CA 94070
(415) 592-1727

American Bikeways Foundation
2019 Q Street N.W.
Washington, D.C. 20009
(202) 462-4900

**Bicycle Federation &
Institute of America**
1818 R Street N.W.
Washington, D.C. 20009
(202) 332-6986

**Bicycle Manufacturers
Association of America**
1055 Thomas Jefferson St. N.W.
Suite 316
Washington, D.C. 20007
(202) 333-4052

Canadian Cycling Association
1600 James Naismith Drive
Gloucester, Ontario K1B 5N4
(613) 748-5692

**International Bicycle
Touring Society**
2115 Paseo Dorado
La Jolla, CA 92037
(619) 459-8775

League of American Wheelman
6707 Whitestone Road
Suite 209
Baltimore, MD 21207
(301) 944-3399

**Nastional Bicycle Dealers
Association**
129 Cabrillo Street
Suite 201
Costa Mesa, CA 92627
(714) 722-6909

**National Off-Road
Bicycle Association**
1750 E. Boulder Street
Colorado Springs, CO 80909
(719) 578-4717

U.S. Cycling Federation
1750 E. Boulder Street
Colorado Springs, CO 80909
(719) 578-4581

**U.S. Professional Cycling
Federation**
Route One, Box 1650
New Tripoli, PA 18066
(215) 298-3262

**Ultra Marathon Cycling
Association**
4790 Irvine Blvd.
Suite 105-111
Irvine, CA 92720
(714) 544-1701

Golf Organizations

**Ladies Professional
Golf Association**
2570 Volusia Avenue
Suite B
Daytona Beach, FL 32114
(904) 254-8800

National Golf Foundation
200 Castlewood Drive
North Palm Beach, FL 33408
(407) 844-2500

**Professional Golf Association
of America**
100 Avenue of Champions
P.O. Box 109601
Palm Beach Gardens, FL 33418
(407) 626-3600

**Professional Golf Association
Men's Tour (PGA)**
Sawgrass
Ponte Vedra, FL 32082
(904) 285-3700

**Professional Golf Association
PGA Seniors Tour**
Sawgrass
Ponte Vedra, FL 32082
(904) 285-3700

**Professional Putters
Association**
P.O. Box 35237
Fayetteville, NC 28303
(919) 485-7131

**Royal Canadian Golf
Association**
Golf House
Oakville, Ontario L6J 4Z3
(416) 844-1800

TPA Golf Tour
4190 Belford Road
Suite 200
Jacksonville, FL 32215
(904) 730-0401

**United States Golf
Association**
Golf House
Far Hills, NJ 07931
(201) 234-2300

**U.S. National Senior's
Open Golf Association**
2140 Westwood Blvd.
Los Angeles, CA 90025
(213) 474-0036

**U.S. Seniors Golf
Association**
60 East 42nd Street
New York, NY 10017
(212) 867-0730

World Amateur Golf
Council
Golf House
Far Hills, NJ 07931
(201) 234-2300

Motor Sports

Listed in this section are associations for autos, air,
power boats, motorcycles, off-road and other racing
organizations.

American Hot Rod
Association
111 N. Hayford Road
Spokane, WA 99204
(509) 244-2372

American Motorcycle
Association (AMA)
PO Box 6114
Westerville, OH 43081
(614) 891-2425

American Power Boat
Association
17640 E. Nine Mile Road
PO Box 377
East Detroit, MI 48021
(313) 773-9700

Continental Motorsports
Club
PO Box 1858
Costa Mesa, CA 92628
(714) 261-6116

Federation of International
du Sport Automobiles (FISA)
8 Place de la Concorde
F 75008 Paris, France
(42) 659 951

Formula One Contractors
Association
Roebuck House
Cox Lane, Surrey,
Chessington, England KIT 1DG
(44) 391 01 21

Formula One Driver's
Association
2 rue Jean Jaures
L-1836 Luxembourg
(45) 0045

Formula One Spectator's
Association
8033 Sunset Blvd.
Suite 60
Los Angeles, CA 90046
(213) 658-5884

Indy Car Racing
390 Enterprise Court
Bloomfield Hills, MI 48302
(313) 334-8500

International Hot Rod
Association (IHRA)
PO Box 3029
Bristol, TN 37625
(615) 764-1164

International Kart
Federation
4650 Arrow Hwy, Suite B4
Montclair, CA 91763
(714) 625-5497

International Motorsports
Association (IMSA)
P.O. Box 10709
Tampa, FL 33679-0709
(813) 877-4672
Fax (813) 876-4604

Mickey Thompson's Off-Road
& Supercross Racing Assoc.
PO Box 25168
Anaheim, CA 92825
(714) 938-4100

National Air Racing Group
1313 Los Arboles
Sunnyvale, CA 94087
(408) 733-7967

**National Association of
Stock Car Racing (NASCAR)**
1801 Speedway Blvd.
PO Box K
Daytona Beach, FL 32015
(904) 253-0611

**National Hot Rod
Association (NHRA)**
2035 Financial Way
PO Box 5555
Glendora, CA 91740
(818) 914-4761

**National Sprint Car
Racing Association**
19785 Deep Harbor
Huntington Beach,
CA 92648
(904) 253-0611

**National Tractor
Pullers Association**
6969 Worthington-
Galena Road, Suite J
Worthington, OH 43085
(614) 436-1761

**Professional Racing
Organization of America**
340 Holly
Denver, CO 80220
(303) 333-2449

**SCORE International Off
Road Racing Association**
31125 Via Colinas, Suite 908
Westlake Village, CA 91362
(818) 889-9216

**Sports Car Club of
America (SCCA)**
1933 E. Easter Place
Englewood, CO 80112
(303) 694-7222

**United States Auto
Club (USAC)**
4910 W. 16th Street
Speedway, IN 46224
(317) 247-5151

The following is a list of Speedways that are on the NASCAR circuit

**Alabama International
Motor Speedway**
PO Box 777
Talladega, AL 35160
(205) 362-2261

**Atlanta International
Raceway**
PO Box 500
Hampton, GA 30228
(404) 946-4211

**Bristol International
Raceway**
PO Box 3966
Bristol, TN 37620
(615) 764-1161

Charlotte Motor Speedway
PO Box 600
Harrisburg, NC 28075
(704) 455-2121

**Darlington International
Raceway**
PO Box 500
Darlington, SC 29532
(803) 393-4041

**Daytona International
Speedway**
PO Drawer S
Daytona Beach, FL 32015
(904) 253-6711

**Dover Downs International
Speedway**
PO Box 843
Dover, DE 19901
(302) 674-4600

Martinsville Speedway
PO Box 3311
Martinsville, VA 24112
(703) 956-3151

**Michigan International
Speedway**
12626 U.S. 12
Brooklyn, MI 49230
(517) 592-6671

**Nashville International
Raceway**
PO Box 40048
Nashville, TN 37204
(615) 242-4343

**North Carolina
Motor Speedway**
PO Box 500
Rockingham, NC 28378
(919) 582-2861

**North Wilkesboro
Speedway**
PO Box 337
North Wilkesboro,
NC 28659
(919) 667-6663

**Pocono International
Raceway**
PO Box 500
Mt. Pocono, PA 18344
(717) 646-2300

**Richmond Fairgrounds
Raceway**
PO Box 9257
Richmond, VA 23337
(804) 233-4178

Sears Point Raceway
Highway 37 & Hwy. 121
Sonoma, CA 95476
(707) 938-8448

The following is a list of Indy Car Racetracks

**Autodromo Ricardo
Rodriquez**
No. 225-B 9th Floor
Mexico 11 D.F.
(905) 574-4896

**Burke Lakefront
Airport**
C.K. Newcomb & Associates
Burke Lakefront Airport
Cleveland, OH 44114
(216) 781-3500

**Detroit Renaissance
Grand Prix**
1000 Renaissance Center
Suite 1760
Detroit, MI 48243
(313) 259-5400

**Indianapolis Motor
Speedway**
4790 West 16th Street
Speedway, IN 46224
(317) 241-2501

Laguna Seca Raceway
PO Box SCRAMP
Monterey, CA 93940
(408) 373-1811

Long Beach Grand Prix
110 West Ocean Blvd.
Suite A
Long Beach, CA 90802
(213) 437-0341

**Meadowlands Complex
Raceway**
N.J. Sports & Exposition
Authority
East Rutherford, NJ 07073
(201) 460-4367

Miami Motorsports
7290 Southwest 48th Street
Miami, FL 33155
(305) 665-7223

**Michigan International
Speedway**
12626 U.S. 12
Brooklyn, MI 49230
(517) 592-6671

**Mid-Ohio Sports
Car Course**
PO Box 3108
Steam Corners Road
Lexington, OH 44904
(419) 884-2295

**Molson Grand Prix
Canadair**
1800 Laurentian Blvd.
Ville St. Laurent
Quebec H3C 3G9
(514) 849-5311

**Phoenix International
Raceway**
PO Box 11388
Phoenix, AZ 85061
(602) 246-7777

**Pocono International
Raceway**
PO Box 500
Mt. Pocono, PA 18344
(717) 646-2300

**Portland Raceway
Rose Festival**
220 NW Second Avenue
Portland, OR 97209
(503) 227-2681

Road America
81 Lake Street
Elkhart Lake, WI 53020
(414) 876-3366

**Wisconsin State Fair
Speedway**
6646 West Fairview Avenue
Milwaukee, WI 53213
(414) 774-1324

Road Running

Listed in this section are Running Organizations &
Marathon committees.

**Association of International
Marathon & Road Races (AINS)**
20 Trongate
Glasgow G1 5ES, Scotland
(41) 227 5093
P.R.: Peter McLean

**Road Runners Club
of America**
629 S. Washington Street
Alexandria, VA 22314
(703) 836-0558

**Association of Road
Running Athletes**
807 Paulsen Building
Spokane, WA 99201
(509) 838-8784

National Marathons

**Adirondack Marathon
Committee**
15 Windy Hill Road
Glens Falls, NY 12801
(518) 792-3804

Atlanta Marathon
Atlanta Track Club
3097 E. Shadowlawn Ave., N.E.
Atlanta, GA 30305
(404) 231-9065

**Atlantic City Marathon
Boardwalk Runners**
PO Box 7336
Atlantic City, NJ 08404
(609) 822-6911

Big Sur Marathon
Box 22620
Carmel, CA 93922
(408) 625-6226

B.A.A. Boston Marathon
20 Park Plaza, Suite 614
Boston, MA 02116
(617) 236-1652

**Bud Light Funfest
Marathon**
1700 Polk Street
Amarillo, TX 79102
(512) 732-1732

Buffalo Marathon
4 Symphony Circle
Buffalo, NY 14201
(716) 882-3365

Cape Cod Marathon
Falmouth Track Club
PO Box 699
West Falmouth, MA 02574
(508) 548-0348

Chicago Old Style Marathon
223 W. Erie Street
Chicago, IL 60610
(312) 951-0660

Dallas White Rock Marathon
PO Box 743335
Dallas, TX 75374
(214) 997-5102

**Denver's Mayor's Cup
Marathon**
1666 Race Street
Denver, CO 80206

**Detroit Free Press
Marathon**
321 W. Lafayette
Detroit, MI 48231
(313) 222-6676

Duke City Marathon
PO Box 14903
Albuquerque, NM 87191
(505) 291-8250

Emerald City Marathon
157 Yesler Way
Suite 208
Seattle, WA 98104
(206) 523-2720

Golden Spike Marathon
PO Box 338
Brigham City, UT 84302
(201) 237-2135

Grandma's Marathon
PO Box 6234
Duluth, MN 55806
(218) 727-0947

High Altitude Bandelier
152 Monterey Drive
Los Alamos, NM 87544

**Heart of San Diego
International Marathon**
2320 Chicago Street
San Diego, CA 92110
(213) 444-5544

**Honolulu Marathon
Association**
3435 Waialae Avenue
Room 208
Honolulu, HI 96816
(808) 734-7200

**Houston-Tenneco
Marathon**
PO Box 2511
Houston, TX 77001
(713) 757-2500

Kansas Relays
Room 143
Allen Field House
Lawrence, KS 66045

Kansas City Marathon
(913) 362-7223

Kilauea Volcano Marathon
PO Box 106
Hawaii Volcanoes Natl.Park,
HI 96718
(808) 967-8222

Las Vegas Marathon
601 S. Maryland Parkway
Las Vegas, NV 89101
(702) 388-6915

Long Beach Marathon
1827 Redondo Avenue
Long Beach, CA 90804
(213) 494-2664

Long Island Marathon
Sport Unit
Eisenhower Park
East Meadow, NY 11554
(516) 542-4439

Los Angeles Marathon, Inc.
11110 W. Ohio Avenue
Suite 100
Los Angeles, CA 90025
(213) 444-5544

Maine Coast Marathon
110 Union Avenue
Old Orchard Beach, ME 04064

Marine Corps Marathon
Box 188
Quantico, VA 22134
(703) 640-2720

Memphis Marathon
Memphis Runners Track Club
PO Box 17981
Memphis, TN 38117
(800) 238-7566

Mayor's Midnight Sun
Marathon
Anchorage Parks &
Recreation
PO Box 196650
Anchorage, AK 99519
(907) 343-4474

Mardi Gras Marathon
Race Director, YMCA
936 St. Charles Avenue
New Orleans, LA 70130
(504) 482-6682

New York City Marathon
9 East 89th Street
New York, NY 10128
(212) 860-4455

OKC-Jim Thorpe
2610 NW Expressway No.1
Oklahoma City, OK 73112
(405) 232-3060

Oakland Marathon
PO Box 32103
Oakland, CA 94604

Phoenix Marathon
4609 E. Thomas Road
Phoenix, AZ 85018
(602) 246-7697

Pittsburgh Marathon
638 USX Tower
Pittsburgh, PA 15219
(412) 391-2800

Portland Marathon
1515 S.W. 5th Avenue
Suite 1000
Portland, OR 97201
(503) 248-1134

Revco Cleveland
Marathon
PO Box 46604
Bedford, OH 44146
(216) 425-9811

San Francisco Marathon
PO Box 27385
San Francisco, CA 94127
(415) 896-1530

Tampa Bay Marathon
415 Cactus Circle
Seffner, FL 33584
(813) 685-3912

Twin Cities Marathon
PO Box 24193
Minneapolis, MN 55424
(612) 341-8400

Wichita Marathon
121 N. River Blvd.
Wichita, KS 67203
(316) 267-6812

Wineglass Marathon
Box 98
Corning, NY 14830
(607) 936-9971

Marathon Committees

Birmingham Vulcan Marathon
(205) 942-1235

**Charleston Almost Heaven
Marathon**
(304) 744-6502

Charlotte Marathon
(704) 379-6896

Cincinnati Marathon
(503) 898-7015

Columbus Marathon
(614) 433-0395

Great Southwest Marathon
(915) 677-8144

Greensboro Marathon
(919) 855-5799

Jacksonville Marathon
(904) 739-1917

**Lake Front Milwaukee
Marathon**
(914) 272-7867

Music City Marathon
(615) 269-4575

Omaha Marathon
(402) 558-9076

Pikes Peak Marathon
(719) 473-2625

Sacramento Marathon
(916) 678-5005

St. Louis Marathon
(314) 367-6577

Tulsa Marathon
(918) 742-4127

International Marathons

**Adelaide Festival City
Marathon**
P.O. Box 6051
Hakifax Street
Adelaide 5000, Australia
(8) 224 6229

Adidas Buenos Aires Marathon
Ave. Eva Peron 2535
C.P. 1650 San Martin
Buenos Aires, Argentina
(1) 735 9040

Amsterdam Marathon
Vardraagzaam 2
1068 SB Amsterdam, Holland
(20) 197 141

Antwerp Marathon
Prosper Slachmuylders
Boomgaardstraat 324
B-2600 Antwerpen, Belgium

Bangkok Marathon
60/17 Silom Road
Bangkok 10500 Thailand
(2) 2353 145

**Barcelona Marathon
Commission**
Catalunya c/o Jonqueres
16-08003 Barcelona, Spain
(3) 301 1230

**Beijing Marathon
Organizing Committee**
9 Tiyuguan Road
Beijing, China

Belgrade Marathon
Kataniceva BB
11000 Belgrade,
Yugoslavia
(11) 44 44 333

Berlin Marathon
Meinekestrasse 13
D-1000 Berlin 15,
Germany
(30) 882 6405

Bermuda Marathon
PO Box DV 397
Devonshire, Bermuda
(809) 296 2428

Berne Grand Prix
Munstergasse 14
CH-3011 Berne,
Switzerland
(41) 31 222 994

Bolton Marathon
Race Headquarters
424 S. Helens Road
Bolton, Gt. Manchester,
England

Bremen Marathon
Postbox 66 04 8
D-2800 Bremen 66
Germany

Broadlands Peoples
Marathon
53 Newry Street
Floreat Park,
Western Australia 6014

Brussels Marathon
17 Rue de la Chapelle
1000 Bruxxelles, Belgium
(2) 511 9000

Budapest Marathon
Vaczi Utca 62-64
1056 Budapest, Hungary
(1) 181 437

China Coast Marathon
GPO 10-368
1, Robinson Road
Hong Kong
(5) 823 1813

Christchurch Marathon
Race Director
PO Box 670
Christchurch, New Zealand

Frankfurt Marathon
Im Fasanengarten 1A
6240 Konigstein, Germany
(6174) 3085

Fukuoka International
Marathon
Japan A.A. Federation
1-1-1 Jinnan
Shibuya-ku, Tokyo 150
Japan
(3) 481 2300

Geneva Marathon
Claude Haegi
Case Postale 519
1211 Geneva 1, Switzerland

Glasgow Marathon
Organizing Committee
20 Trongate
Glasgow G1 5ES, Scotland
(41) 227 5093

Gold Coast International
Marathon
P.O. Box 5251
Gold Coast, Queensland
4217, Australia
(61) 75 931 616

Gothenburg Half Marathon
P.O. Box 7229
402 34 Gothenburg, Sweden
(31) 820 045

Hamburg Marathon
Postfach 10 26 49
D-2000 Hamburg 1, Germany
(40) 336 711

Helsinki City Marathon
Radiokatu 20
SF-00240 Helsinki, Finland
(90) 1581

**Intercontinental Eurasia
Marathon**
1874 Cumburiyet Cadd.
Elmada
Istanbul, Turkey
146 0115

Jakarta Marathon
Jalan Menteng Raya No. 72
Jakarta Pusat, Indonesia
(21) 340 880

Jerusalem Marathon
 9, Aharonovitch Street
Tel Aviv 63566, Israel
972-3-525 1333

Lisbon Marathon
Rua Du Laranjal 7-A
1300 Lisbon, Portugal
(1) 3633 605

London Marathon
P.O. Box 262
Surrey TW10 5JB, England
(1) 948 7935

Marathon de Lyon
Rue Colon
69100 Villeurbanne, France

Macau International Marathon
Caixa Postal 334
Macau
580 762

Madrid Marathon
C/ Linneo 4
28005 Madrid, Spain
(91) 266 9701

**Marrakesh International
Marathon**
estage 13
Ave. de l'Armee Royale
Casablanca 01, Morocco
(212) 331 903

**Melbourne Marathon, Inc.
Race Director**
Olympic Park Adm. Bldg.
Swan Street
Melbourne, Victoria, 3002
Australia

Mexico City Marathon
Av. Division Del Norte Esq.
Rio Churubusco Col.
Portales, Mexico City, Mexico
(5) 881 835

**Mombasa International
Marathon**
P.O. Box 47874
Nairobi, Kenya
(2) 25 884

**Montreal International
Marathon**
PO Box 1570, Station B
Montreal, Quebec H3B 3L2

**Moscow International
Peace Marathon**
18 Markhlevsky Street
Moscow, USSR
924 0824

Mount Meru Marathon
P.O. Box 1779
Arusha, Tanzania
(57) 7011

Munchen Marathon
Birkenleiten 15
8000 Munich 90, Germany
(89) 652 081

Paris Marathon
17 Rue de Sevigne
75004 Paris, France
(1) 48 877 518

**MAS International
Marathon Penang**
C/4 Lebuh Leith
10200 Penang, Malaysia
(4) 638 244

Philippines International Marathon
3679 Bautista Street
Makati, Metro Manila,
Philippines
(2) 831 7359

Prague Marathon
P.O. Box 534
Praha 1-111 21,
Czechoslovakia
(42-2) 263 747

Reykjavik Marathon
Alfabakki 16, Box 9180
129 Reykjavik, Iceland
(1) 603 060

Maraton do Rio
Jose Werneck
Rua da Ajuda no. 35/7o
andar
Rio de Janiero,
200 40 Brasil
(21) 210 3237

Maraton di Roma
Via Paulucci de Calboli
Fulcieri, 60
00195 Roma, Italy
(6) 318) 462

Rotterdam Marathon
Postbus 1627
3000 BP Rotterdam,
Netherlands
(10) 4172 440

Sao Paulo Marathon
Jose Werneck
Rua da Ajuda no. 35/7o
andar
Rio de Janeiro 20040
Brasil
(21) 210 3237

Seoul International Marathon
P.O. Box 566 K.M.W.
Seoul, Korea
(2) 777 4175

Seville Marathon
C/ Ignacio Gomez Millan
41010 Seville, Spain
(1) 266 9701

Stockholm Marathon
Box 10023
100 55 Stockholm, Sweden
(8) 667 1930

Sydney Marathon
Australian Athletic Union
PO Box 700
Strawberry Hills NSW 2013
Australia

Tel Aviv Marathon
P.O. Box 7170
8 Haarbaa Street
64739 Tel Aviv, Israel
(3) 561 3316

Tokyo Men's Marathon
Yomiuri Shimbun
1-2-1 Kiyosumi
Kotoku, Tokyo 135
Japan
(3) 5245 7085

Tokyo Women's Marathon
Asahi Shimbun
5-3-2 Tsukji, Chuo-ku
Tokyo, Japan
(3) 545 0355

Valencia Marathon
Antonio de la Lastra Liern
Pintor Piero 10-4a-7a
46010 Valencia, Spain
(6) 369 2071

Vancouver International Marathon
1033 Davie Street
Suite 600
Vancouver, B.C. V6E 1M7
Canada
(604) 685-5616

**Vardinoyannios Marathon
Crete**
OFI Amateur Club
93, Isavron Street
Heraklion 713 03 Crete
Greece
(081) 261 860

Venice Marathon
Via Felisati 34
30171 Mestre-Venezia,
Italy
(41) 940 644

Vienna Spring Marathon
Columbusgasse 66/B
1100 Wien, Austria
(222) 602 1720

**Split International
Marathon**
Dalmacijaturist
Titova Obala 5/1
5800 Split, Yugoslavia
(58) 40 266

Publications

Runner's World
33 East Minor Street
Emmaus, PA 18049
(215) 967-5171

Running International
6290 Busch Blvd.
Columbus, OH 43216
(614) 433-0393

Running Times
2022 A Opitz Blvd.
Suite 1
Woodbridge, VA 22191
(703) 491-2044

The Walking Magazine
711 Boylston Street
Boston, MA 02116
(617) 236-1885

Rugby

**Federation of International
Amateur Rugby**
7 Cite d'Antin
75009 Paris, France
(011) 33.1 4874 8475

USA Rugby
830 North Tejon
Suite 104
Colorado Springs, CO 80903
(719) 632-1022

Canadian Rugby Union
1600 James Naismith Drive
Gloucester, Ontario KiB 5N4
(613) 748-5657

**Eastern Rugby Union
of America**
4001 Ronson Drive
Alexandria, VA 22310
(703) 841-8616

**Midwest Rugby Football
Union**
814 N. Beatty
Pittsburgh, PA 15205
(412) 256-1286

**Pacific Coast Rugby
Football Union**
P.O. Box 15157
San Francisco, CA 94115
(415) 531-9161

Publications

Rugby
2350 Broadway
New York, NY 10024
(212) 787-1160

Softball

**Amateur Softball Association
International Softball Assoc.**
2801 N.E. 50th Street
P.O. Box 68207
Oklahoma City, OK 73111
(405) 424-5266

Canada Softball Association
1600 James Naismith Drive
Gloucester, Ontario KIB 5N4
(613) 748-5668

Cinderella Softball Association
P.O. Box 1411
Corning, NY 14830
(607) 937-5469

International Softball Congress
6007 E. Hillcrest Circle
Anaheim Hills, CA 92087
(714) 998-5694

**U.S. Slo-Pitch Softball
Association**
P.O. Box 2047
3935 S. Crater Road
Petersburg, VA 23805
(804) 732-4099

Water Sports Organizations

Wind Surfing/Sail Boarding

**American Boardsailing
Industries Association**
99 E. Blithedale Avenue
Mill Valley, CA 94941
(800) 333-ABIA

**International Women's
Boardsailing Association**
P.O. Box 116
Hood River, OR 97031
(503) 386-8708

**Professional Boardsailing
Association**
Gomunder Strasse 9
D-8000 Munich 70, Germany

**U.S. Boardsailing
Association**
P.O. Box 978
Hood River, OR 97031
(503) 386-8708

**World Boardsailing
Association**
Feldafinger Platz 2
DK-8000 Munich 71, Germany
(48.89) 781-074

Surfing

**Association of Surfing
Professionals**
16691 Gothard Street
P.O. Box 309
Huntington Beach, CA 92648
(714) 842-8826

**International Surfing
Association**
"Sunridge" 109
Winston Avenue
Branksome People
Dorset, England

**International Surfing
Commission**
Surfhouse
Box 3432
Palm Beach, FL 33480
(407) 736-4277

**International Surfing
Committee**
P.O. Box 15277
Newport Beach, CA 92660
(714) 548-9599

International Surfing
League
P.O. Box 1315
Beverly Hills, CA 90210
(213) 859-3024

**Professional Surfing
Association of America**
530 Sixth Street
Hermosa Beach, CA 90254
(213) 372-0414

**U.S. Surfing Federation
11 Adams Point**
Barrington, RI 02806
(508) 336-6904

**Women's International
Surfing Association**
P.O. Box 512
San Juan Capistrano, CA 92675
(714) 493-5496

Water Skiing

American Water Ski Association
799 Overlook Drive
Winter Haven, FL 33882
(813) 324-4341

**International Water Skiing
Federation**
Via Verza 4
22035 Canzo (Como), Italy
(39.31) 68 2091

Swimming

**National Association of
Underwater Instructors**
P.O. Box 14650
Montclair, CA 91763
(714) 621-5801

U.S. Lifesaving Association
425 E. McFetridge Drive
Chicago, IL 60605
(312) 294-2333

Winter Sports Organizations

Skiing

Alpine Canada
1600 James Naismith Drive
Gloucester, Ontario K1B 5N4
(613) 748-5661

Alpine Club of Canada
P.O. Box 1026
Banff, Alberta T0L 0C0
(403) 762-4481
(Mountaineering, Skiing)

American Ski Association
1888 Sherman Street
Suite 500
Denver, CO 80203
(303) 861-SNOW

American Ski Federation
207 Constitution Avenue N.E.
Washington, D.C. 20002
(202) 543-1595

**Association of Ski Racing
Professionals**
148 Porters Point Road
Colchester, VT 05446
(802) 862-9498

Biathalon Canada
1600 James Naismith Drive
Gloucester, Ontario K1B 5N4
(613) 748-5617

Canada Ski Association
1600 James Naismith Drive
Gloucester, Ontario K1B 5N4
(613) 748-5710

**Cross Country Ski Areas
Association**
259 Bolton Road
Winchester, NH 03470
(603) 239-4341

Eastern Ski Association
22 High Street
Brattleboro, VT 05301
(802) 254-6077

**National Ski Areas
Association**
P.O. Box 2883
Springfield, MA 01101
(413) 781-4732

National Ski Patrol System
133 S. Van Gordon Street
Lakewood, CO 80228
(303) 988-1111

**National Standard
Racing (NASTAR)**
P.O. Box 4580
Aspen, CO 81611
(303) 925-7864

**North American Snowboard
Association**
P.O. Box 2522
Durango, CO 81301
(303) 259-2181

**Professional Ski Instructors
Association of America**
133 S. Van Gordon #240
Lakewood, CO 80228
(303) 987-9390

Pro Ski International
P.O. Box 3330
Copper Mountain, CO 80443
(303) 968-2849

Ski Council of America
6600 Madison Avenue
New York, NY 10022
(212) 874-3030

Ski Industries America
8377-B Greensboro Drive
McLean, VA 22102
(703) 556-9020

**United States Biathalon
Association**
P.O. Box 5515
Essex Junction, VT 05453
(802) 655-4524

**United States Ski
Association**
1500 Kearns Blvd.
Suite 200
Park City, UT 84060
(801) 649-9070

United States Ski Team
P.O. Box 100
Park City, UT 84060
(801) 649-9090

**U.S. Recreational Ski
Association**
1315 E. Pacifico Avenue
Anaheim, CA 92805
(714) 634-1050

**U.S. Pro Ski Tour
North American Pro Ski**
122 Front Street
Bath, ME 04530
(207) 443-3847
(Sponsors Men's & Women's
Pro ski tour)

**World Loppet-Telemark
Association**
P.O. Box 911
Hayward, WI 54843
(715) 634-5025

Bobsledding/Luge

Professional Bobsledding
340 Cornelia Street
Plattsburgh, NY 12901
(518) 563-5237

**United States Luge
Association**
P.O. Box 651
Lake Placid, NY 12946
(518) 523-2071

U.S. Bobsled & Skeleton Association

P.O. Box 828
Lake Placid, NY 12946
(518) 523-1842

U.S. Ski Bob Federation
P.O. Box 102
Littleton, CO 80120
(303) 979-5722

Curling

International Curling Federation
2424 Olson Drive
Grand Forks, ND 58201
(701) 772-1327

Curl Canada
1600 James Naismith Drive
Gloucester, Ontario K1B 5N4
(613) 748-5713

U.S. Curling Association
P.O. Box 971
Stevens Point, WI 54481
(715) 345-0525

U.S. Women's Curling Association
7 Little John Lane
Stamford, CT 06907
(203) 322-1922

Winter Swimming

Iceberg Athletic Club
3046 W. 22nd Street
Brooklyn, NY 11224
(718) 266-5764

Polar Bear Club
376 Naughton Avenue
Staten Island, NY 10305
(718) 979-8370

Sled Dog Racing

International Sled Dog Racing Association
P.O. Box 446
Nordman, ID 83848
(208) 443-3153

Iditarod Trail Race Committee
P.O. Box 5155
Wasilla, AK 99687
(907) 376-6998

Snowshoe Racing

International Snowshoe Racing Federation
Corinth, NY 12822
(518) 654-7165

Sports Organizations for the Disabled and Handicapped

**Special Olympics
Joseph P. Kennedy**
Foundation
1350 New York Avenue
Suite 500
Washington, DC 20005
(202) 628-3630

**Cerebral Palsy International
Sports and Recreation
Association**
Verdistraat 51
2161 Lisse, Netherlands

**Comite' International
des Sports des Sourds**
Langaavel 41
2650 Hvidovre, Denmark
(45.1) 30 4522

**Internal Blind Sports
Organization**
Postsrasse 4/5
1020 Berlin, Germany
(37.2) 212 4522

**International Coordinating
Committee of World Sports
Organizations for the Disabled**
Heyenoordsweg 5
6813 GG Arnhem
Netherlands
(31.85) 52 6726

**International Sports
Federation for Persons
with Mental Handicap**
Koninginnegracht 101
2514 Den Haag,
Netherlands
(3170) 50 3415

**Internationsl Sports
Organization of the Disabled**
Bondebyv 27
S-610 55 Stigtomta
Sweden
0155-275 05

**International Stoke
Mandeville Games
Federation**
Harvey Road
Aylesbury, Bucks,
England
(44.296) 8 4848

**Winter Games for the
Disabled**
3701 Connecticut Avenue
Suite 236
Washington, DC 20008
(202) 833-1251

**American Athletic
Association for the Deaf**
1134 Davenport Drive
Burton, MI 49529
(313) 239-3969

**American Blind Bowling
Association**
67 Bame Avenue
Buffalo, NY 14215
(716) 836-1472

**American Wheelchair
Bowling Association**
Larkspur Lane
Menomonee Falls, WI 53501
(914) 781-6876

**Blind Outdoor Leisure
Development**
533 E. Main Street
Aspen, CO 81611
(303) 925-8922

Blind Sports Association
1939 16th Avenue
San Francisco, CA 94116
(415) 681-1939

**Canadian Deaf Sports
Association**
218-1367 W. Broadway
Vancouver, B.C. V6H 4A9
(604) 737-3041 Voice
(604) 738-7122 TDD

**Canada Federation of
Sports Organizations for
the Disabled**
1600 James Naismith Drive
Gloucester, Ontario K1B 5N4
(613) 748-5630

Canadian Special Olympics
40 St. Clair Avenue West
Toronto, Ontario M4V 1M6
(416) 928-8100

**National Association for
Disabled Athletes**
17 Lindley Avenue
Tenafly, NJ 07670
(201) 236-6560

**National Association of
Sports for Cerebral Palsy**
66 East 34th Street
New York, NY 10016
(203) 562-1821

**National Deaf Bowling
Association**
9244 E. Mansfield Avenue
Denver, CO 80237
(303) 771-9018

**National Handicapped Sports
& Recreation Association**
1145 19th Street N.W.
Suite 717
Washington, DC 20036
(202) 652-7505

**National Sports Center
for the Disabled**
P.O. Box 36
Winter Park, CO 80482
(303) 726-5514

**National Wheelchair
Athletic Association**
3595 E. Fountain Blvd.
Colorado Springs, CO 80910
(719) 574-1150

**National Wheelchair
Basketball Association**
University of Kentucky
110 Seaton Bldg.
Lexington, KY 40506
(606) 257-1623

**North American Wheelchair
Athletic Association**
PO box 32
Waynesboro, VA 22980
(703) 949-6320

**U.S. Amputee Athletic
Association**
PO Box 210709
Nashville, TN 37221
(615) 662-2323

**U.S. Association for
Blind Athletes**
4708 46th Street N.W.
Washington, DC 20016
(202) 363-1807

**U.S. Cerebral Palsy
Athletic Association**
34518 Warren Road
Suite 264
Westland, MI 48185
(313) 425-8961

**U.S. Deaf Skiers
Association**
159 Davis Drive
Hackensack, NJ 07601
(201) 489-3777 (TDD)

**Amputee Sports
Association**
PO Box 60412
Savannah, GA 31420
(912) 927-5406

Blind Sports Association
1939 16th Avenue
San Francisco, CA 94116
(415) 681-1939

Sports Museums & Halls of Fames

Listed in this section are many fine Museums & Hall of Fames for sports, both in North America and abroad. Please support these fine Museums.

Academy of Sports
4, rue de Teheran
75008 Paris, France
(33) 4562 9715

Alabama Sports Hall of Fame Museum
PO Box 10163
Birmingham, AL 35202
(205) 323-6665
Location: Civic Center Plaza

Amateur Athletic Foundation of Los Angeles
2141 West Adams Blvd.
Los Angeles, CA 90018
(213) 730-9600

Amateur Sports Hall of Fame
211 Bedford Street
Johnstown, PA 15901
(814) 536-5107

American Water Ski Hall of Fame
799 Overlook Drive S.E.
Winter Park, FL 33884
(813) 324-2472

Aquatic Hall of Fame and Museum of Canada
435 Main Street
Winnipeg, Manitoba, R3B 1B2
(204) 947-0131

Australian Gallery of Sport
PO Box 175
East Melbourne, Australia 3002
03-654-8922

Australian Institute of Sport National Sport Information Centre
Leverrier Crescent, Bruce
ACT PO Box 176
Belconnen ACT 2616 Australia
(06) 252 1369

Auto Racing Hall of Fame
4790 West 16th Street
Speedway, IN 46224
(317) 248-6747

Babe Ruth Birthplace Museum
216 Emory Street
Baltimore, MD 21230
(301) 727-1539

Barcelona Museum & Sports Study Center
Buenos Aires Street 56-58
(Torre)
08036 Barcelona, Spain
93/230-61-18

Bermuda Sports Hall of Fame
Box 121
Hamilton, Bermuda

British Columbia Sports Hall of Fame & Museum
PO Box 69020, Station K
Vancouver, B.C., V5K 4W3
(604) 253-2311

Paul W. (Bear) Bryant Museum
The University of Alabama
300 Bryant Drive
Box 870385
Tuscaloosa, AL 35487
(205) 348-4668

California Horse Racing Hall of Fame
201 Colorado Place
Arcadia, CA 91007

Canada's Sports Hall of
Fame
Exhibition Place
Toronto, Ontario, M6K 3C3
(416) 595-1046

Canadian Amateur Sports
Hall of Fame
2380 avenue Pierre Dupuy
Montreal, Quebec H3C 3R4
(514) 861-3371

Canadian Baseball Hall of
Fame
PO Box 4008
Station A
Toronto, Ontario, M5W 2R1

Canadian Figure Skating
Assoc. Hall of Fame
1600 James Naismith Drive
Gloucester, Ontario K1B 5N4
(613) 748-5635

Canadian Football Hall of
Fame
58 Jackson Street West
Hamilton, Ontario, L8P 1L4

Canadian Lacross Hall of
Fame
PO Box 308
New Westminster, B.C.,
V3l 4Y6
(604) 526 4281

Canada Olympic Hall of
Fame
Canada Olympic Park, S.S. 1
Calgary, Alberta, T2M 4N3
(403) 286-2632

College Football Hall of
Fame
5540 Kings Island Drive
Kings Island, OH 45034
(513) 398-5410

Curling Hall of Fame & Museum
219 Winchester Street
Winnipeg, Manitoba, R3N 1C1

Catskill Fly Fishing Center
RD 1, Box 130-C
Livingston Manor, NY 12758
(914) 439-4810

Chicago Sports Hall of Fame
222 West Ontario, Suite 503
Chicago, IL 60610
(312) 943-3085

Delaware Sports Hall of
Fame
21 Molly Lane
Chadds Ford, PA 19317
(215) 459-0728

Detroit Tigers Hall of
Fame
44 Frank Llyod Wright Dr.
PO Box 341
Ann Arbor, MI 48106
(313) 930-3818

Florida Sports Hall of
Fame
PO Box 1847
Lake City, FL 32055
(904) 755-5666
Location: Intersection of
Interstate 75 & U.S.90

Frankfort-Elberta National
Soaring Hall of Fame & Museum
403 Main Street
Frankfort, MI 49635

Georgia Sports Hall of Fame
1627 Peachtree Street N.E.
Suite 325
Atlanta, GA 30309
(404) 634-9138

Greater Cleveland Sports Hall
of Fame
1375 Euclid Avenue, Suite 412
Cleveland, OH 44115

Greater St. Louis Amateur
Baseball Hall of Fame
PO Box 9951
Kirkwood, MO 63122

Green Bay Packers Hall of Fame
1901 South Oneida Street
Green Bay, WI 54307
(414) 499-4281

Greyhound Hall of Fame
407 South Buckeye
Abilene, KS 67410
(913) 263-3000

Harrah (William F.) Automobile Foundation
970 Glendale Avenue
Reno, NV 89431
(702) 355-3500

Hellenic Sports Hall of Fame
180 Bolton Street
Marlboro, MA 01752

Hockey Hall of Fame
Exhibition Place
Toronto, Ontario, M6K 3C3
(416) 595-1345

Indiana Basketball Hall of Fame
One Hall of Fame Court
New Castle, IN 47362
(317) 529-1891

Indiana Football Hall of Fame
PO Box 1035
Richmond, IN 47374

Indiana Museum of Sport
202 N. Alabama Street
Indianapolis, IN 46204
(317) 232-1637

Indianapolis Motor Speedway Hall of Fame Museum
4790 West 16th Street
Indianapolis, IN 46223
(317) 248-6747

International Afro-American Sports Hall of Fame
15011 Strathmoor Street
Detroit, MI 48227
(313) 272-0281
Location: 600 Randolf St.

International Boxing Hall of Fame
PO Box 425
Canastota, NY 13032
(315) 697-7095

International Gymnastics Hall of Fame
227 Brooks Street
Oceanside, CA 92054
(619) 722-0606

International Hockey Hall of Fame and Museum
PO Box 82
York & Alfred Streets
Kingston, Ontario, K7L 4V6

International Jewish Sports Hall of Fame
11500 W. Olympic Blvd.
Suite 303
Los Angeles, CA 90064
(213) 276-1014

International Motor Sports Hall of Fame
PO Box 1018
Talladega, AL 35160
Location: Alabama International Motor Speedway Complex
(205) 362-5002

International Palace of Sports
Camelot Square, PO Box 332
North Webster, IN 46555

International Snowmobile Racing Hall of Fame
PO Box 7
Minocqua, WI 54548 (Summer)
6905 Norway Road
Sun Prairie, WI 53590 (Winter)
(608) 825-6373 or 3366
A permanent Hall is planned in Eagle River, WI

International Surfing Hall
of Fame
5580 La Jolla Blvd.
Suite 373
La Jolla, CA 92037

International Swimming Hall
of Fame
One Hall of Fame Drive
Fort Lauderdale, FL 33316
(305) 464-6536

International Tennis Hall
of Fame and Museum
194 Bellevue Avenue
Newport, RI 62840

International Women's Sports
Hall of Fame
342 Madison Avenue
Suite 728
New York, NY 10173
(212) 972-9170

Japanese Baseball Hall of
Fame
3-61, Koraku-I-chome
Bunkyo-ku, Tokyo 102
(03)811-3600

Lacrosse Hall of Fame
Foundation, Inc.
Newton H. White, Jr. Athletic Ctr.
Homewood, Baltimore MD 21218
(301) 235-6882

Little League Baseball Museum
PO Box 3485
Williamsport, PA 17701
(717) 326-3607

Maine Sports Hall of Fame
and Museum
3 Delano Park
Cape Elizabeth, ME 04107
207) 799-4555

Manitoba Sports Hall of Fame
and Museum
0700 Ellice Avenue
Winnipeg, Manitoba R3H 0B1

Mexican Professional Baseball
Hall of Fame
Banpacifico
Venida Reforma
Ciudad, Mexico, D.F.

Metropolitan Detroit Sports
Museum
PO Box 2532
Detroit, MI 48231
(313) 393-8618

Michigan Jewish Sports
Hall of Fame
17000 West Ten Mile Rd.
Southfield, MI 48075

Michigan Sports Hall
of Fame
1010 Joanne Court
Bloomfield Hills, MI 48013
(313) 646-2216

Ralph W. Miller Golf Library
& Museum
One Industry Hills Parkway
City of Industry, CA 91744
(818) 965-0861

Missouri Basketball
Hall of Fame
Tenth & Roger Streets
Columbia, MO 65216
(314) 875-7413
Location: Columbia College
Dorsey Gymnasium

Motorsports Museum and
Hall of Fame
45225 West Ten Mile Road
Novi, MI 48050
(313) 575-9400

Museum of Polo and Hall
of Fame
Kentucky Horse Park
4059 Iron Works Pike
Lexington, KY 40507
(606) 281-6285

The Museum of Sport
Tervuursevest 101
3030 Leuven, Belgium
(32) 1622-0405

**Museum of Western Australia
Sport**
Superdrome Sports Center
Stephenson Ave., PO Box 57
Claremont, West Australia 6010
(09) 387-8542

Museum of Yachting
Box 129, Fort Adams
Newport, RI 02840
(401) 847-1018

**Muskegon Area Sports Hall
of Fame**
7740 Old Channel Trail
Montague, MI 49437
(616) 894-2923

**Naismith Memorial Basketball
Hall of Fame**
1150 West Columbus Avenue
Springfield, MA 01101
(413) 781-6500

National Art Museum of Sport
University of New Haven
West Haven, CT 06516
(203) 932-7000 x 7197

**National Baseball Hall of
Fame and Museum**
PO Box 590
Cooperstown, NY 13326
(607) 547-9988
Location: Main Street

**National Bowling Museum &
Hall of Fame**
111 Stadium Plaza
St. Louis, MO 63102
(314) 231-6340

Negro League Baseball Museum
1601 East 18th Street
Kansas City, MO 64108
(816) 221-1920

**National Collegiate
Athletic Association (NCAA)
Visitors Center**
6201 College Blvd.
Overland Park, KS 66211
(913) 339-0066

National Collegiate Hall of Fame
PO Box 1745
Lake Havasu, AZ 86403

**National Cowboy Hall of Fame
& Western Heritage Center**
1700 N.E.63rd Street
Oklahoma City, OK 73111

**National Football Foundation
and Hall of Fame**
1865 Palmer Avenue
Larchmont, NY 10538
(914) 834-0474

**National Fresh Water Fishing
Hall of Fame**
One Hall of Fame Drive
Hayward, WI 54843
(715) 634-4440

**National High School Sports
Hall of Fame**
11724 Plaza Circle, Box 20626
Kansas City, MO 64195
(816) 464-5400

**National Italian-American
Sports Hall of Fame**
2625 Clearbrook Drive
Arlington Heights, IL 60005

**National Lawn Tennis Hall
of Fame and Tennis Museum**
Newport Casino
Newport, RI 02840

**National Motorsports Hall
of Fame**
20 Division Street
Coldwater, MI 49036
(515) 278-7223

National Museum of Racing
Union Avenue
Saratoga Springs, NY 12866
(518) 584-0400

**National Polish-American Sports
Hall of Fame**
13450 Keystone
Detroit, MI 48212
(313) 891-3676

National Rivers Hall of Fame
American House
McGregor, IA 52157
(319) 583-1241

National Ski Hall of Fame
PO Box 191, Poplar & Mather
Ishpeming, MI 49849
(906) 486-9281

National Soaring Museum
Harris Hill, RD #1
Elmira, NY 14903

National Soccer Hall of Fame
5-11 Ford Avenue
Oneonta, NY 13820
(607) 432-3351

**National Softball Hall of
Fame and Museum**
2801 N.E. 50th Street
Oklahoma City, OK 73111
(405) 424-5266

**National Sportscasters &
Sportswriters Hall of Fame**
322 E. Innes Street
Salisbury, NC 28144
(704) 633-4275

**National Sprint Car Hall
of Fame & Museum**
1402 N. Lincoln Avenue
Knoxville, Iowa 50138
(800) 874-4488
Location: Marion Cnty. Fairgrounds

**National Track & Field Hall
of Fame**
PO Box 120
Indianapolis, IN 46206
(317) 638-9155

National Wrestling Hall of Fame
405 West Hall of Fame Avenue
Stillwater, OK 74074

**New Brunswick Sports Hall of
Fame**
PO Box 6000, Queen Street
Fredericton, N.B., E3B 5H1
(506) 453-3747B

New England Sports Museum
1175 Soldiers Field Rd.
Boston, MA 02134-9990

**New Foundland Sports Hall
of Fame**
Colonial Building, Rm. 18
Military Road
St.John's, N.F., A1C 2C9

**New Jersey Sports Hall of Fame
Sports & Exposition Authority**
East Rutherford, NJ 07073
(201) 460-4022

**New South Wales Hall of
Champions**
State Sports Centre
PO Box 135
Fleming Market, N.S.W.
2129 Australia
(02) 763-0111

**North Carolina Sports Hall
of Fame**
3316 Julian Drive
Raleigh, NC 27604
(919) 872-9289

Ohio Baseball Hall of Fame
Lucas Co. Rec. Center
2901 Key Street
Maumee, OH 43537
(216) 464-3049

Olympic Museum
Avenue Ruchonnet 18, 1003
Lausanne, Switzerland
22/20-93-31

**Oregon Sports Hall of Fame
and Museum**
PO Box 4381
Portland, OR 97208-4381
(503) 227-7466
Museum Location:
Standard Insurance Center
900 S.W. Fifth Ave., Portland

**Pennsylvania Sports Hall
of Fame**
937 Willow Street
PO Box 1140
Lebanon, PA 17042-1140
(717) 274-3644

PGA Tour Hall of Fame
112 Tournament Players Club Blvd.
Sawgrass
Ponte Vedra, FL 32082
(904) 285-3700

PGA World Golf Hall of Fame
PGA Blvd. PO Box 1908
Pinehurst, NC 28374
(919) 295-6651 or (800) 334-00178

Planes of Fame Air Museum
WWII Cal-Aero Field, Chino Airport
7000 Merrill Avenue
Chino, CA 91710
(714) 597-3722

**Prince Edward Island Sports
Hall of Fame**
42 Newland Crescent
Charlottestown, P.E.I., C1A 4H7

Pro Football Hall of Fame
2121 George Halas Drive, N.W.
Canton, OH 44708
(216) 456-8207

Pro Rodeo Hall of Champions
101 Pro Rodeo Drive
Colorado Springs, CO 80919

**Rome Sports Hall of Fame
and Museum**
City Hall
Rome, NY 13440

Rose Bowl Hall of Fame
PO Box 1050
9161 Las Tunas Drive
Temple City, CA 91780
(818) 449-4100

St. Louis Sports Hall of Fame
100 Stadium Plaza
St. Louis, MO 63102
(314) 421-6790

San Diego Hall of Champions
1649 El Prado, Balboa Park
San Diego, CA 92101
(619) 234-2544

**Saskatchewan Sports Hall
of Fame**
2205 Victoria Avenue
Regina, Sask., S4P 084
(306) 522-3651

Singapore Sports Museum
Singapore Sports Council
National Stadium
Kallang, Singapore 1439
345-7111 x 635

Songwriters Hall of Fame
One Times Square
New York, NY 10021

Sport Australia Hall of Fame
76 Jolimont Street
Jolimont, Victoria, Australia
(613) 654-7633

Sports Hall of Oblivion
9760 E. Houghton Lake Drive
Where, MI 48629
Curator: Chuck Hershberger

Sports Immortals Museum
1130 Onion Drive
Pittsburgh, PA 15235

Swiss Sports Museum
Postfach, Missionstrasse 28
CH-4003 Basel, Switzerland
061-25-12-21

**Sport Nova Scotia Hall
of Fame**
PO Box 3010S.
Halifax, N.S., B3J 3G6

**Texas Sports Hall of Champions
and Texas Tennis Museum**
PO Box 3475
Waco, TX 76707
(817) 756-2307
Location:
14th & Waco Drive, Waco

**Texas Sports Hall of Fame
Foundation**
601 Fidelity Union Life Building
Dallas, TX 75201

**Trapshooting Hall of Fame
& Museum**
601 W. Vandalia Road
Vandalia, OH 45377
(513) 898-1945

**Trotter Horse Museum & Hall
of Fame**
PO Box 590
Goshen, NY 10924
(914) 294-6330
Location:
240 Main St., Goshen

**United States Figure Skating
Association Hall of Fame & Museum**
20 First Street
Colorado Springs, CO 80906
(303) 635-5200

**United States Golf Association
Golf Museum**
Golf House
Far Hills, NJ 07931
(201) 234-2300

**United States Hockey Hall
of Fame**
PO Box 657, Hat Trick Avenue
Eveleth, MN 55734
(218) 744-5167

**United States Olympic
Committee Hall of Fame**
1750 East Boulder Street
Colorado Springs, CO 80909-5760
(719) 632-551

**United States Slo-Pitch Softball
Association Hall of Fame Museum**
PO Box 2047, South Crater Road
Petersburg, VA 23803
(804) 732-4099

**United States Track & Field
Hall of Fame**
PO Box 297
Angola, IN 46703

U.S. Bicycling Hall of Fame
PO Box 8535
1 West Main Street
Somerville, NJ 08876
(201) 722-3620

Virginia Sports Hall of Fame
420 High Street
Portsmouth, VA 23704
(804) 393-8031

Volleyball Hall of Fame
PO Box 1895
444 Dwight Street
Holyoke, MA 01040
(413) 536-5770

**North American Sports
Library Network**
Amateur Athletic Foundation
2141 W. Adams Blvd.
Los Angeles, CA 90018
(213) 730-9696
Dr. Wayne Wilson

Sports Collecting

Listed in this section are the Card Companies for the Major & Minor Leagues as well as Foreign Card Companies and collectible manufacturers of officially licensed sports products.

Fleer Corporation
1120 Route 73
Mt. Laurel, NJ 08054
(609) 231-6200

Goal Line Art, Inc.
PO Box 372
Ridley Park, PA 19078

Hi-Pro Marketing
2000 Bigler Street
Fort Lee, NJ 07024
(201) 947-4007
(action packed card sets)

JOGO Novelties, Inc.
1872 Queensdale Avenue
Gloucester, Ontario K1T 1K1
Canada
(613) 564-1875

Kenner Products
1041 Vine Street
Cincinnati, OH 45202
(513) 579-4000

Leaf-Donruss Company
2355 Waukegan Road
Bannockburn, IL 60015
(708) 940-7500

NBA Hoops
300 North Duke Street
Durham, NC 27702
(919) 683-9301

O-Pee-Chee Co., Ltd.
PO box 6306
London, Ontario N5W 5S1
Canada
(519) 659-3300

Barry Colla Photography
855 Civic Center Drive
Santa Clara, CA 95050
(408) 248-5260

Optigraphics
924 Avenue J East
Grand Prairie, TX 75050
(214) 647-2728
(makers of SCORE &
Sportflies sets)

Panini USA
655 Madison Avenue
New York, NY 10021
(212) 308-0200
(a division of Pannini Cards
of Italy)

Parker Brothers
50 Dunham Road
Beverly, MA 01915
(508) 927-7600
(starting lineup game
and card set)

Perez-Steele Galleries
Box 1776
Fort Washington, PA 19034
(215) 836-1192

Philadelphia Chewing Gum Corp.
Lawrence & Eagle Roads
Havertown, PA 19083-2198
(215)449-1700
(Swell Gum sets)

Playball USA Cards
777 Kapiolani Blvd.
Suite 3309
Honolulu, HI 96813
(808) 625-5379

Pro Set, Inc.
17250 Dallas Parkway
Dallas, TX 75248
(214) 407-2800

Pro Set U.K., Ltd.
87 Wembley Hill Road
Wembley, Middlesex HA9 8BU
England

Score/Major League Marketing
25 Ford Road
Westport, CT 06880
(203) 227-8882

SkyBox
NBA Properties, Inc.
Olymmpic Tower
645 Fifth Avenue
New York, NY 10022

Star Pics, Inc.
PO Box 2573
Farminton Hills, MI 48333
(313) 851-PICS

Topps Chewing Gum, Co.
254 36th Street
Brooklyn, NY 11232
(718) 768-8900
(makers of Bowman card
sets as well as Topps cards)

Topps of Ireland, Ltd.
Innshmore Ballincollig
County of Cork, Republic of
Ireland
(353.21) 871-005
Rep.: Duncan Markam

T & M Sports, Inc.
9950 Campo Road
Suite 303
Spring Valley, CA 92077
(619) 589-8111
(makers of Umpire & Senior
League card sets)

Upper Deck Company
5909 Sea Otter Place
Carlsbad, CA 92008
(619) 929-2070

Players International Ltd.
3417 Meadow Bluff Drive
Charlotte, NC 28226
(704) 541-0446

Minor League & Misc. Sport Card Manufacturers

Boxscores Enterprises
PO Box 280
Neenah, WI 54957

Classic Games, Inc.
Best Cards Division
6488 East Spring Street
Douglasville, GA 30134
(800) 229-1429

**Collector's Marketing
Corp. (CMC)**
220 12th Avenue
New York, NY 10001
(212) 563-2585

College Classics, Inc.
6323 Busch Blvd.
Columbus, OH 43229
(614) 431-2028

Collegiate Collection
201 E. Main Street
Suite 101A
Louisville, KY 40202
(800) 999-1364
(502) 587-8141

Grand Slam Cards
PO Box 27045
Tucson, AZ 85726
(602) 325-2621

HSC Marketing
PO Box 1415
Louisville, KY 40201
(502) 222-5518
(horse racing & jockey cards)

Pacific Trading Cards
18424 Highway 99
Lynwood, WA 98037
(800) 551-2002

ProCards, Inc.
202 S. Hanover Street
Pottstown, PA 19464
(215) 970-5833

Bill Pucko Cards
43 Alpine Drive
Webster, NY 14580

Star International, Inc.
1181 S. Rodgers Circle
Suite 28
Boca Raton, FL 33487
(407) 241-8601

Several firms have recently issued card sets for boxing, soccer, tennis & bowling that are not listed here due to limited information on these card companies.

Minicards Ltd.
64 Clifton Street
London EC2A 4HB, England

Licensed Products

Ace Novelty Company
13434 N.E. 16th Street
Bellevue, WA 98005
(206) 644-1820
(lapel pins & MVP cards)

All World Sports
2903 Saturn Street
Suite G
Brea, CA 92621
(714) 572-6858

Barry Colla Collection
2044 Lynwood Terrace
San Jose, CA 95128
(408) 247-7196
(Photoprints, postcards,
card sets)

Fotoball, USA, Inc.
4901 Morena Blvd.
Suite 505
San Diego, CA 92117
(800) 325-3686

Hartland Plastics, Inc.
PO box 439
Hartland, WI 53029
(statues/figurines)

**Professional Sports
Publications**
PO Box 1750
Grand Central Station
New York, NY 10163
(212) 697-1460
(college & pro programs)

Raymond Enterprises, Inc.
2395 West 2nd Avenue
Unit 10
Denver, CO 80223
(303) 922-3656
(NFL Star-Cal decals)

Sports Impressions
82 Bridge Road
Central Islip, NY 11722
(800) 368-5553
(figurines)

Sports Stamps Collectibles
PO Box 1809
Hicksville, NY 11802
(800) 767-1600

Hobby Guides and Directories

**The American Standard Catalog
of Certified Baseball Cards**
65 High Ridge Road
Stamford, CT 069056
(203) 968-0687

The Autograph Buyers Guide
PO Box 55328
Stockton, CA 95205
(209) 942-2131

**Baseball Card Dealer Directory
Meckler Books**
11 Ferry Lane West
Westport, CT 06880

Baseball Card Price Guide
700 E. State Street
Iola, WI 54990
(715) 445-2214

Baseball Update
405 Tarrytown Road
Suite 405
White Plains, NY 10607

**The Encyclopedia of
Baseball Cards**
Po Box 137
Centereach, NY 11720
(516) 981-3286
Publisher: Lew Lipset

The Charlton Press
2010 Yonge Street
Toronto, Ontario M4S 1Z9
(416) 488-4653
Price Guides on Hockey, Baseball
& Football

Legends Price Guide
429 Hart Drive, Suite 16
El Cajon, CA 92021
(619) 442-3056
(price guide of sports
collectibles)

Matchcover Collector's Price Guide
AMCC
PO Box 18481
Asheville, NC 28814
(704) 254-4487

**MLB Licensed Product
Reference Guide**
MLB Properties
Retail Marketing Dept.
350 Park Avenue
New York, NY 10022
(212) 339-7900

**The Price Guide to Autographs
Autograph House**
PO Box 658
Enka, NC 28728
(704) 667-9835

**The Sports Americana
Baseball Address List**
Jack Smalling
2308 Van Buren
Ames, IA 50010
(515) 232-7599

**The Sport Americana
Price Guides**
Becket Publications
4887 Alpha Road, Suite 200
Dallas, TX 75244
(214) 991-6657
Editor: Dr. James Beckett

The Sports Address Bible
1223 Broadway, Suite 102
Santa Monica, CA 90404
(310) 454-9480
Publisher: Global Sports
Author: Ed Kobak

**The Standard Catalog of
Baseball Cards**
700 E. State Street
Iola, WI 54990
(800) 258-0929
Publisher: Krause Publications

VIP Address Book
PO Box 10190
Marina del Rey, CA 90295-8864
Editor: Jim Wiggins

Foreign Reference Guides

**The Catalog of British & Foreign
Cigarette Cards 1888 -1991**
LCC, Ltd.
Sutton Road, Somerton
Somerset TA11 6QP,
England

Cigarette Card Values
Imperial Collections International
PO Box 10814
Lynchburg, VA 24506
(804) 832-1007
Pub.: Murray Cards Int'l., Ltd./London

The Guide To Cigarette Card Collecting
Albert's of Twickenham
113 London Road
Twickenham TW1 1EE, England

Sports Hobby Periodicals

Listed in this section are publications for the sport
memorabilia and card collecting hobby.

Beckett Monthly Magazines
4887 Alpha Road, Suite 200
Dallas, TX 75244
(214) 991-6657

Canadian Sportscard Collector
103 Lakeshore Rd., Suite 202
St. Catharines, Ontario L2N 2T6
(905) 646-7744

Krause Publications
700 East State Street
Iola, WI 54990
(715) 445-2214
(800) 258-0909
Publishers of
Sports Collectors Digest
Baseball Cards
BB Card Price Guide Monthly
The Postcard Collector
FB, Basketball & Hockey Collector
plus other fine price guides &
collector publications.

Sports Card Trader
990 Grove Street
Evanston, IL 60201
(708) 941-6440

Tuff Stuff
PO Box 1637
Glen Allen, VA 23060
(804) 266-0140

———————

American Collectors Journal
206 W. 4th Street, PO Box 407
Kewanee, IL 61443
(309) 852-2602

**The Autograph Collector's
Magazine**
PO Box 55328
Stockton, CA 95205
(209) 942-2131

The Autograph Review
305 Carlton Road
Syracuse, NY 13207
(315) 474-3516
Publisher: Jeff Morey

**Auto Racing Memories
And Memorabilia**
75 S.E. Fourth Avenue
Delray Beach, FL 33444
Publisher: Ken C. Breslauer

Baseball Autograph News
527 Third Avenue #294
New York, NY 10016
(212) 683-7912

**Baseball Card Investment
Report**
PO Box 9625
Newport Beach, CA 92660
(714) 662-2273

Card News
65 High Ridge Road
Suite 227
Stamford, CT 06905
(203) 968-0687

Collectors News
506 Second Street
Grundy Center, IA 50638
(319) 824-5456

EPSCC Newsletter
PO Box 3037
Maple Glen, PA 19002
(215) 643-0901
President: Bob Schmierer

**Fistic Fever
Boxing Memorabilia
Marketplace**
7010 Brookfield Plaza
Suite 342
Springfield, VA 22150
(703) 765-3610

Football Card News
PO Box 2510
Del Mar, CA 92014
(619) 755-2811
Editor: Alan Kaye

Hobbies
1006 S. Michigan Avenue
Chicago, IL 60605
(312) 939-4767

Insight On Collectables
Hwy. 6, PO Box 130
Durham, Ontario N0G 1R0
(519) 369-5155

Journal of Sports Philately
PO Box 2286
La Grange, IL 60525
Editor: John La Porta

Low & Inside
PO Box 290228
Minneapolis, MN 55429

Manuscripts News
350 N. Niagara Street
Burbank, CA 91505
Editor: David R. Smith

National Hobby News
PO Box 612
New Philadelphia, OH 44663
(216) 339-6338
Editor: Woody Russell

The Old Judge
PO Box 137
Centereach, NY 11720
(516) 981-3286
Editor: Lew Lipset

Olympin Collector's News
1386 Fifth Street
Schenectady, NY 12303
(518) 355-6493

The Pen and Quill
VACC
PO Box 6181
Washington, DC 20044
Sec.: Chris Wilson

The Pin Official Bulletin
3822 St. Damase
Jonquiere, Quebec G7X 2K1

Paper Collector's Marketplace
P.O. Box 128
Scandinavia, WI 54977
(715) 467-2379

Right On Schedule
204 N. Charro
Thousand Oaks, CA 91320
(805) 499-1918
Editor: Keith Gadbury

The Schedule Notebook
8 Fillmore Place
Lawrenceville, NJ 08648
Editor: Marty Falk

**Sports Card News &
Price Guides**
10300 Watson Road
St. Louis, MO 63127
(314) 966-2000
Publisher: Allan Kaye

Sports Card Review
RFD 1, Box 530
Winthrop, ME 04364
Editor: Susan Vogel

Topps Magazine
254 36th Street
Brooklyn, NY 11232
(718) 768-8900
Editor: Bob Woods

Trading Cards
9171 Wilshire Blvd.
Suite 300
Beverly Hills, CA 90210
(310) 858-7155
Editor: Terry Melia

Foreign Collecting Periodicals

Card Times
70 Winifred Lane
Aughton, Ormskirk
Lancs. L39 5DL, England
Editor: David Stuckey
Pub.: Magpie Publiscations

Cartophilic Notes and News
The Cartophilic Society of G.B.
116 Hillview Road
Ensbury Park,
Bournemouth BH10 SBJ, England
Editor: Ken Fox

Cigarette Card News & Trade Card Chronicle
The London Cigarette
Card Co., Ltd.
Sutton Road, Somerton
Somerset TA11 6QP, England

The Football Programme Directory
66 Southend Road
Wickford, Essex SS11 8EN
England
Editor: David Stacey

Hobby Associations & Societies

Sports Collectibles Association International (SCAI)
1450 N.E. 123rd Street
North Miami, FL 33161
(305) 892-2841
(supported by the card manufacturers, hobby publications & dealers)

Sports Collectors Association of America (SCAA)
2690 N.E. 191st Street
Miami, FL 33180
(new club, not to be confused with the SCAI.)
Issues: publication titled,
"The Sports Collector"

Foreign Societies

Australia Cartophilic Society
30 Minerva Avenue
North Balwyn, Victoria 3104
Australia
Pres.: John Etkins

Great Britain Cartophilic Society
116 Hillview Road
Ensbury Park, Bournemouth BH20 5BJ
England
Pres.: Ken Fox

New Zealand Cartophilic Society
8 Tahora Avenue
Remuera, Auckland 5
New Zealand
Pres.: Alan Spurdle
Issues: Card Lines

Collecting Organizations

Listed in this section are hobby collecting clubs from the world of stamps, autographs, post cards, sports memorabilia, matchcovers, beer can collectors, etc., all of which involves sports collectibles. Clubs are listed alphabetically by collecting subject for most listings.

American First Day Covers Society
PO Box 17124
Philadelphia, PA 19105
Pres.: Allen Warren

American Matchcover Collecting Club
PO Box 18481
Asheville, NC 28814
(704) 254-4487
Editor: Bill Retskin

The Autograph Collectors Club
PO Box 158160
Nashville, TN 37215
Editor: Jeff Sanborn

**American Hobby Collectors
Association**
3329 White Castle Way
Decatur, GA 30034
(404) 987-2773
Pres.: Ray E. Brokaw

Amity International
Port Area, Quarter B-12
PO Box 10
Visa-Khapatnam 530 001
India
Director: Zarin Begam
(facilities exchange of
information on hobbies &
collectors interest)

**Universal Autograph
Collectors Club**
PO Box 467
Rockville Center, NY 11571
(516) 766-0093
Pres.: Herman M. Darvick

**Auto Racing Memorabilia
Collectors Association**
PO Box 443057
Delray Beach, FL 33483
Pres.: K. C. Breslauer

**Beer Can Collectors of
America**
747 Merus Court
Fenton, MO 63026
(314) 343-6486
Pres.: Richard Johnson

**Commemorative Collectors
Society**
25 Farndale Close
Long Eaton
Nottinghamshire NG10 3PA
England

**Cover Collectors
Circuit Club**
305 Caliente Drive
San Leandro, CA 94578
(415)351-1033
Pres.: Lt. Col. Lew Scott

Deltiologists of America
Box 8
Norwood, PA 19074
(215) 485-8572
Director: James Lowe
(postcards)

**Ephemera Society
of America**
PO Box 37
Schoharie, NY 12157
(516) 295-7978
Pres.: Wm. Frost Nobley

Golf Collectors Society
235 E. Helena Street
Dayton, OH 45404
(513) 224-0358
Director: Robert Kuntz

**International Seal, Label &
Cigar Band Society**
8915 E. Bellevue Street
Tucson, AZ 85715
(602) 296-1048
Ex. Sec.: Myron Freedman
(also matchbooks, postcards,
etc.)

The Manuscript Society
350 North Niagara Street
Burbank, CA 91505
Exec. Dir.: David R. Smith

**Rathkamp Matchcover
Society**
1359 Surrey Road, Dept. Y
Vandalia, OH 45377
(513) 890-8684
Sec.: John C. Williams

Olympin Collector's Club
1386 Fifth Street
Schenectady, NY 12303
(518) 355-6493

Pages From The Past
Route 12, Box 485
Gray, TN 37615
Pres.: Page Rea
(ephemera)

**National Association of
Paper and Advertising
Collectors**
PO Box 500
Mt. Joy, PA 17552
(717) 653-9797

**International Pin
Collectors Club**
Box 227
Marcy, NY 13403
(315) 736-4019
Pres.: Rev. Rowan Fay

Pin Collector's Club
3822 St. Damase
Jonquiere, Quebec G7X 2K1
Pres.: Michel Tremblay

**National Pop Can
Collectors Club**
1124 Tyler Street
Fairfield, CA 94533
(707) 426-5553
Pres.: Dave Brackett

**International Federation of
Postcard Dealers**
Box 1765
Manassas, VA 21100
(703) 368-2757
Sec.: John McClintock

**International Stamp Collectors
Society**
PO Box 854
Van Nuys, CA 91408
(818) 997-6496

Sugar Packet Collectors Club
2106 Parkwood Avenue
2nd Floor
Richmond, VA 23220
Pres.: Paul Guider

The following sports memorabilia/card collectors clubs
are located in the United States. Please contact the
author if there is a club in your area.

**Greater Arizona Sports
Collectors Association**
515 E. Camelback
Phoenix, AZ 95073
(602) 263-0593
Pres.: Bob Wilke

**Chicagoland Sports
Collectors Association, Inc.**
1877 Waukegan Road
Glenview, IL 60025
(708) 998-5252

**Connecticut Sports
Collectors Club**
164 Sandquist Circle
Hamden, CT 06514
(203) 281-6125
Joe LeGrand

**Eastern Pennsylvania
Sports Collectors Club**
PO Box 3037
Maple Glen, PA 19002
(215) 643-0901
Pres.: Bob Schmierer

**Indiana Sports Collectors
Association**
PO Box 44499
Indianapolis, IN 46204
(317) 881-8337

**Texas Sports Collectors
Association**
14246 Bella Drive
Houston, TX 77429
(713) 955-0734
Al Evans

Twin Cities Sports
Collectors Club
5054 Rainbow Lane
Moundsview, MN 55112
(612) 780-0817
Steve Barker

Wisconsin Sports
Collectors Club
3436 S. First Street
Milwaukee, WI 53207
(414) 769-1407
LeRoy Kilps

Motorsport Research Group
5210 First Avenue, N.W.
Seattle, WA 98107
(206) 782-9295

Sports Research Committees

The following are not collectors clubs, but are research
groups for their sports.

**Society For American Baseball
Research (SABR)**
Box 93183
Cleveland, OH 44101
(216) 575-0500

Listed here are SABR Committees:
**SABR-Negro League Baseball
Research Committee**
 1080 Hull
 Ypsilanti, MI 48198
 Chmn.: Dick Clark
SABR-Women in Baseball Committee
 PO Box 3333
 Kalamazoo, MI 49003
 Chwmn.: Sharon Roepke
SABR-Latin American Committee
 PO Box 2199
 West Lafayette, IN 47908
 Chmn.: Peter Bjarkman
SABR-19th Century Committee
 4518 Wichita Avenue
 St. Louis, MO 63110
 Chmn.: Bob Tiemann
SABR office governs the Committees.
SABR issues a monthly bulletin and
other publications.

**Professional Football Researchers
Association (PFRA)**
12870 Route 30
N. Huntingdon, PA 15642
(412) 863-6345
Pres.: Bob Carroll

Sports Career Development

College Sports Administration & Management Studies

Listed in this section are Colleges & Universities that specialize in offering degree programs in sport & athletic management, sports law & sports medicine. As professional & amateur sports become more specialized, there is a great need for trained professionals who have gained knowledge through these sports programs and internships. This list is incomplete but will be expanded as more institutions begin programs.

Adelphi University
Garden City, NY 11530
(516) 294-8700
Dr. Ronald Feingold
Graduate
Sport Management

Alabama, University of
PO Box 1967
University, AL 35486
(205) 348-6075
Dr. Joseph Smith
Undergraduate
Sports Fitness Management

American College of Sports Medicine
401 W. Michigan Street
Indianapolis, IN 46202
(317) 637-9200
Carol Lemay, Dir.

Appalachian State Univ.
Dept. HLES
Boone, NC 28608
(704) 262-3140
Dr. Beverly Warren
Undergraduate
Sports Management/PE

Ashland University
Ashland, OH 44273
(419) 289-5443
Dr. Allan Hall
Undergraduate
Sports Communication

Averett College
420 W. Main Street
Danville, VA 24541
(804) 791-5759
Norma Roady, Director
Sports Management/PE

Ball State University
University Gymnasium
Muncie, IN 47306
(317) 285-1451
John Reno, Director
Sports Management

Baylor University
CSB 397
Waco, TX 76798
(817) 755-3505
Andy Pitman
Graduate
Sports Management

Bemidji State Univ.
1500 Birchmont Drive
Bemidji, MN 56601
(218) 755-3785
A.P. Loeffler, Chmn.
Sports Management/Studies

Bowling Green State Univ.
School of HPER
Bowling Green, OH 43403
(419) 372-7230
Dr. Janet Parks, Chair
Sports & Athletic Mgt./Admin.

Calif. State Univ. - Fullerton
Gymnasium
Fullerton, CA 92634
(714) 773-2676
Dr. Edward Coates, Dir.
Sport Management

Central Michigan University
108 Rose Center
Mt. Pleasant, MI 48859
(517) 774-6661
Dr. Walter Schneider
Undergrad/Grad.
Sports Administration/PE

Cleveland State University
Euclid Ave. at S. 24th St.
Cleveland, OH 44115
(216) 687-4870
Dr. Annie Clement
Undergrad/Graduate
Sports Management

Concordia University
Montreal, Quebec H4B 1R6
Canada
(514) 848-3334
George Short, Director
Sports Management

Connecticut, Univ. of
2111 Hillside Road
Storrs, CT 06269
(203) 486- 3623
Wm. Servedio, Director
Undergrad./PhD.
Sport Medicine, Athletic
training

SUNY - Cortland
PO Box 2000
Cortland, NY 13045
(607) 753-4955
Dr. Suzanne Wingate
Sport Management/PE

Durham College
Oshawa, Ontario L1H 7L7
(416) 576-0210
Ramona Rickard, Director
Sports Administration

Eastern Illinois Univ.
224 Lantz,
College of HPER
Charleston, IL 61920
(217) 581-6363
Dr. Scott Crawford
Graduate
PE/Sports Adm.& Mgt. Studies

Eastern Kentucky Univ.
202 Weaver Health Bldg.
Richmond, KY 40475
(606) 622-1244
Dr. Wayne Jennings
HPER/Sports Adm.

Elon College
Campus Box 2189
Elon college, NC 27244
(919) 584-2559
Dr. James P. Drummond,
Director
Undergraduate
HPE & R

Florida, Univ. of
303 Florida Gym
Gainesville, FL 32611
(904) 392-0584
Dr. Sue Whidden
Betty Graham
Grad/Undergrad.
Athletic/Sports Adm.

Georgia, Univ. of
Athens, GA 30602
(404) 542-5947
Dr. Stan Brassie
Graduate
Sports Management/PE

Georgia Southern
Statesboro, GA 30460
(912) 681-5266
Dr. Patrick Cobb
Graduate
Sports Management/PE

Georgia State Univ.
University Plaza
Atlanta, GA 30303
(404) 651-2536
Dr. Joe Willis
Graduate
Athletic Adm./Fac.Mgt.
Sports Club Mgt.

Grambling State Univ.
Grambling, LA 71245
(318) 274-2712
Dr. Willie Daniel
Graduate
Sports Adminstration

Greenville College
Greenville, IL 62246
(618) 664-1840
Jack Trager, Chmn.
Undergrad./Spt. Mgt.

Guilford College
5800 W. Friendly Ave.
Greensboro, NC 27419
(919) 292-5511
Dr. Herb Appenzeller
Sports Studies/Sport Mgt.

Harding University
900 East Center
Searcy, AR 72143
(501) 279-4360
Dr. Karyl Bailey
HPE/Sports Management

Idaho, Univ. of
Recreation Dept.
Moscow, ID 83843
(208) 885-6582
Dr. Dorothy Zakrajsek
Graduate
Sport & Rec. Mgt.

Illinois, University of
170 IMPE Bldg.
201 Peabody Drive
Champaign, IL 6182
(217) 333-9780
Dr. David Matthews
Graduate, Ph.D.
Communications, Ath. & Rec.

Indiana State University
HPER Bldg.
Terre Haute, IN 47809
(812) 237-4053
Dr. Mildred Lemon
Undergrad/Grad
Sports Management/Admin.

Indiana University
HPER Bldg.
Bloomington, IN 47405
(812) 335-5523
Dr. Betty Haven, Chr. Under.
Dr. MaryLou Remley, Grad.
Sport Mkt & Management

Iowa State University
PELS
Ames, IA 50011
(515) 294-8042
Dr. Gary R. Gray
Undergrad/Grad.
PE/Sports Management

James Madison University
Harrisonburg, VA 22807
(703) 568-6145
Dr. Joel Vedelli
Undergrad.
Sport Mgt./Exercise Fitness

Kansas, University of
HPER
Lawrence, KS 66045
(913) 864-5552
DR. Marlene Mawson
Undergrad/Grad.
PE/Sport Admin.

Keene State College
229 Main Street
Keene, NH 03431
(603) 352-1909
Dr. Stephen L. Cone
Undergrad.
Sports Mgt./Leisure Adm.

Kent State University
HPER, Memorial Annex
Kent, OH 44242
(216) 672-2990
Dr. Carl Schreibman
Grad.
PE/Sport Adm.

Laurentian University
Sudbury, Ontario P3E 2C6
(705) 675-1151 ext. 1007
Greg Zorbas, Chmn.
Undergrad.
Sports Administration

Liberty University
Sports Adm. Studies
Box 20000
Lynchburg, VA 24506
(804) 582-2330
Coordinator: Dr. Dale Gibson
Internship Dir: Dr. Roy Yarbrough

Long Island University
Brooklyn Campus
M-320
Brooklyn, NY 11201
(718) 834-6000
Dr. Milorad Stricevic
Undergraduate
Sports Science/PE

Loras College
Dubuque, IA 52001
(319) 588-7196
Dr. Robert Tucker
Undergrad./Grad.
Sport Mgt./Ath.Adm.

Louisville, Univ. of
HPER
Louisville, KY 40292
(502) 588-6641
Brendon Pitts
(502) 588-0553
Dr. Lori K. Miller
Undergrad/Grad.
Sport Adm. & Mgt.

Mankato State University
Dept. of Phys. Educ.
Mankato, MN 56001
(507) 389-6112
Gordon Graham,Dir.
Graduate
Sports Management/PE

Marshall University
HPER
400 Hal Greer Blvd.
Huntington, WV 25755
(304) 696-6490
Dr. W. Don Williams
Undergrad/Grad.
Ath. Adm./Sport Mgt.

Maryland Univ. of
Dept of PE
College Park, MD 20742
(301) 454-4916
Dr. Jerry Wrenn
Graduate
Sports Management

Massachusetts, Univ. of
Curry Hicks Bldg.
Amherst, MA 01003
(413) 545-0441
Glenn M. Wong
Undergrad/Graduate
Sport Management

Michigan State University
East Lansing, MI 48824
(517) 355-1643
Dr. Herbert Olson
Graduate
Ath. Admin.

Michigan, Univ. of
401 Wash
Ann Arbor, MI 48109
(313) 747-2688
Joyce Lindeman, Chair.
Undergrad./Grad/
Sport Mgt. & Comm.
Div. of Kinesiology

Mississippi, Univ. of
Turner University
University, MS 38677
(601) 232-5521
Dr. Don Cheek, Chmn.
Undergrad.
Sports Management

Montana State Univ.
Bozeman, MT 59717
(406) 994-4001
Dr. Gary Stevens
Undergrad/ Grad
Sport Management

Mount Union College
1972 Clark Avenue
Alliance, OH 44601
(216) 821-5320
Dr. James Thoma
Undergrad.
Sport Management

New Mexico, Univ. of
HPER
Johnson Center
Albuquerque, NM 87131
(505) 277-5151
DR. Bill De Groot, Chmn.
MS, Ph.D.
Sports Administration

New York University
Management Institute
48 Cooper Square
New York, NY 10003
(212) 998-7217
Dr. Ronald Janoff, Dir.
Undergrad/Grad.
Certificate in Sports &
Special Event Mkt.
Summer Institute in Sports.

North Carolina State Univ.
Box 8004
Raleigh, NC 27695
(191) 737-3276
Phillip S. Rea, Chmn.
DR. Carolyn S. Love
Undergrad./Grad.
Sports Management

North Carolina, Univ. of
CB #8700, Fetzer Gym
Chapel Hill, NC 27599
(919) 962-0017
Dr. John Billing
Graduate
PE/Sports Admin.

Northeastern University
360 Huntington Avenue
Boston, MA 02115
(617) 437-3166
Dr. Carl Christensen, Chmn.
Rec., Sport & Fitness Mgt.

Ohio Northern University
King Horn Center - HPESS
Ada, OH 45810
(419) 772-2443
Dr. Donn A. Bennice, Dir.
Undergraduate
HPE/Sports Studies

Ohio State University
HPER - Larkims Hall
337 W. 17th Avenue
Columbus, OH 43210
(614) 292-7701
Dr. Wm. Sutton
M.S., Ph.D.
Sports Mkt./Ath. Admin.

Ohio University
Grover Center - Office 11
Athens, OH 45701
(614) 593-4666
Dr. Charles R. Higgins, Coord.
Undergrad/Grad.
Sports Admn.

Penn State University
]105 White Bldg.
University Park, PA 16802
(814) 863-7367
Dr. Terry R. Haggerty
B.S., M.S., Ph.D.
Exercise & Spsort Science
Sport Management

Rice University
PO Box 1892
Houston, TX 77251
(713) 527-4058
T. Jesse Wilde, Dir.
Undergrad.
Sport Management

THE UNIVERSITY OF SOUTH CAROLINA
SPORT ADMINISTRATION

**Preparation for careers
in sports business**

**Research and information
dissemination services for the
sports industry**

The Department of Sport Administration
is uniquely located in the College of Applied
Professional Sciences. An equally
distinguishing characteristic of the USC's
program is its full-time faculty who are
responsible for the curriculum.

Executive Development Seminars are
offered, in collaboration with the Daniel
Management Center, College of Business
Administration, USC, as a service to the
sports industry.

for additional information contact:

Dr. Guy M. Lewis, Chairman
Department of Sport Administration
College of Applied Professional Sciences
Columbia, South Carolina   292208
Phone: 803--777-4690
Fax: 803-777-6427

Richmond, Univ. of
Robins Center
Richmond, VA 23173
(804) 289-8358
Dr. Donald W. Pate, Dir.
Graduate
Sport Management

Robert Morris College
Narrows Run Road
Coraopolis, PA 15108
(412) 262-8416
Dr. Robert D. McBee, Chmn.
Dr. Susan Hofacre
Undergrad/Gradiate
Sport Management
Exchange program in Sport
Management with Victoria
College of Australia

Rutgers University
Loree Gym, Lipman Dr.
New Brunswick, NJ 08903
(201) 932-9525
Nancy K. Mitchell, Chair
Undergraduate
Sport Management

South Carolina, Univ. of
College of Applied Spec. Sciences
Columbia, SC 29208
(803) 777-4690
Dr. Guy M. Lewis, Chair
Undergraduate
Sport Administration

Southeastern Louisiana Univ.
PO Box 845
Hammnond, IA 70402
(504) 549-2129
Betty S. Baker, Dept. Head
HPED/Sport Management

Southern Illinois Univ.
Phy. Ed. - Davies
Carbondale, IL 62901
(618) 453-5478
Charlotte West, Dir.
M.S., Ph.D.
Sport Management

**Southern Mississippi,
Univ. of HPR**
Southern Sta. Box 5142
Hattiesburg, MS 39406
(601) 266-5370
Dr. C. Newton Wilkes
Undergrad/Grad.
Sports Administration

Springfield College
263 Alden Street
Springfield, MA 01109
(413) 788-3275
Dr. Nicholas Moutis, Dir.
Undergraduate
Sport Management

Tampa, Univ. of
Tampa, FL 33606
(813) 253-3333
Dr. Eric Vlahov, Coord.
Undergraduate
Sport Management

Temple University
Pearson Hall - 133
Philadelphia, PA 19122
(21) 787-8712
Dr. Michael Jackson
Dr. Bonnie Parkhouse
Undergrad/Graduate
Sports Administration

Tennessee, Univ. of
1914 Andy Holt Avenue
Knoxville, TN 37996
(615) 974-5711
Dr. Dennie Ruth Kelley
Undergraduate
Sport Studies/Management

Toledo, Univ. of
2801 W. Bancroft
Toledo, OH 43606
(419) 537-2743
Undergrad/Grad.
Athletic Admin

United States Sports Academy
One Academy Drive
Daphne, Al 36526
(205) 626-3303
Dr. Donn Renwick
Graduate
Sport Medicine & Sport Adm.,
Journalism

Utah, University of
College of Health
Salt Lake City, UT 84112
(801) 581-7586
Dr. Jim Ewers, Dir.
Graduate
Sport Management

Washington State Univ.
Dept. of Phys. Education
Pullman, WA 99164
(509) 335-6363
Joanne Washburn, Dir.
Undergraduate
Sport Management

Wayne State Univ.
266 Matthaei Bldg.
Detroit, MI 48202
(313) 577-4269
Dr. Vernon K. Gale, Dir.
Sports Administration

Western Illinois Univ.
Macomb, IL 61455
(309) 295-1414
Dr. David Beaver
Dr. William Bradley
Grad./Sport Management

Winston-Salem State University
Station A
Winston-Salem, NC 27110
(919) 761-2109
Undergraduate
Sports Management

Wisconsin, Univ. of
129 Mitchell Hall
La Crosse, WI 54601
(608) 785-8182
Dr. Mary I. McLellan, Dir
Undergraduate
PE/Sports Management

University of Oklahoma
Dept. of HPER
1401 Asp Avenue
Norman, OK 73019
(405) 325-5211
Director: Scott Branvold
Sports Adm. Grad. Studies

Sports Career & Sports Business Conferences

Listed here are a few of the Conferences & Seminars that specialize in sports business for the career-oriented and the executive. This is not a complete listing.

American College of Sports Medicine
401 W. Michigan Street
Indianapolis, IN 46202
(317) 637-9200
Dir.: Carol Lemay

The Athletic Business Conference
1842 Hoffman Street,
Suite 201
Madison, WI 53704
(800) 722-8764
Dir.: Anne Straka

International Conference on Sports Business
Univ. of South Carolina
Columbia, SC 29208
(803) 777-4690
Dr. Guy Lewis

Seton Hall Sports Law Symposium
School of Law
1111 Raymond Blvd
Newark, NJ 07102
(201) 642-8810

Sport, Physical Education Recreation & Law Conference
Sport Management Dept.
HPER
University of Louisville
Louisville, KY 40292
(502) 588-0553
Lori K. Miller

Sport Summit
7315 Wisconsin Ave.
Suite 420 East
Bethesda, MD 20814
(301) 986-7800
Pres.: Ned Krause

Sports Careers
PO Box 10129
Phoenix, AZ 85064
(602) 954-8106
Pres.: Jay Abraham

**Sports Management
Institute**
Univ. of Southern California
Los Angeles, CA 90089
(213) 743-2771
Dir.: Bill Shumard

Sports Marketing Institute
109 58th Avenue
St. Petersburg Beach, FL 33706
(813) 367-5668
Dir.: H. Robert Pennington

University Paris Dauphine
U.F.R. Economie Appliquee
Economie et Gestion du Sport
Place du Marechal de Lattre-de- Tassigny 75775
Paris Cedex 16 France
Director of Sports Adm: Dr. Alain Michel

**National Sports Law
Institute**
Marquette Univ. Law School
1103 W. Wisconsin Ave.
Milwaukee, WI 53233
(414) 288-5815

National Sports Placement
501 W. South Street
South Bend, IN 46601
(800) 837-1593
PR: Julie Magrane

*NSP offers a placement service,
seminars and newsletter.*

National State High School Federations

National Federation of State High School Associations

11724 Plaza Circle
P.O. Box 20626
Kansas City, MO 64195
(816) 464-5400
Fax (816) 464-5571
Exec. Dir.: Brice B. Durbin

Alabama High School Athletic Association
926 Pelham Street
PO Box 5014
Montgomery, AL 36103-5014
(205) 263-6994
Exec. Dir.: Herman L. Scott

Alaska School Activities Association
650 W. International Airport Rd.
Anchorage, AK 99518
(907) 563-3723
Fax (907) 561-0720
Exec. Dir.: Ed Nash

Arizona Interscholastic Assoc.
2606 West Osborn Road
Phoenix, AZ 85017-5194
(602) 257-0272
Fax (602) 254-9141
Exec. Dir.: Dr. Voie Stuart Coy

Arkansas Activities Association
2900 Willow
North Little Rock, AR 7114-2233
(501) 771-2205
Fax (501) 771-1027
Exec. Dir.: Lamar Cole

California Interscholastic Federation
2282 Rosecrans
Fullerton, CA 92633
(714) 680-4285
Fax (714) 447-0161
Comm.: Thomas E. Byrnes

Colorado High School Activities Association
14855 E. Second Avenue
Aurora, CA 80011
(303) 344-5050
Fax (303) 344-5053
Comm.: Bob Ottewill

Connecticut Interscholastic Athletic Conference
30 Realty Drive
Cheshire, CT 06410
(203) 250-1111
Exec. Dir.: Michael H. Savage

Delaware Secondary School Athletic Association
John G. Townsend Building
Dover, MD 19901
(302) 739-4181
Exec. Dir.: Dale C. Farmer

D. C. Interscholastic Athletic Association
Lovejoy School
12th & D Streets
Washington, D.C. 20002
(202) 724-4988
Fax (202) 724-4997
Ath. Dir.: Claude E. Moten

Florida High School Activities Association
240 S.W. First Street
PO Box 1173
Gainesville, FL 32602
(904) 372-9551
Fax (904) 373-1528
Comm.: Fred E. Rozelle

Georgia High School Assoc.
150 So. Bethel Street
PO Box 271
Thomaston, GA 30286
(404) 647-7473
Fax (404) 647-2638
Exec. Dir.: William C. Fordham

**Hawaii High School
Athletic Association**
1302 Queen Emma Street
Room 201
Honolulu, HI 96813
(808) 548-6082
Fax (808) 528-0047
Exec. Sec.: Edward S. Kiyuna

**Idaho High School
Activities Association**
9422 Fairview Avenue
PO Box 4667
Boise, ID 83704
(208) 375-7027
Fax (208) 322-5505
Exec. Dir.: Bill Young

Illinois High School Assoc.
2715 McGraw Drive
PO Box 2715
Bloomington, IL 61702-2715
(309) 663-6377
Fax (309) 663-7479
Exec. Sec.: Lavere L. Astroth

**Indiana High School
Athletic Association**
9150 No. Meridian St.
PO Box 40650
Indianapolis, IN 46240
(317) 846-6601
Comm.: C. Eugene Cato

**Iowa High School
Athletic Association**
1605 S. Story
PO Box 10
Boone, IA 50036
(515) 432-2011
Fax (515) 432-2961
Exec. Sec.: Bernie Saggau

**Kansas State High School
Activities Association**
520 S.W. 27th Street
PO Box 495
Topeka, KS 66601
(913) 235-9201
Fax (913) 235-2637
Exec. Dir.: Nelson L. Hartman

**Kentucky High School
Athletic Association**
560 E. Cooper Drive
PO Box 22280
Lexington, KY 40522
(606) 252-4436
Fax (606) 233-0911
Exec. Dir.: Tom Mills

**Louisiana High School
Athletic Association**
1681 Wooddale Blvd.
Baton Rouge, LA 70806
(504) 925-0100
Fax (5040 925-0104
Comm.: Tommy Henry

**Maine Secondary School
Principals Association**
16 Winthrop Street
PO Box 2468
Augusta, ME 04338
(207) 622-0217
Exec. Dir.: Richard W. Tyler

**Maryland Public Secondary Schools
Athletic Association**
200 W. Baltimore Street
Baltimore, MD 21201
(301) 333-2339
Fax (301) 333-2379
Exec. Sec.: Edward F. Sparks

**Massachusetts Interscholastic
Athletic Association**
83 Cedar Street
Milford, MA 01757
(508) 478-5641
Fax (508) 634-3044
Exec. Dir.: Richard F. Neal

**Michigan High School
Athletic Association**
1019 Trowbridge Road
East Lansing, MI 48823
(517) 332-5046
Fax (517-332-4071
Exec Dir.: Jerry Cvengros

**Minnesota State High School
League**
2100 Freeway Blvd.
Brooklyn Center, MN 55430
(612) 560-2262
Fax (612) 569-0499
Exec. Dir.: David V. Stead

**Mississippi High School
Activities Association**
152 Millsaps Avenue
PO Box 4521
Jacskson, MS 39296
(601) 354-4117
Dir. Act.: Woodrow L. Marsh

Missouri State High School
Activities Association
1808 1-70 Drive, S.W.
PO Box 1328
Columbia, MO 65205
(314) 445-4443
Fax (314) 445-2502
Exec. Dir.: Jack Miles

Montana High School Assoc.
1 South Dakota Avenue
Helena, MN 59601
(406) 442-6010
Exec. Dir.: Dan L. Freund

**Nebraska School
Activities Association**
8230 Beechwood Drive
PO Box 5463
Lincoln, NE 68505
(402) 489-0386
Exec. Dir.: James Riley

**Nevada Interscholastic
Activities Association**
400 W. King Street
Capitol Complex
Carson City, NV 89710
(702) 687-4390
Fax (702) 687-5660
Exec. Dir.: Dr. Jerry A. Hughes

**New Hampshire Interscholastic
Athletic Association**
101 North State Street
Concord, NH 03301
(603) 228-8671
Exec. Dir.: James W. Desmarais

**New Jersey State Interscholastic
Athletic Association**
Route 130
PO Box 487
Robbinsville, NJ 08691
(609) 587-4855
Fax (609) 259-3047
Exec. Dir.: Robert F. Kanaby

New Mexico Activities Assoc.
1721 University, S.E.
Albuquerque, NM 87196
(505) 243-7991
Fax (505) 842-6848
Exec. Dir.: Dan Salzwedel

**New York State Public High School
Athletic Association**
88 Delaware Avenue
Delmar, NY 12054-1599
(518) 439-8872
Exec. Dir.: Dr. Sandra E. Scott

**North Carolina High School
Athletic Association**
Finley Golf Course Road
UNC Campus
PO Box 3216
Chapel Hill, NC 27515
(919) 962-2345
Fax (919) 926-1686
Exec. Dir.: Charles H. Adams

North Dakota High School
Activities Association
134 N.E. Third Street
PO Box 817
Valley City, ND 58072
(701) 845-3953
Fax (701) 845-4953
Exec. Sec.: Robert D. King

Ohio High School
Athletic Association
4080 Roselea Place
Columbus, OH 43214
(614) 267-2502
Fax (614) 267-1677
Comm.: Clair Muscaro

Oklahoma Secondary School
Activities Association
222 N.E. 27th Street
PO Box 53464
Oklahoma City, OK 73152
(405) 528-3385
Exec. Sec.: H.J. Green

Oregon School
Activities Association
6900 S. W. Haines Road
Suite 120
Tigard, OR 97223
(503) 639-9656
Fax (503) 639-5399
Exec. Dir.: Donald R. Peterson

Pennsylvania Interscholastic
Athletic Association
550 Gettysburg Road
PO Box 2008
Mechanicsburg, PA 17055-0785
(717) 697-0374
Fax (717) 697-7721
Exec. Dir.: Dr. Russell Werner

Rhode Island Interscholastic
League
2212 Post Road
Warwick, RI 02886
(401) 738-0530
Exec. Dir.: Rev. Robert Newbold

South Carolina High School
League
University of South Carolina
Room 408, Carolina Coliseum
Columbia, SC 29208
(803) 777-3116
Fax (803) 777-2642

South Dakota High School
Activities Association
204 N. Euclid
PO Box 1217
Pierre, SD 57501
(605) 224-9261
Fax (605)224-9262
Exec. Sec.: Marlyn Goldhammer

Tennessee Secondary School
Athletic Association
3333 Lebanon Road
Hermitage, TN 37076
(615) 889-6740
Fax (615) 889-0544
Exec. Dir.: Ronny Carter

Texas University
Interscholastic League
2622 Wichita Street
Austin, TX 78705
(512) 471-5883
Fax (512) 471-5908
Dir: Bailey M. Marshall

Utah High School
Activities Association
199 East 7200
Midvale, UT 84047
(801) 566-0681
Fax (801) 561-4579
Exec. Dir.: Glen L. Beere

Vermont Headmaster' Assoc,
Two Prospect Street
PO Box 126
Montpelier, VT 05601-0126
(802) 229-0547
Exec. Dir.: W. Scott Blanchard

Virginia High School League
1642 State Farm Blvd.
Charlottesville, VA 22901
(804) 977-8475
Fax (804) 977-5943
Exec. Dir.: Earl S. Gillespi

**Washington Interscholastic
Activities Association**
4211 W. Lake Sammamish Blvd. S.E.
Bellevue, WA 98008
(206) 746-7102
Fax (206) 747-WIAA
Exec. Dir.: Cliff A. Gillies

**West Virginia Secondary School
Activities Commission**
Rt. 9, Box 76
Parkersburg, WV 26101
(304) 485-5494
Fax (304) 428-5431
Exec. Sec.: Jim Hamrick

**Wisconsin Interscholastic
Athletic Association**
41 Park Ridge Drive
PO Box 267
Stevens Point, WI 54481
(715) 344-8580
Fax (715) 344-4241
Exec. Dir.: Douglas Chickering

**Wyoming High School
Activities Association**
731 E. 2nd Street
Casper, WY 82601
(307) 577-0614
Fax (307) 577-0637
Comm.: Mike Colbrese

Canada

**Canadian School Sports
Federation**
10 Kenmore
Three Oaks Senior High School
Summerside, P.E.I., C1N 4C9
(709) 282-6838
Pres.: Garth Turtle

Alberta Schools' Athletic Assoc.
11759 Groat Road
Edmonton, Alberta, T5M 3K6
(403) 453-8670
Fax (403) 453-8553
Exec. Dir.: April Rukus

BC School Sports
1367 West Broadway #330
Vancouver, B.C., V6H 4A9
(604) 737-3066
Exec. Dir.: Gay Gale

Manitoba High Schools
Athletic Association
200 Main Street
Winnipeg, Manitoba, R3C 4M2
(204) 985-4225
Fax (204) 985-4224
Exec. Dir.: Morris Glimcher

**New Brunswick Interscholastic
Athletic Association**
Department of Education
PO Box 804
Fredericton, N.B., E3B 5B4
(506) 453-2770
Exec. Dir.: W.S. Ritchie

**Newfoundland-Labrador
High School Athletic Federation**
Provincial Recreation Centre
Bldg. 25, Torbay Airport
St. John's, Newfoundland, A1C 5T7
(709) 576-2795
Exec. Dir.: Karen Keough

**Nova Scotia School
Athletic Federation**
5516 Spring Garden Road
PO Box 3010-S
Halifax, N.S., B3J 3G6
(902) 425-5450
Fax (902) 425-5606
Exec. Dir.: Ron O'Flaherty

**Ontario Federation of School
Athletic Associations**
255 Yorkland Blvd. Suite 213
Willowdale, Ont., M2J 1S3
(416) 494-0022
Exec. Dir.: Andy Gibson

**Prince Edward Island School
Athletic Association**
Department of Education
PO Box 2000
Charlottetown, P.E.I., C1A 7N8
(902) 368-4600
Exec. Sec.: Lyall Huggan

Quebec Student Sport Federation
4545 Avenue Pierre-de-Coubertin
C.P. 1000
Succursale M
Montreal, Que., H1V 3R2
(514) 252-3300
Fax (514) 252-3172
Dir. Gen.: Claude Parent

**Saskatchewan High Schools
Athletic Association**
16-395 Park Street
Regina, Sask., S4N 5B2
(306) 721-2151
Fax (306) 721-2659
Exec. Dir.: Bryan Matehson

Others

**Philippine Secondary Schools
Athletic Association**
George Dewey High School
USNS Box 70
FPO San Francisco, CA 96651
Exec. Sec.: John J. Stauffer

**St. Croix Interscholastic
Athletic Association**
PO Box 513
Christiansted, St. Croix
U.S. Virgin Islands, 00821
(809) 773-1520
Admistrator: Peggi S. Morris

**St. Thomas - St. John
Interscholastic Athletic Assoc.**
PO Box 11102
St. Thomas
U.S. Virgin Islands, 00801
Chairman: William I. Frett

Media

Listed in this section are the Networks for Television.

National Television & Cable Networks

ABC Sports
47 West 66th Stret
13th Floor
New York, NY 10023
(212) 887-4867

Canadian Broadcasting Corporation (CBC)
1500 Bronson Avenue
PO Box 8478
Ottawa, Ontario K1G 3J5

Canadian Television Network (CTV)
42 Charles Street East
Toronto, Ontario M4Y 1T5
(416) 928-6000

CBS Sports
51 West 52nd Street
30th Floor
New York, NY 10019
(212) 975-5230

Fox Broadcasting Company
10201 West Pico Blvd.
Los Angeles, CA 90035
(213) 203-3266

German Television Network
251 West 57th Street
Suite 428
New York, NY 10019
(212) 307-0242

Global Television Network
81 Barber Green Road
Don Mills, Ontario M3C 2A2
(416) 446-5311

Hughes Television Network
260 Madison Avenue
19th floor
New York, NY 10016
(212) 684-7900

The International Televion Network
919 Third Avenue, 6th Floor
New York, NY 10022
(212) 223-2635

Miziou Television Network
352 Seventh Avenue, 7th Floor
New York, NY 10001
(212) 244-3750

NBC Sports
30 Rockefeller Plaza
New York, NY 10036
(212) 664-4444

Public Broadcasting Service
1320 Braddock Place
Alexandria, VA 22314-1698
(703) 739-5000

Spanish International Network
460 West 42nd St., 4th Floor
New York, NY 10036
(212) 502-1300

TVA
1600 de Maisonneuve Blvd. Est.
Montreal, Quebec H2L 4P2
(514) 526-0476

Univision
9200 Sunset Blvd., Suite 1100
Los Angeles, CA 90069
(213) 859-7200

Oldtyme
Baseball
News
The newspaper that remembers
the glory days of baseball!

Special Free Offer!
Free 1988 Premier Issue with each paid
subscription. Great Collectors Item!

"It's Like a Baseball Time Machine"

For more information and a sample copy of Oldtyme
Baseball News - Send your name and address plus $3.50 to:

OLDTYME BASEBALL NEWS
P.O. Box 833-K
Petoskey, Michigan 49770

(check or money order, please)

National Cable Television Networks

Black Entertainment Network (BET)
1232 31st Street N.W.
Washington, D.C. 20007
(202) 337-5260

Cable News Network (CNN)
One CNN Center Box 105366
Atlanta, GA 30348-5366
(404) 827-1500

Consumer News & Business Channel (CNBC)
30 Rockefeller Plaza
New York, NY 10112
(212) 664-2812

Entertainment & Sports Programming Network (ESPN)
ESPN Plaza
Bristol, CT 06010
(203) 585-2000

Home Box Office (HBO)
1100 Avenue of the Americas
New York, NY 10036
(212) 512-1000

The Nashville Network
250 Harbor Plaza Drive
Box 10210
Stamford, CT 06904
(203) 965-6000

SCORE
6701 Center Drive West
Los Angeles, CA 90045
(213) 450-2412

Showtime/The Movie Channel
1633 Broadway, 37th Floor
New York, NY 10020
(212) 708-1600

SportsChannel America
150 Crossways Park West
Woodbury, NY 11797
(516) 364-2222

The Sports Network (TSN)
1155 Leslie Street
Don Mills, Ontario M3C 2Z6
(416) 449-2244

Turner Network Television (TNT)
One CNN Center
Box 10566
Atlanta, GA 30348
(404) 827-1647

USA Network
1230 Avenue of the Americas
New York, NY 10020
(212) 408-9100

Viewers Choice
909 Third Avenue, 2nd Floor
New York, NY 10022
(212) 486-6600

Superstations

TBS Superstation
One CNN Center
Box 105366
Atlanta, GA 30348
(404) 827-1700

WGN-TV
3801 S. Sheridan
Tulsa, OK 74145
(918) 665-6690

WWOR-TV
112 Northern Concourse
Syracuse, NY 13221
(315) 455-5955
(800) 448-3322

National Radio Networks

ABC Radio
125 West End Avenue
New York, NY 10023
(212) 887-5851

CBS Radio
51 West 52nd Street
New York, NY 10019
(212) 975-4321

NBC Radio
1700 Broadway
3rd Floor
New York, NY 10019
(212) 237-2500

American Public Radio
700 Meritor Tower
444 Cedar Street
St. Paul, MN 55101

AP Network News
1825 K Street N.W.
Suite 615
Washington, D.C. 20006
(202) 955-7200

CNN Radio Network
1050 Techwood Drive N.W.
Box 105264
Atlanta, GA 30348
(404) 827-1500

Mutual Radio News
1755 S. Jefferson Davis Hwy.
Arlington, VA 22202
(703) 685-2000

National Black Network
10 Columbus Circle
New York, NY 10019
(212) 586-0610

National Public Radio
2025 M Street N.W.
Washington, D.C. 20036
(202) 822-2000

Radiomutuel Inc.
1717 Est. boul. Rene Levesque
Montreal, Quebec H2L 4E8

Sheridan Broadcasting Network
One Times Square Plaza
New York, NY 10036
(212) 575-0099

Sun Radio Network
Box 7000
Tampa, FL 33673
(813) 238-3145

United Stations Radio Network
1440 Broadway
New York, NY 10018
(212) 575-6100

UPI Radio Network
1400 Eye Street N.W.
9th Floor
Washington, D.C. 20005
(202) 898-8000

USA Radio Network
2290 Springlake Road
Suite 107
Dallas, TX 75234
(214) 484-3900

Radio & TV News Services

Some of the following services also provide information
to the print media.

American Radio News
345 W. 85th Street
Suite 46
New York, NY 10024
(212) 713-5207

Associated Press
1825 K Street N.W.
Suite 615
Washington, D.C. 20006
(202) 955-7200

Audio-Video News
6130 Beachway Drive
Falls Church, VA 22041
(703) 671-1049

Black Radio Network
166 Madison Avenue
New York, NY 10016
(212) 686-6850

Broadcast News Ltd.
36 King Street East
Toronto, Ontario M5C 2L9
(416) 364-3172

Cable SportsTracker
3801 S. Sheridan
Tulsa, OK 74145
(918) 665-6690

Copley News Service
PO Box 190
San Diego, CA 92112
(619) 293-1818

Cox Cable Communications
1400 Lake Hearn Drive
Atlanta, GA 30319
(404) 843-5127

Dunkel Sports Research Service
PO Box 2167
Ormond Beach, FL 32074
(904) 677-6100

Feature-Net TM Radio Network
3000 Town Center, Suite 777
Southfield, MI 48075
(313) 355-1776

George Michael's Sports Machine
4001 Nebraska Avenue
Washington, D.C. 20016

INN: The Independent News
11 WPIX Plaza
New York, NY 10017
(212) 949-1100

Lorimar Sports Network
7475 Skillman, 101B
Dallas, TX 75231
(214) 340-1404

The Newsfeed Network
888 Seventh Avenue
New York, NY 10106
(212) 307-3218

Newsradio
30 Carlton Street
Toronto, Ontario M5B 2E9
(416) 591-6390

NFL Films
330 Fellowship Road
Mt. Laurel, NJ 08054
(609) 778-1600

Nippon TV Network Corp.
50 Rockefeller Plaza
Suite 940
New York, NY 10020
(212) 765-5076

Radio America
499 S. Capitol Street S.W.
Suite 417
Washington, D.C. 20003
(202) 488-7226

Reuters News Agency
1700 Broadway, 2nd Floor
New York, NY 10019
(212) 730-2739
London:
85 Fleet Street
London EC4P 4AJ, England

The Sports Network
701 Mason's Mill Business Park
Huntingdon Valley, PA 19006
(215) 947-2400

Sportsticker Plus
670 White Plains Road
Scarsdale, NY 10583
(914) 725-3100

Standard Broadcast News/Wire
2 St. Clair Avenue West
Toronto, Ontario M4V 1L6
(416) 924-5711

United Press International
1400 Eye Street N.W.
Washington, D.C. 20005
(202) 898-8238

UPDATE
Regency Plaza One
4643 S. Ulster Street
Suite 340
Denver, CO 80237
(303) 721-1062

Western Information Network
815 McBride Plaza
New Westminster, B.C. V3L 2C1
(604) 522-2711

Worldwide Television News Corp.
WTN House
31 - 36 Foley Street
London W1P 7LB England
(44) 1-323-3255

Worldwide Information Services
360 First Avenue
New York, NY 10010
(212) 677-7839

National Newspapers & Services

The following is a list of national newspapers
information services for the print media.

The New York Times
National Edition
229 West 43rd street
New York, NY 10036
(212) 556-1234

USA Today
1000 Wilson Blvd.
Arlington, VA 22229
(703) 276-3735

The European Newspaper
PO Box 860
Canal Street Station
New York, NY 10013
(800) 927-6477
London:
Oxford OX3 OBW, England
(44) 865-743372

Services

Associated Press
1825 K Street N.W.
Suite 615
Washington, D.C. 20006
(202) 955-7200

Chicago Tribune-New York News
Syndicate
220 E. 42nd Street
News Building
New York, NY 10017
(212) 949-3400

European Sports Press Union
Daily Mirror Sports
33 Holborn
London EC1P 1DQ, England

Howe Sports Data International
Boston Fish Pier
West Bldg. 2, Suite 306
Boston, MA 02210
(617) 269-0304

International Sports Press Association
Via Paolo da Cannobio 9
20122 Milan, Italy

International Sports Writer's Association
46 Oak Hill Crescent
Woodford Green
Essex 1G8 9PW, England

King Features Syndicate
235 East 45th Street
New York, NY 10017
(212) 682-5600

Los Angeles Times Syndicate
Times Mirror Square
Los Angeles, CA 90053
(213) 972-5000

News Flash International
508 Atlanta Avenue
N. Massapequa, NY 11758
(516) 731-0662

Newspaper Enterprises Association
200 Park Avenue, 6th Floor
New York, NY 10166
(212) 692-3700

Reuters Information Services
1700 Broadway
New York, NY 10019
(212) 603-3573

Sports Features Syndicate, Inc.
PO Box 660
Maple Shade, NJ 08052

Tass News Agency
10 Tverskoi Bulvar
Moscow, U.S.S.R.
(7095) 290-1493

United Feature Syndicate, Inc.
United Media
200 Park Avenue
New York, NY 10166
(212) 557-2333

United Press International
1400 Eye Street N.W.
Washington, D.C. 20005
(202) 898-8238

Regional Cable Television Sports Networks

Listed in this section are the regional cable networks throughout the United States & Canada.

Arizona Sports Program Network (ASPN)
P.O. Box 37827
7602 N. Black Canyon Hwy.
Phoenix, AZ 85069
(602) 866-0072

Home Sports Entertainment
2080 N. State Highway, Suite 260
Grand Prairie, TX 75050
(214) 988-9222

Home Team Sports
1111 18th St. N.W., Suite 200
Washington, DC 20036
(202) 728-5300

KBL Entertainment Network
294 W. Steuben Street
Pittsburgh, PA 15205
(412) 922-9610

Madison Square Garden Network
2 Penn. Plaza, Suite 1800
New York, NY 10121
(212) 563-8100
Fax (212) 563-3794

Midwest Sports Channel
11th on the Mall
Minneapolis, MN 55403
(612) 330-2637

New England Sports Network (NESN)
70 Brookline Avnue
Boston, MA 02215
(617) 536-9233

Pacific Sports Network
5924 Stoneridge Drive
Pleasanton, CA 94566
(415) 463-0870

Prime Sports Network
250 Steele Street
Suite 300
Denver, CO 80206
(303) 355-7777

Prime Sports Northwest
18 West Mercer Street
Seattle, WA 98119
(206) 281-7800

Prime Ticket Network
10000 Santa Monica Blvd.
Los Angeles, CA 90067
(213) 286-3800

PRISM
225 City Line Avenue
Bala Cynwyd, PA 19004
(215) 668-2210

Pro Am Sports System (PASS)
24 Frank Llyod Wright Dr.
Box 3812
Ann Arbor, MI 48106-3812

San Diego Cable Sports Network
c/o TBS Sports
1050 Techwood Drive N.W.
Atlanta, GA 30348
(404) 827-1700

Sportschannel
PO Box 530
San Antonio, TX 78292
(512) 224-4611

Sportschannel Bay Area
901 Battery Street
Suite 220
San Fraancisco, CA 94111
(415) 296-8900

Sportschannel Chicago
820 W. Madison
Oak Park, IL 60302
(312) 524-9444
Fax (312) 524-9484

Sportschannel Florida
Executive Court I
2295 Corp. Blvd. N.W.
Boca Raton, FL 33431
(407)-994-0250

Sportschannel Los Angeles
1546 26th Street
Santa Monica, CA 90404-4180
(213) 453-1985

Sportschannel New England
10 Tower Office Park
Suite 600
Woburn, MA 01810
(617) 933-9300
Fax (617) 933-3877

Sportschannel New York
200 Crossways Park Drive
Woodbury, NY 11797
(516) 364-3650
Fax (516) 364-4020

Sportschannel Ohio
Metro Center
6500 Rockside Road
Suite 340
Independence, OH 44131
(216) 328-0350

Sportschannel Philadelphia
c/o PRISM
225 City Line Avenue
Bala Cynwyd, PA 19004
(215) 668-2210

Sunshine Network
1 DuPont Centre
390 N. Orange Avenue
Orlando, FL 32801
(407) 648-1150

Canada

Le Reseau des Sports
1755 boul. Rene Levesque Est.
Montreal, Quebec H2K 4P6
(514) 599-2244
Fax (514) 599-2299

Superchannel
5324 Calgary Trail
Edmonton, Alberta T6H 4J8
(403) 437-7744
Fax (403) 437-31882

International Radio & Television

Listed here are some of the major radio & television networks from around the world. Some are commercial or private networks, as well as government run networks. Many of these networks carry sports & sports news programming.

Television

Armed Forces Network
Bertramstrasse 6
D-6000 Frankfurt/Main,
Germany
(49.611) 1516101

Asia-Pacific Broadcasting Union (ABU)
P.O. Box 1164
Jalan Pantai Bahru
59700 Kuala Lumpur, Malaysia
(60.3) 274.3592

BBC-TV Europe
Woodlands
80 Wood Lane
London W12 0TT, England
(41.1) 576.2510

Caribbean Broadcasting Union (CBU)
Wanderers Gap
Dayrells Road
Christ Church, Barbados
(809) 429-9146

CNN News-Europe
25-28 Old Burlington Street
London W1X 1LB, England
(41.1) 434.9323

European Broadcasting Union
Ave. Albert Lancaster 32
1180 Brussels, Belgium
(32.2) 375.5990

**Union of National Radio
& Television Organizations**
of Africa (URTNA)
101 Rue Carnot
B.P. 3237 Dakar, Senegal
(22.1) 21. 1625

Argentina
Asociacion De Teleradiodifusoras
Argentinas (ATA)
Av. Cordoba 323, 6to
1054 Buenos Aires
(54.1) 312.4208

Australia
Australian Broadcasting Corp.
ABC House
150 William Street
Sydney, NSW 2000
(61.2) 339.0211

**Federation of Australian
Commercial Television Stations**
44A Avenue Road
Mossman, NSW 2088
(61.2) 858.7777

Austria
Osterreichischer Rundfunk
ORF-Zentrum Wien
Wurzburgasse 30
A-1136 Wien, Austria

Brazil
**Associacao Brasileira de Emissoras
de Radio e Televisao (ABERT)**
Hotel Nacional
s/5 e 7, C.P. 040-280
70322 Brasilia, DF

Bulgaria
Balgarska Televizija
Ul. San Stefano 29
1504 Sofia 4, Bulgaria
(359.2) 43481

Czechoslovakia
Ceskoslovenska Televize
Jindrisska 16
1150 Pravda 1, Czechoslovakia
(42.2) 221247

Denmark
TV2
Rugaardsvej 25
DK-5100 Odense C., Denmark
(45.65) 91 1244

England
British Broadcasting Corp.
Television Centre
London W12
(44.1) 749.7520

Independent Broadcasting Authority (IBA)
70 Brompton Road
London SW3 1EY
(44.1) 584.7011

Independent Television News Ltd.
ITN House
48 Wells Street
London W1P 4DE

Lifestyle & Screen Sport
180 Wardour Street
London W1V 4AE
(44.1) 439 1177

Super Channel
19-21 Rathbone Place
London W1P 1DF
(44.1) 631.5050

France
Television Francaise 1 (TF1)
Societe Nationale TF1
15 rue Cognacq Jay
F-75330 Paris Cedex 07
(33.1) 42.75 1234

TV Sport
13 rue de Castellane
75008 Paris
(33.1) 4266.9966

TV5-Europe
21 rue Jean Goujon
5008 Paris
(33.1) 299.4125

Germany
ARD
Arnulfstrasse 42
8000 Munich 2
(49.89) 590001

Hungary
Magyar Televizio
Szabadsag ter 17
1810 Budapest
(36.1) 533200

Ireland
Radio/Television Ireland
Donnybrook
Dublin 4
(353.1) 693111

Israel
Israel Broadcasting Authority (IBA)
P.O. Box 7139
Jerusalem 91071
(972.2) 301.333

Italy
Radiotelevisione Italiana
Direzione Centrale TV
Viale Mazzini 14
00195 Rome

Japan
Nippon Hoso Kyokai
2-2-1 Jinnan, Shibuya-ku
Tokyo 150
(81.3) 465.1111

Nippon Television Network (NTN)
14 Niban-cho, Chiyodaku
Tokyo 102
(81.3) 265.2111

Mexico
Televisa, S.A.
Av. Chapultepec 28
06724 Mexico, D.F.
(52.5) 709.3333

Netherlands
NOS
P.O. Box 444
1200 JJ Hilversum
(31.35) 779222
(TV/Radio)

New Zealand
Television New Zealand
P.O. Box 3819
Auckland
(64.9) 770.630

Norway
Norsk Rikskringkasting
Oslo 3
(47.2) 459050
(TV/Radio)

Poland
Telewizja Polska
ul. J.P. Woronicza 17
P-35, 00950 Warsaw
(48.22) 478501

Portugal
RadioTelevisao Portuguesa SARL
Av. 5 de Outubro 187
1000 Lisbon
(351.1) 731774

Romania
Radioteleviziunea Romana
Cale Dorobanti 191
71281 Bucharest
(40.90) 793290

South Africa
SABC-TV
Broadcasting Center
Auckland Park
Johannesburg 2092
(27.11) 714.9111

Spain
Radiotelevision Espanola
Apartado de Correos 26002
Madrid 11
(34.1) 711.0400

Sweden
Sveriges Television AB
S-105
10 Stockholm
(46.8) 784.0000

Switzerland
Swiss Broadcasting Corp.
Giacomettistrasse 3
CH-3000 Berne 15
(41.31) 439111

Turkey
Turkish Radio Television Corp.
Nevzat Tandogan Caddesi 2
Kavaklidere, Ankara
(90.41) 280.546

U.S.S.R.
Soviet Television
Tsentralnaja studija televidenija
ul. Korolijova 12
Moscow 12700

Yugoslavia
Jugoslovenska Radiotelevizija
Borisa Kidrica 70
11000 Belgrade
(38.11) 433.718

Radio

Armed Forces Network (Europe)
Bertramstrasse 6
6000 Frankfurt/Main 1, Germany
(49.611) 115.6101

Radio Free Europe
Oettingenstrasse 67
8000 Munich 22, Germany
(49.89) 2102.3960
New York:
1775 Broadway
New York, NY 10019
(212) 397-5300
Washington:
1201 Connecticut Avenue, N.W.
Washington, D.C. 20036
(202) 254-8040

Radio Australia
P.O. Box 428G, G.P.O.
Melbourne, Victoria 3001
(61.2) 352.222

Radio Austria International
Wurzburggasse 30
A-1136 Vienna
(43.222) 8291.2130

Belgium
BRT International
P.O. Box 26
B-1000 Brussels
(32.2) 737.3805

Canada
CBC/Radio Canada International
P.O. Box 6000
Montreal, Quebec H3C 3A8
(514) 285-3211
Or:
CBC Radio
P.O. Box 500
Station A
Toronto, Ontario M5W 1E6
(416) 975-3311

England
BBC Radio Broadcasting House
London W1A 1AA
(44.1) 580.4468
(Radio 3-Sports)

Radio France
116 Ave. du President Kennedy
F-75786 Paris Cedex 16
(33.1) 4230.2222

Germany
Deutschlandfunk
Raderberggurtel 40
5000 Koln 51
(49.221) 345-1

Deutsche Welle
Postfach 10 04 44
D-5000 Koln 1
(49.221) 3890

All India Radio
P.O. Box 500
New Delhi 110001
(91.11) 382.021

Radio Japan
2-2-1 Jinnan, Shibuya-ku
Tokyo
(81.3) 465.1234

Radio Netherlands International
P.O. Box 222
1200 JG Hilversum, Netherlands
(31.35) 724.211

Radio New Zealand
P.O. Box 2092
Wellington, NZ
(64.4) 741.555

Scotland
BBC Radio Scotland
Broadcasting House
Queen Margaret Drive
Glasgow G12 8DG
(44.41) 330.2345

Radio South Africa
P.O. Box 4559
Johannesburg 2000
(27.11) 714.9111

Spain
Radio Nacional de Espana
Casa de la Radio
Prado del Rey
28023 Madrid
(34.7) 118000

Radio Exterior de Espana
Apartado 156.202
28080 Madrid
(34.1) 711 2742

Radio Sweden
S-105
10 Stockholm
(46.8) 784.0000

Swiss Radio International
Giacomettistrasse 1
3000 Berne 15
(41.31) 439.222

U.S.S.R.
Soviet Radio Broadcasting
Pyatnitskaya ulitsa 25
113 326 Moscow
(7.095) 2177898

   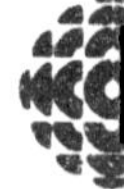

Sports Organizations & Associations

**Aerobics & Fitness Assoc.
of America**
15250 Ventura Blvd.
Suite 310
Sherman Oaks, CA 91403
(818) 905-0040

All American Soap Box Derby

789 Derby Downs Drive
Akron, OH 44306
(216) 733-8723

Alpine Club of Canada
P.O.Box 1026
Banff, Alberta, Canada T0L 0C0
(403) 762-4481

Amateur Athletic Union
3400 W. 86th Street
P.O. Box 68207
Indianapolis, IN 46268
(317) 872-2900

**Amateur Bicycle League
of America**
924 Cherry Street
San Carlos, CA 94070
(415) 592-1727

**Amateur Skating Union
of the U.S.**

1033 Shady Lane
Glen Ellyn, IL 60137
(312) 790-3230

**American Academy of
Sports Physicians**
17113 Gledhill Street
Northridge, CA 91325
(818) 886-7891

**American Alliance for Health,
Physical Education, Recreation
and Dance (AAHPERD)**
1900 Association Drive
Reston, VA 22091
(703) 476-3409

**American Amateur Baseball
Congress**
118 Redfield Plaza, Box 467
Marshall, MI 49068
(616) 781-2002

**American Amateur Racquetball
Association**
815 N. Weber, Suite 101
Colorado Springs, CO 80903
(719) 635-5396

American Archery Council
200 Castlewood Road
North Palm Beach, FL 33408
(407) 842-4100

**American Arm Wrestling
Association**
P.O. Box 132
Scranton, PA 18504
(717) 342-4984

**American Association for
Leisure & Recreation**
1900 Association Drive
Reston, VA 22091
(703) 476-3400

**American Association of
School Administrators**
1801 N. Moore Street
Arlington, VA 22209
(703) 528-0700

**American Athletic Association
for the Deaf**

1134 Davenport Drive
Burton, MI 48529
(313) 239-3962

**American Athletic Trainers
Association**
660 W. Duarte Road
Arcadia, CA 91007
(818) 445-1978

**American Baseball Coaches
Association**
P.O. Box 3545
Omaha, NE 68108
(402) 733-0374

American Bicycle Association
P.O. Box 718
Chandler, AZ 85226
(602) 961-1903

American Bikeways Foundation
2019 Q Street N.W.
Washington, D.C. 20009
(202) 462-4900

American Billiard Association
1660 Lin Lor Court
Elgin, IL 60120
(312) 741-6836

**American Blind Bowling
Association**
150 N. Bellaise Avenue
Louisville, KY 40206
(502) 896-8039

**American Boat & Yacht
Council**

190 Ketcham Avenue
Amityville, NY 11701
(516) 598-0550

American Canoe Association
P.O. Box 1190
Newington, VA 22122
(703) 550-7523

**American College Health
Association**
1300 Piccard Drive
Suite 200
Rockville, MD 20850
(301) 963-1100

**American College of
Sports Medicine**
P.O. Box 1440
Indianapolis, IN 46206
(317) 637-9200

**American Council on
International Sports**
817 23rd Street N.W.
Washington, D.C. 20052
(703) 476-3462

**American Grand Prix
Association**
722 National City Bank Bldg.
Cleveland, OH 44114
(216) 781-2051

**American Greyhound Track
Operators Association**
1065 N.E. 125th Street
Suite 219
North Miami, FL 33161
(305) 893-2101

American Horse Council, Inc.
1700 K Street N.W.
Suite 300
Washington, D.C. 20006
(202) 296-4031

American Horse Shows Assn.
220 E. 42nd Street
New York, NY 10017
(212) 872-2472

**American Equipment
Managers Association**
723 Keil Court
Bowling Green, OH 43402
(419) 352-1207

American Horse Vaulting
Association
P.O. Box 3663
Saratoga, CA 95070
(408) 867-0402

American Hospital Association
840 North Lake Shore Drive
Chicago, IL 60611
(312) 280-6000

American Kitefliers Assn.
1559 Rockville Pike
Rockville, MD 10852
(312) 642-8692

American Medical Association
515 North State Street
Chicago, IL 60610
(312) 280-6000

American Morgan Horse
Association
P.O. Box 960
Shelburne, VT 05482
(802) 985-4597

American Orthopaedic Society
for Sports Medicine
2250 E. Devon Avenue
Suite 115
Des Plaines, IL 60018
(708) 803-8700

American Osteopathic Academy
of Sports Medicine
P.O. Box 623
Middleton, WI 53562
(608) 831-4400

American Platform Tennis
Association
P.O. Box 901
Upper Montclair, NJ 07043
(201) 744-1190

American Professional
Racquetball Association
5089 N. Granite Reef Rd.
Scottsdale, AZ 85253
(602) 945-0143

American Quarter Horse
Association
P.O. Box 200
Amarillo, TX 79168
(806) 376-4811

American Recreation Coalition
1331 Pennsylvania Ave., N.W.
Suite 726
Washington, D.C. 20004
(202) 662-7420

American Rowing Association
251 N. Illinois Street
Suite 980
Indianapolis, IN 46204
(317) 237-2769

American Running & Fitness
Association
9310 Old Georgetown Rd.
Bethesda, MD 20814
(301) 897-0197

American Ski Federation
207 Constitution Ave. N.E.
Washington, D.C. 20002
(202) 543-1595

Amer. Society for Testing & Materials
1916 Race Street
Philadelphia, PA 19101
(215) 299-5499

American Sportscasters
Association
150 Nassau Street
New York, NY 10038
(212) 227-8080

American Swimming Coaches
Association
One Hall of Fame Drive
Fort Lauderdale, FL 33316
(305) 462-6267

American Tennis Federation
200 Castlewood Drive
North Palm Beach, FL
(407) 848-1026

**American Trapshooting
Association of America**
601 W. National Road
Vandalia, OH 45377
(513) 898-4638

**American Youth Soccer
Organization**
5403 W. 138th Street
P.O. Box 5045
Hawthorne, CA 90251
(213) 643-6455

Appaloosa Horse Club
Box 8403
Moscow, ID 83843
(208) 882-5578

The Aquatic Exercise Association
P.O. Box 497
Port Washington, WI 53074
(414) 284-3416

**Association for Fitness
in Business**
310 N. Alabama, Suite A100
Indianapolis, IN 46204
(317) 636-6621

Association of Cricket
Statisticians
3 Radcliffe Road
West Bridgeford
Nottinghampshire, England

**The Association of Oldtime
Barbell & Strongmen**
611 Banner Avenue
Suite 4D
Brooklyn, NY 11235
(718) 648-5254
Pres.: Vic Boff

**Association of Physical
Fitness Centers**
600 Jefferson Street
Suite 202
Rockville, MD 20852
(301) 424-7744

**Association of Physical Plant
Administrators or Universities
& Colleges**
1446 Duke Street
Alexandria, VA 22314
(703) 684-1446

**The Association of
Professional Rodeo Cowboys**
2929 W. 19th Avenue
Denver, CO 80204
(303) 534-8637

**Association of Professional
Triathletes**
666 Baker St., Suite 367
Costa Mesa, CA 92626
(714) 432-8226

**Association of Road
Racing Athletes**
807 Paulsen Bldg.
Spokane, CA 99201
(509) 838-8784

**Association of School Business
Officials**
11401 North Shore Drive
Reston, VA 22090
(703) 478-0405

Athletes In Action
4790 Irvine Blvd.
Suite 105-325
Irvine, CA 92720
(714) 669-1720

**Athletic Equipment Managers
Association**
723 Keil Court
Bowling Green, OH 43402
(419) 352-1207

Athletic Institute
200 Castlewood Drive
North Palm Beach, FL 33408
(407) 842-3600

The Athletics Congress (TAC)

One Hoosier Dome
Suite 140
Indianapolis, IN 46225
(317) 261-0500

**Balloon Federation
of America**
829 15th Street N.W.
Suite 430
Washington, D.C. 20005
(202) 737-0897

**Bandy International
Federation**
Kopmangatum 25
S-95 132 Lulea, Sweden
(46-920) 50060

Baseball Chapel
P.O. Box 785
Butler, NJ 07405
(201) 838-8111

**Bicycle Federation of
America**
1818 R Street N.W.
Washington, D.C. 20009
(202) 332-6986

**Bicycle Manufacturers
Association of America**
1055 Thomas Jefferson St., N.W.
Washington, D.C. 20007
(202) 333-4052

Bicycle Travel Association
113 Main Street
Missoula, MT 59807
(406) 721-1776

**Billiards & Bowling Institute
of America**
200 Castlewood Drive
North Palm Beach, FL 33408
(407) 842-4100

Black Coaches Association
P.O. Box 5371
Coralville, IA 52241
(319) 237-9595

Booster Clubs of America
200 Castlewood Drive
North Palm Beach, FL 33408
(407) 842-3600

Boston Athletic Association
20 Park Plaza
Boston, MA 02116
(617) 338-5709

**Bowling Proprietor's
Association of America**
P.O. Box 5802
Arlington, TX 76011
(817) 460-2121

**Boy Scouts of America
National Headquarters**
1325 Walnut Hill Lane
P.O. Box 152079
Irving, TX 75015
(214) 580-2423

**Boys & Girls Clubs
of America**
771 First Avenue
New York, NY 10017
(212) 351-5900

Canadian Olympic Association
2380 avenue Pierre Dupuy
Montreal, Quebec H3C 3R4
(514) 861-3371
Fax (514) 861-2896

**Canadian National Sports and
Recreation Centre**
1600 James Naismith Drive
Gloucester, Ontario K1B 5N4
(613) 746-0060

The Centre is the governing body for
most sports in Canada. Listed here are
the sports organizations that occupy the
Centre as their national office.

Alpine Canada	(613) 748-5661
Archery Canada	(613) 748-5604
Athletics Canada	(613) 748-5678
Badminton Canada	(613) 748-5605
Baseball Canada	(613) 748-5606
Basketball Canada	(613) 748-5607
Biathalon Canada	(613) 748-5617
Boxing Canada	(613) 748-5611
Canoe Canada	(613) 748-5623
College Athletic Assoc.	(613) 748-5626
Coaching Association	(613) 748-5624
Cross Country Running	(613) 748-5713
Cross Country Skiing	(613) 748-5662
Curl Canada	(613) 748-5713
Disabled Sports	(613) 748-5630
Amateur Diving	(613) 748-5631
Equestrian Canada	(613) 748-5632
Fencing Canada	(613) 748-5633
Field Hockey Canada	(613) 748-5634
Figure Skating	(613) 748-5635
Football Canada	(613) 748-5636
Health, P.E. & Recreation	(613) 748-5622
Intramural Recreation	(613) 748-5639
Judo Canada	(613) 748-5640
Ladies Golf	(613) 748-5642
Gymnastics Canada	(613) 748-5654
Rythmic Gymnastics	(613) 748-5654
Team Handball	(613) 748-5706
Amateur Hockey	(613) 748-5613
Old Timers Hockey	(613) 748-5646
Inter-University Athletics	(613) 748-5619
Amateur Lacrosse	(613) 748-5706
Orienteering Canada	(613) 748-5647
Canada Racquetball	(613) 748-5653
Ringette Canada	(613) 748-5706
Rowing Canada	(613) 748-5656
Rugby Union	(613) 748-5657
Ski Association	(613) 748-5710
Canada Soccer	(613) 748-5667
Canada Softball	(613) 748-5668
Speed Skating	(613) 748-5669
Sports Medicine Council	(613) 748-5671
Sports Sciences	(613) 748-5768
Athletic Therapists	(613) 748-5671
Canada Squash	(613) 748-5672
Swimming Canada	(613) 748-5673
Syncro-Swimming	(613) 748-5674
Tennis Canada	(613) 746-5593
Table Tennis	(613) 748-5675
Track & Field	(613) 748-5678
Volleyball Canada	(613) 748-5681

Water Polo	(613) 748-568
Water Skiing	(613) 748-56
Amateur Wrestling	(613) 748-566
Yachting Canada	(613) 748-568

The Sports Centre may have other spor
organization listings within the comple

**Canadian Recreational
Canoeing Association**
1029 Hyde Park Road
Suite 5
Hyde Park, Ontario N0M 1Z0
(519) 473-2109

**Canadian School Sport
Federation**
Colonel Gray High School
Charlottetown, PEI C1A 4S6

Canadian Special Olympics
40 St. Clair Avenue, West
Suite 209
Toronto, Ontario M4V 1M6
(416) 927-9050

**Canadian Sporting Goods
Association**
4550, rue St. Antoine St. W.
Suite 510
Montreal, Quebec H2Z 1J1
(514) 393-1132

Catholic Youth Organization
1011 First Avenue
New York, NY 10022
(212) 371-1000

**Club Managers Association
of America**
7615 Winterbury Place
Bethesda, MD 20817
(301) 229-3600

**College Football
Historical Society**
24 Rockbluff Way
Lockport, IL 60441
(708) 349-4798

College Rodeo Association
2925 Isaacs Avenue
Walla Walla, WA 99362
(509) 529-4402

**Commonwealth Games Association
of Canada, Inc.**
P.O. Box 3763, Sta. C
Hamilton, Ontario L8H 7NI

**Council of Parks and
Recreation Association**
1500 Lakeland Avenue
Bohemia, NY 11716
(516) 563-4800

Dwarf Athletic Association
3725 W. Holmes Road
Lansing, MI 58911
(517) 393-3116

**Eastern Marathon
Swimming Association**
541 Guy Lombardo Avenue
Freeport, NY 11520

**Eastern Rugby Union
of America**
226 Lauriston Street
Philadelphia, PA 19128
(215) 483-1399

Federation of Fly Fishers
P.O. Box 1088
West Yellowstone, MT 59758
(406) 646-9541

**Fellowship of Christian
Athletes**
8701 Leeds Road
Kansas City, MO 64129
(816) 921-0909

**Field Hockey Association
of America (Men)**
1750 E. Boulder Street
Colorado Springs, CO 80909
(719) 578-4587

**Fish & Wildlife Service
Department of the Interior**
Washington, D.C. 20240
(202) 343-5634

Fitness and Amateur Sport
365 Laurier Avenue West
Journal Tower South
Ottawa, Ontario KIA 0X6
(613) 992-9187

**Football Writers Association
of America**
P.O. Box 1022
Edmond, OK 73003
(405) 231-3314

Girl Scouts of the USA
830 3rd Ave. at 51st St.
New York, NY 10022
(212) 940-7500

Harness Tracks of America
35 Airport Road
Morristown, NJ 07960
(201) 285-9090

Iceberg Athletic Club
3046 W. 22nd Street
Brooklyn, NY 11224
(718) 266-5764

**Ice Skating Institute
of America**
355 West Dundee Road
Buffalo Grove, IL 60089
(708) 808-SKAT

**International Amateur
Wrestling Federation**
Ave. Ruchonnet 3
CH-1003 Lausanne,
Switzerland
(41.21) 22 8426

**International Association
of Auditorium Managers**
4425 W. Airport Freeway
Suite 590
Irving, TX 75062
(214) 255-8020

**International Badminton
Federation**
Unit 4, Manor Park
Mackenzie Way
Cheltenham, Gloucestershire
GL51 9TX, England
(44) 242 234-904

**International Bicycle
Touring Society**
2115 Paseo Dorado
La Jolla, CA 92037
(619) 459-8775

International Bocce Association
400 Rutger St., P.O. Box 170
Utica, NY 13503
(315) 733-9611

**International Frisbee
Association**
P.O. Box 970
San Gabriel, CA 91776
(818) 287-2257

**International Game Fish
Association**
3000 E. Las Olas Blvd.
Fort Lauderdale, FL 33316
(305) 467-0161

**International Grass Skiing
Association**
42 rue de Bale, B.B. 3131
F-68063 Mulhouse Cedex,
France

**International Jai Alai
Association**
5 Calle Aldamar, 1 Dcha
San Sebastian 3, Spain
(34.43) 42 8425

**International Jousting
Association**
328 Bush Chapel Road
Aberdeen, MD 21001
(301) 272-3086

**International Association of
Fairs & Expositions**
P.O. Box 985
Springfield, MO 65801
(417) 862-5771

**International Professional
Gymnastics Association**
2953 Wyandot Street
Denver, CO 80211
(303) 695-3858

**International Professional
Rodeo Association**
P.O. Box 615
Pauls Valley, OK 73705
(405) 238-6488

**International Racquetball
Federation**
815 North Weber
Colorado Springs, CO 80903
(719) 635-5396

**International Racquet
Sports Association**
132 Brooklyn Avenue
Boston, MA 02215
(617) 734-8000

**International Roller
Skating Federation**
P.O. Box 6579
1500 South 70th Street
Lincoln, NE 68506
(402) 483-7551

**International Shuffleboard
Association**
1701 Commerce Avenue #11
Haines City, FL 33844
(813) 422-4202

**International Table
Tennis Association**
53 London Road
St. Leonards-on-Sea
East Sussex TN37 6AY,
England

**Interservice Military
Sports Commission**
HQDA DACF-15-afs
Alexandria, VA 22331-0522
(703) 325-8871

Izaack Walton Fishing
League of America
1401 Wilson Blvd.
Level B
Arlington, VA 22209
(703) 528-1818

Jewish Sports Congress
134 Middle Neck Rd., Suite 210
Great Neck, NY 11023
(516) 482-5550

Jockey Club
380 Madison Avenue
New York, NY 10017
(212) 599-1919

Jockey's Guild
555 Fifth Avenue
Room 1501
New York, NY 10017
(212) 687-7746

Licensing Industry
Merchandisers Association
850 Fifth Avenue
Suite 6210
New York, NY 10018
(212) 244-1944

National Academy
of Sports
220 East 63rd Street
New York, NY 10021
(212) 838-5860

National Aeronautic
Association
821 15th Street N.W.
Suite 430
Washington, D.C. 20005
(202) 347-2808

National Archery Association
1750 East Boulder Street
Colorado Springs, CO 80909
(719) 578-4576

National Association for
Girls & Women in Sports
1900 Association Drive
Reston, VA 22091
(703) 476-3450

National Association for Sport
and Physical Education
1900 Association Drive
Reston, VA 22091
(703) 476-3410

National Association
of Concessionaires
35 East Wacker Drive
Suite 1849
Chicago, IL 60601
(312) 236-3858

National Association of
Educational Buyers
180 Froelich Farm Blvd.
Woodbury, NY 11797
(516) 364-6000

National Association of
Police Athletic Leagues
200 Castlewood Drive
North Palm Beach, FL 33408
(407) 844-1823

National Association of
Sports Officials
2017 Lathrop Avenue
Racine, WI 53405
(414) 632-5448

National Association of
State Racing Commissions
P.O. Box 4216
Lexington, KY 40504
(606) 278-5460

National Athletic Trainers
Association, Inc.
1001 East 4th Street
Greenville, NC 27834
(919) 752-1725

National Board YWCA
726 Broadway
New York, NY 10003
(212) 564-1300

National Boating
Federation
629 Waverly Lane
Bryn Athyn, PA 19009
(215) 947-0158

National Club Association
1625 I Street N.W.
Suite 609
Washington, D.C. 20006
(202) 466-8424

National Field Archery
Association

31407 Outer I-l04
Redlands, CA 92373
(714) 794-2133

National Fitness Foundation
2250 E. Imperial Hwy.
El Segundo, CA 90245
(213) 640-0145

National Girls Athletic
Association
1201 16th Street N.W.
Washington, D.C. 20036
(202) 833-5540

National Golf Foundation
1150 S. U.S. Hwy. One
Jupiter, FL 33477
(407) 744-6006

National Handicapped Sports
2246 S. Albion
Denver, CO 80222
(303) 759-8123

National Horseshoe
Pitchers Association
P.O. Box 810
Circleville, OH 43113
(614) 474-7727

National Institute on Park
& Ground Management
P.O. Box 1936
Appleton, WI 54913
(414) 733-2301

National Intramural Recreation
Sports Association
850 S.W. 15th Street
Corvallis, OR 97333
(503) 737-2088

National Park &
Recreation Association
3101 Park Center Drive
Alexandria, VA 23202
(703) 820-4940

National Rifle Association
1600 Rhode Island Ave., N.W.
Washington, D.C. 20036
(202) 828-6000

National Rowing Foundation
P.O. Box 6030
Arlington, VA 22206
(703) 379-2974

National School Board
Association
1680 Duke Street
Alexandria, VA 22314
(703) 838-6722

National School Supply
& Equipment Association
8300 Colesville Road
2nd Floor
Silver Spring, MD 20910
(703) 524-8819

**National Senior Sports
Association**
10560 Main Street
Suite 205
Alexandria, VA 22030
(703) 385-7540

**National Skateboarding
Association**
P.O. Box 1916
Vista, CA 92083
(619) 941-1844

**National Skeet Shooting
Association**
P.O. Box 68007
San Antonio, TX 78268
(512) 688-3371

**National Spa & Pool
Institute**
2111 Eisenhower Avenue
Alexandria, VA 22314
(703) 838-0083

**National Sporting
Goods Association**
1699 Wall Street
Mt. Prospect, IL 60056
(708) 439-4000

**National Sportscasters &
Sportswriters Association**
P.O. Drawer 559
Salisbury, NC 28745
(704) 633-4275

**National Strength &
Conditioning Association**
P.O. Box 81410
Lincoln, NE 68501
(402) 472-3000

**National Youth Sports
Coaches Association**
2611 Old Okeechobee Road
West Palm Beach, FL 33409
(407) 684-1141

**New York State Athletic
Commission**
270 Broadway
New York, NY 10007
(212) 587-5700

**North American Youth Sport
Institute**
4985 Oak Garden Drive
Suite 91
Kernersville, NC 27284
(919) 784-4926

Olympian International
Penn Center House
1900 John F. Kennedy Blvd.
Philadelphia, PA 19103
(215) 563-1886

**Ontario Sports Administration
Centre**
1200 Sheppard Avenue East
Willowdale, Ontario M2K 2X1
Canada
(416) 495-4000
(Most Ontario sports
organizations operate out of
the Centre.)

**People to People Sports
Committee**
40 Cutler Mill Road
Great Neck, NY 11021
(516) 482-5158

**President's Council on
Physical Fitness & Sports**
450 5th Street, N.W.
Suite 20001
(202) 272-3421

**Professional Racing
Organization of America**
340 Holly
Denver, CO 80220
(303) 333-2449

**Professional Rodeo Cowboys
Association**
101 Pro Rodeo Drive
Colorado Springs, CO 80919
(719) 593-8840

Professional Skaters Guild
P.O. Box 5904
Rochester, MN 55903
(507) 281-5122

**Resort & Commercial
Recreation Association**
P.O. Box 1208
New Port Richey, FL 33552
(813) 845-7373

Roller Skating Associations
7700 A Street
Lincoln, NE 68510
(402) 489-8811

**Roller Skating Foundation
of America**
515 Madison Avenue
New York, NY 10022
(212) 753-4153

**Roller Skating Rink
Operators Association**
P.O. Box 83067
Lincoln, NE 68501
(402) 483-7551

Sail America
1904 Hotel Circle North
San Diego, CA 92108
(619) 296-9224

**Senior Games Development
Council**
200 Castlewood Drive
North Palm Beach, FL 33408
(407) 842-3600

**Soaring Society of
America**
P.O. Box E
Hobbs, NM 88241
(505) 392-1177

Special Olympics
Joseph P. Kennedy
Foundation
1350 New York Avenue
Suite 500
Washington, D.C. 20005
(202) 628-3630

Sport Balloon Society
Menlo Oaks Balloon Field
Drawer 2247
Menlo Park, CA 94026
(415) 326-7679

Sport Fishing Institute
1010 Massachusetts Ave., N.W.
Suite 100
Washington, D.C. 20001
(202) 898-0770

**Sporting Goods Agents
Association**
P.O. Box 998
Morton Grove, IL 60053
(708) 296-3670

**Sporting Goods Manufacturers
Association**
200 Castlewood Drive
North Palm Beach, FL 33408
(407) 842-4100

Sports Ambassadors
25 Corning Avenue
Milpitas, CA 95035
(408) 249-7111

Sports America
301 Fourth Street S.W.
Room 561
Washington, D.C. 20547
(202) 485-6671

Sports Lawyers Association
2017 Lathrop Avenue
Racine, WI 53405
(414) 632-4040

Sports Licensing Corporation of America
75 Rockefeller Plaza
16th Floor
New York, NY 10019
(212) 484-8807

Sports Turf Managers Association
P.O. Box 94857
Las Vegas, NV 89193
(702) 739-8052

Thoroughbred Club of America
P.O. Box 8147
Lexington, KY 40503
(606) 277-8202

Thoroughbred Racing Association
3000 Marcus Avenue
Suite 2W4
Lake Success, NY 11040
(516) 328-2666

Union of World Karate Organizations
Senpake Shinko Bldg.
1-15-16 Toran Omon
Minato-ku, Tokyo 105
Japan

United States Amateur Confederation of Roller Skating

P.O. Box 83067
7700 A Street
Lincoln, NE 68501
(402) 483-7551

United States Badminton Association
920 O Street, 4th Floor
Lincoln, NE 68508
(402) 438-2473

United States Judo, Inc.
P.O. Box 10013
El Paso, TX 79991
(915) 565-8754

United States Olympic Committee
1750 East Boulder Street
Colorado Springs, CO 80909
(719) 632-5551

United States Parachute Association
1440 Duke Street
Alexandria, VA 22314
(703) 836-3495

USA Rugby Football Union
3595 E. Fountain Blvd.
Colorado Springs, CO 80910
(719) 637-1022

USA Wrestling
225 South Academy Blvd.
Colorado Springs, CO 80910
(719) 597-8333

USA Triathalon Federation
P.O. Box 1010
Colorado Springs, CO 80901
(719) 630-2255

U.S. Base Parachute Assoc.
12619 S. Manor Drive
Hawthorne, CA 90250
(213) 678-0163

U.S. Canoe & Kayak Association
201 S. Capitol
Suite 470
Indianapolis, IN 46225
(317) 237-5690

U.S. Chess Federation
186 Route 9W
New Windsor, NY 12553
(914) 562-8350

U.S. Commission: Sports
for Israel
275 S. 19th Street
Suite 1203
philadelphia, PA 19103
(215) 546-4701

U.S. Croquet Association
500 Avenue of Champions
Palm Beach, FL 33418
(407) 624-3128

U.S. Diving, Inc.
201 S. Capitol Avenue
Suite 430
Indianapolis, IN 46225
(317) 237-5252

U.S. Equestrian Team
17 East 45th Street
New York, NY 10017
(212) 370-4160

U.S. Figure Skating
Association
20 First Street
Colorado Springs, CO 80906
(719) 635-5200

U.S. Gymnastics Federation
201 S. Capitol Avenue
Suite 300
Indianapolis, IN 46225
(317) 237-5050

U.S. Handball Association
930 N. Benton Avenue
Tucson, AZ 85711
(602) 795-0434

U.S. Hang Gliding Association
P.O. Box 8300
Colorado Springs, CO 80933
(719) 632-8300

U.S. International
Sailing Association
P.O. Box 209
Newport, RI 02840
(401) 849-5200

U.S. Karate Organization
2910 N. Santiago Blvd.
Orange, CA 92666
(714) 282-USKO

U.S. Lifesaving Association
425 E. McFetridge Drive
Chicago, IL 60605
(312) 578-4578

U.S. Modern Pentathalon
Association
530 McCullough
San Antonio, TX 78215
(512) 246-3000

U.S. Paddle Tennis
Association
189 Seeley Street
Brooklyn, NY 11218

U.S. Parachute Association
1440 Duke Street
Alexandria, VA 22314
(703) 836-3495

U.S. Professional Tennis
Association, Inc.
3535 Briarpark Drive
Houston, TX 77042
(713) 97-USPTA

U.S. Rowing Association
201 S. Capitol Avenue

Indianapolis, IN 46225
(317) 237-5656

U.S. Squash Racquets
Association
P.O. Box 1216
Bala Cynwyd, PA 19004
(215) 667-4006

U.S. Syncronized Swimming, Inc.
201 S. Capitol Avenue
Indianapolis, IN 46225
(317) 237-5700

U.S. Tennis Association
707 Alexander Road
Princeton, NJ 08540
(609) 452-2580

U.S. Trotting Association
750 Michigan Avenue
Columbus, OH 43215
(614) 224-2291

U.S. Volleyball Association
3595 E. Fountain Blvd.
Colorado Springs, CO 80910
(719) 637-8300

U.S. Water Polo, Inc.
201 S. Capitol Avenue
Suite 520
Indianapolis, IN 46225
(317) 237-5599

U.S. Wrestling
405 W. Hall of Fame Avenue
Stillwater, OK 74075
(405) 377-5242

U.S. Yacht Racing Union
P.O. Box 209
Newport, RI 02840
(401) 849-5200

Winter Games for the Disabled
3701 Connecticut Avenue
Suite 236
Washington, D.C. 20008
(202) 833-1251

**Women's Professional
Racquetball Association**
1001-C North Harlem
Oak Park, IL 60302
(708) 383-9437

Women's Sports Foundation
342 Madison Avenue
Suite 728
New York, NY 10173
(212) 972-9170

**World Arm Wrestling
Federation**
P.O. Box 132
Scranton, PA 18504
(717) 342-4984

**World Leisure & Recreation
Association**
University of Ottawa
559 King Edward Avenue
Room 108
Ottawa, Ontario, Canada
(613) 231-6812

**World Pro Arm Wrestling
Association**
3020 Earlman Drive
Los Angeles, CA 90064
(213) 837-8370

**World Pro Squash
Association**
12 Sheppard Street
Suite 500
Toronto, Ontario M5H 3A1
Canada
(416) 869-3499

World Taekwondo Federation
San 76 Yuksamdong,
Kangamku, Seoul
Korea (135)

World Wrestling Federation
1055 Summer Street
P.O. Box 3857
Stamford, CT 06905
(203) 352-8699

**World's Wristwrestling
Championship Association**
423 E. Washington Street
Petaluma, CA 94952
(707) 778-0210

Yachting Club of America
P.O. Box 487
Islamorada, FL 33036
(305) 664-4102

YMCA of the USA
101 North Wacker Drive
Chicago, IL 60606
(312) 977-0031

Youth Basketball of America, Inc.
P.O. Box 36108
Orlando, FL 32823
(407) 363-0599

YWCA of the USA
726 Broadway
Fifth Floor
New York, NY 10003
(212) 614-2700

The following sports organizations are U.S. national governing bodies for amateur sports that are part of the Olympic family and make their home in Colorado Springs at the USOC Complex.

United States Olympic Committee
1750 East Boulder Street
Colorado Springs, CO 80909
(719) 632-5551
(719) 578-4500 (To reach an athlete in Complex)
(719) 578-4654 (Telecopier)

National Archery Association	(719) 578-4576
USA Amateur Boxing Federation	(719) 578-4506
USA Basketball	(719) 632-7687
U.S. Cycling Federation	(719) 578-4581
U.S. Fencing Federation	(719) 578-4511
U.S. Men's Field Hockey Association	(719) 578-4587
U.S. Women's Field Hockey	(719) 578-4567
U.S. Soccer Federation	(719) 578-4678
U.S. Speed Skating	(719) 593-0465
U.S. Swimming, Inc.	(719) 578-4578
U.S. Table Tennis Association	(719) 578-4583
U.S. Taekwondo Union	(719) 578-4632
U.S. Handball Association	(719) 578-4582
U.S. Weightlifting Federation	(719) 578-4508
U.S. Olympic Training Center	(719) 578-4500

The following sports federations are part of the USOC family located in Colorado Springs but outside the USOC Complex.

USA Hockey	(719) 576-499
USA Racquetball	(719) 635-539
USA Rugby Football Union	(719) 637-102
USA Triathalon	(719) 630-225
USA Wrestling	(719) 597-833
U.S. Figure Skating	(719) 635-520
U.S. Volleyball	(719) 637-830

U.S. Olympic Training Center
1776 East Boulder Street
Colorado Springs, CO 80909
(719) 578-4500

U.S. Olympic Training Center
20 Lake Placid Drive
Lake Placid, NY 12946
(518) 523-2600

U.S. Olympic Center
Northern Michigan University
Marquette, MI 49855
(906) 227-2849

U.S. Olympic Training Center News Bureau
1776 East Boulder Street
Colorado Springs, CO 80909
(719) 578-4623

Sports Publications

Listed in this section are Multi-Sport and International publications. Some may be duplicated from other sections of the book.

All Star Sports Report
PO Box 955
Lenoir, NC 28645
(704) 758-5827

Amateur Wrestling News
PO Box 60387
Oklahoma City, OK 73146
(405) 236-2808

American Canoeist
PO Box 1190
Newington, VA 22122
(703) 550-7523

American Fencing Magazine
1750 East Boulder St.
Colorado Spring, CO 80909
(719) 578-4511

American Hockey Magazine
2997 Broadmoor Vallley Road
Colorado Spring, CO 80906
(719) 576-4990

American Outdoors
1331 Pennsylvania Avenue
Suite 726
Washington, D.C. 20004
(202) 662-7420

American Rowing Magazine
201 S. Capitol, Suite 400
Indianapolis, IN 46225
(317) 237-5656

American Sports
PO Box 6100
Rosemead, CA 91770
(818) 572-4727

Amusement Business
PO Box 24970
Nashville, TN 37202
(615) 321-4250

Athletic Administration
24651 Detroit Road
Cleveland, OH 44115
(216) 892-4000

Athletic Business
1842 Hoffman Street
Suite 201
Madison, WI 53704
(608) 249-0186

Athletic Director
319 Barry Avenue S.
Wayzata, MN 55391
(612) 476-2200

Athletic Director and Coach
450 Lafayette Street
Salem, MA 01970
(617) 744-1793

Athletics Magazine
IAAF
3 Hans Crescent
Knightsbridge OLN
London SWIX England
(44) 581-8771

Athlon's Pro & College Publications
220 25th Avenue North
Nashville, TN 37203
(615) 297-7581
(800) 251-1201

Australia's Hockey Circle
PO Box 127
Glen Iris Victoria 3146
Australia
(03) 885-7235

Auto Racing Digest
990 Grove Street
Evanston, IL 60201
(708) 941-6440

TAC News
3400 West 86th Street
Indianapolis, IN 46208

**BAA Boston Marathon
Magazine**
100 Massachusetts Avenue
Boston, MA 02115
(617) 536-5390

Backpacker
33 E. Minor Street
Emmaus, PA 18098
(215) 967-5171

Basketball Weekly
17820 E. Warren Avenue
Detroit, MI 48224
(313) 881-9554

B. C. Soccer Magazine
17231-57A Avenue
Surrey, B.C., V3S 5AB

Beach Culture
PO Box 1028
Dana Point, CA 92629
(714) 496-5922

The Big Eight Magazine
PO Box 20688
11018 Quail Creek Road
Oklahoma City, OK 73120
(405) 521-9396

Big League
PO Box 261
Randwick 2031, Australia
(Rugby Magazine)

Black Belt Magazine
1813 Victory Place
Burbank, CA 91510
(818) 843-4444

Black Sports
31 East 28th Street
New York, NY 10016
(212) 725-9196

The Blue Chips
PO Box 20688
Oklahoma City, OK 73120
(405) 364-1050

Boating
1515 Broadway
New York, NY 10036
(212) 719-6000

Bowlers Journal
875 North Michigan Avenue
Chicago, IL 60611
(312) 266-7171

Bowling Digest
990 Grove Street
Evanston, IL 60201
(708) 491-6440

Boxing Update
PO Box 789
Capitola, CA 95010
(408) 476-6223

Breakout Magazine
2691 State Street
Carlsbad, CA 92008
(619) 434-3322
(Surfing)

**California Basketball/
Football**
1801 S. Catalina Avenue
Suite 301
Redondo Beach, CA 90277
(213) 375-9860

Canadian Curling News
1108 Centre Street North
Calgary, Alberta, T2E 2R2

**Canadian Old Timers
Sports News**
Box 951
Peterborough, Ont., K9J 7A5

Championship Wrestling
1115 Broadway
New York, NY 10010
(212) 807-7100

China Sports Magazine
8 Tiyuguan Road
Beijing, China

City Sports
PO Box 3693
San Francisco, CA 94119
(415) 456-6150

Coffin (FB) Corner
12870 Route 30
North Huntingdon, PA 15642
(412) 863-6345

College Athletic Management
438 W. State Street
Ithaca, NY 14850
(607) 272-0265

College & Pro Football News
18 Industrial Park Drive
Port Washington, NY 11050
(516) 484-3300

Collegiate Baseball
PO Box 50566
Tucson, AZ 87703
(602) 623-7195

Cross Country Skier
PO Box 1203
Brattleboro, VT 05301
(802) 257-1304

Cross Country Skiing Magazine
380 Madison Avenue
New York, NY 10017
(212) 687-3000

English Basketball Monthly
12 Rumford Place
Liverpool, England

The European Hockey Report
12275 Cote de Liesse Road
Dorval, Quebec, H9P 1B4

Fairway Magazine
2 Park Avenue
New York, NY 10016
(212) 779-5000

FIBA Basketball Monthly
Station Road
Stanstead Abbotts, Ware
Herts, SG12 8DJ, England
(0920) 870808

Field & Stream
1515 Broadway
New York, NY 10036
(212) 719-6685

FIFA News
PO Box 85
CH-8030 Zurich,
Switzerland
(01) 55 5400

Flying
1515 Broadway
New York, NY 10036
(212) 719-6000

Football Action
18 Industrial Park Drive
Port Washington, NY 11050
(516) 484-3300

Football Digest
990 Grove Street
Evanston, IL 60201
(708) 491-6440

The Football News
17820 E. Warren Avenue
Detroit, MI 48224
(313) 881-9554

Football Today
16 Lancaster Gate
London W2 3LW, England

Game Day/Goal
600 Third Avenue
New York, NY 10016
(212) 697-1460

The Gold Sheet
9255 Sunset Blvd.
Suite 200
Los Angeles, CA 90069
(213) 273-9025

Golf Digest/Golf World
5520 Park Avenue
Trumbull, CT 06611
(203) 373-7000

Golf Magazine
2 Park Avenue
New York, NY 10016
(212) 779-5000

High School Sports
1230 Avenue of the
Americas, Suite 2000
New York, NY 10020
(212) 765-3300

Hockey Digest
990 Grove Street
Evanston, IL 60201
(708) 491-6440

Hockey Digest Magazine
Elm Lawn, Staines Road
Leleham on Thames
TW18 2TD, England

The Hockey News
Hockey Pictoral
85 Scarsdale Road
Suite 100
Don Mills, Ontario, M3B 2R2
(416) 445-5702

Hoop
600 Third Avenue
New York, NY 10016
(212) 697-1460

Inside Lacrosse
559 Jarvis Street
Toronto, Ontario, M4Y 2J1

Inside Running
8100 Bellaire
Suite 1318
Houston, TX 77036
(713) 777-9084

Jewish Sports & Fitness
P.O. Box 4549
Old Village Station
Great Neck, NY 11023
(516) 482-5550

Inside Sports
990 Grove Street
Evanston, IL 60201
(708) 491-6440

International Basketball
438 W. 37th Street,
Suite 3B
New York, NY 10018

**International Boxing
Magazine**
PO Box 48
Rockville Center, NY 11571
(516) 546-3700

**International Field
Hockey News**
Avenue des Arts (Bte 5)
1040 Brussels, Belgium

**International Ice Hockey
Guide/Eishockey Magazin'**
WIBA Druck Gmbh
Haunstetter Strasse 26
8900 Augsburg, Germany
(08.21) 574-006

**Interscholastic Athletic
Administration**
11724 Plaza Circle
PO Box 20626
Kansas City, MO 64195
(816) 464-5400

**Japan Pro Baseball
Fan Handbook**
1-15-13 Fijimachi
Hoya-shi, Tokyo-to
Japan 202
(0424) 65 4792
Editor: Wayne Graczyk

**The Journal of Physical
Education, Recreation & Dance**
1900 Association Drive
Reston, VA 22091
(703) 476-3400

Journal of Sport Management
Box 5076
Champaign, IL 61825
(217) 351-5076

**Journal of the Philosophy
of Sport**
PO Box 5076
Champaign, IL 61825
(217) 351-5076

JUCO Review
PO Box 7305
Colorado Springs, CO 80933
(719) 590-9788

Kicker Sportsmagazin
Sammelbilder,
Postfach 3411
8500 Nurnberg, Germany

KO Magazine
PO Box 48
Rockville Center, NY 11571
(516) 546-3700

**Let's Play Hockey
Let's Play Softball**
2721 E. 42nd Street
Minneapolis, MN 55406
(612) 729-0023

Michigan Basketball G
415 Detroit Street
Ann Arbor, MI 48104

Michigan Hockey Weekly
25042 West Warren Road
Dearborn Heights, MI 48127
(313) 563-9130

MultiSport Facility News
1450 N.E. 123rd Street
North Miami, FL 33161
(305) 893-8771

NAIA News
1221 Baltimore Avenue
Kansas City, MO 64105
(816) 842-5050

NASCAR Newsletter
PO Box K
Daytona Beach, FL 32015
(904) 253-3220

National Coach Magazine
1515 E. Silver Springs Rd.
Ocala, FL 32678
(904) 622-3660

**National High School
Federation News**
11724 Plaza Circle
PO Box 20626
Kansas City, MO 64195
(816) 464-5400

National Sports Review
333 First Avenue South
Seattle, WA 98119
(206) 282-2322

NCAA News & Publications
6201 College Blvd.
Overland Park, KS 66211
(913) 339-1906

North American Curling News
214 Summit Street
Portage, WI 53901
(608) 742-3853

The Olympian
U.S. Olypic Society
PO Box 1699
Colorado Springs,
CO 80901-9938
(719) 632-5551

Olympic Horizons
Angel Kanchev Street
Sofia 4, Bulgaria

Outdoor Life
2 Park Avenue
New York, NY 10016
(212) 779-5000

Outside Magazine
1165 N. Clark Street
Chicago, IL 60610
(312) 951-0990

**Parks & Recreation
Magazine**
3101 Park Center Drive
Alexandria, VA 22302
(703) 820-4940

**Petersen's Pro Football
Annual**
8490 Sunset Blvd.
Los Angeles, CA 90069
(213) 657-5100

PGA Magazine
100 Avenue of Champions
Palm Beach Gardens, FL 33410
(407) 626-3600

Physical Education Digest
111 Kingsmount Blvd.
Sudbury, Ontario P3E 1K8
(705) 675-7055

**The Physician and
Sportsmedicine**
4530 W. 77th Street
Suite 350
Minneapolis, MN 55435
(612) 835-3222

Polo Magazine
656 Quince Orchard Road
Gaithersburg, MD 20878
(301) 977-0200

Press Magazine
Krekelstraat 13
B9300 Aalst, Belgium

Pro Football News
666 Dundee Road
Suite 11011
Northbrook, IL 60662
(312) 272-1237

Propeller Magazine
17640 East 9 Mile Road
PO Box 377
East Detroit, MI 48021
(313) 773-9700

Pro Rodeo News
PO Box 585
Pauls Valley, OK 73075
(405) 238-3310

Pro Wrestling Illustrated
PO Box 48
Rockville Center, NY 11571
(516) 546-3700

Referee Magazine
PO Box 161
Franksville, WI 53126
(414) 632-8855

Rugby
2350 Broadway
New York, NY 10024
(212) 787-1160

Runner's World
PO Box 366
Mountain View, CA 94040
(415)965-8777

Running & Triathalon News
5111 Santa Fe Street
Suite 206
San Diego, CA 92109
(619) 270-4974

Sailing World
5520 Park Avenue
Trumbull, CT 06611
(203) 373-7000

Salt Water Fishing
2 Park Avenue
New York, NY 10016
(212) 779-5000

Skating
20 First Street
Colorado Springs, CO 80906

Ski Magazine
2 Park Avenue
New York, NY 10016

Skiing
2 Park Avenue
New York, NY 10016
(212) 779-5000

Ski Racing International
PO Box 125
Waitsfield, VT 05673
(802) 496-7700

Ski X-C
1515 Broadway
New York, NY 10036
(212) 719-6061

Skin Diver Magazine
8490 Sunset Blvd.
Los Angeles, CA 90069
(213) 854-2960

Skybox
1328 Elam Street
Cincinnati, OH 45225
(513) 541-0269

Snowboarding Magazine
PO Box 6
Cardiff-by-the-Sea
CA 92007
(619) 722-7777

Soccer America
PO Box 23704
Oakland, CA 94623
(415) 528-5000

Soccer Digest
990 Grove Street
Evanston, IL 60201
(708) 491-6440

Soccer International
PO Box 246
Artesia, CA 90702
(213) 860-2831

Soccer Match
PO Box 39A27
Los Angeles, CA 90039
(818) 242-9970

Softball World
PO Box 10151
Grand Lake Station
Oakland, CA 94610
(415) 428-2000

Sport Intern
Alescher Strass 7
Postfach 710 420
D-8000 Munich 71, Germany

Sport Magazine
8490 Sunset Blvd.
Los Angeles, CA 90069
(213) 854-2222

Sporting Goods Business
1515 Broadway
New York, NY 10036
(212) 869-1300

Sporting Goods Intelligence
PO Box 908
Concordville, PA 19331
(215) 558-1601

The Sporting News
1212 North Lindbergh Blvd.
PO Box 56
St. Louis, MO 63166
(314) 997-7111

Sports Afield
250 W. 55th Street
New York, NY 10019
(212) 262-8852

The Sport Psychologist
PO Box 5076
Champaign, IL 61825
(217) 357-5076

Sports Illustrated
1271 Avenue of the Americas
New York, NY 10020
(212) 586-1212

Sports Illustrated For Kids
1271 Avenue of the Americas
New York, NY 10020
(212) 522-1212

Sports Industry News
PO Box 946
Camden, ME 04843
(207) 236-8346

The Sports Journal
7 Glenbrook Place S.W.
Calgary, Alberta, T3E 6W4
(403) 240-3258

The Sports Journal
105 Berkeley Place
Glen Rock, NJ 07452
(201) 445-2288

Sports Management News
1167 Woodside Road
Yardley, PA 19067
(215) 493-2720

Sports Reporter
306 Broadway
Lynnbrook, NY 11563
(516) 599-2121

Sport USSR & World
Arena
8 Ulitsa Moskuina
Moscow 103772, USSR

Street & Smith's
Yearbooks
304 East 45th Street
New York, NY 10017
(212) 880-8698

Super Star Hockey
Annual
1115 Broadway
New York, NYT 10010
(212) 807-7100

Surfer Magazine
33046 Calle Aviada
San Juan Capistrano,
CA 92675
(714-496-5922

Surfing Magazine
950 Calle Amanecer
PO Box 3010
San Clemente, CA 92672
(714) 492-7873

Team Marketing Report
1147 West Ohio
Suite 506
Chicago, IL 60622
(312) 829-7060

Team Sports Business
4141 N. Scottsdale Road
Suite 316
Scottsdale, AZ 85251
(602) 483-0014

Tennis
5520 Park Avenue
Trumbull, CT 06611
(203) 373-7000

Tennis USA
3 Park Avenue
New York, NY 10016
(212) 340-9200

Texas/Arkansas Football
PO Box 47420
Dallas, TX 75247
(214) 631-1160

Track & Field News
2570 El Camino Real
Suite 606
Mountain View, CA 94040
(415) 948-8188

Triathlete
1415 Third Street
Suite 303
Santa Monica, CA 90401
(213) 394-1321

Velo-News (Cycling)
Box 1257
Brattleboro, VT 05301
(802) 254-2305

Volleyball Monthly
PO Box 3137
San Luis Obispo, CA 93403
(805) 541-2294

Volley World
FIVB
12 Avenue de La Gare
CH-1001 Lausanne,
Switzerland
(41) 21-208932

The Water Skier
799 Overlook Drive
Winterhaven, FL 33880
(813) 324-4341

Who's Who in Baseball
1115 Broadway
New York, NY 10010
(212) 807-7100

Wind Surf Magazine
Box 561
Dana Point, CA 92629
(714) 661-4888

Women's Sports & Fitness
1919 14th Street
Suite 421
Boulder, CO 80302
(303) 440-5111

Women's Sports Pages
PO Box 151534
Chevy Chase, MD 20825
(301) 913-0450

World Baseball Magazine
Pan American Plaza
201 S. Capitol Avenue
Suite 490
Indianapolis, IN 46225
(317) 237-5757

World Handball Magazine
Klaus-Dieter Kimmel
Seelower Strasse 9
Berlin 1071, Germany
(372) 221 2240

World Soccer
Central House
27 Park Street
Croydon, CRO 1YD, England
(44) 081-686-9777

World Tennis
3 Park Avenue
New York, NY 10036
(212) 719-6000

World Weightlifting
IWF
1054 Budapest, Hold u.1,
Hungary
(36-1) 131-8153

Wrestling USA
55 Maple Avenue
Rockville Center, NY 11570
(516)764-0300

Yachting
2 Park Avenue
New York, NY 10016
(212) 779-5000

Women's Sports Pages
PO Box 151534
Chevy Chase, MD 20825
(301) 913-0450

Intercollegiate Athletics

NCAA College Bowl Games

SEC Championship Game
Birmingham Football Foundation
PO Box 11304
Birmingham, AL 35202
(205) 252-5507
Ex. Dir: Jim Simmons

Alamo Bowl
100 Montana Street
San Antonio, TX 78203
(210) 226-2695
Ex. Dir: Derrick S. Fox

Aloha Bowl
1110 University Avenue
Suite 403
Honolulu, Hawaii 96826
(808) 947-4141
Ex. Dir: Marcia Cherner

Blue-Gray All-American
Classic
PO Box 94
Montgomery, AL 36101
(205) 265-1266

California Raisin Bowl
P.O. Box 1469
Fresno, CA 93716
(209) 233-4651
Ex. Dir: Susan Tatnam

Copper Bowl
440 S. Williams Blvd.
Suite 100
Tucson, AZ 85711
(602) 790-5510
Ex.Dir.: Merle A. Miller

Cotton Bowl Classic
1300 W. Mockingbird, Suite 400
Dallas, TX 75247
(214) 634-7525
Ex.Dir.: Jim L. Brock

East-West Shrine Game
1651 19th Avenue
San Francisco, CA 94122
(415) 661-4000

Fiesta Bowl
120 S. Ash Avenue
Tempe, AZ 85281
(602) 350-0900
Ex. Dir: John Junker

Florida Citrus Bowl
One Citrus Bowl Place
Orlando, FL 32805
(407) 423-2476
Ex. Dir: Charles Rohe

Freedom Bowl/
Disneyland Classic
2000 South State
College Blvd.
Anaheim, CA 92806
(714) 634-1984
Ex.Dir.: Don Anderson

Gator Bowl
4080 Woodcock Drive
Suite 130
Jacksonville, FL 32207
(904) 396-1800
Ex.Dir.: John T. Bell

Hall of Fame Bowl
4511 N. Himes Avenue
Suite 260
Tampa, FL 33614
(813) 874-2695
Ex. Dir: James P. McVay

Holiday Bowl/
Sunshine Football Classic
9449 Friars Road, Gate P
San Diego, CA 92108
(619) 283-5808
Ex.Dir.: John Reid

Hula Bowl
P.O. Box 11270
Honolulu, HI 96828
(808) 956-4854
Ex. Dir: Roy Nagel

Independence Bowl

'PO Box 1723
Shreveport, LA 71166
(318) 221-0712
Ex.Dir.: Mrs. Pat Tiller

Japan Bowl
2975 Wilshire Blvd.
Suite 711
Los Angeles, CA 90010
(213) 384-2235
Pres.: Matsujiro Kawana

John Hancock Bowl
2609 North Stanton
El Paso, TX 79902
(915) 533-4416
Ex. Dir: Craig Helwig

Kickoff Classic
Giants Stadium
East Rutherford, NJ 07073
(201) 460-4361
Ex. Dir: Robert Mulcahy 111

Liberty Bowl
4735 Spottswood, Suite 102
Memphis, TN 38117
(901) 767-7700
Ex. Dir: A.F. "Bud" Dudley

Las Vegas Bowl
2030 East Flamingo
Suite 200
Las Vegas, NV 89119
(702) 731-2115
Ex. Dir: Herb McDonald

Orange Bowl

601 Brickell Key Drive
Suite 206
Miami, FL 33131
(305) 371-4600
Ex. Dir: Keith Tribble

Peach Bowl
235 International Blvd.
Atlanta, GA 30303
(404) 586-8500
Ex. Dir: Robert Dale Morgan

Rose Bowl
391 S. Orange Grove Blvd.
Pasadena, CA 98114
(818) 449-4100
Ex.Dir.: John H.B.French

Senior Bowl
63 S. Royal Street, Suite 107
Mobile, AL 36602
(205) 438-2276

Sugar Bowl
Louisiana Superdome
1500 Sugar Bowl Drive
New Orleans, LA 70112
(504) 525-8573
Ex. Dir: Troy Mathieu

Carquest Sunshine Bowl
915 Middle River Drive
Suite 120
Fort Lauderdale, FL 33304
(305) 564-5000
Ex. Dir: Brian Flajole

College Athletic Associations

National Collegiate Athletic Association
6201 College Blvd.
Overland Park, KS 66211-2422
(913) 339-1906
Fax (913) 339-1950

National Association of Intercollegiate Athletics
1221 Baltimore Avenue
Kansas City, MO 64105
(813) 842-5050
Fax (816) 421-4471
Exec. Dir.:
Dr. Jefferson D. Farris

National Junior College Athletic Association
PO Box 7305
Colorado Springs, CO 80933
(719) 590-9788
Fax (719) 590-7324
Exec. Dir.: George E. Killian

National Small College Athletic Association
1884 College Heights
New Ulm, MN 56073
(507) 359-9791
Commissioner: Gary Dallmann

National Christian College Athletic Association
PO Box 1312
Marion, IN 46952
(317) 674-8401
Fax (317) 674-8487
Pres.: Mike Fratzke

National Invitational Tournament
Downtown Athletic Club
19 West St., Suite 2010
New York, NY 10004
(212) 425-6510
Fax (212) 785-0594

NCAA Member Universities and Conferences

Listed in this section are the major conferences and universities that are members of the NCAA. All contact names are that of the Athletic Director.

National Collegiate Athletic

American West Conference (I, I-AA Football)
5855 Brookline Lane
San Luis Obispo, CA 93401
(805) 756-1412
Fax (805) 756-7273
Comm: Victor A. Buccola

Conference Members

American South Athletic Conference (I)

One Galleria Blvd.
Suite 2016
Metairie, LA 70001
(504) 834-6600
Fax (504) 834-6806
Commissioner: Craig Thompson
Publicity: Tom Burnett

Arkansas State University
State University, AR 72467
(501) 972-3880
Charles Thornton

Central Florida, Univ. of
Orlando, FL 32816
(407) 823-2994
Gene McDowell

Lamar University
Beaumont, TX 77710
(409) 880-8313
Gary Gallup

Louisiana Tech University
Ruston, LA 71272
(318) 257-4111
Paul A. Miller

New Orleans, University of
New Orleans, LA 70148
(504) 286-7020
Ronald J. Maestri

Pan American University
Edinburg, TX 78539
(512) 381-2221
Sam Odstrcil

**Southwestern Louisiana,
University of**
Lafayetter, LA 70506
93180 231-6318
Nelson Stokely

Association of Mid-Continent Conference (I)
40 Shuman Blvd.
Suite 118
Naperville, IL 60563
(708) 416-7560
Fax (708) 416-7564
Comm: Jerry Ippoliti
Publicity: Tom Lessig

Akron, University of
Akron, OH 44325
(216) 972-7080
Jim Dennison

**Cleveland State
University**
Cleveland, OH 44115
(216) 687-4808
John Konstantinos

**Eastern Illinois
University**
Charles, IL 61920
(217) 581-2106
Michael Ryan

**Illinois-Chicago,
University of**
Chicago, IL 60680
(312) 996-2695
Thomas Russo

**Northern Illinois
University**
DeKalb, IL 60115
(815) 753-0888
Gerald O'Dell

**Northern Iowa,
University of**
Cedar Fall, IA 50614
(319) 273-2470
Robert A. Bowlsby

Valparaiso University
Valparaiso, IN 46383
(219) 464-5230
William L. Steinbrecher

**Western Illinois
University**
Macomb, IL 61455
(309) 298-1106
Gil Peterson

**Wisconsin-Green Bay,
University of**
Green Bay, WI 54311
(414) 465-2145
Daniel Speillmann

Atlantic Coast Conference (I, Football I-A)

PO Drawer ACC
Greensboro, NC 27419
(919) 854-8787
Fax (919) 854-8797
Comm.: Eugene Corrigan
Publicity: Thomas Mickle

Clemson University
Clemson, SC 29631
(803) 656-2218
Robert Robinson

Duke University
Durham, NC 27706
(919) 684-2431
Tom Butters

Florida State University
Tallahassee, FL 32316
(904) 644-1079
Bob Goin

**Georgia Institute
of Technology**
Atlanta, GA 31332
(404) 894-5411
Homer C. Rice

Maryland, University of
College Park, MD 20740
93010 454-4705
Ferdinand Geiger

**North Carolina,
University of**
Chapel Hill, NC 27514
(919) 962-6000
John D. Swofford

**North Carolina
State University**
Raleigh, NC 27695
(919) 737-2109
William Turner

Virginia, University of
Charlottesville, VA 22903
(804) 982-5100
James Copeland, Jr.

Wake Forest University
Winston-Salem, NC 27109
(919) 759-5616
Gene E. Hooks

Atlantic 10 Conference (I)

10 Woodbridge Center Drive
Woodbridge, NJ 07095
(201) 634-6900
Fax (201) 634-6923
Comm.: Ron Bertovich
Publicity: John Wooding

Duquesne University
Pittsburg, PA 15282
(412) 434-6565
Brian Colleary

**George Washington
University**
Washington, D.C.20052
(202) 994-6650
Steve Bilsky

Massachusetts, University of
Amherst, MA 01003
(413) 545-2460
Frank P. McInerney

Rhode Island, University of
Kingston, RI 02881
(401) 792-5245
McKinley Boston

Rutgers University
New Brunswick, NJ 08903
(201) 932-8610
Fred E. Gruninger

**St. Bonaventure
University**
St. Bonaventure, NY 14778
(716) 375-2210
Lawrence J. Weise

St. Joseph's University
Philadelphia, PA 19131
(215) 660-1707
Don J. DiJulia

Temple University
Philadelphia, PA 19122
(215) 787-7447
Charles Theokas

West Virginia University
Morgantown, WV 26506
(304) 293-5621
Fred A. Schaus

Big East Conference
(I, Football I-A)

56 Exchange Terrace
Providence, RI 02903
(401) 272-9108
Fax (401) 751-8540
Comm: Michael Tranghese
Publicity: W. John Paquette, Jr.

Boston College
Chestnut Hill, MA 02167
(617) 552-4681
William J. Flynn

Connecticut, University of
Storrs, CT 06269
(203) 486-3863
Lewis Perkins

Georgetown University
Washington, D.C. 20057
(202) 687-2435
francis X. Rienzo

Miami, University of
Coral Gables, FL 33124
(305) 284-3822
David L. Maggard

Pittsburgh, University of
Pittsburgh, PA 15260
(412) 648-8230
Edward Bozik

Providence College
Providence, RI 02918
(401) 865-2265
John M. Marinatto

St. John's University
Jamaica, NY 11439
(718) 990-6224
John W. Kaiser

Seton Hall University
South Orange, NJ 07079
(201) 761-9497
Laurence C. Keating, Jr.

Syracuse University
Syracuse, NY 13244
(315) 443-2385
Jack Crouthamel

Villanova University
Villanova, PA 19085
(215) 645-4111
Ted Aceto

Big Eight Conference
(I, Football I-A)

104 W. Ninth Street, Suite 408
Kansas City, MO 64105
(816) 471-5088
Foz (816) 4714601
Comm.: Carl C. James
Information: Jeff Bollig

Colorado, University of
Boulder, CO 80309
(303) 492-7931
William Marolt

Iowa State University
Ames, IA 50011
(515) 294-3662
Max Urick

Kansas, University of
Lawrence, KS 66045
(913) 864-3143
Robert Frederick

Kansas State University
Manhattan, KS 66506
(913) 532-6910
Steve Miller

Missouri, University of
Columbia, MO 65211
(314) 882-6501
Richard Tamburo

Nebraska, University of
Lincoln, NE 68588
(402) 472-3644
Robert S. Devaney

Oklahoma, University of
Norman, OK 73019
(405) 325-8200
Donnie Duncan

Oklahoma State University
Stillwater, OK 74078
(405) 744-5733
James Garner

Big Sky Conference
(I, I-AA Football)

PO Box 1736
Boise, ID 83701
(208) 345-5393
Fax (208) 345-0281
Comm.: Ron Stephenson
Information: Arnie Sgalio

Boise State University
Boise, ID 83725
(208) 385-1981
Gene Bleymaier

**Eastern Washington
University**
Cheney, WA 99004
(509) 359-2463
Darlene Bailey

Idaho, University of
Moscow, ID 83843
(208) 885-0200
D. Gary Hunter

Idaho State University
Pocatello, ID 83201
(208) 236-2771
Randy Hoffman

Montana, University of
Missoula, MT 59812
(406) 243-5331
William Moos

Montana State University
Bozeman, MT 59717
(406) 994-4226
Doug Fullerton

Nevada-Reno, University of
Reno, NV 89557
(702) 784-6900
Chris Ault

Northern Arizona University
Flagstaff, AZ 86011
(602) 523-5353
Tom Jurich

Weber State University
Ogden, UT 84408
(801) 626-6817
Richard Hannan

Big South Conference (I)

1551 21st Avenue, Suite 13
Myrtle Beach, SC 29577
(803) 448-9998
Fax (803) 626-7167
Comm.: George "Buddy" Sasser
Publicity: Tom Collins

Big Ten Conference (I, Football I-A)

1500 W. Higgins Road
Park Ridge, IL 60068
(708) 696-1010
Fax (708) 696-1110
Comm: James Delany
Publicity: Mark Rudner

Illinois, University of
Champaign, IL 61820
(217) 333-3678
John Mackovic

Indiana University
Bloomington, IN 47405
(812) 855-1966
Ralph N. Floyd

Iowa, University of
Iowa City, IA 52242
(319) 335-9435
Chalmers W. Elliot

Michigan, University of
Ann Arbor, MI 48109
(313) 764-6227
Jack Weidenbach

Michigan State University
East Lansing, MI 48824
(517) 355-1623
George Perles

Minnesota, University of
Minneapolis, MN 55455
(612) 625-9579
Richard M. Bay

Northwestern University
Evanston, IL 60208
(708) 491-8880
Bruce A. Corrie

Ohio State University
Columbus, OH 43210
(614) 292-7572
James L. Jones

Pennsylvania State University
University Park, PA 16802
(814) 865-1086
James Tarman

Purdue University
West Lafayette, IN 47907
(317) 494-3189
George S. King, Jr.

Wisconsin, University of
Madison, WI 53706
(608) 262-5068
Pat Richter

Big West Conference (I, Football I-A)

2 Corporate Park, Suite 206
Irvine, CA 92714
(714) 261-2525
Fax (714) 261-2528
Comm: Dennis Farrell

California-Irvine, University of
Irvine, CA 92717
(714) 856-6979
Thomas J. Ford

Calif.-Santa Barbara, University of
Santa Barbara, CA 93106
(805) 893-3400
John V. Kasser

Fresno State University
Fresno, CA 93740
(209) 278-3178
Gary Cunningham

Fullerton State University
Fullerton, CA 92634
(714) 773-2677
Edward O. Carroll

Hawaii, University of
Honolulu, HI 96822
(808) 956-7301
Stanley B. Sheriff

Long Beach State University
Long Beach, CA 90840
(213) 985-4655
Corey Johnson

Nevada-Las Vegas, University of
Las Vegas, NV 89154
(702) 739-3983
Dennis Finfrock

New Mexico State University
Las Cruces, NM 88003
(505) 646-1211
Albert Gonzalez

Pacific, University of
Stockton, CA 95211
(209) 946-2248
Edward Leland

San Jose State University
San Jose, CA 95192
(408)924-1200
Tom Brennan

Utah State University
Logan, UT 84322
(801) 750-1862
Rod Tueller

Central Collegiate Conference
1705 Evanston Street
Kalamazoo, MI 49008
(616) 349-1009
Comm.: George G. Dales

Central Collegiate Hockey Association (I)

1000 South State Street
Ann Arbor, MI 48109
(313) 764-2590
Comm.: Bill Beagan
Publicity: Jeff Weiss

Bowling Green State University
Bowling Green, OH 43403
(419) 372-2401
Jack Gregory

Ferris State University
Big Rapids, MI 49307
(616) 592-2860
Dean Davenport

Illinois-Chicago, University of
Chicago, IL 60680
(312) 996-2695
Tom Russo

Lake Superior State University
Sault Ste. Marie, MI 49783
(906) 635-2366
James Fallis

Miami University
Oxford, OH 45056
(513) 529-3108
R.C.Johnson

Michigan, University of
Ann Arbor, MI 48109
(313) 764-6227
Jack Weidenbach

Michigan State University
East Lansing, MI 48824
(517) 355-1623
George Perles

Ohio State University
Columbus, OH 43210
(614) 292-7572
James L. Jones

Western Michigan University
Kalamazoo, MI 49008
(616) 387-3120
Leland E. Byrd

Central Intercollegiate Athletic Association

303 Butler Farm Road
Suite 110
Hampton, VA 23666
(804) 865-0071
Fax (804) 865-8436
Comm: Leon King
Publicity: Wallace Dooley, Jr.

Colonial Athletic Association (I)

2550 Professional Road
Suite 16
Richmond, VA 23235
(804) 272-1616
Fax (804) 272-1688
Comm.: Tom Yeager
Publicity: Tripp Sheppard

American University
Washington, D.C. 20016
(202) 885-3000
Joseph O'Donnell

East Carolina University
Greenville, NC 27858
(919) 757-4501
David R. Hart, Jr.

George Mason University
Fairfax, VA 22030
(703) 323-3462
Jack E. Kvancz

James Madison University
Harrisonburg, VA 22807
(703) 568-6164
O. Dean Ehlers

North Carolina,
University of
Wilmington, NC 28403
(919) 395-3230
William J. Brooks

Richmond, University of
Richmond, VA 23173
(804) 289-8370
Charles S. Boone

U.S. Naval Academy
Annapolis, MD 21402
(301) 267-2429
Jack Lengyel

William & Mary, College of
Williamsburg, VA 23187
(804) 221-3330
John H. Randolph

East Coast Conference (I)

946 Farnsworth Avenue
Bordentown, NJ 08505
(609) 298-4009
Fax (609) 298-6023
Comm.: John B. Carpenter
Publicity: Marie Wozniak

Central Connecticut
State University
New Britian, CT 06050
(203) 827-7347
Judith A. Davidson

Delaware, University of
Newark, DE 19716
(302) 451-1818
Edgar N. Johnson

Drexel University
Philadelphia, PA 19104
(215) 590-8930
John Semanik

Hofstra University
Hempstead, NY 11550
(516) 560-6749
Jim Garvey

Maryland-Baltimore County,
University of
Baltimore, MD 21228
(301) 455-2207
Charles R. Brown

Rider College
Lawrenceville, NJ 08648
(609) 896-5054
Marty Devlin

Towson State University
Towson, MD 21204
(301) 830-2758
Bill Hunter

Eastern College Athletic Conference (I)

PO Box 3
Craigville Beach Road
Centerville, MA 02632
(508) 771-5060
Fax (508) 771-9481
Comm.:Clayton W. Chapman
Publicity: John W. Garner, Jr.

Eastern College Hockey Association (ECHA)

PO Box 3
Centerville, MA 02632
(508) 771-5060
Comm.: Clayton Chapman

Gateway Collegiate Athletic Conference (I, Football I-AA)

100 N. Broadway
Suite 1135
St. Louis, MO 63102
(314) 421-2268
Fax (314) 421-3505
Comm: Patricia Viverito
Publicity: Mike Kern

Bradley University
Peoria, IL 61625
(309) 677-2671
Ron Ferguson

Drake University
Des Moines, IA 50311
(515) 271-2889
Robert W. Ash

Eastern Illinois University
Charleston, IL 61920
(217) 581-2106
Michael Ryan

Illinois State University
Normal, IL 61761
(309) 438-3636
Ronald D. Wellman

Indiana State University
Terre Haute, IN 47809
(812) 237-4040
Brian Faison

Northern Iowa, University of
Cedar Falls, IA 50614
(319) 273-2470
Robert A. Bowlsby

Southern Illinois University
Edwardsville, IL 62026
(618) 692-2871
Cynthia Jones

Southwest Missouri State University
Springfield, MO 65804
(417) 836-5244
Bill Rowe, Jr.

Western Illinois University
Macomb, IL 61455
(309) 298-1106
Gil Peterson

Wichita State University
Wichita, KS 67208
(316) 689-3250
Tom Shupe

Great Midwest Conference (1)

35 East Wacker Drive
Suite 650
Chicago, IL 60601
(312) 553-0483
Fax (312) 553-0495
Comm: Michael L. Slive
Publicity: Tim Stephens

Members: U. Ala.-Birmingham, U. of Cincinnati, DePaul, Marquette, Memphis State U. & St. Louis U.

Gulf South Conference

4 Office Park Circle
Suite 218
Birmingham, AL 35223
(205) 870-9750
Fax (205) 870-9751
Comm: Sonny Moran
Publicity: Bryan Arnold

High Country Athletic Conference (I)

2317 Sherman Hill Road
Laramie, WY 82070
(307) 766-3282
Exec.Dir.: Margie McDonald

Hockey East Association (I)

PO Box 69
Orono, ME 04473
(207) 866-2244
Fax (207) 866-7524
Comm.:Stuart P. Haskell, Jr.
Publicity: Dr. Norinne H. Daly

Ivy League
120 Alexander Street
Princeton, NJ 08544
(609) 258-6426
Fax (609) 258-1690
Ex. Dir.: Jeffrey Orleans
Publicity: Chuck Yrigoyen 111

Brown University
Providence, RI 02912
(401) 863-2343
David T. Roach

Columbia University
New York, NY 10027
(212) 854-2537
Alvin R. Paul

Cornell University
Ithaca, NY 14850
(607) 255-7265
Laing E. Kennedy

Dartmouth College
Hanover, NH 03755
(603) 646-2465
Richard Jaeger

Harvard University
Cambridge, MA 02138
(617) 495-2204
Wm. J. Cleary, Jr.

Pennsylvania, University of
Philadelphia, PA 19104
(215) 898-6121
Paul R. Rubincam, Jr.

Princeton University
Princeton, NJ 08544
(609) 258-3535
Robert J. Myslik

Yale University
New Haven, CT 06520
(203) 432-1414
Harold E. Woodsum, Jr.

Metro Atlantic Athletic Conference (I)

1090 Amboy Avenue
Edison, NJ 08837
(908) 225-0202
Fax (908) 225-5332
Comm: Richard J. Ensor
Publicity Carolanne McAuliffe

Canisius College
Buffalo, NY 14208
(716) 888-2970
Daniel P. Starr

Fairfield University
Fairfield, CT 06430
(203) 254-4040
Harold Menninger

Iona College
New Rochelle, NY 10801
(914) 633-2311
Richard Petriccione

LaSalle University
Philadelphia, PA 19141
(215) 951-1516
Robert Mullen

Loyola College
Baltimore, MD 21210
(301) 323-1010
James Smith

Manhattan College
Riverdale, NY 10471
(212) 920-0230
Robert J. Byrnes

Niagara University
Niagara University, NY 14109
(716) 285-1212
Michael Jankowski

St. Peter's College
Jersey City, NJ 07306
(201) 915-9098
William Stein

Sienna College
Loudonville, NY 12211
(518) 783-2531
William J. Kirsch

Metropolitan Collegiate Athletic Conference (I)

Two Ravina Drive,
Suite 210
Atlanta, GA 30346
(404) 395-6444
Fax (404) 395-6423
Comm.: Ralph McFillen
Publicity: Jamie Kimbrough

Cincinnati, University of
Cincinnati, OH 45221
(513) 556-2330
Charles F. Taylor

Louisville, University of
Louisville, KY 40292
(502) 588-5732
William C. Olsen

Memphis State University
Memphis, TN 38152
(901) 678-2335
Charles Cavagnaro

**Southern Missippi,
University of**
Hattiesburg, MS 39406
(601) 266-5017
Bill McLellan

Tulane University
New Orleans, LA 70118
(504) 865-5502
Chester Gladchuk

**Virginia Polytechnic
Institute**
Blacksburg, VA 24061
(703) 231-6796
David T. Braine

Mid-American Conference (I, Football I-A)

Four Sea Gate, Suite 102
Toledo, OH 43604
(419) 249-7177
Fax (419) 249-7199
Comm.: Karl Benson

Ball State University
Muncie, IN 47306
(317) 285-8225
Don Purvis

**Bowling Green State
University**
Bowling Green, OH 43403
(419) 372-2401
Jack Gregory

Central Michigan University
Mount Pleasant, MI 48859
(517) 774-3046
David Keilitz

**Eastern Michigan
University**
Ypsilanti, MI 48197
(313) 487-1050
Eugene D. Smith

Kent State University
Kent, OH 44242
(216) 672-3120
Paul V. Amodio

Miami University
Oxford, OH 45056
(513) 529-3108
R.C.Johnson

Ohio University
Athens, OH 45701
(614) 593-1174
Harold N. McElhaney

Toledo University of
Toledo, OH 43606
(419) 537-4987
Allen R. Bohl

**Western Michigan
University**
Kalamazoo, MI 49008
(616) 387-3120
Leland Byrd

Mid-East Athletic Conference (I, Football I-AA)

PO Box 21205
Greensboro, NC 27420
(919) 275-9961
Fax (919) 275-9964
Comm.: Kenneth Free
Publicity: Larry Barber

**Bethune Cookman
College**
Daytona Beach, 32115
(904) 255-1401
Lloyd Johnson

Coppin State College
Baltimore, MD 21216
(301) 333-5488
Ronald K. DeSouza

Delaware State College
Dover, DE 19901
(302) 736-4928
John C. Martin

Florida A & M University
Tallahassee, FL 32307
(904) 599-3868
Walter Reed

Howard University
Washington, DC 20059
(202) 806-7140
William P. Moultrie

**Maryland-Eastern Shore,
University of**
Princess Anne, MD 21853
(301) 651-2200
Hallie E. Gregory

Morgan State University
Baltimore, MD 21239
(301) 444-3050
Leonard C. Braxton

North Carolina A & T
State University
Greensboro, NC 27411
(919) 334-7686
Willie James Burden

South Carolina State College
Orangeburg, SC 29117
(803) 536-7242
Willie E. Jeffries

Midwestern Collegiate
Conference (I)

201 South Capitol Avenue
Suite 500
Indianapolis, IN 46225
(317) 237-5622
Fax (317) 237-5620
Comm.: Daniel DiEdwardo
Publicity: Mike Hermann

Butler University
Indianapolis, IN 46208
(317) 283-9375
John C. Parry

Dayton, University of
Dayton, OH 45469
(513) 229-2111
Thomas J. Frericks

Detroit, University of
Detroit, MI 48221
(313) 927-1720
Brad Kinsman

Evansville, University of
Evansville, IN 47722
(812) 479-2238
James A. Byers

Loyola University
Chicago, IL 60611
(312) 508-2560
Charles T. Schwarz

Marquette University
Milwaukee, WI 53233
(414) 288-6303
William L. Cords

Notre Dame, University of
Notre Dame, IN 46556
9219) 239-6107
Richard A. Rosenthal
(all sports except Men's
Basketball & Football)

St. Louis University
St. Louis, MO 63108
(314) 658-3187
Deborah Yow

Xavier University
Cincinnati, OH 45207
(513) 745-3413
Jeffrey Fogelson

Missouri Valley Conference

100 N. Broadway
Suite 1135
St. Louis, MO 63102
(314) 421-0339
Fax (314) 421-3505
Comm.: J. Douglas Elgin
Publicity: Ron English

Bradley University
Peoria, IL 61625
(309) 677-2671
Ron Ferguson

Creighton University
Omaha, NE 68178
(402) 280-2720
Dick Myers

Drake University
Des Moines, IA 50311
(515) 271-2889
Robert W. Ash

Illinois State University
Normal, Il 61761
(309) 438-3636
Ronald D. Wellman

Indiana State University
Terre Haute, In 47809
(812) 237-4040
Brian Faison

Southern Illinois
University
Carbondale, IL 62901
(618) 453-7250
Jim Hart

Southwest Missouri State
University
Springfield, MO 65804
(417) 836-5244
Bill Rowe, Jr.

Tulsa, University of
Tulsa, OK 74104
(918) 631-2391
Rick Dickson

Wichita State University
Wichita, KS 67208
(316) 689-3250
Tom Shupe

New South Women's Athletic
Conference
C.S.V., Box 731
Atlanta, GA 30303
(404) 651-4402
Comm.: Sherman Day

North Atlantic Conference (I)

PO Box 69
Orono, ME 04473
(207) 866-2383
Fax (207)866-7524
Comm.: Stuart P. Haskell, Jr.
Media: Len Harlow
          Brook Merrow

Boston University
Boston, MA 02215
(617) 353-4630
Gary Strickler

Delaware, University of
Newark, DE 19716
(302) 451-1818
Edgar N. Johnson

Drexel University
Philadelphia, PA 19104
(215) 590-8930
John Semanik

Hartford, University of
West Hartford, CT 06117
(203) 243-4989
C. Donald Cook

Maine, University of
Orono, ME 04469
(207) 581-1057
Kevin White

New Hampshire, University of
Durham, NH 03824
(603) 862-1850
Gilbert Chapman

Northeastern University
Boston, MA 02115
(617) 437-2672
Irwin Cohen

Vermont, University of
Burlingtonb, VT 05405
(802) 656-3074
Denis E. Lambert

Northeast Conference (I)

900 Route 9. Suite 120
Woodbridge, NJ 07095
(201) 636-9119
Fax (201) 636-6496
Comm: Chris Monasch
Publicity: Ray Cella

Fairleigh Dickinson
University
Teaneck, NJ 07666
(201) 692-3980
Roy Danforth

Long Island University
Brooklyn Center
Brooklyn, NY 11201
9718) 403-1030
Paul Lizzo

Marist College
Poughkeepsie, NY 1260a
(914) 575-3699
Eugene Doris

Monmouth College
West Long Branch, NJ 07764
(201) 571-4295
Wayne Szoke

Mount St. Mary's College
Emmitsburg, MD 21717
(301) 447-5296
J. Thomas Balistree

Robert Morris College
Coraopolis, PA 15108
(412) 262-8302
Robert McBee

St. Francis College
Brooklyn, NY 11201
(718) 522-2300
Carlo Tramontozzi

St. Francis College
Loretto, PA 15940
(814) 472-3276
Frank Pergolizzi

Wagner College
Staten Island, NY 10301
(718) 390-3433
Walt Hameline

North Star Conference (I)

310 S. Peoria Street, Suite 210
Chicago, IL 60607
(312) 733-0214
Fax (312) 733-0216
Comm.: Arnold D. Fielkow

Akron, University of
Akron, OH 44325
(216) 972-7080
Jim Dennison

Cleveland State University
Cleveland, OH 44115
(216) 687-4808
John Konstantinos

DePaul University
Chicago, IL 60604
(312) 362-8413
Bill Bradshaw

**Illinois-Chicago,
University of**
Chicago, IL 60680
(312) 996-2695
Thomas Russo

Northern-Illinois University
DeKalb, IL 60115
(815) 753-0888
Gerald O'Dell

Valparaiso University
Valparaiso, IN 46383
(219) 464-5230
Wm. L. Steinbrecher

**Wisconsin-Green Bay,
University of**
Green Bay, WI 54311
(414) 465-2145
Daniel Spielmann

Wright State University
Dayton, Oh 45435
(513) 873-2771
Michael J. Cusack

Ohio Valley Conference (I, Football I-AA)

278 Franklin Road
Suite 103
Brentwood, TN 37027
(615) 371-1698
Fax (615) 371-1788
Comm.: Dan Beebe

**Austin Peay State
University**
Clarksville, TN 37044
(615) 648-7903
Tim Weiser

**Eastern Kentucky
University**
Richmond, KY 40475
(606) 622-3654
Donald G. Combs

**Middle Tennessee State
University**
Murfreesboro, TN 37132
(615) 898-2450
John E. Stanford

Morehead State University
Morehead, KY 40351
(606) 783-2386
Steve Hamilton

Murray State Universitty
Murray, KY 42071
(502) 762-6184
Michael D. Strickland

Tennessee State University
Nashville, TN 37209
(615) 320-3598
William Thomas

**Tennessee Technological
University**
Cookeville, TN 38505
(615) 372-3949
David Larimore

Pacific 10 Conference
(I, Football I-A)

800 South Broadway
Suite 400
Walnut Creek, CA 94596
(510) 932-4411
Fax (510) 932-4601
Comm: Thomas C. Hansen

Arizona, University of
Tucson, AZ 85721
(602) 621-2200
Cedric Dempsey

Arizona State University
Tempe, AZ 85287
(602) 965-3482
Charles S. Harris

California, University of
Berkeley, CA 94720
(415) 642-5316
Robert Driscoll

**California-Los Angeles,
University of (UCLA)**
Los Angeles, CA 90024
(213) 825-8699
Peter T. Dalis

Oregon, University of
Eugene, OR 97403
(503) 346-5464
Bill Byrne

Oregon State University
Corvallis, OR 97331
(503) 737-2547
Dutch Baughman

**Southern California,
University of (USC)**
Los Angeles, CA 90089
(213) 743-2221
Michael McGee

Stanford University
Stanford, CA 94305
(415) 723-1413
Alan Cummings

Washington, University of
Seattle, WA 98195
(206) 543-2212
Milo Lude

Washington State Univ.
Pullman, WA 99164
(509) 335-0200
Jim Livengood

Patriot League
(I, Football I-AA)

3897 Adler Place
Bldg. C, Suite 310
Bethlehem, PA 18017
(215) 691-2414
Fax (215) 691-8414
Exec. Dir: Carl F. Ullrich

Bucknell University
Lewisburg, PA 17837
(717) 524-3301
Rick Hartzell

Colgate University
Hamilton, NY 13346
(315) 824-1000
Fred Dunlap

Fordham University
Bronx, NY 10458
(212) 579-2447
Francis X. McLaughlin

Holy Cross College
Worcester, MA 01610
(508) 793-2582
Ronald S. Perry

Lafayette College
Easton, PA 18042
(215) 250-5470
Eve Atkinson

Lehigh University
Bethlehem, PA 18015
(215) 758-4320
Joseph D. Sterrett

U.S. Military Academy
West Point, NY 10996
(914) 938-3701
Al Vanderbush

Southeastern Conference
(I, Football I-A)

2201 Civic Center Blvd.
Birmingham, AL 35203
(205) 458-3000
Fax (205) 458-3032
Comm: Roy Kramer
Publicity: Mark Whitworth

Alabama, University of
Tuscaloosa, AL 35487
(205) 348-3697
Cecil Ingram

Arkansas, University of
Fayetteville, AR 72467
(501) 575-3753
J. Frank Broyles

Auburn University
Auburn, AL 36849
(205) 844-4750
Pat Dye

Florida, University of
Gainesville, Fl 32604
(904) 375-4683
William Arnsparger

Georgia, University of
Athens, GA 30613
(404) 542-1307
Vincent J. Dooley

Kentucky, University of
Lexington, KY 40506
(606) 257-8000
C.M. Newton

Louisiana State University
Baton Rouge, LA 70803
(504) 388-3600
Joe Dean

Mississippi, University of
University, MS 38677
(601) 232-7241
Warner Alford

Mississippi State University
Mississippi State, MS 39762
(601) 325-2532
Larry Templeton

South Carolina, Univ. of
Columbia, SC 29208
(803) 777-4202
King Dixon

Tennessee, University of
Knoxville, TN 37996
(615) 974-1224
Douglas A. Dickey

Vanderbilt University
Nashville, TN 37212
(615) 322-4831
Paul Hoolahan

Southern Conference
(I, Football I-AA)

One West Pack Square
Suite 1508
Asheville, NC 28801
(704) 255-7872
Fax (704) 251-5006
Comm: Wright Waters
Publicity: Geoff Cabe

Appalachian State University
Boone, NC 28608
(704) 262-4010
(704) 262-4010
Roachel Laney

The Citadel
Charleston, SC 29409
(803) 792-5030
Walt Nadzak

East Tennessee
State University
Johnson City, TN 37614
(615) 929-4343
Janice Shelton

Furman University
Greenville, SC 29613
(803) 294-2150
W. Ray Parlier

Marshall University
Huntington, WV 25715
(304) 696-5408
William Lee Moon, Sr.

Tennessee-Chattanooga,
University of
Chattanooga, TN 37403
(615) 755-4495
Edward Farrell

**Virginia Military
Institute**
Lexington, VA 24450
(703) 464-7251
Eric Hyman

**Western Carolina
University**
Cullowhee, NC 28723
(704) 227-7338
Bobby N. Setzer

Southland Conference
(I, Football I-AA)

1309 W. 15th Street
Suite 303
Plano, TX 75075
(214) 424-4833
Fax (214) 424-4099
Comm: Bill Belknap
Publicity: Pam Rapkin

McNeese State University
Lake Charles, LA 70609
(318) 475-5215
Robert G. Hayes

North Texas, University of
Denton, TX 76203
(817) 565-2451
Corky Nelson

**Northeast Louisiana
University**
Monroe, LA 71209
(318) 342-5361
Benny Hollis

**Northwestern State
University**
Natchitoches, LA 71497
(318) 357-5251
Tynes Hildebrand

**Sam Houston State
University**
Huntsville, TX 77341
(409) 294-1160
Robert Case

**Southwest Texas
State University**
San Marcos, TX 78666
(512) 245-2114
Billy M. Miller

**Stephen F. Austin
State University**
Nacogdoches, TX 75962
(409) 568-3501
Steve McCarty

Texas, University of
Arlington, TX 76019
(817) 273-2261
William C. Bill

Southwest Athletic
Conference (I)

1300 West Mockingbird
Suite 444
Dallas, TX 75247
(214) 634-7353
Fax (214) 638-5482
Comm.: Fred Jacoby
Publicity: Bo Carter

Baylor University
Waco, TX 76798
(817) 754-4648
Bill Menefee

Houston, University of
Houston, TX 77204
(713) 749-3772
Rudy Davalos

Rice University
Houston, TX 77251
(713) 527-9851
John May

Southern Methodist University
Dallas, TX 75275
(214) 692-4301
Forrest Gregg

Texas, University of
Austin, TX 78712
(512) 471-5757
DeLoss Dodds

Texas A & M University
College Station, TX 77843
(409) 845-2227
John David Crow

Texas Christian University
Fort Worth, TX 76129
(817) 921-7965
Frank Windegger

Texas Tech University
Lubbock, TX 79409
(806) 742-3355
Robert L. Bockrath

Southwestern Athletic Conference (I, Football I-AA)

1500 Sugar Bowl Drive
New Orleans, LA 70112
(504) 523-7574
Fax (504) 523-7513
Commn.: James Frank
Publicity: Lonza Hardy, Jr.

Alabama State University
Montgomery, AL 36101
(205) 293-4440
Houston Markham, Jr.

Alcorn State University
Lorman, MS 39096
(601) 877-3762
James A. Brooks

Grambling State University
Grambling, LA 71245
(318) 274-2481
Fred C. Hobdy

Jackson State University
Jackson, MS 39217
(601) 968-2291
Howard Davis

Mississippi Valley State University
Itta Bena, MS 38941
(601) 254-6641
Charles Prophet

Prairie View A & M
Prairie View, TX 77446
(409) 857-2224
George H. Stafford

Southern University
Baton Rouge, LA 70813
(504) 771-3170
Marino H. Casem

**Texas Southern
University**
Houston, TX 77004
(713) 527-7271
Wilbert C. Williams

Sun Belt Conference (I)

One Galleria Blvd.
Suite 2115
Metairie, LA 70001
(504) 834-6600
Fax (504) 834-6806
Comm: Craig Thompson
Publicity: Tracey Judd

**Alabama-Birmingham,
University of**
Birmingham, Al 35294
(205) 934-3402
B. Gene Bartow

Jacksonville University
Jacksonvile, FL 32211
(904) 744-3950
Donald O. Jacobs

**North Carolina-Charlotte,
University of**
Charlotte, NC 28223
(704) 547-4920
Judy Rose

Old Dominion University
Norfolk, Va 23529
(804) 683-3369
James Jarrett

**South Alabama,
University of**
Mobile, AL 36688
(205) 460-7121
Joe Gottfried

South Florida, University of
Tampa, FL 33620
(813) 974-2125
Paul Griffin

Virginia Commonwealth
University
Richmond, VA 23284
(804) 367-1280
Richard L. Sander

**Western Kentucky
University**
Bowling Green, OH 42101
(502) 745-3542
Jimmy Feix

Trans America Athletic Conference (I)

The Commons
3370 Vineville Avenue
Suite 108-B
Macon, GA 31204
(912) 474-3394
Fax (912) 474-4272
Comm: Bill Bibb
Publicity: Jed Gumbart

Campbell University
Buies Creek, NC 27506
(919) 893-4111
Tom Collins

Central Florida, U. of
Orlando, FL 32816
(407) 823-2342
Gene McDowell

Centenary College
Shreveport, LA 71134
(318) 869-5275
Walt Stevens, Jr.

College of Charleston
Charleston, SC 29424
(803) 792-5556
Andrew L. Abrams

Florida International
University
Miami, FL 33199
(305) 348-2761
Richard Young

Georgia State University
Atlanta, GA 30303
(404) 651-2772
Orby Moss, Jr.

Mercer University
Macon, GA 311207
(912) 752-2994
Bobby Pope

Samford University
Birmingham, AL 35229
(205) 870-2966
Stephen C. Allgood

Stetson University
DeLand, FL 32720
(904) 822-8100
Robert J. Jacoby

Southeastern Louisiana U.
Hammond, LA 70402
(504) 549-2253

U.S. Intercollegiate Lacrosse Association

Cornell Athletics
Ithaca, NY 14850
(607) 255-7332
Pres: Richie Moran
Publicity: Doyle Smith
(804) 982-5500
Fax (804) 982-5525

West Coast Conference (I)

400 Oyster Point Blvd.
Suite 221
South San Francisco, CA 94080
(415) 873-8622
Comm: Michael M. Gilleran
Publicity: Don Ott

Gonzaga University
Spokane, WA 99258
(509) 328-4220
Dan Fitzgerald

Loyola Marymount
University
Los Angeles, CA 90045
(213) 338-2765
Brian Quinn

Pepperdine University
Malibu, CA 90263
(213) 456-4242
Wayne Wright

Portland, University of
Portland, OR 97203
(503) 283-7117
Joseph A. Etzel

St. Mary's College
Moraga, CA 94575
(415) 631-4383
Richard Mazzuto

San Diego, University of
San Diego, CA 92110
(619) 260-4803
Thomas Iannacone

San Francisco, University of
San Francisco, CA 94117
(415) 666-6891
Rev. Robert A. Sunderland

Santa Clara University
Santa Clara, CA 95053
(408) 554-5344
Thomas J. O'Connor

Western Athletic Conference (I, Football I-A)

14 W. Dry Creek Circle
Littleton, CO 80120
(303) 795-1962
Fax (303) 795-1960
Comm: Karl Benson
PR: Jeff Hurd

Brigham Young University
Provo, UT 84602
(801) 378-6164
Glen C. Tuckett

Colorado State University
Fort Collins, CO 80523
(303) 491-5300
L. Oval Jaynes

Hawaii, University of
Honolulu, HI 96822
(808) 956-7301
Stan Sheriff

New Mexico, University of
Albuquerque, NM 87131
(505) 277-6375
Gary Ness

San Diego State University
San Diego, CA 92182
(619) 594-5162
Dr. Fred Miller

Texas-El Paso, University of
El Paso, TX 79968
(915) 747-5347
Brad Hovious

U.S. Air Force Academy
USAF Academy, CO 80840
(719) 472-4008
Col. John J. Clune

Utah, University of
Salt Lake City, UT 84112
(801) 581-5605
Christopher Hill

Wyoming, University of
Laramie, WY 82071
(307) 766-2292
Paul Roach

Western Collegiate Hockey Association (WCHA)

PO Box 14599
Madison, WI 53714
(608) 251-4003
Fax (608) 283-6412
Comm: Bruce McLeod

Colorado College
Colorado Springs, CO 80903
(719) 389-6493
Max Taylor, Jr.

Denver, University of
Denver, CO 80208
(303) 871-3399
TBA

Michigan Technological University
Houghton, MI 49931
(906) 487-2715
J. Ricnard Yeo

**Minnesota-Duluth,
University of**
Duluth, MN 55812
(218) 726-8168
Bruce McLeod

Minnesota, University of
Minneapolis, MN 55455
(612) 625-9579
Richard M. Bay

**North Dakota,
University of**
Grand Forks, ND 58202
(701) 777-2234
John Gasparini

**Northern Michigan
University**
Marquette, MI 49855
(999906) 227-1211
Richard Comley

**St. Cloud State
University**
St. Cloud, MN 56301
(612) 255-3102
Morris Kurtz

Wisconsin, University of
Madison, WI 53706
(608) 262-5068
Pat Richter

Western Intercollegiate Volleyball Association

University of California
16 Blake Court
Irvine, CA 92715
(714) 856-5366
Fax (714) 856-8441
Comm.: Robert Newcomb

Western Football Conference

5825 Brookline Place
San Luis Obispo, CA 93401
(805) 543-9104
Fax (805) 756-7273
Comm: Vic Buccola

Western Water Polo Association (I)

580 Brambles Way
Orange, CA 92669
(714) 639-9106
Comm.: John Montrella

Yankee Conference (I, Football I-AA)

University of Richmond
PO Box 8
Richmond, VA 23173
(804) 289-8371
Fax (804) 289-8371
Comm: Charles S. Boone
James Madison University and William & Mary are new members.

Boston University
Boston, MA 02215
(617) 353-4630
Gary Strickler

Connecticut, University of
Storrs, CT 06269
(203) 486-3863
Lewis Perkins

Delaware, University of
Newark, DE 19716
(302) 451-1818
Edgar N. Johnson

Maine, University of
Orono, ME 04469
(207) 581-1057
Kevin White

**Massachusetts,
University of**
Amherst, MA 01003
(413) 545-2460
Frank P. McInerney

**New Hampshire,
University of**
Durham, NH 03824
(603) 862-1850
Gilbert Chapman

Rhode Island, University of
Kingston, RI 02881
(401) 792-5245
McKinley Boston, Jr.

Richmond, University of
Richmond, VA 23173
(804) 289-8370
Charles S. Boone

Villanova University
Villanova, PA 19085
(215) 645-4111
Ted Aceto

Corresponding Members

Catholic University
Ponce, Puerto Rico 00731
(809) 844-4150
Rosario Lopez Cepero

Puerto Rico, University of
Box 23311
University Station
Rio Piedras, P. R. 00931
(809) 751-5590
Dr. Rafael Ojeda

Major Independents

Listed in this section are the major independent colleges & universities from the NCAA. Even though they may play in a conference, these institutions will usually be an independent in one of the major revenue sports.

**Alaska-Anchorage,
University of**
Anchorage, AK 99508
(907) 786-1230
Ronald J. Petro

**Alaska-Fairbanks,
University of**
Fairbanks, AK 99775
(907) 474-7205
G. Lynn Lashbrook

Chicago State University
Chicago, IL 60628
(312) 995-2295
Al Avant

Davidson College
Davidson, NC 28036
(704) 892-2000
Terry Holland

DePaul University
Chicago, IL 60614
(312) 341-8413
Bill Bradshaw

De Pauw University
Greencastle, IN 46135
(317) 658-4834
Ted Katula

**Florida Atlantic
University**
Boca Raton, FL 33431
(407) 367-3710
Jack Mehl

Kentucky State University
Frankfort, KY 40601
(502) 227-6011
TBA

Liberty University
Lynchburg, VA 24502
(804) 582-2100
Chuck Burch

**Memphis State
University**
Memphis, TN 38152
(901) 678-2331
Charles Cavagnaro

**Missouri-Kansas City,
University of**
Kansas City, MO 64110
(816) 276-1036
Lee Hunt

**Northeastern Illinois
University**
Chicago, IL 60625
(312) 583-4050
Dr. Dennis Keihn

**Northern Illinois
University**
DeKalb, IL 60115
(815) 753-1295
Gerald O/Dell

Notre Dame University
Notre Dame, IN 46556
(219) 239-6107
Richard A. Rosenthal

Portland State University
Portland, OR 97207
(503) 725-4000
Roy Love

**San Francisco State
University**
San Francisco, CA 94132
(415) 338-2218
William Partlow

Seattle Pacific University
Seattle, WA 98119
(206) 281-2085
Keith R. Phillips

**Southeastern Louisiana
University**
Hammond, LA 70402
(504) 549-2253
Al LeBlanc

Southern Utah State College
Cedar City, UT 84720
(801) 586-1937
Jack Bishop

Texas, University of
San Antonio, TX 78285
(512) 691-4161
Bobby Thompson

**U.S. International
University**
San Diego, CA 92131
(619) 693-4732
Al J. Palmiotto

Wright State University
Dayton, OH 45435x
(513) 873-2771
Michael J. Cusack

**Youngstown State
University**
Youngstown, OH 44555
(216) 742-3478
Joseph F. Malmisur

NCAA Conferences

**Atlantic Football
Conference (III)**
15 Tulipwood Drive
Commack, NY 11725
(516) 543-0730
Comm.: Stan Gural

**Big Central Soccer
Conference**
S.I.U.
Box 1129
Edwardsville, IL 62026
(618) 692-2869
Comm.: Cindy Jones

**California Collegiate
Athletic Association (II)**
'40 Via Di Roma Walk
Long Beach,l CA 90803
(213) 985-4051
Comm.: Tom D. Morgan

**Centennial Football
Conference (III)**
Dickinson College
Carlisle, PA 17013
(717) 245-1507
Pres: Carmen Neuberger

**Central Intercollegiate
Athletic Association (II)**
PO Box 7349
303 Butter Farm Rd., Ste. 110
Hampton, VA 23666
(804) 865-0071
Comm.: Leon Kerry

**City University of New York
Athletic Conference (III)**
University of the South
Juhan Gymnasium
Sewanee, TN 37375
(615) 598-1388
Comm.: Bill Huyck

**College Conference of
Illinois and Wisconsin (III)**
Wheaton College
Wheaton, IL 60187
(708) 260-5167
Comm.: Jack Swartz

**Colorado Athletic
Conference**
1364 Nissen Place
Broomfield, CO 80020
(303) 460-7713
Comm.: Irv Brown

**Commonwealth Coast
Conference (III)**
Wentworth Institute of Tech.
Boston, MA 02115
(617) 442-9010
Comm.: Francis Nestor

**Continental Divide
Conference (II)**
University of Alaska
105 Patty Center
Fairbanks, AK 99775
(907) 474-7205
G. Lynn Lashbrook

**Dixie Intercollegiate
Athletic Conference (III)**
3400 Wesleyan Blvd.
Rocky Mount, NC 27804
(919) 977-7171
Pres: C. Michael Fox

**Eastern Intercollegiate
Baseball League/Wrestling
Association (I)**
PO Box 3
Centerville, MA 02632
(508) 771-5060
Comm.: Clayton Chapman

**Eastern State Athletic
Conference (III)**
1101 Camden Avenue
Salisbury, MD 21801
(301) 543-6340
Pres: William E. Lide

**Eastern Water Polo
Association (I)**
Water Polo Coach
U.S. Naval Academy
Annapolis, MD 21402
(301) 267-3958
Pres: Mike Schofield

**Eastern Wrestling
League (I)**
Asst. Dir. of Athletics
Penn. State University
University Park, PA 16802
(814) 863-0420
Pres: Richard J. Lucas

**Golden State Athletic
Conference**
3900 Lomaland Drive
San Diego, CA 92106
(619) 221-2266
Pres: Carroll Land

**Great Lake Intercollegiate
Athletic Conference (II)**
5015 Tressa Drive
Lansing, MI 48910
(517) 394-5015
Comm.: Vern L. Norris

**Great Lakes Valley
Conference (II)**
Box 1012, College Station
Rensselaer, IN 47978
(219) 866-5217
Comm.: Richard F. Scharf

**Great Northwest
Conference (II)**
PO Box 2002
Billings, MT 59103
(406) 656-4369
Comm.: Elwood B. Hahn

**Great West Intercollegiate
Hockey Conference (II)**
Northern Arizona University
Flagstaff, AZ 86011
(602) 523-03031
Comm.: Lawrence D. Garrett

Gulf South Conference (II)
4 Office Park Circle,
Suite 218
Birmingham, Al 35223
(205) 870-9750
Comm.: "Sonny" Moran, Jr.

**Heartland Collegiate
Conference (II)**
3600 W. Petty Road
Muncie, IN 47304
(317) 282-9446
Comm.: John "Jim" Hinga

**Independent College
Athletic Conference (III)**
McLane Center, Alfred University
Alfred, NY 14802
(607) 871-2193
Pres: Gene Castrovillo

**Iowa Intercollegiate
Athletic Conference (III)**
608 33rd Street
West Des Moines, IA 50265
(515) 225-3021
Comm.: John Van Why

**Liberty Football
Conference (III)**
St. John's University
Grand Central & Utopia Pkwys.
Jamaica, NY 11439
(718) 990-6224
Pres: John Kaiser

Little East Conference III
Southeaster Mass. Univ.
Old Westport Road
North Dartmouth, MA 02747
(508) 999-8722
Comm.: Robert A. Dowd

Lone Star Conference (II)
Texas A & I University
Kingsville, TX 78363
(512) 595-2677
Pres: Pence Dacus

**Massachusetts State College
Athletic Conference (III)**
Salem State College
352 Lafayette St.
Salem, MA 01970
(508) 741-6570
Comm.: John Galaris

**Michigan Intercollegiate
Athletic Association (III)**
PO Box 63
Spring Lake, MI 49456
(616) 842-7865
Comm.: Albert L. Deal

**Mideast Collegiate
Conference (II)**
Pace University
861 Bedford Road
Pleasantville, NY 10570
(914) 773-3411
Pres: Chris Bledsoe

**Middle Atlantic States
Collegiate Athletic**
Conference (III)
Schwartz Center,
Widener University
Chester, PA 19013
(215) 499-4525
Comm.: Nathan N. Salant

**Midwest Athletic
Conference for Women (III)**
Beloit College
Beloit, WI 53511
(608) 365-2681

**Midwest Collegiate
Athletic Conference (III)**
Lake Forest College
Lake Forest, IL 60045
(708) 234-3100
Comm.: Ralph L. Shively

**Midwest Intercollegiate
Football Conference (II)**
3752 E. 71st St., Suite D
Indianapolis, IN 46220
(317) 842-4680
Comm.: William Sylvester

**Minnesota Intercollegiate
Athletic Conference (III)**
405 Laurie Lane
Stillwater, MN 55082
(612) 439-7768
Coordinator: Wm. D. Herzog

**Missouri Intercollegiate
Athletic Association (II)**
PO Box 508
Maryville, MO 64468
(816) 582-5655
Comm.: Ken B. Jones

**New England College Conference
Wrestling Association (III)**
Wesleyan University
Middletown, CT 06457
(203) 344-7907
Exec. Dir: John Biddiscombe

**New England Collegiate
Conference (II)**
Keene State College
229 Main Street
Keene, NH 03431
(603) 358-2813
Comm.: Joanne Fortunato

**New England Football
Conference (III)**
Framingham State College
100 State Street
Framingham, MA 01701
(508) 626-4614
Pres: Lawrence P. Boyd

**New England University
Wrestling Association (I)**
University of New Hampshire
Durham, NH 03824
(603) 862-3424
Pres: Jim Urquhart

New England Women's 8 (III)
Smith College
Ainsworth Gymnasium
Northampton, MA 01063
(413) 585-2701
Pres: Linda C. Hackett

**New Jersey Athletic
Conference (III)**
Montclair State College
Upper Montclair, NJ 07043
(201) 893-5234
Pres: Greg Lockard

**New York Collegiate
Athletic Conference (II)**
65-30 Kissena Blvd.
Flushing, NY 11367
(718) 520-7215
Pres: Richard Wettan

**New York State
Women's Collegiate
Athletic Association (III)**
Cortland State University
Box 2000
Cortland, NY 13045
(607) 753-4930
Pres: Delores Bogard

**North Central Intercollegiate
Athletic Conference (II)**
Ramkota Inn
2400 N. Louise
Sioux Falls, SD 57107
(605) 338-0907
Comm.: Noel W. Olson

**North Coast Athletic
Conference (III)**
PO Box 16679
Cleveland, OH 44116
(216) 871-8100
Exec.Dir.: Dennis M. Collins

Northeast-10 Conference (II)
AIC
1000 State Street
Springfield, MA 01109
(413) 737-7000
Comm.: Robert E. Burke

**Northern California
Athletic Conference (II)**
2551 Garfield Avenue
Carmichaell, CA 95608
(916) 488-4243
Comm.: James P. Jorgensen

**Northern Collegiate
Hockey Conference (III)**
University of Wisconsin
1800 Grand Superior, WI 54880
(715) 394-8371
Pres: Steve BEcker

**Northwest Conference of
Independent Colleges**
PO Box 328
Gig Harbor, WA 98335
(206) 858-9404
Publicity: Jack Sareault

**Ohio Athletic
Conference (III)**
Four Sea Gate, Suite 102
Toledo, OH 43604
Comm.: Jamie McCloskey

**Old Dominion Athletic
Conference (III)**
PO Box 971
Salem, VA 24153
(703) 389-7373
Comm.: Daniel E. Woolridge

**Pennsylvania State
Athletic Conference (II)**
Lock Haven University
105 Zimmerli Bldg.
Lock Haven, PA 17745
(717) 893-1572
Pres: Rodney C. Kelchner

**President's Athletic
Conference (III)**
Bethany College
Old Main, Room 110
Bethany, WV 26032
(304) 829-7111
Pres: Diane Cummins

**Rocky Mountain Athletic
Conference (II)**
2940 E. Bates Avenue
Denver, CO 80210
(303) 753-0600
Comm.: Wanda Brechler

**St. Louis Intercollegiate
Athletic Conference (III)**
843 Greenlantern Lane
St. Louis, MO 63011
(800) 633-0419
Comm.: Walter Schoenke

Skyline Conference (III)
SUNY-Stony Brook
Stony Brook, NY 11794
(516) 632-7196
Pres: Paul Dudzick

**South Atlantic Field
Hockey/Lacrosse Conference (I)**
American University Sports Ctr.
Washington, D.C. 20016
(202) 885-3024
Pres: Barbara J. Reimann

**Southern California
Intercollegiate Athletic
Conference (III)**
Whittier College
13046 E. Philadelphia
Whittier, CA 90608
(231) 693-0771
Pres: Joseph Price

**Southern Intercollegiate
Athletic Conference (II)**
Box 4186
Ft. Valley State College
Fort Valley, GA 31030
(912) 825-6281
Comm.: J.E.Hawkins

**State University of
New York Athletic**
Conference (III)
Fredonia State University
Fredonia, NY 14063
(716) 673-3105
Comm.: Patrick R. Damore

**Suburban Intercollegiate
Soccer League (II)**
125 Purchase Street
Purchase, NY 10577
(914) 694-2200
Pres: John Cassidy

Sunshine State Conference
500 Ocean Trail Way
Suite 306
Jupiter, FL 33477
(407) 575-7702
Comm.: Bob Vanatta

**University Athletic
Association (III)**
668 Mt. Hope Avenue
Rochester, NY 14620
(716) 275-3814
Pres: G. Dennis O'Brien

**Western Football
Conference (II)**
651 Patricia Avenue
San Luis Obispo, CA 93405
(805) 756-1412

**Wisconsin State University
Conference (III)**
PO Box 8010
Madison, WI 53708
(608) 263-4402
Comm.: Max R. Sparger

**Wisconsin Women's
Intercollegiate Athletic**
Conferee (III)
1930 Monroe Street
Madison, WI 53711
(608) 263-4407
Comm.: Judy Kruckman

**Women's Intercollegiate
Athletic Conference (III)**
Centre College
Danville, KY 40422
(606) 236-6081
Pres.: Kitty R. Baird

Affiliated Members

**American Baseball Coaches
Association**
PO Box 3545
Omaha, NE 68103
(402) 733-0374
Exec.Dir.: Jerry Miles

**American Foobtall Coaches
Association**
7758 Wallace Rd., Suite 1
Orlando, FL 32819
(407) 351-6113
Ex. Dir.: Charles McClendon

American Hockey Coaches Association
Boston University
285 Babcock Street
Boston, MA 02115
(617) 353-4639
Pres: Jack Parker

American Volleyball Coaches Association
122 Second Ave., Suite 201
San Mateo, CA 94401
(415) 375-8113
Exec.Dir.:Sandra Vivas

American Water Polo Coaches Association
324 Esther Street
Costa Mesa, CA 92607
(714) 642-7083
Pres: Ed Newland

Black Coaches Association
PO Box J
Des Moines, IA 50311
(515) 271-3994
Ex.Dir.: Rudy Washington

College Athletic Business Management Association
University of Minnesota
516 15th Ave. S.E.
Minneapolis, MN 55455
(612) 624-3354
Pres: Kenneth Buell

College Division Commissioner's Association
2551 Garfield Avenue
Carmichael, CA 95608
(916) 488-4243
Sec.: James Jorgenson

College Field Hockey Coaches Association
Ohio State University
411 Woody Hayes Drive
Columbus, OH 43210
(614) 292-5952
Pres: Karen Weaver

College Football Association
6688 Gunpack Drive,
Ste. 201
Boulder, CO 80301
(303) 530-5566
Exec.Dir.: Charles Neinas

College Sports Information Directors of America
Vanderbilt University
Nashville, TN 37212
(615) 322-2888
Pres: June Stewart

College Swimming Coaches Association of America, Inc.
901 West N.Y. Street
Indianapolis, IN 46202
(317) 274-3376
Exec.Dir: Dale Neuburger

Collegiate Commissioners Association
14 West Dry Creek Circle
Littleton, CO 80120
(303) 795-1962
Pres: Joseph L. Kearney

Collegiate Independents Football Officiating Association
Temple University
Philadelphia, PA 19122
(215) 787-7449
Pres: Charles Theokas

Division I-A Directors Association
PO Box 16428
Cleveland, OH 44116
(216) 892-4000
Adm.: Michael Cleary

Football Writers Association of America
Box 1022
Edmond, OK 73083
(405) 341-4731
Exec.Dir: Volney Meece

**Golf Coaches Association
of America**
PO Box 215
Raymore, MO 64083
(816) 322-3180
Exec.Dir: Jim Hames

**Intercollegiate Soccer
Association of America**
417 South 14th Street
Quincy, IL 62301
(217) 223-9408
Exec.Dir: Frank Longo

**Intercollegiate Tennis
Coaches Association**
Princeton University
PO Box 71
Princeton, NJ 08544
(609) 258-6332
Exec.Dir: David A. Benjamin

**Intercollegiate Women's
Lacrosse Coaches Assoc.**
Bates College
Lewiston, ME 04240
(207) 786-6341
Sec.: Suzanne Coffey

**Midwestern Independent
Collegiate Officials
Association**
5001 Brentwood Stair Road
Suite 100
Fort Worth, TX 76112
(817) 457-2262
Pres: Tommy Taylor

**National Association of
Academic Advisors for Athletics**
University of Virginia
PO Box 3785
Charlottesville, VA 22903
(804)982-5300
Pres: Richard McGuire

**National Association of
Basketball Coaches**
12 Pine Orchard Road
PO Box 307
Branford, CT 06405
(203) 488-1232
Exec.Dir: Joseph R. Vancisin

**National Association of
Collegiate Directors of
Athletics**
PO Box 16428
Cleveland, OH 44116
(206) 892-4000
Exec. Dir: Michael J. Cleary

**National Association of
Collegiate Gymnastics
Coaches (Men)**
US Air Force Academy
Colorado Springs, CO 80840
(719) 472-2281
Pres: Lou Burkel

**National Association of
Collegiate Gymnastics
Coaches (Women)**
University of Kentuckky
Lexington, KY 40506-0019
(606) 257-6483
Pres: Leah Little

**National Association of
Division I Independents**
Rutgers University
College Ave., PO Box 5061
New Brunswick, NJ 08903
Pres: Fred Gruninger

**National Athletic Steering
Committee**
Florida A & M University
Box 982
Tallahassee, FL 32307
(904) 599-3868
Pres: Walter Reed

**National Athletic Trainers
Association**
2952 Stemmons Hwy.
Suite 200
Dallas. TX 75247
(214) 637-6282
Exec.Dir: Alan A. Smith, Jr.

**National Soccer Coaches
Association of America**
RD #5, Box 5074
Stroudsburg, PA 18360
(717) 421-8720
Exec.Dir: John McKeon

**National Softball Coaches
Association**
PO Box 321
Louisville, CO 80027
(303) 666-0686
Exec.Dir: Kim Vance

**National Wrestling
Coaches Association**
Bloomsburg University of
University of Pennsylvania
Bloomsburg, PA 17815

**NCAA Division Track
& Field Coaches Association**
3031 Dutton Street
Waco, TX 76711
(817) 754-4648
Pres: Clyde Hart

**NCAA Division III Track
Coaches Association**
Augustana College
Rock Island, IL 61201
(309) 794-7257
Pres: Paul Olsen

**United States Cross Country
Coaches Association**
University of Arizona
Tucson, Ariz 85721
Pres: Dave Murray

**United States Fencing
Coaches Association**
19181 Eldridge Lane
Southfield, MN 48076
(313) 647-1928
Pres: Guglielmo A. Pezza

**United States Intercollegiate
Lacrosse Association**
Cornell University
Teagle Hall
Ithaca, NY 14850
(607) 255-7332

**United States Lacross
Coaches Association**
University of Delaware
Newark, DE 11716
(302) 451-8661
Pres: Robert Shillinglaw

**University Commissioners
Association**
2550 Professional Road
Suite 16
Richmond, VA 23112
(804) 272-1616
Pres: Thomas E. Yeager

**Women's Basketball Coaches
Association**
North Carolina State Univ.
Box 8501
Raleigh, NC 27695-8501
(919) 737-2880
Pres: Kay Yow

**Women's Intercollegiate
Cross Country Coasches
Association**
Brigham Young University
295 Richards Building
Provo, UT 84602
(801) 378-7508
Pres: Patrick Shane

College Tournaments

Basketball Hall of Fame
Tip-Off Classic
72 Lawrence Drive
Longmeadow, MA 01106
(413) 567-5025
Pres: John O'Donnell

National Invitation
Tournament /Dodge NIT
19 West Street
New York, NY 10004
(212) 425-6510
Fax (212) 785-0594
Ex.Dir: John Powers
Dodge NIT Pre-Season
NIT Post-Season

Canadian Colleges & Universities

Canadian Interuniversity
Athletic Union

1600 James Naismith Drive
Gloucester, Ontario KIB 5N4
(613) 748-5619
Fax (613) 748-5764

Regional Associations

Athletic Universities A.A.
Director of Athletics
University of New Brunswick
Frederick, N.B. E3B 5A3
(506) 453-4580
Pres.: James Born

Atlantic Universities A.A.
Director of Athletics
University of New Brunswick
Frederick, N.B. E3B 5A3
(506) 453-4580
Pres.: James Born

Quebec Student Sports
Federation
Director of Athletics
McGill University
475 Pine Avenue West
Montreal, Quebec H2W 1S4
(514) 398-7000
Pres.: Robert Dubeau

Ontario Universities A.A.
Director of Athletics
University of Waterloo
University Avenue
Waterloo, Ontario N2L 3G1
(519) 885-1211

Ontario Women's
Intercollegiate A.A.
Assistant Director
Carleton University
Colonel By Drive
Ottawa, Ontario K1S 5B6
Pres.: Gail Blake

Great Plains Athletic
Conference
Director of Athletics
University of Manitoba
Faculty of P.E. &
Recreation Studies
Winnipeg, Manitoba R3T 2N2
(204) 474-9140
Pres.: Mike Moore

Canada West Universities A.A.
Director of Athletics
University of Calgary
2500 University Drive, N.W.
Calgary, Alberta T2N 1N4
(403) 220-4310
Pres.: Dr. Robert Corran

CIAU Members

Acadia University
Wolfville, Nova Scotia B0P 1X0
(902) 542-2201
A.D.: Donald G. Wells

University of Alberta
87th Avenue & 114 Street
Edmonton, Alberta T6G 2H9
(403) 492-3413
A.D.: Dale Schulha

Bishop's University
Lennoxville, Quebec J1M 1Z7
(819) 822-9673
A.D.: Bruce Coulter

Brandon University
20th & Louise
Brandon, Manitoba R7A 6A9
(204) 727-7431
A.D.: Mark Arnett

University of British Columbia
208-6081 University Blvd.
Vancouver, B.C. V6T 1W5
(604) 228-4279
A.D.: Dr. R.G. Hindmarch

Brock University
St. Catharines, Ontario L2S 3A1
(416) 688-5550
A.D. Bob Davis

University of Calgary
2500 University Drive N.W.
Calgary, Alberta T2N 1N4
(403) 220-3409
A.D.: Dr. Robert Corran

**University College of
Cape Breton**
PO Box 5300
Sydney, Nova Scotia B1P 6L2
(902) 564-1344
A.D.: Dr. J.I. Albrecht

Carleton University
Colonel By Drive
Ottawa, Ontario K1S 5B6
(613) 788-5627
A.D.: Keith Harris

Concordia University
7141 Sherbrooke Street West
Montreal, Quebec H4B 1R6
(514) 848-3862
A.D.: Robert Phillip

Dalhousie University
University Avenue
Halifax, Nova Scotia B3H 3J5
(902) 494-2139
A.D.: Tony Martin

University of Guelph
Guelph, Ontarion N1G 2W1
(519) 824-4120
A.D.: Dave Copp

Lakehead University
Oliver Road
Thunder Bay, Ontario
P7B 5E1
(807) 343-8601
A.D.: Clyde Tuyl

Laurentian University
Ramsey Lake Road
Sudbury, Ontario P3E 2C6
(705) 675-1151
A.D.: Peter Ennis

Universite Laval
Cite Universitaire
Sainte Foy, Quebec G1K 7P4
(418) 656-2807
A.D.: Gilles D'Amboise

The University of Lethbridge
4401 University Drive
Lethbridge, Alberta T1K 3M4
(403) 329-2681
A.D.: Murray McAuley

University of Manitoba
Faculty of Physical Education
Winnipeg, Manitoba R3T 2N2
(204) 474-9140
A.D.: Mike Moore

McGill University
475 Pine Avenue West
Montreal, P.Q. H2W 1S4
(514) 398-7000
A.D.: Robert Dubeau

McMaster University
Hamilton, Ontario L8S 4K1
(416) 525-9140
A.D.: Therese Quigley

**Memorial University of
Newfoundland**
Elizabeth Avenue
St. John's, Newfoundland
A1C 5S7
(709) 737-8129
A.D.: Keith Taylor

Universite de Moncton
Moncton, New Brunswick E1A 3E9
(506) 858-4165
A.D.: Daniel O'Carroll

Universite de Montreal
CEPSUM 2100
Edouard-Montpetit
Montreal, Quebec H3C 3J7
(514) 343-7714
A.D.: Bernard Goyette

Mount Allison University
Sackville, New Brunswick E0A 3C0
(506) 364-2400
A.D.: Leon Abbott

University of New Brunswick
Fredericton, New Brunswick
E3B 5A3
(506) 453-4580
A.D.: James Born

University of Ottawa
Montpetit Hall
125 University Avenue
Ottawa, Ontario K1N 6N5
(613) 564-5913
A.D.: Wanda Pilon

**University of Prince
Edward Island**
University Avenue
Charlottetown, P.E.I.
C1A 4P3
(902) 566-0305
A.D.: Ed Hilton

**Universite du Quebec a
Chicoutimi**
P.Q. G7H 2B1
(418) 545-5050
A.D.: Normand Delisle

**Universite du Quebec a
Trois Rivieres**
C.P.500, Pavillion des Sports
(819) 376-5254
A.D.: Jean-Francois Grenier

Queen's University
Physical Education Centre
Union Street
Kingston, Ontario K7L 3N6
(613) 545-2666
A.D.: J.G. Reid

University of Regina
Regina, Saskatchewan S4S 0A2
(306) 584-4048
A.D.: TBA

**Royal Military College
of Canada**
Athletic Department
Kingston, Ontario K7K 5L0
(613) 541-6422
A.D.: Major W.J. Oliver

Ryerson Polytechnical Institute
350 Victoria Street
Toronto, Ontario M5B 2K3
(416) 979-5089
A.D.: Bob Fullerton

St. Francis Xavier University
Antigonish, Nova Scotia B2G 1C0
(902) 867-2280
A.D.: George Kehoe

Saint Mary's University
Halifax, Nova Scotia B3H 3C3
(902) 420-5427
A.D.: Dr. Susan Nattrass

St. Thomas University
Fredericton, New Brunswick
E3B 5G3
(506) 452-0539
A.D.: LeRoy J. Washburn

University of Saskatchewan
Saskatoon, Sask. S7N 0W0
(306) 966-6490
A.D.: Val Schneider

Universite de Sherbrooke
2500 Boul Universite
Sherbrooke, Quebec J1K 2R1
(819) 821-7570
A.D.: TBA

University of Toronto
Department of Athletics &
Recreation
55 Harbord Street
Toronto, Ontario M5S 2W6
(416) 978-2136
A.D.: Dr. Ian McGregor

Trent University
Box 4800
Peterborough, Ontario K9J 7B8
(705) 748-1252
A.D.: P.S.B. Wilson

University of Victoria
PO Box 3015
McKinnon Bldg., Room 181
Victoria, British Columbia
V8W 2P1
A.D.: Wayne MacDonald

University of Waterloo
University Avenue
Waterloo, Ontario N2L 3G1
(519) 885-1211
A.D.: Wally Delahey

The University of Western Ontario
Richmond Street N.
London, Ontario N6A 3K7
(519) 661-3088
A.D.: Darwin Semotiuk

Wilfred Laurier University
75 University Avenue West
Waterloo, Ontario N2L 3C5
(519) 884-1970
A.D.: Rich Newbrough

University of Windsor
Windsor, Ontario N9B 3P4
(519) 253-4232
A.D.: Dr. Bob Bucher

University of Winnipeg
515 Portage Avenue
Winnipeg, Manitoba R3B 2E9
(204) 786-9419
A.D.: Aubrey Ferris

York University
4700 Keele Street
North York, Ontario M3J 1P3
(416) 736-5182
A.D.: Mike Dinning

Canadian Colleges Athletic Association

1600 James Naismith Drive
Gloucester, Ontario K1B 5N4
(613) 748-5626
Fax (613) 748-5757
Exec. Dir.: Clare Gillespie

British Columbia Colleges A.A.

British Columbia Tech.
3700 Willingdon
Burnaby, British Columbia V5G 3H2
(604) 432-8613
A.D.: Jim Mitchell

Capilano College
2055 Purcell Way
North Vancouver, British Columbia
V7J 3N5
(604) 986-1911
A.D.: Neil Chester

Cariboo College
PO Box 3010
Kamloops, British Columbia V2C 5N3
(604) 828-5000
A.D.: Mr. Pat O'Brian

College of New Caledonia
3330 - 22nd Avenue
Prince George, British Columbia
V2N 1P8
(604) 562-2131
A.D.: David Wharrie

Columbia Bible College
2940 Clearbrook Road
Clearbrook, British Columbia
V2T 2Z8
(604) 854-1862
A.D.: Norbert Bargen

Douglas College
PO Box 2503
New Westminister,
British Columbia V3L 5B2
(604) 527-5043
A.D.: Betty Lou Hayes

Fraser Valley College
33844 King Road
Abbotsford, British Columbia
V2S 4N2
(604) 853-7441
A.D.: Jane Antil

Malaspina College
900 Fifth Avenue
Nanaimo, British Columbia V9R 5S5
A.D.: Les Malbon

Okanagan College
1000 K.L.O. Road
Kelowna, British Columbia V1Y 4X8
(604) 762-5445
A.D.: Alex Recsky

Royal Roads Military College
FMO Victoria, British Columbia
V0S 1B0
(604) 380-4629
A.D.: Captain Al Kimick

Selkirk College
PO Box 1200
Castlegar, British Columbia
V1N 3J1
(604) 365-7292
A.D.: Rob Johnson

Trinity Western College
7600 Glover Road
Langley, British Columbia V3A 6H4
(604) 888-7511
A.D.: Murray Hall

Vancouver Community College
100 West 49th Avenue
Vancouver, British Columbia
V5Y 2Z6
(604) 324-5511
A.D.: Duncan McCallum

Alberta Athletic Conference

Camrose Lutheran College
4901 - 46 Avenue
Camrose, Alberta T4V 2R3
(403) 679-1160
A.D.: Yvonne Becker

Grande Prairie Regional College
7319 - 29 Avenue
Grande Prairie, Alberta T8V 4C4
(403) 539-2911
A.D.: Leigh Goldie

Grant McEwan Community College
7319 - 29 Avenue
Edmonton, Alberta T6E 2P1
(403) 462-5517
A.D.: Bill Dean

Keyano College
8115 Franklin Avenue
Fort McMurray, Alberta T9H 2H7
(403) 791-4800
A.D.: Ian Allan

Lakeland College
Vermilion, Alberta T0B 4M0
(403) 853-8470
A.D.: Ingo Henstchel

Lethbridge Community College
3000 College Drive, S.
Lethbridge, Alberta T1K 1L6
(403) 382-6900
A.D.: Tim Tollestrup

Medicine Hat College
299 College Drive S.E.
Medicine Hat, Alberta T1A 3Y6
(403) 529-3836
A.D.: Mike Havey

Mount Royal College
4825 Richard Road S.W.
Calgary, Alberta T3E 6K6
(403) 240-6517
A.D.: Al Bohonus

Northern Alberta Tech.
11762 - 106 Street
Edmonton, Alberta T5G 2R1
(403) 471-00KS
A.D.: Irwin Strifler

Olds College
Olds, Alberta T0M 1P0
(403) 556-8281
A.D.: Al Qually

Red Deer College
PO Box 5005
Red Deer, Alberta T4N 5H5
A.D.: Allan Ferchuk

Southern Alberta Tech.
1301 - 16 Avenue N.W.
Calgary, Alberta T2M 0L4
(403) 284-8457
A.D.: Phil Allen

Briercrest Bible Institute
Caronport, Saskatchewan
S0H 0S0
(306) 756-3317
A.D.: Stan Peters

Canadian Bible College
4400 - 4th Avenue
Regina, Saskatchewan S4T 0H8
(306) 545-1515
A.D.: Don Jaspar

Kelsey Institute
PO Box 1520
Saskatoon, Sask. S7K 3R5
(306) 933-8349
A.D.: Al Peterson

Conestoga College
299 Doon Valley Drive
Kitchener, Ontario N2G 4M4
(519) 748-3512
A.D.: Dan Young

Confederation College
PO Box 398
Thunder Bay, Ontario P7C 4W1
(807) 475-6231
A.D.: Ron Fearon

Durham College
PO Box 385
Oshawa, Ontario L1H 7L7
(416) 576-0210
A.D.: Dave Stewart

Fanshawe College
PO Box 4005
1460 Oxford Street E.
London, Ontario N5W 5H1
(519) 452-4202
A.D.: Mike Lindsay

Fleming College
Brealey Drive
Peterborough, Ontario K95 7B1
(416) 749-5552
A.D.: Fred Batley

George Brown College
200 King Street E.
Toronto, Ontario M5A 3W8
(416) 867-2099
A.D.: Alex Barbier

Georgian College
1 Georgian Drive
Barrie, Ontario L4M 3X9
(705) 722-1577
A.D.: James Martin

Humber College
205 Humber College Blvd. N.
Rexdale, Ontario M9W 5L7
(416) 675-3111
A.D.: Doug Fox

Lambton College
1457 london Road
Sarnia, Ontario N7T 7K4
(519) 542-7751
A.D.: Dave Gotts

Loyalist College
Box 4200
Belleville, Ontario K8N 5B9
(613) 969-1913
A.D.: Greg Gavin

Sask. Indian Federated College
118 College West
University of Regina
Regina, Sask. S4S 0A2
(306) 584-8333
A.D.: Milton Tootoosis

Saskatchewan Tech.
PO Box 1420
Moose Jaw, Sask. S6H 4R4
(306) 694-3267
A.D.: Roy Rowley

Saskatchewan Institute
PO Box 3003
Prince Albert, Sask. S6V 6G1
(306) 953-7117
A.D.: Don Laing

Wascana Institute
PO Box 556
Regina, Sask. S4S 5X1
(306) 787-5338
A.D.: Nancy Jacoby

Ontario Athletic Conference

Algonquin College
1385 Woodroffe Avenue
Nepean, Ontario K2G 1V8
(613) 727-7709
A.D.: Ron Port

Cambrian College
1400 Barrydown Road
Sudbury, Ontario P3A 3V8
(705) 566-8101
A.D.: Bob Piche

Canadore College
Box 5001, 100 College Drive
North Bay, Ontario P1B 8K9
(705) 474-7600
A.D.: Bill Ramore

Centennial College
PO Box 631, Station "A"
Scarborough, Ontario M1K 5E9
(416) 694-3241
A.D.: Mary Zettel

Mohawk College
PO Box 2034
Fennel & West 5th
Hamilton, Ontario L8N 3T2
(416) 575-2072
A.D.: Laurie Cahill

Niagara College
PO Box 1005
Welland, Ontario L3B 5S2
(416) 735-2211
A.D.: Peter Rylander

Northern College
640 Latchford Street
PO Box A
Hailbury, Ontario P0J 1K0
(705) 672-3376
A.D.: Carlo Cattarello

Northern College
PO Box 2002
South Porcupine, Ontario P0N 1H0
(705) 235-7225
A.D.: Wayne Bozzer

Northern College
140 Government Road
Kirkland Lake, Ontario P2N 3L8
(705) 529-9291
A.D.: Francine Poirier

St. Clair College
2000 Talbot Road
Windsor, Ontario N9A 6S4
(519) 966-1656
A.D.: Bob Weepers

St. Lawrence College
2288 Parkdale Avenue
Brockville, Ontario K6V 5X3
(613) 345-0660
A.D.: Tyler Forkes

St. Lawrence College
King & Portsmouth Avenue
Kingston, Ontario K7L 5A6
(613) 544-5400
A.D.: Judy Buck

Seneca College
1750 Finch Avenue E.
North York, Ontario M2J 2X5
(416) 491-5050
A.D.: Ernie Armstrong

Sheridan College
1430 Trafalgar Road
Oakville, Ontario L6H 2L1
(416) 845-9430
A.D.: Dick Ruschiensky

Redeemer College
777 Rymal Road
Ancaster, Ontario L9G 3N6
(416) 648-2131
A.D.: Jane Devos-Kors

Royal Military College
Kingston, Ontario K7K 5L0
(613) 541-6422
A.D.: W.J. Oliver

St. Lawrence College
1 Belmont Street
Windmill Point, Cornwall
K6H 4Z1
(613-933-6080
A.D.: Bonnie Bacvar

Quebec Athletic Conferen

College Abitibi-Temiscamingue
426 Boul. du College
Rouyn Noranda, Quebec J9X 5E5
A.D.: Ghislain Hamel

College Ahuntsic
9155 Rue St. Hubert
Montreall, Quebec H2M 1Y8
(514) 389-5921
A.D.: Christian Muisan

College Bois-de-Boulogne
10555 Avenue Bois-de-Boulogne
Montreal, Quebec H4N 1L4
(514) 332-3000
A.D.: Normand Masson

Centennial Academy
3641 rue Prud'homme
Montreal, Quebec H4A 3H6
(514) 486- 5533
A.D.: Laurie Traylen

College Champlain-St. Lambert
900 Riverside Drive
St. Lambert, Quebec J4P 3P2
(514) 672-7360
A.D.: Andre Lebianc

College Champlain - Lennoxville
Campus Lennoxville
Lennoxville, Quebec J1M 2A1
(819) 564-3670
A.D.: Tony Addena

College Chicoutimi
534 Jacques Cartier
Chicoutimi, Quebec G7H 1Z6
(418) 549-9520
A.D.: Guy Wauthier

Dawson College
3040 Sherbrooke St. Ouest
Westmount, Quebec H3Z 1A4
(514) 931-8731
A.D.: John Davidson

Drummondville College
960 rue St. Georges
Drummondville, Quebec J2C 6A2
(819) 478-4671
A.D.: Andre Lamy

F.X. Garneau
1660 Boul. de l'Entente
Quebec, Quebec G1T 2S5
(418) 688-8310
A.D.: Serge Laliberte

College Granby
235 rue St. Jacques
Granby, Quebec J2G 9H7
(514) 372-6614
A.D.: Gilles Fortin

John Abbott College
C.P. 2000
Montreal, Quebec H9X 3L9
(514) 457-6610
A.D.: Glenn Ruiter

College L'Assomption
270 Blvd. l'Ange-Gardien
L'Assomption, Quebec J0K 1G0
(514) 589-5621
A.D.: Michel Villeneuve

College Levis-Lauzon
205 rue Mgr. Bourget
Lauzon, Quebec G6V 6Z9
(418) 833-5110
A.D.: Laurent Fallon

College Limoilou
1300 8e Avenue
Quebec, Quebec G1K 7H3
(418) 647-6784
A.D.: Gisele Huot

College Maisonneuve
3800 Est. Sherbrooke
Montreal, Quebec H1X 2A2
(514) 254-7131
A.D.: Michel Biron

College Montmorency
475 boul. L'Avenir
Laval, Quebec H7N 5H9
(514) 667-5100
A.D.: Sylvain Cheron

College L'Outaovais
3333 Boul. Cite des Jeunes
C.P. 5220, Succ. A
Hull, Quebec J84 6M5
(819) 770-4012
A.D.: Luc Maurice

College Riviere du Loup
80 rue Frontenac
Riviere du Loup, Quebec
G5R 1S8
(418) 862-6903
A.D.: Gaetan St. Pierre

St. Jean sur Richelieu
30 boul. du Seminaire
St. Jenn sur Richelieu
Quebec, J3B 7B1
(514) 347-5301
A.D.: Levis Lessard

College St. Jerome
455 Fournier
St. Jerome, Quebec J7Z 4V2
(514) 436-1580
A.D.: Richard Campeau

College St. Laurent
625 Boul. Ste. Croix
Montreall, Quebec H4L 3X7
(514) 747-6521
A.D.: Robert Bondaz

College Ste.Foy
2410 Chemin Ste.Foy
Ste.Foy, Quebec G1V 1T3
(418) 659-6600
A.D.: Robert Goulet

College Sherbrooke
475 Parc
Sherbrooke, Quebec J1H 5M7
(819) 564-6234
A.D.: George Laurent

Vanier College
821 Boul. Ste. Croix
Montreal, Quebec H4L 3X9
(514) 744-7126
A.D.: Alex Sidorenko

College Victoriaville
475 rue Notre Dame, Est.
Victoriaville, Quebec G6P 4B3
(819) 758-6401
A.D.: Yvon Pare

College Vieux Montreal
255 est, rue Ontario
C.P. 144, Station "N"
Montreal, Quebec H2X 3M8
(514) 982-3438
A.D.: Michel Arseneault

Nova Scotia Athletic Conference

Canadian Coast Guard College
PO Box 4500
Sydney, Nova Scotia B1P 6L1
(902) 564-3660
A.D.: Marc Comeau

University College of
Cape Breton
PO Box 5300
Sydney, Nova Scotia B1P 6L2
(02) 539-5300
A.D.: Dr. J.I. Albrecht

University of Kings
College
6350 Colburg Road
Halifax, Nova Scotia
B3M 2J6
(902) 422-1277
A.D.: Bob Quigley

Mount Saint Vincent
University
166 Bedford Highway
Halifax, Nova Scotia B3M 2J6
(902) 443-4450
A.D.: June Lumsden

Nova Scotia Agricultural
College
PO Box 550
Truro, Nova Scotia B2N 5G5
(902) 895-5347
A.D.: Wilf McCormack

University Sainte-Anne
Pointe-de-l'Eglise,
Nova Scotia B0W 1M0
(902) 769-2114
A.D.: Pierre Norbert

Saint Thomas University
PO Box 4569
Fredericton, New Brunswick
E3B 5G3
(506) 452-0539
A.D.: LeRoy Washburn

RARE SPORTSFILMS

Here's baseball action at it's nostalgic best - 1940's and 1950's teams, plays and players are now available on beautiful quality videotapes and in outstanding COLOR. See action in all those old ballparks which have long since left the baseball scene: Braves Field, the Polo Grounds, Ebbets Field, Seals Stadium, Forbes Field, Shibe Park, Crosley Field, Sportsman's Park, etc. All tapes have original narration and soundtrack, just as they appeared over 30 years ago! "RARE SPORTSFILMS" tapes are the nostalgic videos that sports fans are asking for with picture quality and sharpness that is unsurpassed! Only $29.95 + $2.50 for first class shipping. VHS or Beta

1951 Baseball News Highlights - B & W
1955 - 56 Baseball News, B & W (1 Hr. 24 Min.) - $36.95
1955 Washington Senators "The Washington Nationals" - Color
1965 New York Mets "Expressway To The Big Leagues" - Color
1956 Kansas City Athletics "The K.C.A.'s In Action" - Color
1948, 1952 & 1955 All-Star Games (One Tape) - B & W
1956 All-Star Game at Washington plus "Ruth To Mays"
1947 Boston Braves "The Braves Family" - Color
1954 Milwaukee Braves "Home Of The Braves" - Color
1955 Milwaukee Braves "Baseball's Main Street" - Color
1957 Milwaukee Braves "Hail To The Braves!" - Color
1954 Boston Red Sox "Baseball In Boston" - Color
1956 Boston Red Sox "Pride Of New England" - Color
1957 Boston Red Sox "Play Ball With The Red Sox" - Color

MOVING???
BE SURE TO SUPPLY
THE AUTHOR WITH
YOUR NEW ADDRESS!

Ed Kobak, Jr.
Global Sports Productions
1223 Broadway, Suite 102
Santa Monica, CA 90404
(310) 454-9480

State Games

Listed in this section are the State Games program, which introduce young athletes to Olympic traditions.

National Congress of State Games
PO Box 2318
Billings, MT 59103
(406) 245-8106
Fax: (406) 248-7414
Ex.Dir.: Tom Osborne

Alabama Sports Festival
PO Box 1110
Montgomery, AL 36101
(205) 263-3411
Fax: (205) 262-4147
Ex.Dir.: Ron Creel

Alaska State Games
2075 Glenn Highway
Palmer, AK 99645
(907) 745-4827
Fax (907) 746-2699
Ex.Dir.: Dean Phillips

Arizona State Games
3800 N. Central, Suite 1400
Phoenix, AZ 85012
(602) 280-1236
Fax (602) 280-1305
Ex.Dir.: Paul Pugmire

Arkansas State Games
Pomfret Center
Box 176
Fayetteville, AR 72701
(501) 575-4646
Ex.Dir.: Dawn Machiarelli

Badger State Games
PO Box 1377
Madison, WI 53701
(608) 251-3333
Fax (608) 283-6412
Ex.Dir.: Otto Breitenbaach

Bay State Games
PO Box 8336
Boston, MA 02114
(617) 727-3227
Fax(617) 727-3204
Ex.Dir.: Doug Arnot

Big Sky State Games
PO Box 2318
Billings, MT 59103
(406) 245-8106
Fax (406) 248-7414
Ex.Dir.: Tom Osborne

Blue Grass State Games
200 East Main Street
Lexington, KY 40507
(606) 258-3900
Ex.Dir.: Shirley Watts

California State Games
PO Box 126698
San Diego, CA 92112
(213) 489-1991
Ex.Dir.: Sandi Mabry

Capitol Games
PO Box 2196
Falls Church, VA 22042
(202) 530-4140
Fax (703) 883-0492
Ex.Dir.: John Henson

Colorado State Games
12 E. Boulder Street
Colorado Springs, CO 80903
(719) 634-7333
Fax (719) 634-5198
Ex.Dir.: Fred Whitacre

Cornhusker State Games
PO Box 82411
Lincoln, NE 68501
(402) 471-2544
Ex.Dir.: Tom Ash

Cowboy State Games
PO Box 3485
Casper, Wy 82602
(307) 577-1125
Ex.Dir.:Eileen Ford

Empire State Games
Agency Bldg. One
Empire State Plaza
Albany, NY 12238
(518) 474-8889
Fax (518) 474-7944
Ex.Dir.: Brendan McCann

First State Games
PO Box 9998
Newark, DE 19714
(302) 454-1000
Fax (302) 737-8450
Ex.Dir.: Eric Conrad

Garden State Games
PO Box 6923
Edison, NJ 08818
(908) 225-0303
Fax (908) 225-0357
Ex.Dir.: Raymond Funkhouser

Georgia State Games
1201 W. Peachtree Street
Suite 3450
Atlanta, GA 30309
(404) 853-0250
Fax (404) 874-7830
Ex.Dir.:Nick Gailey

Great Lakes State Games
Sports Training Center
Northern Michigan University
Marquette, MI 49855
(906) 227-2888
Fax (906) 227-2848
Ex.Dir.: Jeff Kleinschmidt

Green Mountain State Games
University of Vermont
201 Patrick Gymnasium
Burlington, VT 05405
(802) 656-7707
Ex.Dir.: Janice Lange

Hawaii State Games
1088 Bishop Street
Suite 1110
Honolulu, HI 96813
(808) 522-0700
Fax (808) 522-0703
Ex.Dir.: Barbara Velasco

Idaho Summer Games
PO Box 873
Pocatello, ID 83204
(208) 233-0022
Fax (208) 234-8026
Ex.Dir.: Harriett Clark

Idaho Winter Games
PO Box 1582
McCall, ID 83638
(208) 634-2945
Fax (208) 634-4153
Ex.Dir.: Irene LaMarche

Iowa Games
PO Box 2350
Ames, IA 50010
(515) 292-3251
Fax (515) 292-3254
Ex.Dir.: Joyce Durlam

Keystone State Games
31 South Hancock Street
Wilkes-Barre, PA 18702
(717) 823-3164
Fax (717) 822-6558
Ex.Dir.: Owen Costello

Louisiana State Games
1520 Sugar Bowl Drive
New Orleans, LA 70112
(504) 525-5678
Ex.Dir.: Bill Gulledge

Maryland State Games
PO Box 311
Sykesville, MD 21783
(301) 549-3360
Fax (301) 795-6048
Ex.Dir.: Jim Gordon

**State Games of
North Carolina**
PO Box 12727
Research Triangle Park,
NC 27709
(919) 941-6227
Fax (919) 941-5717
Ex.Dir.: Winkie La Force

Nutmeg State Games
290 Roberts Street
East Hartford, CT 06108
(203) 528-4588
Fax: (203) 291-8032
Ex.Dir.: William Mudano

Ocean State Games
2212 Post Road
Warwick, RI 02908
((401)272-3434
Fax (401) 421-0824
Ex.Dir.: Ed O'Brien

Ohio Sports Festival
11000 Cedar Avenue,
Suite 207
Cleveland, OH 44106
(216) 721-5605

State Games of Oregon
700 N.E. Multnomah, Ste.455
Portland, OR 97232
(503) 234-2013
Ex.Dir.: Ken Allen

Palmetto State Games
2600 Bull Street
Columbia, SC 29201
(803) 734-4137
Fax (803)737-3946
Ex.Dir.: James Testor

Prairie Rose State Games
1424 West Century Avenue
Bismark, ND 58501
(701) 224-4887
Fax (701) 224-3000
Ex.Dir.: Tim Mueller

Prairie State Games
525 West Jefferson
Springfield, IL 62706
(217) 785-8216
Fax (217) 782-3987
Ex.Dir.: Jim Sunderlin

Show Me State Games
University of Missouri
404 Jesse Hall
Columbia, MO 65211
(314) 882-2101
Fax (314)882-6957
Ex.Dir.: Gary Filbert

Sooner State Games
PO Box 26567
Oklahoma City, OK 73126
(405) 235-4222
Fax (405) 236-5008
Ex.Dir.: Susan Jones

**Star of the North
State Games**
1700 - 105th Ave., N.E.
Blaine, MN 55434
(612) 785-5600
Ex.Dir.: Jeff Mordhorst

Sunflower State Games
PO Box 312
Lawrence, KS 66044
(913) 749-2244
Ex.Dir.: Craig White

Sunshine State Games
1330 N.W. 6th Street
Suite D
Gainesville, FL 32601
(904) 336-2120
Fax: (904) 373-8879
Ex.Dir.: Jose Rodriquez

Tennessee Sportsfest
315 Deaderick Street
Suite 2050
Nashville, TN 37238
(615) 254-3787
Fax (615) 242-1829
Ex.Dir.: Allen Newton

Texas State Games
12015 Park 35 Circle
Austin, TX 78753
(512) 835-1434
Fax (832-1646
Ex.Dir.: Cliff Warrick

Utah Summer Games
PO Box 71
Cedar City, UT 84721
(801) 586-7228
Fax (801) 586-4362
Ex.Dir.: Rich Wilson

Utah Winter Games
PO Box 25204
Salt Lake City, UT 84125
(801) 973-8824
Fax (801) 649-1559
Ex.Dir.: Brad Barber

Virginia State Games
412 Shenandoah Bldg.
Roanoke, VA 24011
(703) 343-0987
Fax (703) 343-7407
Ex.Dir.: Doug Fonda

Washington State Games
1001 4th Avenue Plaza
Suite 3135
Seattle, WA 98154
(206) 682-4263
Fax (206)682-4986
Ex.Dir.: Tim Davidson

West Virginia State Games
PO Box 1659
Huntington, WV 25717
(304) 696-5540
Ex.Dir.: Buddy Graham

**White River Park
State Games**
201 South Capitol Avenue
Suite 1200
Indianapolis, IN 46225
(317) 237-5000
Fax (317) 237-5041
Ex.Dir.: Jim Titus

Sports Commissions

Listed in this section are sports commissions that are responsible for their community's involvement in professional and amateur sports for scheduling of events, attracting sports franchises and organizations, etc.

Arkansas Major Sports Association
1 Spring Building
Little Rock, AR72201
(501) 374-4871

Arkansas Major Sports Association
1 Spring Building
Little Rock, AR 72201
(501) 374-4871

Atlanta Sports Council
235 International Blvd.
Atlanta, GA 30303
(404) 586-8510

Greater Cleveland Sports Council
690 Huntington Bldg.
Cleveland, OH 44115
(216) 621-3300

Colorado Amateur Sports Corp.
12 East Boulder Street
Colorado Springs, CO 80937
(719) 634-7333

Florida Amateur Sports Council
1330 N.W. 6th Street
Gainesville, FL 32606
(904) 377-0134

Great Lakes Sports
(Michigan)
602 Cohodas
Administration Center
Northern Michigan University
Marquette, MI 49855

Greater Hartford Sports and Events Council
250 Constitution Plaza
Hartford, CT 06103
(203) 525-4451

Houston Sports Foundation
3300 Main Street
Houston, TX 77002
(713) 523-5050

Indiana Sports Corp.
201 S. Capitol Avenue
Indianapolis, IN 46225
(317) 237-5000

Jacksonville Sports and Entertainment Commission
1145 East Adams Street
Jacksonville, FL 32202
(904) 630-3933

Kansas City Sports Commission
800 Westport Road
Kansas City, MO 64111
(816) 561-4652

Los Angeles Sports Council
404 South Bixel
Los Angeles, CA 90017

Maryland State Athletic Commission
501 St. Paul Place
Baltimore, MD 21202
(301) 333-6315

Metropolitan Sports Facilities Commission
900 South Fifth Street
Minneapolis, MN 55415
(612) 332-0386

Sports Council of
Greater Miami
1601 Biscayne Blvd.
Miami, FL 33132
(305) 350-7700

Minneapolis Amateur
Sports Commission
899 American Center
150 East Kellogg Blvd.
St. Paul, MN 55101
(612) 296-4845

Nebraska Sports Industry
Commission
555 South 10th
County City Bldg.
Lincoln, NE 68508
(402) 464-1260

New Jersey Sports and
Exposition Authority
50 State Highway 20
East Rutherford, NJ 07073
(201) 460-4011

New Orleans Sports
Foundation
Louisiana Superdome
1520 Sugar Bowl Drive
New Orleans, LA 70112
(504) 525-5678

New York Sports Commission
375 Hudson Street
New York, NY 10014
(212) 463-2004

North Carolina Amateur
Sports
PO Box 12727
Research Triangle Park
NC 27709
(919) 941-6227

North Carolina Sports
Development
430 N. Salisbury Street
Raleigh, NC 27603
(919) 733-9015

Attractions & Development
Committee
Oakland Convention &
Visitors Bureau
Transpacific Center
1000 Broadway, Suite 200
Oakland, CA 94607
(415) 839-9000

Greater Omaha Sports
Committee
Mid-American Exposition
666 Farnam Bldg.
Omaha, NE 68103
(402) 346-8003

Greater Orlando Sports
Organizing Committee
250 North Orange Avenue
Orlando, FL 32801
(407) 423-2532

Pensacola Sports
Association
Civic Center
PO Box 12463
Pensacola, FL 32582
(904) 434-2800

Philadelphia Sports
Congress
1515 Market Street
Philadelphia, PA 19102
(215) 636-3417

Pinella's County Sports
Authority
204 16th Street South
St. Petersburg, FL 33705
(813) 870-3060

Sacramento Sports Commission
4623 T Street
Sacramento, CA 95819
(916) 449-5500

St. Louis Sports Commission
100 S. Fourth Street
Suite 500
St. Louis, MO 63102
(314) 231-5555

**San Antonio Sports
Foundation**
PO Box 830386
San Antonio, TX 78283
(512) 246-3480

**Greater Spokane Sports
Association**
1020 W. Riverside
Spokane, WA 99210
(509) 624-1393

Syracuse Sports Corporation
100 E. Onondaga Street
Syracuse, NY 13202
(315) 470-1386

Tampa Sports Authority
4201 North Dale Mabry
Tampa, FL 33607
(813) 870-3060

**Sports Foundation of
Metro Tulsa**
616 South Boston
Tulsa, OK 74119
(918) 585-1201

Utah Sports Foundation
180 S.W. Temple
Salt Lake City, UT 84101
(801) 364-7607

**Worcester Chamber of Commerce
Sports Committee**
33 Waldo Street
Worcester, MA 06108
(508) 753-2924

Sports Business Industry

Corporate Sports Sponsorship

Listed in this section are corporations and firms that are involved in sports sponsorship through advertising and promotion. This is a representation confirmed by questionaire & telephone and is not a complete listing. Listed are contact members whenever possible from advertising/promotion or sports marketing departments.

American Airlines, Inc.
PO Box 619616
Dallas-Ft. Worth Airport
TX, 75261
(817) 355-1234
Spo.Mkt.: Kevin Murphy

American Express Co.
200 Vesey Street
New York, NY 10285
(212) 640-2904
Spo. Mkt.: Anne Graham

American Telephone & Telegraph Company (AT&T)
550 Madison Avenue
New York, NY 10022
(212) 605-6719
Corp. Events: Chris Christman

Anheuser-Busch, Inc.
One Busch Place
721 Pestalozzi Street
St. Louis, MO 63118
(314) 577-2000
Spo. Mkt.: Mark Lamping

Best Western International
PO Box 10203
Phoenix, AZ 85064
(602) 957-4200
Adv. Dir.: Vicki Cabianca

Bridgestone U.S.A., Inc.
P.O. Box 140991
Nashville, TN 37214
(615) 391-0088
Dir. of Motorsports:
Bob Graham

Budget Rent-A-Car Corp.
200 N. Michigan Avenue
Chicago, IL 60601
(312) 580-5000
Spec.Events: Garry Bricker

Bulova Watch Co.
One Bulova Avenue
Woodside, NY 11377
(718) 204-3300
Public Rel.: Elaine Wnukowski

Burger King Corp.
PO Box 520783
Miami, FL 33150
(305) 378-7011
Spo. Mkt.: Richard Fallon

Cadillac Motor Car/GMC
2860 Clark Avenue
Detroit, MI 48232
(313) 554-6112
Adv. Dir.: Peter R. Levin

Caesars World Sports
1801 Century Park East
Suite 2600
Los Angeles, CA 90067
(213) 552-2711
Pres.: Richard Rose

Cannon USA
One Cannon Plaza
Lake Success, NY 11042
(516) 488-6700
Mkt. Dir.: Ted Ando

Castrol, Inc.
1500 Valley Road
Wayne, NJ 07470
(201) 633-2261
Spo. Mkt.: John A. Howell

Chevrolet/GMC
30007 Van Dyke Avenue
Warren, MI 48090
(313) 492-1816
Mkt.: Terry Dolan

Chrysler Corp.
12000 Chrysler Drive
Highland Park, MI 48288-0857
(313) 252-7320
Mkt. Dir.: Bill Klinger

Coca Cola USA
One Coca Cola Plaza
Atlanta, GA 30313
(404) 676-8717
Spo. Mkt.: Hal Price

Adolph Coors Co.
311 W. 10th Street
Golden, CO 80401
(303) 277-6465
Spo. Mkt.: Tim Simmons

Days Inn of America, Inc.
2751 Buford Hwy., N.E.
Atlanta, GA 30324
(404) 728-4281
Spo. Mkt.: David Kemp

Duracell, Inc.
Berkshire Ind. Park
Bethel, CT 06801
(203) 796-4516
Adv.: Robert Giacolone

Eastman Kodak Co.
343 State Street
Rochester, NY 14650
(716) 724-2208
Mkt.: John Barr

Federal Express Corp.
2003 Corporate Avenue
Memphis, TN 38132
(901) 395-3520
Spo.Mkt.: Nancy Attenburg

Ford Motor Co.
300 Renaissance Center
Detroit, MI 48243
(313) 322-4927
Corp. Adv.: Fred Wuellner

Goodyear Tire & Rubber Co.
1144 E. Market Street
Akron, OH 44316
(216) 796-2121
Adv.Dir.: Davis M. Jones

GTE Company
351 Phelps Court
Irving, TX 75038
(214) 718-3747
Spo. Mkt.: Gene Lloyd

Hewlett-Packard Co.
19091 Pruneridge Avenue
Cupertino, CA 95014
(408) 447-1074
Spo.Mkt.: Jerry L. Gross

Hilton Hotels Corp.
15 W. Sixth Street
Cincinnati, OH 45202
(800) 331-3858
Spo.Mkt.: Patty Stevens

Holiday Inns
3796 Lamar Avenue
Memphis, TN 38195
(901) 362-4294
Spo. Mkt.: J.D. Henning

Hospitality Franchise Systems
1850 Parkway Place
Suite 400
Marietta, GA 30067
(404) 423-7755
Spo. Mkt.: John Hansen
Ramada Inns & Howard Johnsons
Worldwide.

International Business
Machines Corp (IBM)
Old Orchard Road
Armonk, NY 10504
(917) 765-6560
Spec. Events: Jim Doherty

Kellogg Company
One Kellogg Square
Battle Creek, MI 49016
(616) 961-3799
Product Pub.: Karen MacLeod

Labatt Breweries
2 First Canadian Place
Suite 3200
Toronto, Ontario M5X 1E7
(416) 361-5050
Sports Mkt.: Terry Zuk

Loew's Hotels Corp.
569 Lexington Avenue
New York, NY 10022
(212) 752-7000
Mkt.: Steven L. Liebman

Manufacturers Hanover
140 E. 45th Street
New York, NY 10016
(212) 270- 8505
Spo. Mkt.: Barbara Paddock

Marriott Hotels Corp.
Marriot Drive
Washington, CC 20058
(301) 380-9000
VP Sports: Sam Huff

Mastercard International
888 Seventh Avenue
New York, NY 10003
(212) 649-5451
Spo.Mkt.: Debbie Hughes

Mazda Motors, Inc.
7755 Irvine Center Drive
Irvine, CA 92718
(714) 727-1990
Dir. of Prom.: Elaine Matsuda

McDonald's Corp.
Campus Office Bldg.
Kroc Drive
Oak Brook, IL 60521
(708) 575-6594
Spo. Mkt.: Jackie Woodward

Mercedes Benz N.A.
One Mercedes Drive
Montvale, NJ 07645
(201) 573-0600
Dir. of Prom.: Rolf Waldeis

Miller Brewing Co.
3939 W. Highland Blvd.
Milwaukee, WI 53208
(414) 931-3195
Spo. Mkt.: Kevin Wulff

Molson Breweries, Inc.
175 Bloor Street East
North Tower, 2nd Floor
Toronto, Ontario M4W 3S4
Canada
(416) 975-1786
Spo. Mkt.: Norm Webb

Panasonic Company
One Panasonic Way
Secaucus, NJ 07094
(201) 348-7000
Adv.Dir.: Robert Greenberg

Pepsi-Cola Company
One Pepsi Way
Somers, NY 10589-2201
(914) 767-6028
Spo. Mkt.: Lisa Squeo

Philip Morris Companies, Inc.
120 Park Avenue
New York, NY 10017
(212) 880-5000
Event Mkt.: Leo McCullagh

Pizza Hut, Inc.
9111 E. Douglas
Wichita, KS 67207
(316) 681-9000
Spo.Mkt: Mark Mears

Ricoh Corp.
5 Dedrick Place
West Caldwell, NJ 07006
(201) 882-2000
VP Comm.: Jack Matyka

R.J. Reynolds Co.
401 N. Main Street
Winston-Salem, NC 27102
(919) 741-5000
Spo. Mkt.: John Powell

Subaru of America, Inc.
575 North Main Street
Heber City, UT 84032
(801) 654-5550
Dir.of Prom.: Molly Laramie

Timex Corporation
PO Box 2126
Waterbury, CT 06722
(203) 573-5000
Spo. Mkt.: Ken Strominger

Uniroyal Goodrich Tire Co.
600 South Main
Akron, OH 44309
(216) 374-3000
Adv.Dir.: Robert E. Hatton

USA Today
1000 Wilson Blvd.
Arlington, VA 22229
(703) 276-3400
Spo. Mkt.: Keith Cutler

Valvoline, Inc.
PO Box 14000
Lexington, KY 40512
(606) 264-7572
Spo.Mkt.: Mark Coughlin

Xerox Corp.
800 Long Ridge Road
Stamford, CT 06904
(203) 968-4485
Adv.Dir.: Tom Creighton

Athletic, Fitness & Outdoor Sporting Goods Manufacturers

Listed in this section is a sampling of the major manufacturers of equipment, apparel, activewear & accessories. Due to space limitations, only a random sampling is listed. Please contact the SGMA & NSGA for a more detailed listing.

Sporting Goods Manufacturers Association
200 Castlewood Drive
North Palm Beach, FL 33408
(407) 842-4100
Fax (407) 863-8984

National Sporting Goods Association
1699 Wall Street
Mt. Prospect, IL 60056
(708) 439-4000
Fax (708) 439-0111

World Federation of Sporting Goods Industry
P.O. Box 1051
Kloten-Zurich,
CH 8302, Switzerland

Publications

Sporting Goods Business
1515 Broadway
New York, NY 10036
(212) 869-1300

The Sporting Goods Dealer
1212 N. Lindbergh Blvd.
St. Louis, MO 63132
(314) 997-7111

Footwear News
7 East 12th Street
New York, NY 10003
(212) 741-4026

Listing of Manufacturers

Above the Rim International
620 C Street, 6th Fl.
San Diego, CA 92101
(619) 238-8540
Activewear

Academy Broadway
1455 Michael Drive
Wood Dale, IL 60191-1015
(708) 350-2400
Outdoor equipment

Accusplit, Inc.
2290-A Ringwood Avenue
San Jose, CA 95131
(800) 538-9750
Training timer devices

Action & Leisure
45 E. 30th Street
New York, NY 10016-7323
(212) 684-4470
Footwear & clothing

Action Wear
1901 Brown Road
St. Louis, MO 63114-5682
(314) 427-1147

Acutrak/MBI Corp.
115 Hurley Road
Oxford, CT 06483-1011
(203) 264-2702
Sports timers

Adams USA, Inc
PO Box 489
Cookeville, TN 38501-0489
(615) 526-2109
Athletic equipment

Adidas USA, Inc.
15 Independence Blvd
Warren, NJ 07060
(201) 580-0700
Apparel & footwear

Aerobics, Inc.
385 Main Street
Little Falls, NJ 07424-1207
(201)256-9700

Air-Omatic
7207 B 114th Avenue N.
Largo, FL 34643
(813) 544-4001
Health

Airwalk
2042 Corte Del Nogal
Carlsbad, CA 92009
(619) 931-6868
Footwear

Ajay Leisure Products, Inc.
1501 E. Wisconsin Street
Delavan, WI 53115-1471
(414) 728-5521
Golf bags & accessories

Alain
14500 SW 119 Avenue
Miami, FL 33186
(800) 292-5589
Activewear

Alix
45 E. 30th Street
New York, NY 10016-7323
(212) 684-4470
Footwear & clothing

Allied Golf Co.
4538 W. Fullerton
Chicago, IL 60639-1992
(312) 772-7710

All-Star Knitwear
331 N. 6th Street
Griffin, GA 30224
(404) 227-5016

Altus Athletic
Manufacturing Co.
PO Box 736
Altus, OK 73522
(405) 482-0891
Accessories

American Athletic, Inc.
200 American Avenue
Jefferson, IA 50129-2801
(800) 247-3978
Strength/conditiong equip.

American Recreation
Products
PO Box 7048-A
St. Louis, MO 63177-0048
(314) 576-8000

Apex Fitness Products
392 Locust Lane E.
York, PA 17402
(717) 846-7769
Fitness equipment

Apolio Athletic
4250 Pacific Hwy #210-B
San Diego, CA 92110
(619) 226-1911
Exercise products

Apple/Dorson Sports, Inc.
195 Lauman Lane
Hicksville, NY 11801-6522
(800) 645-7215
Equipment & accessories

Aqua Leisure Industries
Avon Industrial Park
Avon, MA 02322-1098
(508) 587-5400
Accessories: training
devices

Arena USA, Inc.
28 Englehard Drive
Cranberry, NJ 08512
(609) 655-1515
Fitness swimwear

Asahi, Inc.
1800-R Macleod Drive
Lawrenceville, GA 30243-5717
(404) 962-8442
Footwear

Asics Tiger Corp.
10540 Talbert Avenue
W. Bldg.
Fountain Valley, CA 92708
(714) 962-7654
footwear & apparel

Atec
115 Post Street
Santa Cruz, CA 95060-2128
(408) 425-1484
Baseball, softball equip.

Athletic Bag Co.
2020 Industrial Circle
Salt Lake City, UT 84104
(801) 972-4866
Custom bags

Augusta Sportswear
PO Box 14939
Augusta, GA 30919-0939
(800) 237-8681
Activewear

Austin Athletic
1005 E. 39th
Shawnee, OK 74801-2240
(405) 273-8681
Equipment

Avia Athletic Footwear
16160 SW Upper Boones Ferry Rd.
Portland, OR 97234-7744

Avita
7140 180th Avenue NE
Redmond, WA 98052-4972
(800) 222-9995
Exercise equipment

Baden Sports, Inc.
1120 SW 16th Avenue
Renton, WA 98055-2698
(206) 235-1830
Athletic balls

Bags Unlimited
3209 E. Empire
Benton Harbor, MI 49022
(616) 926-8568

Bard Sports Corp.
14516 SW 119th Avenue
Miami, FL 33186-6100
(305) 233-2200
Accessory product lines

Barracuda Swim Products
0224 SW Hamilton Street
Portland, OR 97201
(503) 241-0528
Sales & Marketing

Battle Creek Equipment Co.
307 W. Jackson Street
Battle Creek, MI 49017-2385
(616) 962-6181
Exercise equipment

Bauer
50 Jonergin Drive
Swanton, VT 05488-1312
(800) 362-3146
Hockey & figure skates

M Z Berger & Co.
Wilson Room
33-00 Northern Blvd.
Long Island City, NY 11101
(718) 361-7720
Athletic watches

Betra Headwear
Chesnee Hwy.
PO Box 6325
Spartanburg, SC 29304-6325
(803) 599-0855

Beuchat USA, Inc.
2900 SW 2nd Avenue
Fort Lauderdale, FL 33315-3123
(305) 523-7242
Scuba & skin diving equip.

Bike Athletic Co.
PO Box 666
Knoxville, TN 37901-0666
(615) 546-4703
Sportsgear

Bison Recreational Products
603 L Street
Lincoln, NE 68508-2432
(800) 247-7668

Bitchin Apparrel
4125 S. 6000 W.
West Valley City, UT 84120-2339
(800) 477-0747

Body Glove Fitness
PO Box 47031
Gardena, CA 90247
(800) 827-5611

Brine, Inc.
47 Sumner Street
Milford, MA 01757-1696
(800) 227-2722
Equipment; apparel

British Knights
138 Duane Street
New York, NY 10013
(212) 227-6236
Footwear; apparel

Brooks Shoe, Inc.
9341 Courtland Drive NE
Rockford, MI 49351-0001
(616) 866-5500

Brunswick Corp.
525 W. Laketon
Muskegon, MI 49441-2697
(616) 725-3300
Bowling products & equip.

Brutini Athletic Footwear
PO Box 222
N. Attleboro, MA 02761
(508) 699-9000

Champion Products
3141 Monroe Avenue
Rochester, NY 14618-4689
(716) 385-3200
Apparel; activewear

Converse, Inc.
1 Fordham Road
N. Reading, MA 01864-2685
(508) 664-7564
Athletic shoes

Cooper
50 Jonergin Drive
Swanton, VT 05488-1312
(800) 362-3146
Hockey Equipment

Daignault-Rolland Ltee.
2567 Rouen
Montreal, PQ, H2K 1M7
(514) 255-1419
Sports equipment

Danskin
111 W. 40th Street
18th Floor
New York, NY 10018-2506
(212) 764-4630
Activewear; dancewear

Diadora America, Inc.
6529 S. 216th
Bldg. E
Kent, WA 98032-2301
Footwear & accessories

Diamond Sports Co.
10537 Humbolt Street
PO Box 637
Los Alamitos, CA 90720
(800) 366-2999
Baseball & protective gear

Diversified Products
309 Williamson Avenue
Opelika, AL 36802-7313
(205) 745-1432
Exercise & fitness equip.

**Dudley Sports/ Div. of
Spalding Sports Worldwide**
PO Box 7055
Chicopee, MA 01021-7055
(413) 539-2051
Equipment

Dunlop Slazenger Corp.
PO Box 3070
Greenville, SC 29602-3070
(803) 241-2200
Racquet & sports

Easton Sports, Inc.
577 Airport Blvd.
Burlingame, CA 94010
(800) 357-3901
  equipment & accessories

Ektelon
8929 Aero Drive
San Diego, CA 92123
(619) 560-0066
Racquet sports

Etonic
147 Centre Street
Brockton, MA 02402-2787
(508) 583-9100
Shoes

Everlast Sporting Goods
Manufacturing
750 E. 132nd
Bronx, NY 10454-3480
(212) 993-0100
Baseball bases

Fila Athletic Footwear
200 International Cir.
#2000
Hunt Valley, MD 21030-1341
(301) 785-7530

Forster Manufacturing Co.
PO Box 657
Wilton, ME 04294-0657
(516) 436-7240

FTM Sports
14500 SW 119 Avenue
Miami, FL 33186
(800) 292-5589
Tennis & golf equip.

Gamemaster Athletic Co.
582 Goddard Avenue
Chesterfield, MO 63005-1198
(314) 532-4646

Head Sports, Inc.
4801 N. 63rd Street
Boulder, CO 80301-3238
(303) 530-2000

High Sierra
880 Corporate Woods Pkwy.
Vernon Hills, IL 60061-3154
(708) 913-1100
Foul weather gear; tents

Hillerich & Bradsby Co.
PO Box 35700
Louisville, KY 40232-5700
(800) 282-2287
Batting gloves; hockey sticks

Hot Sports USA
3101 W. Pacific Coast Hwy
#307
Newport Beach, CA 92663
Wet suits; catamarans

Insport
1870 NW 173
Beaverton, OR 97006
(800) 652-5200

Intersport Limited
22633 Davis Drive
Sterling, VA 22170
(703) 709-7155

Itech Sport Products
Swanton Rd. Rte. 7 N.
PO Box 309
St. Albans, VT 05478-0309
(802) 524-9095
Facial & eye protection

Ivanko Barbell Co.
PO Box 1470
San Pedro, CA 90733-1470
(800) 247-9044
Fitness & exercise equip.

Jag
1825 S. Hill Street
Los Angeles, CA 90015
(800) 421-9371
Swimwear; beachwear

Jayfro Corp.
976 Hartford Tpke.
Waterford, CT 06385-4002
(203) 447-3001
Physical Ed. equip.

Jugs, Inc.
PO Box 365
Tualatin, OR 97062-0365
(503) 692-1635
Pitching machines

Kaepa, Inc.
5410 Kaepa Court
San Antonio, TX 78218-5535
(800) 776-9899
Tennis & athletic footwear

Kangaroos
1809 Clarkson Road
Chesterfield, MO 63017-5038
(314) 532-3357
Rugged outdoor footwear

Keds Corp
5 Cambridge Center
Cambridge, MA 02142
(800) 537-3336

Keys Fitness Products
11251 Leo Lane
Dallas, TX 75229
(800) 683-1236

K-Swiss
12300 Montague
Pacoima, CA 91331
(818) 897-3433
Athletic shoes

L. A. Gear
4221 Redwood Avenue
Los Angeles, CA 90066-5619
(800) 252-4327
Activewear & accessories

**Jack La Lanne
Fitness Products**
17150 New Hope Street
#408
Circleville, NY 10919
(914) 361-1700

Le Coq Sportif/Arena
28 Englehard Drive
Center Point 8A
Cranbury, NJ 08512-9599
(609) 655-1515
Activewear

Lifetime Products, Inc.
PO Box 1525
Clearfield, UT 84016
(801) 776-1532
Full line basketball

Lotto USA, Inc.
2301 Mc Daniel Drive
Carrollton, TX 75006-6868
(214) 351-2537
Soccer & tennis shoes, access.

Louisville Slugger Co. Inc.
PO Box 35700
Louisville, KY 40232-5700
(502) 585-5226

**Mac Gregor
Sporting Goods, Inc.**
336 Trowbridge Drive
Fond Du Lac, WI 54935
(414) 921-8200
Athletic equipment

Marcy Fitness Products
1900 S. Burgundy Place
Ontario, CA 91761
Exercise & fitness equip.

Merrygarden Athletic Wear
3500 Parkdale Avenue
Baltimore, MD 21211-1442
(301) 669-4400
Team uniforms

Mikasa Sports
17500 Redhill Avenue #180
Irvine, CA 92714
(714) 863-1588
Athletic balls

Mitre Sports
Genesco Park #690
PO Box 731
Nashville, TN 37202-0731
(615) 367-7475
Athletic footwear

Mizuno Sports
577 Airport Blvd.
Burlingame, CA 94010-2020
(415) 342-4100

Molten America
Box 70310
Reno, NV 89570-0310
(702) 358-4060
Footwear & access.

**New Balance
Athletic Shoe, Inc.**
38-42 Everett Street
Boston, MA 02134
(617) 783-4000

Nico/Boco
214 W. 39th Street
#705
New York, NY 10018
(212) 768-2679
footwear;sportswear

Nike
9000 SW Nimbus
Beaverton, OR 97500-7197
(503) 644-9000
Footwear & apparel

**Northern Cap
Manufacturing Co.**
510 1st Avenue N
Minneapolis, MN 55403-1681
(612) 332-8979

Patrick USA
PO Box 2308
Rohnert Park, CA 94927
(707) 586-0292
Soccer shoes and access.

Penn Athletic Products
306 S. 45th Avenue
Phoenix, AZ 85043-3998
(602) 269-1492
Racquets & racquetballs

Pony Sports & Leisure, Inc.
201 Rte. 17 N.
Rutherford, NJ 07070
(201)896-0101
Athletic footwear

Precor, Inc.
PO Box 3004
Bothell, WA 98041-3004
(800) 477-3267
Exercise equipment

Prince Manufacturing, Inc.
PO Box 2031
Princeton, NJ 08543-2031
(609) 896-2500
Tennis racquets & access.

Pro Kennex
9606 Kearny Villa Road
San Diego, CA 92126-4589
(619) 271-8390
Racquets & accessories

Puma, USA
147 Centre Street
Brockton, MA 02403
(508) 583-9100
Footwear & apparel

Rawlings
Sporting Goods
PO Box 22000
St. Louis, MO 63126-0090
(314) 349-3500

Reebok International, Ltd.
100 Technology Center Dr.
Stoughton, MA 02072
(617) 341-5000
Footwear & apparel

Riddell
3670 N. Milwaukee
Chicago, IL 60641-3032
(312) 794-1994
Protective gear

Rollerblade, Inc.
One Rollerblade Park
9700 W. 76th Street
Minneapolis, MN 55344-3714
(612) 944-6726
Skates; access; apparel

Ross Bicycles USA/Rand
51 Executive Blvd.
Farmingdale, NY 11735-4710
(516) 249-6000

Russell Athletic
PO Box 272
Alexander City, AL 35010-0272
(205) 329-5089
Teamwear apparel

Saranac Glove Co.
1201 Main Street
PO Box 786
Green Bay, WI 54305-4797
(800) 558-7302
Sport gloves

Spaulding Sports
Worldwide
425 Meadow Street
Chicòpee, MA 01021-2234
(413) 536-1200
Sporting goods & access.

Speedo
22nd Floor
11111 Santa Monica Blvd.
Los Angeles, CA 90025
(213) 473-0032
Swimwear

Spot-Bilt
Centennial Industrial Pk.
Centennial Dr. Box 6046
Peabody, MA 01961
(508) 532-9000
Athletic footwear

Stubbies
1900 Oakdale Avnue
San Francisco, CA 94124-20004
(415) 282-9100
Recreation apparel

S T X , Inc.
1500 bush Street
Baltimore, MD 21230-1987
(800) 368-2250
Equipment

Tachikara Ltd.
9742 Pflumm Road
Lenexa, KS 66215
(913) 888-5874
Athletic balls

Timex
Box 2126
Waterbury, CT 06722-2126
(203) 573-6912
Watches & timing devices

Titan Cycle Products
41 W. Yokuts #116
Stockton, CA 95207-5722
(209) 952-7512

Titan Exercise Equipment
1440 Lemay #110
Carrollton, TX 75007-4854
(214) 245-3000

Trace Athletic Corp
PO Box 1844
Bellevue, WA 98009
(206) 453-1055
Protective equip.

Tretorn Footwear
147 Centre Street
Brockton, MA 02402-2734
(508) 583-9100

Umbro USA
25 E. Court Street
Greenville, SC 29601-2819
(800) 762-2371
Sportswear

Universal Industries
5 Industrial Drive
Mattapoisett, MA 02739
(800) 225-8194

Wilson
Sporting Goods Co.
2233 West Street
River Grove, IL 60171-1895
(708) 456-6100

Yamaha Corp.of America
6722 Orangethorpe Ave.
Buena Park, CA 90620-1347
(714) 522-9437

York Barbell Co.Inc.
PO Box 1701
York, PA 17402-9409
(717) 767-6481

Sports Marketing/Management & Promotion Agencies

Listed in this section is a random sampling of sports marketing firms. This section is not a complete listing of firms, and will be expanded in future editions of The Sports Address Bible.

Advantage International
1025 Thomas Jefferson St., N.W.
Washington, D.C. 20007
(202) 333-3838

The American Consulting Corporation
55 Fifth Avenue
17th Floor
New York, NY 10003
(212) 627-4100

Bevilaqua International, Inc.
3490 Piedmont Road
Suite 1515
Atlanta, GA 30305
(404) 261-8882

Big Fights, Inc.
9 East 40th Street
New York, NY 10016
(212) 532-1711

Blumenfeld & Associates
130 W. 42nd Street
New York, NY 10036
(212) 764-1690

Burns Sports Celebrity Service
230 N. Michigan Avenue
Chicago, IL 60601
(312) 236-2377

Capital Sports, Inc.
Metro Center
One Station Place
Stamford, CT 06902
(203) 353-9900

Championship Group, Inc.
3690 N. Peachtree Road
Atlanta, GA 30341
(404) 457-5777

Custom Event Marketing
633 Third Avenue
20th Floor
New York, NY 10017
(212) 692-4080

DelWilber + Associates
1430 Springhill Road
Suite 250
McLean, VA 22102
(703) 749-9300

Don King Productions
32 East 69th Street
New York, NY 10021
(212) 744-7583

Edelman Public Relations Worldwide
456 Montgomery Street
Suite 800
San Francisco, CA 94104
(415) 433-5381

Events Internationale, Inc.
10 Lewis Street
Lincoln, MA 01773
(617) 259-1580

Events International, Inc.
637 N. 18th Street
Philadelphia, PA 19130
(215) 232-9333

Garvey Marketing Group
4320 La Jolla Village Dr.
Suite 300
San Diego, CA 92122
(619) 453-6666

Heritage Sports
34555 Chagrin Blvd.
Cleveland, OH 44022
(216) 247-6500

Hill and Knowlton, Inc.
One Illinois Center
111 E. Wacker Drive
Suite 1700
Chicago, IL 60017
(312) 565-1200

International Management Group
22 East 71st Street
New York, NY 10021
(212) 772-8900

ISL Marketing USA, Inc.
645 Fifth Avenue
Suite 901
New York, NY 10022
(212) 826-3730

The Management Company
625 Madison Avenue
11th Floor
New York, NY 10022
(212) 418-6990

Marketing Werks, Inc.
620 N. Michigan Avenue
Suite 530
Chicago, IL 60611
(312) 988-9385

Millsport Inc.
909 Third Avenue
15th Floor
New York, NY 10022
(212) 755-3090

Network International
701 Market Street
Suite 4400
Philadelphia, PA 19106
(215) 922-7824

ProServ, Inc.
888 17th Street, N.W.
Suite 1200
Washington, D.C. 20006
(202) 457-8800

SCA Promotions, Inc.
8300 Douglas Avenue
Suite 625
Dallas, TX 75225
(214) 363-8744

Sports Etcetera
2 Pennsylvania Plaza
New York, NY 10001
(212) 465-6565

**Sports Licensing Group
of America**
75 Rockefeller Plaza
16th Floor
New York, NY 10019
(212) 484-8807

Sports Programmers, Inc.
125 East 38th Street
New York, NY 10016
(212) 684-6100

Top Rank, Inc.
919 Third Avenue
New York, NY 10022
(212) 371-3232

West Nally, Inc.
3 East 54th Street
12th Floor
New York, NY 10022
(212) 759-2601

Olympic Games & Multi-Sport Games

Olympic Games

Albertville 1992
Winter Olympics
Organizing Committee
11 rue Pargoux
73200 Albertville
France
(33.7) 937 9242

Barcelona 1992 Summer Olympics

Barcelona Olympic
Organizing Committee
Edificio Hellas
C/Mejia Leguerica
S/N 08028
Barcelona, Spain
(34.3) 421 1992
Pres: Pasqual Maragall

Lillehammer 1994 Winter Olympics

Lillehammer Olympic
Organizing Committee
P.O. Box 106
Elvegaten 19
2601 Lillehammer,
Norway
(47.62) 71 994
Fax (47.62) 58 860
Pres.: Gerhard Heiberg

Atlanta 1996 Summer Olympics

Atlanta Olympic Organizing
Committee
P.O. Box 1996
250 Williams Street
Suite 6000
Atlanta, GA 30303
(404) 224-1996
Fax (404) 224-1997
Pres.: William Payne

Multi-Sport Games

Nagano 1998
Winter Olympics

Nagano Olympic
Organizing Committee
Fujin Kaikan Building
688-2 Minami Agata-machi
Nagano City 380, Japan
(81.262) 32 1998
Fax (81.262) 33 2004
Pres.: Eishiro Saito

World Masters Games
Vestergade 48 1
DK-8000 Aarhus C.
Denmark
(45.6) 20 9989

International Olympic Federations

International Olympic
Committee
Chateau de Vidy
CH-1007, Lausanne,
Switzerland
(41.21) 25 32 71
Pres: Juan Antonio Samaranch

International Amateur
Athletic Federation (IAAF)
3 Hans Crescent
Knightsbridge
London SWIX OLN,
England
(44.1) 581 87 71

Federation International des
Societes D' Aviron (FISA)
Case Postale 352
2001 Neuchatel,
Switzerland
(41.38) 25 72 22

International Badminton
Federation (IBF)
24 Winchcombe House
Winchcombe Street
Cheltenham, Gloucestershire
GL52 2NA, England
(44.242) 349 04

International Baseball
Association (IBA)
Pan American Plaza
Suite 490
201 S. Capitol Avenue
Indianapolis, IN 46225
(317) 237-5757
Pres: Dr. Robert E. Smith
Pres. Tel: (618) 664-1840

Federation of International
Basketball (FIBA)
PO Box 700607
Kistlerhofstr. 168
8000 Munich 70,
Germany
(49.89) 78 30 36

Federation of International
Bobsleigh and Tobogganing (FIBT)
Via Piranesi 44/b
20137 Milan, Italy
(39.2) 7197 51

Association of International
Amateur Boxing (AIBA)
Postamt Volkrdstr.,
Postlagernd
1137 Berlin, GDR,
Germany
(37.2) 22 93 413

Federation International
de Canoe (FIC)
G. Massaia 59
50134 Florence,
Italy
(39.55) 48 40 52

Federation of International
Amateur Cycling (FIAC)
Via Cassia, N. 490
00198 Rome, Italy
(39.6) 366 88 27

Federation of International
Equestrian (FEI)
PO Box 3000
Bolligenstrasse 54,
Berne 32, Switzerland
(41.31) 42 93 42

Federation of International
d'Escrime (Fencing)
32 rue de la Boetie
(33.1) 45 6114 72

Federation International de
Football Association (FIFA)
PO Box 85, Hitzigweg 11
CH-8030 Zurich, Switzerland
(015) 55400

Federational International
de Gymnastics (FIG)
Juraweg 12
3250 Lyss, Switzerland
(41.32) 84 19 60

International Handball
Federation (IHF)
Lange Gasse 10
4052 Bale, Switzerland
(41.61) 50 50 15

Federation de International
Hockey (FIH)
Avenue des Arts 1 (bte 5)
1040 Brussels, Belgium
(32.2) 219 45 37

International Ice Hockey
Federation (IIHF)
Bellevuestrasse 8
A-1190 Vienna, Austria
(43.1) 32 52 52

International Judo
Federation (IJF)
Avenida del Trabajo 2666
C.P. 1406
Buenos Aires, Argentina
(54.1) 632.5002

International Skating
Union
Promenade 73
7270 Davos-Platz,
Switzerland
(41.83) 3 75 77

Federation de
International Ski (FIS)
Worbstrasse 210
3073 Gumligen B. Bern,
Switzerland
(41.31) 52 58 15

International Table
Tennis Federation (ITTF)
53 London Road
St. Leonards-on-Sea
East Sussex TN37 6AY,
England
(44.424) 72 12 12

International Tennis
Federation (ITF)
Palliser Road,
Barons Court, London W14 9EN
(44.1) 381 8060

Union International
de Tir (Rifle)
Bavariaring 21
8000 Munich 2, Germany
(49.89) 53 42 93

Federation International
de Tir a l'Arc (Archery-FITA)
Via Cerva 30
20122 Milan, Italy
(39.2) 79 60 38

International Volleyball
Federation (FIVB)
Avenue de la Gare 12
1003 Lausanne, Switzerland
(41.21) 20 89 32

International Weightlifting
Federation (IWF)
Rosemberg Hp. U.1
1374 Budapest P.F. 614,
Hungary
(36.1) 311 162

International Yacht
Racing Union (IYRU)
60 Knightsbridge,
Westminster
London SWEX 7JX, England
(44.1) 235 6221

International Luge
Federation (FIL)
Olympiadestrasse 168
8786 Rottenmann, Austria
(43.3614) 22 66

Federation International
de Lutte Amateur (FILA)
Avenue Ruchonnet 3
1003 Lausanne, Switzerland
(41.21) 22 84 26

International Amateur
Nation Federation (FINA)
Avenue Mon-Repos 14
1005 Lausanne, Switzerland
(41.21) 22 80 76

Union of International
Pentathlon and Modern
Biathalon (UIPMB)
Birger Jarsgatan 113: C,3,TR
11356 Stockholm, Sweden
(46,8) 3108 40

Recognized International Federations

The following international organizations are recognized by the IOC but do not participate in the Olympic Games as medal sports

**International Aéronautic
Federation (FAI)**
6 rue Galilee
75782 Paris cedex 16,
France
(33.1) 47 20 91 85

**Confederation Mondiale du
Sport de Boules**
Stade Bouliste Rainier III
Principal de Monaco
(33.93) 50 95 14

**International Curling
Federation (ICF)**
2 Coates Crescent
Edinburgh EH3 7AN,
Great Britain
(O31) 220 1351

**World Union of Karate
Organizations (WUKO)**
Senpaku Shinko Bldg.
1-15-16 Toranomon,
Minato-ku,
Tokyo 105, Japan
(81.3) 503 6638

**Federation International
de Pelota Vasca (Jai Alai-FIPV)**
5 Calle Aldamar, I Dcha
San Sebastian 3, Spain
(34.43) 42 84 15

**International Orienteering
Federation (IOF)**
PO Box 76
Solientuna, Sweden
(46) 8 35 34 55

**Federation International
des Quilleurs (Bowling-FIQ)**
5301 S. 76th Street
Greendale, WI 53129
(414) 421-6400
Pres: Roger Tessman

**International Racquetball
Federation (IRF)**
815 North Weber
Colorado Springs, CO 80903
(719) 635-5396
Pres: Luke St. Onge

**International Roller
Skating Federation (FIRS)**
PO Box 6579
1500 S. 70th Street
Lincolln, NE 68506
(402) 483-7551
Pres: Budd Van Roekel

**International Softball
Federation (ISF)**
PO Box 11437
2801 N.E. 59th Street
Oklahoma City, OK 73111
(405) 424-5266
Pres: Don E. Porter

**International Federation of
Sports Acrobatics (IFSA)**
18 Tolbouhin Blvd.
1000 Sofia, Bulgaria
(359.2) 66 1556

**World Taekwondo
Federation (WTF)**
San 76 Yuksam-Dong
Kangnam-Ku, Seoul,
Korea
(82.2) 566 2505

International Squash
Racquets Federation (ISRF)
93 Cathedral Road
Cardiff, Wales CF1 9PG,
Great Britain
(44.222) 374 771

International Water Ski
Federation (IWSF)
Via August 18
08006 Barcelona, Spain
(34.3) 238 3003

Confederation Mondiale de
Activites Subaquatics (CMAS)
47 rue du Commerce
75015 Paris, France
(33.1) 4575 4275

International Trampoline
Federation (ITF)
Otzbergstrasse 10
6000 Frankfurt/Main 71,
Germany

National Olympic Committees

Listed below are the National Olympic Committees recognized by the International Olympic Committee (IOC)

International Olympic
Committee
Chateau de Vidy
CH-1007 Lausanne,
Switzerland
(412) 25 32 17
Pres: Juan Antonio Samaranch

Afghanistan Olympic
Committee
Kabul, Afghanistan

Albania Olympic
Committee
Rruga Dervish Hima 31
Tirana, Albania

Algeria Olympic
Committee
B.P. 64, El Biar
Alger R.P., Algeria

Andoran Olympic
Committee
Barbot Camp No. 2-3-2
Andoree-la-Vieille,
Andora

Angola Olympic
Committee
B.P. 5466
Luanda, Angola

Antigua Olympic
Committee
PO Box 747
St. John',
Antigua W.I.

Argentina Olympic
Committee
Juncal N. 1662
Codigo Postal 1062
Buenos Aires,
Argentina

Aruba Olympic
Committee
PO Box 253
San Nicolaas,
Aruba

Australia Olympic
Committee
Level 1, Sports House
157 Gloucester Street
Sydney, NSW 2000
Australia

Austria Olympic
Committee
Prinz-Eugen-Strasse 12
1040 Vienna, Austria

Bahamas Olympic
Association
PO Box 6250 (SS)
Nassau, Bahamas

Bahrain Olympic
Committee
PO Box 26406
Bahrain

Bangladesh Olympic
Association
Tennis Complex,
Ramna Green
Dacca 2, Bangladesh

Barbados Olympic
Association
PO Box 659
Bridgetown,
Barbados W.I.

Belgium Olympic
Committee
Avenue de Bouchout 9
1020 Brussels,
Belgium

Belize Olympic Association
PO Box 103
Belize City, Belize

Benin Olympic Committee
B.P. No. 032767
Cotonou, Benin

Bermuda Olympic
Association
PO Box 1665
Hamilton 5, Bermuda

Bhutan Olympic
Committee
PO Box 103
Thimphu, Bhutan

Bolivia Olympic
Committee
Casilla 4481
La Paz, Bolivia

Botswana Olympic
Committee
PO Box 918
Gaborone, Botswana

Brazil Olympic
Committee
Rua da Assembleia
10-32 Andar
Salas 32/11
20011 Rio de Janeiro,
Brazil

Brunei National
Olympic Council
PO Box 2008
Bandar Seri Begawan
Negara Brunei
Darussalam

Bulgaria Olympic
Committee
Rue Anghel Kanchev 4
1000 Sofia, Bulgaria

National Olympic &
Sports Council of Burkinabe
B.P. 3925
Ouagadougou, Burkina Faso

Burma Olympic Committee
Aungsan Stadium
Mingal Taungnyunt Township
Rangoon Division 11221
Burma

Cameroon Olympic Committee
B.P. 528
Yaounde, Cameroun

Canada Olympic Association
2380 Pierre Dupuy
Montreal, Quebec H3C 3R4
(514) 861-3371

Cayman Islands Olympic
Committee
PO Box 1529
Grand Cayman,
British West Indies

Central Africa Olympic Committee
B.P. 154
Bangui, Central Africa

Chad Olympic Committee
B.P. 519
N'Djamena, Chad

Chile Olympic Committee
Vicuna Mackenna 44
Casilla 2239
Santiago, Chile

Chinese Olympic Committee
9 Tiyuguan Road
Beijing, People's
Republic of China

Chinese Taipei Olympic Committee
PO Box 3420
Nr.3, Lane 153,
Chang An Road East
Section 2, Taipei,
China

Colombia Olympic Committee
Carrea 16, No. 37-20
Apartado Aereo (Postal) 5093
20 Bogota, Colombia

Congo Olympic Committee
B.P. 1007
Brazzaville, Congo

Cook Islands Sports and Olympic Association
PO Box 569
Rarotonga, Cook Islands

Costa Rica Olympic Committee
PO Box 5388
1000 San Jose,
Costa Rica

Cuba Olympic Committee
Zona Postal 4
Calle 13, No. 601
Havana, Cuba

Cyprus National Olympic Committee
20 Ionos Street
PO Box 3931
Nicosie, Cyprus
Fed. Republic of Czechoslovakian Olympic Committee
Narodni 33
11000 Prague 1,
Czechoslovakia

Denmark Olympic Committee
Idraettens Hus
Brondby Stadion 20
Denmark

Djibouti Olympic Committee
B.P. 16
Djibouti

Dominican Republic Olympic Committee
Calle Pedro Henriquez
Urena 107
Apartado Postal 406
Santo Domingo,
Domican Republic

German Olympic Committee
Postfach 710130
Otto-Fleck-Scheneise 12
6000 Frankfurt/Main 71,
Germany

Egypt Olympic Committee
Kasr-el-Nil 13
PO Box 2055
Cairo, Egypt

El Salvador Olympic Committee
Apartado Postal No. 759
Gimnasio Nacional
Jose Adolfo Pineda
San Salvador,
El Salvador

Equador Olympic Committee
Avenida de las Americas
PO Box No. 4567
Guayaquil, Equador

Ethiopia Olympic Committee
B.P. 3241
Addis-Abeba, Ethiopia

Fiji Olympic Committee
PO Box 1279
Suva, Fiji

Finnish Olympic Committee
Radiokatu 12
SF-00240 Helsinki,
Finland

France Olympic Committee
23 rue D'Anjou
75008 Paris, France

Gabon Olympic Committee
B.P. 2266
Libreville, Gabon

Gambia National Olympic Committee
Independence Stadium
PO Box 605
Banjul, Gambia

Ghana Olympic Committee
PO Box M. 439
Ministries Branch
Accra, Ghana

The British Olympic Association
1 Wandsworth Plain
London SW18 1EH,
England

Greece (Hellenic) Olympic Committee
4 rue Kapsali
10674 Athens, Greece

Grenada Olympic Association
Ministry of Sports
Carenage, St. George's,
Grenada

Guam National Olympic Committee
PO Box 21809
GMF Guam, Marshall
Islands 96921

Guatemala Olympic Committee
Palacio de Deportes,
Zona 4
Guatemala, Central America

Guinean Olympic Committee
Ministry of Sport and Arts
B.P.262
Conakry, Guinea

Equatorial Guinea National Olympic Committee
Ministry of Education &
Sports
Malabo, Equatoriale Guinea

Guyana Olympic Association
PO Box 10133
Georgetown, Guyana

Haitian Olympic Committee
PO Box 2405
Av. Marie-Jeanne No. 21
Cite de l'Expositon
Port-au-Prince, Haiti

**Honduras Olympic
Committee**
C.A. Apartado Postal 36C
Tegucigalpa, Honduras

**Hong Kong Olympic
Committee**
Prince's Building 1211
Hong Kong

Hungary Olympic Committee
Balog Tihamer 4
1118 Budapest, Hungary

**Iceland Olympic
Committee**
Laugardal
105 Reykjavik, Iceland

**Indian Olympic
Association**
Room 1104, Block 'F'
Jawahar Lal Nehru Stadium
New Delhi 110003
India

**Indonesia Olympic
Committee**
c/o Koni Pusat Senayan
Djakarta, Indonesia

**Iranian Olympic
Committee**
PO Box 15815/1589
Teheran, Iran

Iraqui Olympic
PO Box 441
Kharbandah,
Baghdad, Iraq

**Ireland Olympic
Committee**
14 Herbert Street
Dublin 2, Ireland

**Olympic Committee of
Israel**
6, Haarbaa Street
Tel-Aviv 64739, Israel

**Italiano Olympic
Committee**
Foro Italico
Rome 00194, Italy

**Ivory Coast Olympic
Committee**
B.P. 979
Abidjan 08,
Ivory Coast

**Jamaica Olympic
Association**
PO Box 544
Kingston 10, Jamaica

**The Japanese Olympic
Committee**
1-1-1 Jinan,
Shibuya-Ku
Tokyo 150, Japan

**Jordan Olympic
Committee**
PO Box 19258
Amman, Jordan

**Kenya Olympic
Association**
PO Box 46888
Nairobi, Kenya

**Olympic Committee of
the Democratic People's
Republic of Korea**
PO Box 56
Pyong Yang, Democratic
People's Rep. of Korea

Korea Olympic Committee
C.P.O. Box 1106
Seoul, Korea

Kuwait Olympic Committee
PO Box no. 795
Safat, 13008, Kuwait

Laos Olympic Committee
B.P. 819
Vientiane, Laos

**Lebanese Olympic
Committee**
PO Box 23
Hazmieh-Beyrouth,
Lebanon

**Lesotho Olympic
Committee**
PO Box 138
Maeru, Lesotho

**Liberian Olympic Games
Association**
PO Box 481
Monrovia, Liberia

**Libyan Olympic
Committee**
Jamahiriya Street
PO Box 879
Tripoli, Libya

**Liechtenstein Olympic
Committee**
P.O.B. Rathaus 19
9494 Schaan,
Liechtenstein

**Luxembourg Olympic
Committee**
7 Victor Hugo Avenue
Luxembourg 1750

**Madagascar Olympic
Committee**
B.P. 4188
Tananarive,
Madagascar

**Olympic Association
of Malawi**
PO Box 867
Blantyre, Malawi

**Olympic Council of
Malaysia**
Stadium Negara,
Hang Jebat Road
05-05 Kuala Lumpur,
Malaysia

**Maldives Olympic
Committee**
Male, Republic of Maldives

**Malien Olympic
Committee**
B.P. 88
Bamako, Mali

**Malta Olympic
Committee**
PO Box 39
Valletta, Malta

**Mauritanein Olympic
Committee**
B.P. 1360
Nouakchott, Mauritania

**Mauritius Olympic
Committee**
8, Felicien Mallefille St.
Port-Louis, Mauritius

Mexico Olympic Committee
Ave. del Conscripto
y Anillo Periferico
Mexico 10 DF, Mexico

**Monaco Olympic
Committee**
Nouveau Stade
Louis 11
Av. Prince Hereditaire
Albert
98000 Monaco

**Mongolia Olympic
Committee**
Baga Toirog 55
Oulan-Bator, Mongolia

Moroco Olympic
Committee
Centre de Belle-Vue
Rabat, Aquedal,
Moroco

Mozambique Olympic
Committee
19 r/c, Avenida Mao Tse Tung
Caixa postal 1404
Maputo, Mozambique

Nepal Olympic
Committee
Dashrath Rangashala
Tripureswore 2090
Kathmandu, Nepal

Netherlands Olympic
Committee
Surinamestraat 33
La Have 2585
Netherlands Antilies

Papua New Guinea
Olympic Committee
PO Box 467
Boroko, Papua,
New Guinea

New Zealand Olympic
Association
PO Box 643
Wellington, New Zealand

Nicaragua Olympic
Committee
PO Box 4981
Managua, Nicaragua

Nigerien Olympic
Committee
B.P. 11975
Niamey, Niger

Nigeria Olympic
Committee
PO Box 3156
Lagos, Nigeria

Norwegian Olympic
Committee
Hauger Skolevei 1
1351 Rud, Norway

National Olympic
Committee of Oman
PO Box 5842
Ruwi, Oman

Pakistan Olympic
Association
Olympic House
Temple Road 2
Lahore, Pakistan

Panama Olympic
Committee
Apartado 66203
El Dorado, Panama

Paraquay Olympic
Committee
Casilla Postal 1420
Asuncion, Paraguay

Peru Olympic Committee
Estadio Naciona]
Puerta 4, Lima, Peru

Philippine Olympic
Committee
Rizal Memorial Sports
Complex, Vito Cruz
Manilla 2800, Philippines

Poland Olympic
Committee
Rue Frascati 4
00483 Varsovie, Poland

Portugal Olympic
Committee
Rue Bramcamp 12,
R.C.esq.
1200 Lisbon, Portugal

**Puerto Rico
Olympic Committee**
Apartado 8
San Juan, Puerto Rico 00902

Qatar Olympic Committee
PO Box 7494
Doha, Qatar

Romania Olympic Committee
Str. Vasile Conta nr. 16
Bucarest, Section I,
Romania

**Rwanda National
Olympic Committee**
B.P. 1044
kigali, Rwanda

**Sammarinese Olympic
Committee**
P.O. Box 22
Via Venticinque Marzo 11
47031 Domagnano

**Saint Vincent and the
Grenadines Olympic**
Association
P.O. Box 1644
Kingstown, Saint Vincent

**American Samoa National
Olympic Committee**
PO Box 3040
Pago Pago,
American Samoa 96799

**Western Samoa Mateur
Sports Federation &
Olympic Committee**
Ministry of Youth
Sports & Cultural
Affairs
Private Bag
Apia, Western Samoa

**Saudi Arabia Olympic
Committee**
PO Box 5844
Riyadh 11442
Saudi Arabia

**Senegal National
Olympic Committee**
B.P. 356
blvd. de la Republique
Dakar, Senegal

**Seychelles National
Olympic Committee**
PO Box 580
Victoria-Mahe,
Seychelles

**Sierra Leone Olympic
and Overseas Games
Committee**
c/o National Sports
Council, PO Box 1181
Siaka Stevens Stadium
Freetown, Sierra Leone

**Singapore National
Olympic Council**
National Stadium
Singapore 1439
Singapore

**Solomon Islands
National Olympic
Committee**
PO Box 532
Honiara, Solomon Islands

**Somali National Olympic
Committee**
PO Box 523
Mogdiscio, Somali

**Espanol Olympic
Committee**
Nunez de Balboa 120
28006 Madrid, Spain

**National Olympic
Committee of Sri Lanka**
Rakshan Mandiraya
21 Vauxhall Street
Colombo 2, Sri Lanka

**Sudanese Olympic
Committee**
PO Box 1938
Baladia Street
Kartoum, Sudan

**Surinam Olympic
Committee**
PO Box 1171
Van Roosmalenstraat
30-Sunecon
Paramaribo,
Surinam

**Swaziland Olympic and
Commonwealth Games**
Association
PO Box 835
Mbabane, Swaziland

**The Swedish Olympic
Committee**
Idrottens Hus
12387 Farsta, Sweden
Switzerland Olympic
Committee
Case Postale
8907 Wettswil,
Switzerland

**Syria Olympic
Committee**
PO Box 3375
Damas, Syria

**Tanzania Olympic
Committee**
PO Box 2182
Dar-es-Salaam,
Tanzania

**Olympic Committee
of Thailand**
226 Sriayuhya Road
Box 3-44 Dusit
Bangkok, Thailand

**Togo National Olympic
Committee**
B.P. 1320
Lome, Togo

**Tonga Amateur Sports
Association and Olympic**
Committee
PO Box 1278
Nuku'Alofa, Tonga

**Trinidad and Tobago
Olympic Association**
PO Box 529
Port-of-Spain,
Trinidad W.I.

**Tunisia Olympic
Committee**
rue Pierre de
Coubertin 2bis
Tunis, Tunisia

**Turkish Olympic
Committee**
Yerebatan Cad. No. 2
Sultanahmet 34410
Istanbul, Turkey

**Uganda Olympic
Committee**
PO Box 2610
Kampala, Uganda

**United Arab Emirates
Olympic Committee**
PO Box 4350
Dubai, United Arab
Emirates

**United States Olympic
Committee**
1750 East Boulder Street
Colorado Springs, CO 80909
(719) 578-4529

**Uruguay Olympic
Committee**
Canelones 1044
PO Box 6193
Montevideo, Uruguay

**U.S.S.R. Olympic
Committee**
Luzhnetskaya Nab.8
Moscow, Russia (U.S.S.R)

Vanuatu Olympic
Committee
PO Box 284
Port Vila, Vanuatu

Venezuela Olympic
Committee
Apartado Postal 6370
Caracas 1010, Venezuela

Vietnam Olympic
Committee
36 Bouldevard Tran Phu
Hanoi, Vietnam

Virgin Islands
Olympic Committee
PO Box 1576
Frederiksted, St. Croix,
Virgin Islands 00840

British Virgin Islands
Olympic Committee
PO Box 335, Road Town
Tortola, British V.I.

Yemen Arab Republic
Olympic Committee
PO Box 2701
Sanaa, Arab Republic
of Yemen

Yemen Olympic Committee
PO Box 933
Crater-Aden,
Democratic Republic of
Yemen

Yugosiavia Olympic
Committee
Ada Cingalija 10
11030 Belgrade,
Yugoslavia

Zaire Olympic
Committee
B.P. 3626
Kinshasa, Gombe,
Zaire

Olympic Committee
of Zambia
PO Box 20728
Kitwe, Zambia

Zimbabwe Olympic
Committee
PO Box 4718
Harare, Zimbabwe

Recognized Sports Associations

Association of the International Winter Sports Federation
Worbstrasse 210
3073 Gumbligen b. Bern,
Switzerland
(41.31) 52 58 15
 Association of the IOC
Recognized International
Sports Federations
San 76 Yuksam-Dong
Kangnam-Ku, Seoul,
South Korea

National Olympic Committee of Africa
B.P. 1363
Yaounde, Cameroun,
Africa

International Olympic Academy
4, rue Kapsali
10674 Athens,
Greece

Olympic Council of Asia
PO Box 6706
Hawalli, Kuwait 32042

National Olympic Committee of Europe
Ave. de Bouchout 9
1020 Brussels,
Belgium
(32.2) 479 19 40

**Central American &
Caribbean Sports
Organization**
Aave. del Conscripto y
Anillo Periferico
Apartado Postal 77-175
Mexico 10, D.F.,
Mexico
(52.5) 557 36 32

**International Sports
Committee of the
Mediterranean**
4, rue Kapsali
10674 Athens, Greece
(30.1) 721 23 13

**Oceania National
Olympic Committee**
G.P.O. Box 284
South Melbourne 3205,
Victoria, Australia
(61.3) 699 38 66

**Pan American Sports
Organization**
Apartado Postal 36-24
Ave. de Conscripto y
Anillo Periferico
Mexico 10, D.F., Mexico

**International Sports
Medicine Federation**
Felipe Becker, 95
91330 Porto Alegre,
Brazil
(55.512) 348 083

**Association of International
Sports Press**
Via Paola da Cannobio 9
20 122 Milan, Italy
(39.2) 87 77 85

**European Sports
Press Union**
I Franz Mehring Platz
1017 Berlin, Germany
(37.2) 585 22 23

**Federation of International
Sports Universities**
Rue General Thys 12
1050 Brussels, Belgium
(32.2) 640 68 73

**The International Association
of Olympic Medical Officers**
The Hospital of the Cross
Rugby-Warwickshire,
England
(0788) 7 28 31

**International World Games
Association**
Gaylingstrasse 5
7800 Freiburg, Germany
761 65 017

**Federation of International
Sports Cinema & Television**
47, via Delia Mendola
00135 Rome, Italy
(39.6) 320 16 55

Academy of Sports
4, rue de Teheran
75008 Paris, France
(33.1) 45 62 97 15

**International Assembly
of National Organizations
of Sport**
PO Box 22
East Melbourne,
3002 Victoria, Australia

International Baseball

**International Baseball
Association**
Greenville College
Greenville, IL 62246
(618) 664-1840
Pres: Dr. Robert Smith

**Argentina Beisbol
Federation**
Avenida Cordoba
3543-20 piso
H-1168, Buenos Aires,
Argentina

**Australia Baseball
Federation**
PO Box 506
Cowandilla, S.A. 5003,
Australia
08.354.0577

**Osterreichister
Baseball V.S.**
Prinz-Eugen Strasse 33
4024 Linz, Austria

**Bahamas Baseball
Association**
PO Box N1747
Nassau, Bahamas

**Belgium Baseball &
Softball Federation**
Galgenweellaan 16
Antwerp 2050, Belgium
3.325.49.10

**Bolivia Beisbol &
Softball Federation**
Edificio Santa Isabel,
Block A
Piso 19, officina 1902
Casilla 20392
La Paz, Bolivia

**British Amateur Baseball
Federation**
197 Newbridge Road
North Humberside
Hull HU9 2LR, England

Canada Baseball
1600 James Naismith Drive
Gloucester, Ontario K1B 5N4

**Chile Beisbol
Federation**
Casilla 13186
Santiago, Chile
(56.2) 22.99

**Baseball Association
of the Peoples Republic
of China**
9, Tiyuguan Road
Beijing, China

**Chinese Taipei Amateur
Baseball Association**
c/o Broadcasting Corp.
of China
No. 53, Sec. 3
Jen-Al Road
Taipei, Taiwan

**Colombiana Beisbol
Federacion**
Edificio Concasa of 404
2253 Cartagena de Indias
Colombia

**Cubana Beisbol
Federacion**
Calle 13, No. 601
Zona Postal 4,
Vedado, Havana, Cuba

Czech Baseball & Softball Asso.
VSEH Rdodva 16
110 00 Pravda 1
Czechoslovakia

**Dominicana Beisbol
Federacion**
Mozart 152
Feria III, Zona 7
Santo Domingo, Dominican Repub.
(809) 566-9515

Ecuador Beisbol Federacion
Estadio "Yeyo Uraga"
Guayaquil, Ecuador S.A.

**Savadorena Beisbol
Federacion**
Col. Miramonte
San Salvador,
Salvador, C.A.

Finland Baseball Federation
Westendintie 40
02160 Espoo, Finland

**Francaise Baseball
Federation**
73 rue Curial
Paris, 75019 France

**German Baseball
Federation DBV**
Lubecker Strasse 8
5000 Koin 40
Germany

Guam Major League Baseball
Association PO Box 1617
Agana, Guam 96910
(671) 477-9125

**Nacional Beisbol Federacion
Diamante Enrique**
Torrebiarte
Au Simeon Canas,
Final, Zona 2 Guatemala,
Guatemala C.A.

**Honduras Amateur Baseball
Federation**
Parque de Lempira
Reina Zepada
Apartado Postal T-159
Tegucigalpa D.C.,
Honduras C.A.

**Amateur Baseball Federation
of India**
112-14 Onkar Nagar-B
Delhi 110035, India

**Indonesia Amateur
Baseball Federation**
9,J1, Panglima
Polim Raya
Kebayorn Baru
Jakarta Selatan, Indonesia

Italiana Baseball Federazione
Viale Tiziano 70
Rome 00196, Italy

**Japan Amateur Baseball
Federation**
Palaceside Building
1-1-1, Hitotsubashi
Chiyoda-Ku
Tokyo 100, Japan

**Korea Amateur Baseball
Association**
No. 19 Mookyo-Dong
Choong-Ku, Seoul,
Korea
(82.2) 77-4050

**Mexicana Ametur Beisbol
Federacion**
Plaza de la Republica 51
4 to, Piso
Mexico, D.F., Mexico
(52.5) 535.19.30

**Royal Dutch Baseball
Association**
PO Box 60
2080 AB Santpoort-Zuid,
Netherlands

**Netherlands Antilliaanse
Baseball Federation**
Saint Rosa 62
PO Box 488
Curacao, Netherlands
Antilles

**Nicaragua Beisbol
Federacion**
Centro Civico,
Camino Ortega S.
Monduio R
Managua, Nicaragua

**Panama Beisbol
Federacion**
Apartado 6075
Zona 2
Panama, Panama C.A.

**Philippine Amateur
Baseball Association**
PO Box 130
College Laguna 3720
Philippines

Polski Baseball Federation
ul. Sygnaly 62
44-251 Rybnick-Gotartowice,
Poland

**Federacion de Beisbol A
de Puerto Rico**
Apartado 41058
Minillas Station
Santurce, Puerto Rico 00940
(809) 722-3340

**Soviet Union National
Baseball Association**
Lushbetsky Embankment
NR.8
Nr.1, Goskmsport
Moscow, USSR

**Espanola Beisbol y Softbol
Federacion**
Caspe 172, 20 A
Barcelona, 08013 Spain

**Sri Lanka Amateur Baseball
Association**
Maligawatte Secretariat
Colombo, 10 Sri Lanka

Swedish Baseball Federation
Idrottens Hus
Farsta S-123
87 Sweden
(46.87) 13.6336

Swiss Baseball Federation
Bleich, CH-9470 Werdenberg
Switzerland

U.S. Baseball Federation
2160 Greenwood Avenue
Trenton, NJ 08609
(609) 586-2381

**Venezuela Beisbol
Federacion**
Animas a Platanal
Edif. Las Marias
Piso 4-401, Av. Urdaneta
Caracas, Venezuela

**British Virgin Islands
Amateur Baseball Association**
PO Box 231
Road Town, Tortola
British Virgin Islands

**Virgin Islands Amateur
Baseball Federation**
c/o First Pennsylvania Bank
PO Box 1737
St. Thomas, U.S.
Virgin Islands, 00801
Pres: Valentino I. McBean

**Yugoslavia National Baseball
Komision**
Zrinsko Frankopanska 17
Split, 58000 Yugoslavia
Pres: Dekovic Edo.

International Basketba

The following addresses are a list of International
Amateur Basketball Federations (FIBA)

FIBA

PO Box 70067
Kistlerhofstr. 168
D-8000 Munchen,
Germany 70

Affiliated National Federations

AFGHANISTAN:
Afghanistan Amateur Basketball Association Olympic
Kabul, Afghanistan

ALBANIA:
Albanian Basketball Federation
Rruga 'Abdi Totptani: 3
Tirana, Albania

ALGERIA
Federation Algerienne de Basketball
B.P 88, El Biar-Alger, Algeria

AMERICAN SAMOA;
American Samoa Amateur Athletic Association
PO Box 607, Pago Pago
American Samoa 96799

ANGOLA
Federacao Angolana de Basketball (F.A.B.)
C.P.6711, Luanda

ANTIQUA:
Antigua Amateur Basketball Association
PO Box 747.
St John's

ARGENTINA;
Confederacion Argentina de Basketball
Alsina 1569, 20-203
Buenos Aires

AUSTRALIA;
Australian Basketball Federation
First Floor, 203 New South Head Rd.
Edgecliff, N.S.W.2027

AUSTRIA
Osterreichischer Basketball-Verband Haus Des Sports.
Prinz-Eugen-Strasse 12
A-1040 Wien

BAHAMAS;
Bahamas Amateur Basketball Association
PO Box No. 5143,
Manama

BAHRAIN
Bahrain Basketball Association
PO Box No. 5143

BANGLADESH;
Bangladesh Basketball federation
Room No. 3, 2nd Floor,
Dacca Stadium, Dacca-2

BARBADOS:
Barbados Amateur Basketball Association
Y.M.C.A., Pinfold Street
St. Michael

BELGIUM:
Federation Royale Beige des Societes de Basketball
27 Avenue P.H. Spaak
B-1070 Bruxelies

BELIZE:
Belize Amateur Basketball Association
PO Box 1188
Belize City

BENIN, PEOPLE'S REPUBLIC OF:
Federation Beninoise de Basketball
B.P. 36 Porto Novo

BHUTAN:
Bhutan Basketball Federation
PO Box 103
Thiumphu

BOLIVIA:
Federacion Boliviana de Basquetbol
Casilla 3310
La Paz

BRAZIL:
Conferacao Brasileira de
Basketball
Edificio Avenida Central,
Avenida Rio Branco
156, salas 2132/3
Rio de Janeiro

BRITISH VIRGIN ISLANDS:
British Virgin Islands
Amateur Basketball Federation
c/o Mark Vanterpool
PO Box 70
Road Town, Tortola

BRUNEI:
Brunei State Amateur Basketball
Association
PO Box 194
Bandar Seri Begawan
Seria, Negara Brunei Darussalam

BULGARIA:
Bulgarian Basketball Federation
Bouldevard Tolboukhine 18
Sofia

BURMA:
Burma Basketball Federation
Aung San Stadium
Rangoon

CAMERON;
Federation Camerounaise de
Basketball
B.P. 2733, Yaounde-Messa

CANADA:
Canadian Amateur Basketball
Association
1600 James Naismith Drive
Gloucester, Ontario K1B 5N4

CAYMAN ISLANDS:
Cayman Islands Amateur Basketball
Association
PO Box 291
West Bay, Grand Cayman B.W.I.

CENTRAL AFRICA:
Federation Centrafricaine de
Basketball
B.P. 943, Bangui

CHAD:
Federation Omnisport Tchadienne
De Basketball
B.P. 758, N'Djamena

CHILI:
Federacion de Basquetbol de Chile
Nataniel No. 190
Santiago de Chile

CHINA, PEOPLE"s REPUBLIC OF:
Basketball Association of the
People's Republic of China
9 Tiyuguan Road, Beijing

COLOMBIA:
Federacion Colombiana de Baloncesto
Apartado Aereo 6698
Bogota

CONGO:
Federacion Congolaise de Basketball
B.P. 2061, Brazzaville

COSTA RICA:
Federacion Costarricense de Baloncesto
Apartado 5009
1000 San Jose

CUBA
Federacion Cubana de Baloncesto
Calle 13 601
Zona Postal 4
La Habana

CYPRUS:
The Cyprus Basketball
Federacion
1 Stassinou Street
PO Box 2448
Engomi, Nicosia

CZECHOLSOVAKIA:
Federation Tchecoslavaque de
Basketball
Na Porici 12
11530 Praha 1

DENMARK:
Dansk Basquetball-Forbund
Rysenteensgade 6
DK-1564 Copenhagen V

DJIBOUTIE:
Federacion Djiboutieene de
Basketball
Comite National des Sports,
Rue Pierre Pascal
B.P. 406, Djibouti

DOMINICA:
Dominica Amateur Basketball
Association
PO Box 71, Roseau

DOMINICAN REPUBLIC
Federacion Dominicana de
Baloncesto
Palacio de los Deportes
Centro Olimpico, Juan Pablo Duarte
Santo Domingo, Zona 6

ECUADOR:
Associacion Ecuatoriana de
Basket-ball
Correo Apartado 3409
Guayaquil

EGYYPT:
Egyptian Basketball Federation
26th of July Street 10
Cairo

EL SALVADOR:
Federacion Salvadorena de Basketbol
Gimnacio Nacional 6a-10a
Calle Poniente
San Salvador

ENGLAND:
English Basket-Ball
Association
Calomax House
Lupton Avenue
Leeds LS97EE

ETHIOPIA:
Ethiopian Amateur Basketball
Federation
PO Box 324
Addis Abeba

FIJI
Fiji Amateur Basketball Federation
PO Box 2348
Suba

FINLAND:
Finnish Basketball Association
Topeliuksenkatu 41 A,
SF-00250 Helsinki 25

FRANCE:
Federacion Francaise de
Basket-Ball
14 rue Froment, B.P. 49
F-75521 Paris Cedex 11

GABON:
Federation Gabonaise de
Basketball
B.P. 679, Libreville

GAMBIA:
Gambia Basketball Federation
c/o Department of Youth
Sports and Culture
8c Marina Parade, Banjul

GAZA:
The Palestinean Basketball
Federation
PO Box 204, Gaza

GERMANY
Deutscher Basketball Bund
Postfach 708
D-5800 Hagen 1

GHANA:
**Amateur Basketball Association
of Ghana**
National Sports Council
PO Box 1272, Accra

GREECE:
Hellenic Basketball Federation
30 Averof Street
6R-10433
Athens

GRENADA:
Grenada Basketball Association
c/o Tyrone Belfon
Young Street
St. George's

GUAM:
Guam Amateur Basketball Union
PO Box 3967
Agana, Guam 96910

GUATEMALA:
**Federacion Baloncesto de
Guatemala**
12 Ave. 25 Calle, Zona 5
Ciudad Guatemala

GUINEA:
**Federation Guinneenne de
Basket-ball**
B.P. 262, Conakry

GUYANA:
**Guyana Amateur Basketball
Federacion**
PO Box 10563
Georgetown

HAITI:
Federation Haitienne de Basketball
PO Box 2538
Port-au-Prince

HONDURAS:
**Federacion Nacional Deportiva
Extraescolar**
Apartado Postal 331
Tegucigalpa, D.C.

HONG KONG:
**Hong Kong Amateur Basketball
Association**
PO Box 13761
Hong Kong

HUNGARY:
Magyar Kosariabda Szovetseg
Dozsa Gyorgy ut. 1-3
H-1143 Budapest XIV

ICELAND:
Icelandic Basketball Association
PO Box 864
Reykjavik

INDIA:
Basketball Federation of India
Mr. P.N. Sankaran
No. 14, A-Road
Jamshedpur-1, 831001

INDONESIA:
Indonesian Basketball Association
c/o Gedung Koni
Senajan, Djakarta

IRAN:
Iranian Basketball Federation
c/o Sports Federations Joint Bureau
PO Box 11-1642
Tehran

IRAQ:
The Iraque Basketball Federation
c/o The Iraque National
Olympic Committee
PO Box No. 441
Baghdad

IRELAND:
**Irish Basketball
Association**
53 Middle Abbey Street
Dublin 1

ISRAEL:
Basketball Association
of Israel
PO Box 20163
10 Marmorek Street
Tel Aviv

ITALY:
Federazione Italian
Pallacanestro
Via Fogliano 15
1-00199

IVORY COAST:
Federation Ivoirienne
de Basket-Ball
01 B.P. 1746
Abidjan 01

JAMAICA:
Jamaica Amateur Basketball
Association
PO Box 751
Kingston

JAPAN:
Japan Amateur Basketball
Association
Kishi Memorial Hall
1-1-1 Jinnan Shibuya,
Tokyo

JORDAN:
The Basketball Federation
of Jordan
PO Box 1005
Amman

KAMPUCHEA:
Federation Kampuchea de
Basketball Amateur
Complexe Sportif National
Boite Postale 101
Phenom Penh

KENYA:
Kenya Basketball Association
PO Box 52107
Nairobi

KOREA:
Korean Basketball Association
C.P.O. Box 1106
Seoul

KOREA (D.P.R.K.)
Korean Sports Guidance
Committee
Munsingdong 2
Dondae Wong District
Pyongyang

KUWAIT:
Basket Ball Association
Al Sharq, Khalid Ibn Alwaleed St.
Shaker Alkazimi Bldg. Flatt No.4
PO Box 3792
Kuwait

LAOS:
Federation de Basketball
du Laos
c/o Direction Generale de la
Jeunesse et de Sports
B.P. 268, Vienetiane

LEBANON:
Federation Libanaise
de Basketball
B.P. 2558
Beyrouth

LIBERIA:
Liberia Basketball Federation
PO Box 9040
Monrovia

LIBYA:
The Libyan General Amateur
Basketball Federation
PO Box 428
Benghazi

LUXEMBURG:
Federation Luxembourgeolse
de Basketball
B.P. 458, L-2014
Luxembourg-Ville

MACAU
Macau Amateur Basket-Ball
Association
10 Caixa Excolar de Macau

MADAGASCAR:
Federation Malgache de
Basketball
Ministere de la Jeunesse
Direction du Sport
et de l'Education Physique

MALAYSIA:
Malaysia Amateur Basketball
Association
PO Box 10842
Kuala Lumpur 05-05

MALI:
Federation Malienne de
Basketball
B.P. 1015
Bamako

MALTA:
Malta Basketball Association
c/o Mr. Louis Borg,
"The Daffodils"
Anglu Gatt Street
Mosta

MAURITANIA:
Federation de Basket Ball de la
Republique Islamique de Mauritanie
B.P. 612, Nouakchott

MAURITIUS:
Mauritius Sports Association
B. Felicien Mallefille Street
Port Louis

MEXICO:
Federacion Mexicana de Basquetbol
Apartado Postal 4-860
Mexico 4, D.F.

MONTSERRAT
Montserrat Amateur Basketball
Association
PO Box 103
Plymouth, W.I.

MOROCCO:
Federation Royale Marocaine
De Basket-Ball
B.P. 379, Casablanca

MOZAMBIQUE:
Federacao Mocambiciana de
Basquetbol
B.P. Box 4589
Maputo

NAURU ISLAND:
The Island Basketball
Association
Mr. Paul Aingimea
Nauru Island, Central Pacific

NETHERLANDS:
Nederlandse Basketball Bond
Frederksplein 21,
NL-1017 XK Amsterdam

NETHERLANDS ANTILLES:
Netherland Antilles Basketball
Federation
PO Box 782
Willemstad, Curacao N.A.

NEW CALEDONIA:
Region Federale de Nouvelle
Caleonie de Basket-Ball
c/o Mrs. C. Gaveau

NEW HEBRIDES:
Federation Neo Hebridaise de
Basketball
B.P. 484, Port Vila

NEW ZEALAND:
New Zealand Basketball
Federation Inc.
PO Box 1624
Christchurch

NICARAGUA:
Federacion Nacional de Basquetbol
de Aficionados de Nicaragua
Apartado Postal 2208
Managua

NIGER:
Federation Nigienne de Basketball
B.P. 11650
Niamey

NIGERIA:
Nigeria Amateur Basketball Assn.
c/o National Sports Commission
National Stadium, Suruler.
PO Box 145, Lagos

NORWAY:
Norwegian Basketball Association
Hauger Skolevei 1
N - 1351 Rud

PAKISTAN:
Pakistan Amateur Basketball
Federation
Khalid Bashir
16 Sharra-e-Quaid-e-Azam,
Lahore

PANAMA:
Federacion Panamena de
Baloncesto
Apartado Postal 8529

PAPUA NEW GUINEA:
Amateur Basketball Federation
of Papua New Guinea
PO Box 868
Port Moresby

PARAGUAY
Confederacion Paraguaya de
Basquetbol
Casilla Correo 1952
Asuncion

PERU:
Federacion Peruana de Basquetbol
Casilla de Correo 1747
Lima

PHILIPPINES:
Basketball Association of the
Philippines
Rizal Memorial Coliseum
PO Box 2272
Manila

POLAND:
Polski Zwiazek Koszykowski
ul. Sienkiewicza 12/14
PL-00-010 Warsaw

PORTUGAL:
Federacao Portuguesa de
Basquetbol
rua da Madalena 179-20
P-1100 Lisboa

PUERTO RICO:
Federacion de Baloncesto de
Puerto Rico
G.P.O. Box 3947
San Juan, Puerto Rico 00936

QATAR:
Qatar Basketball Association
c/o Mr. Ahmed Ghanim Al Rumahi
Youth Welfare Department
PO Box 2511, Doha

ROMANIA:
Federatia Romana deBaschet
str. Vasile Cona 16
70139 Bucharest

RWANDA:
Federation Rwandaise des
Sports
c/o Ministere de la Jeunesse
B.P. 1044, Kigali

ST. KITTS:
St. Kitts Amateur Basketball
Association
52 Upper Market Street
Basseterre

SAINT VINCENT & THE GRENADINES:
Saint Vincent and the Grenadines
Basketball Association
PO Box 883
Kingstown

SAIPAN:
Saipan Amateur Basketball
Association
PO Box 222, Capitol Hill
Saipan CM 96950

SAN MARINO:
Ferazione Sammarinese
Pallacanestro
Viz del Bando, Borgo Maggiore

SAUDI ARABIA
Saudi Arabia Basketball
Association
PO Box 4697, Riyadh

SCOTLAND:
Amateur Basketball Association
of Singapore
8 Frederick Street
Edinburgh EH2, 2HB

SENEGAL:
Senegalaise Basket-Ball
Federation
B.P. 448, Dakar

SEYCHELLES:
Amateur Basketball Association
of the Seychelles
PO Box 398
Victoria

SINGAPORE:
Basketball Association of
Singapore
Room 23, Sports House
Rutland Road, Singapore 8

SOMALIA:
Somali Amateur Basketball
Federation
PO Box 2829
Mogadisho

SPAIN:
Federacion Espanola de
Baloncesto
Ferraz 16, E-28008 Madrid

SRI LANKA:
Sri Lanka Basketball
Federation
PO Box 553
Sri Lanka Army, Colombo

S. TOME E PRINCIPE:
Ministerio da Sude e Desporto
Cx. Postal 42, S. Tome

SUDAN:
Sudan Basquetball Association
PO Box 186, Khartoum

SURINAM:
Surinaamse Basketball Bond
PO Box 1378
Paramaribo

SWEDEN:
Svenska Basketbolforbundet
Djurgardsslatten 96
S-11521 Stockholm

SWITZERLAND:
Federation Suisse de
Basket-Ball Amateur
Place de l'Hotel de Ville 145
Case Postale 314,
CH-1701 Fribourg

SYRIA:
Syrian Basketball Federation
PO Box 421
Damascus

TAHITI:
Federation Generale des Societes
Sportives
c/o Mr. Lewis Chaavez
B.P. 1644, Papeete

TAIPEI, CHINA:
Chinese Taipei Basketball
Association
PO Box 1223, Tapei

TANZANIA:
Basketball Association of
Tanzania
c/o National Sports Council
PO Box 2182
Dar-es-Salaam

THAILAND:
**Basketball Association of
Thailand**
Gymnasium 1 National Stadium
Rama 1 Road, Bangkok

TOGO:
**Federation Togolaise de
Basketball**
BP. 1320, Lome

TRINIDAD and TOBAGO
**National Basketball Federation of
Trinidad and Tobago**
National Stadium,
Wrightson Road Extension
Port of Spain

TUNISIA:
**Federation Tunisienne de
Basket-Ball**
36, rue du Niger, Tunis

TURKEY:
Turkish Basketball Federation
Spor Sergi Sarayi
Harbiye-Istabul

UGANDA:
Amateur Basketball Association
PO Box 3356
Kampala

UNITED ARAB EMIRATES:
**United Arab Emirates
Basketball Association**
Po Box 5130, Dubai

UNITED STATES
**Amateur Basketball Association
of the United States of America**
1750 East Boulder Street
Colorado Springs, CO 80909
(719) 632-7687

UPPER VOLTA:
**Federation Voltaique de
Basketball**
Colonel Mamadou Djerma
B.P. 677, Ouagadogou

URUGUAY:
**Federacion Uruguaya de
Basketball**
Canelones No. 1029, Montevideo

U.S.S.R.:
Federatia Basketbola S.S.S.R.
Luzhnetskaja Naberezhnaja 8
Moscow 119270
Soviet Union

VENEZUELA:
**Federacion Venezolana de
Baloncesto**
I.N.D. Velodromo "Teo Capriles"
La Vega, Caracas

VIETNAM:
**Association de Basket-Ball
Amateur**
R.S. Viet-Nam
No. 36 Bd. Tran Phu,
Hanoi

VIRGIN ISLANDS:
**Virgin Islands Amateur
Basketball Federation**
PO Box 23
Frederiksted, St. Croix

WALES:
**Basketball Association of
Wales**
Mr. David Gwynn
Bay View Penrice, Oxwich
Swansea, West Glamorgan,
South Wales

WESTERN SAMOA:
**Western Samoa Amateur
Basketball Association**
PO Box 286
Apia

YEMEN
Yeman Basketball Union
c/o The Supreme Council
of the Youth Welfare
PO Box 4045
Crater Aden

YUGOSLAVIA:
Kosarkaski Savez Jugoslavje
Cetinjska 20-22
YU-11000 Belgrade

ZAIRE:
Federation Nationale Zairoise
de Basket-Ball Amateur
B.P. 14530, Kinshasa 1

ZAMBIA:
Zambia Basketball Association
PO Box 20594, Kitwe

ZIMBABWE:
Zimbabwe Basketball Association
PO Box 4102
Harare

International Football Federations

Federation International de
Football Association
FIFA House
PO Box 85
Hitzigweg 11
8030 Zurich, Switzerland
(01) 55 54 00
Fax: (01) 55 62 39
Telex: 817 240 fif ch

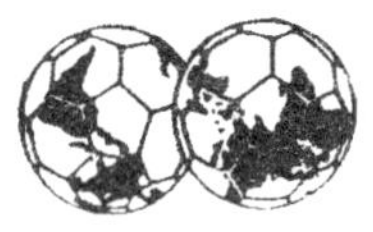

Confederations

Asia
Asian Football Confederation (AFC)

93-E Jalan Maharajalela (Jalan Birch)
Kuala Lumpur 50150
Malaysia

Africa
Confederation Africaine
de Football (CAF)

5 Shareh Gabalaya
Guezira, Cairo
AR Egypt

America - North and Central
and Caribbean
Confederacion Norte-
Centroamericana y del Caribe
de Futbol (CONCACAF)

717 Fifth Avenue, 13th Floor
New York, NY 10022

South America
Confederacion Sudamericana
de Futbol (CONMEBOL)

Ed. Banco do Braxil - Piso 4
Nuestra Senora de la Asuncion 540
Asuncion/Paraguay

**Europe
Union of European Football
Associations (UEFA)**

Jupiterstrasse 33
PO Box 16
3000 Berne 15
Switzerland

**Oceania
Oceania Football
Confederation (OFC)**

Mt. Smart Stadium,
PO Box 35-210
Browns Bay, Auckland, 10
New Zealand

National Associations

**Afghanistan
The Football Federation of
National Olympic Committee**
Olympic Kabul
Kabul

**Albania
Federation Albanaise de Football**
Rruga Dervish Hima NR. 31
Tirana, Albania

**Algeria
Federation Algerienne de Football**
Route Ahmed Ouaked
Boite Postale No. 39
Alger-Dely-Ibrahim, Algeria

**Angola
Federation Angolaise de Football**
B.P. 3449
Luanda, Angola

**Antigua
The Antigua Football Association**
PO Box 773
St. John's, Antigua

**Argentina
Asociacion del Futbol Argentino**
Viamonte 1366/76
1053 Buenos Aires, Argentina

**Aruba
Arubaanse Voetbal Bond**
PO Box 376
Oranjestad, Aruba

**Australia
Australian Soccer Federation**
First Floor
23-25 Frederick Street
Rockdale, NSW 2216 Australia

**Austria
Oesterreichischer Fussball-Bund**
Praterstadion, Sektor A/F
Meireistr. Postfach 340
A-1021 Wien, Austria

**Bahamas
Bahamas Football Association**
PO Box N 8434
Nassau, N.P. Bahamas

**Bahrain
Bahrain Football Association**
PO Box 5464, Bahrain

Bangladesh Football Federation
Stadium
Dhaka 1000, Bangladesh

Barbados Football Association
PO Box 1362
Bridgetown, Barbados

Belgium
Union Royale Belge des Societes
de Football Association
Aavenue Houba de Strooper 145
B-1020 Bruxelles, Belgium

Belize
Belize National Football Association
PO Box 1742
Belize City, Belize, Central America

Benin
Federation Beninoise de Football
B.P. 965
Cotonou, Benin PR

Bermuda
The Bermuda Football Association
PO Box HM 745
Hamilton HM CX, Bermuda

Bolivia
Federacion Boliviana de Futbol
AV. 16 de Julio No.N.0782
Casilla Postal No. 484
Cochabamba, Bolivia

Botswana
Botswana Football Association
PO Box 1396
Gaborone, Botswana

Brazil
Confederacao Brasileira de Futebol
Rua da Alfandega, 70
PO Box 1078
20.070 Rio de Janeiro, Brazil

Brunei
The Football Association of
Brunei Darussalam
PO Box 2010
1920 Bandar Seri Begawan, Brunei

Bulgaria
Bulgarian Football Union
Gotcho Gopin 19
1000 Sofia, Bulgaria

Burkina Faso
Federation Burkinabe de Football
O1 B.P. 57
Ouagadougou, Burkina Faso

Burundi
Federation de Football du Burundi
B.P. 3426
Bujumbura, Burundi

Cameroon
Federation Camerounaise de Football
B.P. 1116
Yaounde, Cameroon

Canada
The Canadian Soccer Association
1600 James Naismith Drive
Gloucester, Ontario K1B 5N4

Cape Verde Islaind
Federacao Cabo-Verdiana de Fubebol
C.P. 234
Praia, Cape Verde Islands

Central Arica
Federation Centrafricaine de Football
B.P. 344
Bangui, Central Africa

Chad
Federation Tchadienne de Football
B.P. 886
N'Djamena, Chad

Chile
Federacion de Fubol de Chile
Calle Erasmo Escala 1872
Casilla No. 3733
Santiago de Chile, Chile

China, People's Republic of
Football Association of the
People's Republic of China
9 Tiyuguan Road
Beijing, China

Chinese Taipei
Chinese Taipei Football Association
100, Kuang-Fu South Road
Taipei, Taiwan

Colombia
Federacion Colombiana de Futbol
Avenida 32, No. 16-22
Apartado Aereo No. 17.602
Bogota, D.E., Colombia

Congo
Federation Congolaise de Football
P.B.4041
Brazzaville, Congo

Costa Rica
Federacion Costarricense de Futbol
Apartado 670-1000
Calle 40-Ave. Ctl 1
San Jose, Costa Rica

Cote D'Ivoire
Federation Ivoirienne de Football
Av. 1, Treichville
B.P. 1201
Abidjan 01, Cote D'Ivoire

Cuba
Asociacion de Futbol de Cuba
c/o Comite Olimpico Cubano
Calle 13 No. 601, Esq. C. Vedado
La Habana, ZP 4, Cuba

Cyprus
Cyprus Football Association
Stasinos Str. 1, Engomi 152
PO Box 5071
Nicosia, Cyprus

Czechoslovakia
Ceskoslovenska Fotbalova Asociace
Diskarska 100
16900 Praha 6-Strahov, Czechoslovakia

Denmark
Dansk Boldspil-Union
Ved Amagerbanen 15
DK-2300 Copenhagen S, Denmark

Dominican Republic
Federacion Dominicana de Futbol
Apartado de Correos No. 1953
Santo Domingo, Dominican Rep.

Ecudor
Federacion Ecuatoriana de Futbol
Calle Jose Mascote 1.103
(Piso 2) y Luque, Casilla 7447
Guayaquil, Ecuador

Egypt
Egyptian Football Association
5, Shareh Gabalaya, Guezira
Al Borg Post Office
Cairo, Egypt

El Salvador
Federacion Salvadorena de Futbol
Av. J.M. Delgado, Col.Escalon
Centro Espanol,I Apartado 1029
San Salvador, El Salvador

England
The Football Association
16 Lancaster Gate
London, W2 2LW England

Equatorial Guinea
Federacion Ecuatoguineana de Futbol
Malabo, Equatorial Guinea

Ethiopia
Ethiopian Football Federation
Addis Ababa Stadium
PO Box 1080
Addis Ababa, Ethiopia

Faroe Islands
Fotboltssamband Foroya
The Faroe's Football Assn.
Gundadalur
PO Box 1028
FR-110 Torshavn, Faroe Islands

Fiji
Fiji Football Association
Mr. J.D. Maharaj, Hon. Secretary
Government Bldgs., POB 2514
Suva, Fiji

Finland
Suomen Palloliitto Finlands Bollfoerbund
Kuparitie 1
PO Box 29
SF-00441 Helsinki

France
Federation Francaise de Football
60 bis, Avenue d'Iena,
F-75783 Paris Cedex 16, France

Gabon
Federation Gabonaise de Football
B.P. 181
Libreville, Gabon

Gambia
Gambia Football Association
c/o Dept. of Youth & Sports
Banjul, Gambia

Germany FR
Deutscher Fussball-Bund
Otto-Fleck-Schneise 6
Postfach 710265
D-6000 Frankfurt (Main) 71,
Germany

Ghana
Ghana Football Association
PO Box 1272
Accra, Ghana

Greece
Federation Hellenique ᴊe Football
Singrou Avenue 137
Athens, Greece

Grenada
Grenada Football Association
No.2 Hillsborough Street
PO Box 326,
Grenada, West Indies

Guatemala
Federacion Nacional de Futbol
de Guatemala C.A.

Guinea
Federation Guineenne de Football
PO Box 262
Conakry, Guinea

Guinea-Bissau
Federacao de Football da
Guinea-Bissau
Rua 4 No. 10-C, Apartado 375
1035 Bissau - Codex

Guyana
Guyana Football Association
PO Box 10727
Georgetown, Guyana

Haiti
Federation Haitienne de Football
B.P. 2258
Stade Sylvio-Cator
Port-au-Prince, Haiti

Honduras
Federacion Nacional Autonoma
de Futbol de Honduras
Apartado Postal 827
Costa Oeste del Est.Nac.
Tegucigalpa, D.C., Honduras

Hong Kong
The Hong Kong Football Association Ltd.
55 Fat Kwong Street, Homantin
Kowloon, Hong Kong

Hungary
Magyar Labdarugo Szovetseg
Hungarian Football Federation
PO Box 325
Nepkoztarsasag Utja 47
H-1061 Budapest VI, Hungary

Iceland
Knattspyrnusamband Island
PO Box 8511
128 Reykjavik, Iceland

India
All India Football Federation
Green Lawns, Talap
P.B. No.429
Cannanore 670 002, India

Indonesia
All Indonesia Football Federation
Main Stadium Senayan, Gate VII
PO Box 2305
Jakarta, Indonesia

Iran
Football Federation of the Islamic
Republic of Iran
Ave Varzandeh No. 10
PO Box 11/1642
Tehran, Iran

Ireland, Northern
Irish Football Association Ltd.
20 Windsor Avenue
Belfast, BT9 6EG, Northern Ireland

Ireland, Republic of
The Football Association of Ireland
(Cumann Peile Na H-Eireann)
80, Merrion Square, South
Dublin 2, Republic of Ireland

Israel
Israel Football Association
12 Carlibach Street
PO Box 20188
Tel Aviv 61201, Israel

Italy
Federazione Italiana Giuoco Calcio
Via Gregorio Allegri, 14
C.P. 2450
1-00198 Roma, Italy

Jamaica
Jamaica Football Federation
Attn: A. James, President
Room 8, National Arena
Institute of Sports
Kingston 19, Jamaica

Japan
The Football Association of Japan
1-1-1 Jinnan, Shibuya-Ku
Tokyo, Japan

Jordan
Jordan Football Association
PO Box 1054
Amman, Jordan

Kampuchea
Federation Khmere de Football
Association
C.P. 101
Complex Sportif National
Phnom-Penh, Kampuchea

Kenya
Kenya Football Federation
NYAYO National Stadium
PO Box 40234
Nairobi, Kenya

Korea DPR
Football Association of the
Democratic People's Republic of Korea
Munsin-Dong 2, Dongdaewon District
Pyongyang, Korea, DPR.

Korea, Republic of
Korea Football Association
110-39, Kyeonji-DG, Chongro-Ku
Seoul, Korea Republic

Kuwait
Kuwait Football Association
PO Box 6040
11442 Riyakh, Kuwait

Laos
Federation de Football Lao
c/o Director des Sports-Education
Physique et Artistique
Vientiane, Laos

Lebanon
Federation Libanaise Football
PO Box 4732
Omar IBN Al Khattab Street
Beirut, Lebanon

Lesotho
Lesotho Sports Council
PO Box 138
Maseru 100, Lesotho

Liberia
The Liberia Football Association
PO Box 10-1066
1000 Monrovia 10, Liberia

Libya
Libyan Arab Jamahiriya Football Federatic
PO Box 5137
Tripoli, Libya

Liechtenstein
Liechtensteiner Fussball-Verband
Postfach 165
FL-9490 Vaduz, Liechtenstein

Luxemburg
Federation Luxembourgeoise de Football
(F.L.F.)
50, rue de Strasbourg
L-2560 Luxembourg

Macao
**Associacao de Futebol de
Macau (AFM)**
PO Box 920
Macau, Macao

Madagascar
Federation Malagasy de Football
c/o Comite Nat. de Coordination
de Football, B.P. 4409
Antananarivo 101, Madagascar

Malawi
Football Association of Malawi
PO Box 865
Blantyre, Malawi

Malaysia
Football Association of Malaysia
Wisma FAM, Tingkat 4
Jalan SS 5A/9, Kelana Jaya
47301 Petaling Jaya
Selangor, Malaysia

**Maldives Republic
Football Association of Maldives**
Attn: Mr. Bandhu Ahamed Saleem
Sports Div. G. Banafsa Magu20-04
Male, Maldives Republic

Mali
Federation Malienne de Football
Stade Mamadou Konate
B.P. 1020
Bamako, Mali

Malta
Malta Football Association
280, St. Paul Street
Valletta, Malta

Mauritania
**Federation de Football de la
Republique Islamique de Mauritanie**
B.P. 566
Nouakchott, Mauritania

Mauritius
Mauritius Football Association
Chancery House, 2nd Floor Nos. 303-305
14 Lislet Geoffroy Street
Port Louis, Mauritius

Mexico
Federacion Mexicana de Futbol Asoclac
Abraham Gonzalex 74
C.P. 06600, Col. Juarez
Mexico 6, D.F., Mexico

Morocco
Federation Royale Morocaine de Footba
Av. IBN Sina, C.N.S. Bellevue
B.P. 51
Rabat, Morocco

Mozambique
Federacao Mocambicana de Futebol
Av. Samora Machel, 11-2
Caixa Postal 1467
Maputo, Mozambique

**Myanmar
Myanmar Football Federation**
Aung San Memorial Stadium
Kandawgalay Post Office
Yangon, Myanmar

Nepal
All-Nepal Football Association
Dasharath Rangashala
Tripureshwor
Kathmandu, Nepal

Netherlands
Koninklijke Nederlandsche Voebalbond
Woudenbergsweg 56
Postbus 515
NL-3700 AM Zeist, Netherlands

Netherlands Antilles
Nederlands Antiliaanse Voebal Unie
PO Box 341
Curacao, N.A.

New Zealand
New Zealand Football Association
PO Box 62-532
Central Park, Greenlane
Auckland 6, New Zealand

Nicaragua
Federacion Nicaraguense de Futbol
Inst. Nicaraguense de Deportes
Apartado Postal 976 0 383
Managua, Nicaragua

Niger
Federation Nigerienne de Football
Stade National Niamey
B.P. 10299
Niamey, Niger

Nigeria
Nigeria Football Association
National Stadium
PO Box 466
Lagos, Nigeria

Norway
Norges Fotballforbund
Ullevaal Stadion, Postboks 3823
Ulleval Hageby
0805 Oslo 8, Norway

Oman
Oman Football Association
PO Box 6462
Ruwi-Muscat, Oman

Pakistan
Pakistan Football Federation
Mr. Sardar Khair Muhammad Khan,
General Secretary
46-A Gulistan Town, Toghi Road
Quetta, Pakistan

Panama
Federacion Nacional de Futbol de Panama
APDO Postal 6-1811
El Dorado, Panama

Papua, New Guinea
Papua New Guinea Football (Soccer)
Association, Inc.
PO Box 1716
Boroko, Papua New Guinea

Paraguay
Liga Paraguaya de Futbol
Estadio de Sajonia, Calles
Mayor Martinez y Alejo Garcia
Asuncion, Paraguay

Peru
Federacion Peruana de Futbol
Estadio Nacional - Puerta No.4
Calle Jose Diaz
Lima, Peru

Philippines
Philippines Football Federation
Room 207 Administration Bldg.
Rizal Memorial Sports Complex
Vito Cruz
Metro-Manila, Philippines

Poland
Federation Polonaise de Football
Al. Ujazdowskie 22
00-478 Warszawa, Poland

Portugal
Federacao Portuguesa de Futebol
Praca da Alegria N.25
Apartado 21.100
P.1128 Lisboa Codex, Portugal

Puerto Rico
Federacion Puertorriquena de Futbol
Coliseo Roberto Clemente
PO Box 4355
Hato Rey, PR 00919-4355

Qatar
Qatar Football Association
PO Box 5333
Doha, Qatar

Romania
Federatia Romana de Fotbal
Vasile Conta 16
Bucharest 70130, Romania

Rwanda
Federation Rwandaise de Football Amate
B.P. 2000
Kigali, Rwanda

San Marino
Federazione Sammarinese Giuoco Calcio
Palazzo C.O.N.S.
Via XXV Marzo, 11
47031 Domagnano, San Marino

Sao Tome e Principe
Federation Santomense de Futebol
PO Box 42
Sao Tome, Sao Tome e Principe

Saudi Arabia
Saudi Arabian Football Federation
North Al-Morabbaa'Quarter
PO Box 5844
Riyakh 11432, Saudi Arabia

Scotland
The Scottish Football Association Ltd.
6 Park Gardens
Glasgow G3 7YF, Scotland

Senegal
Federation Senegalaise de Football
Stade de l'amitie, Route de
l'Aeroport de Yoff, B.P. 7021
Dakar, Senegal

Seychelles
Seychelles Football Federation
PO Box 580
Mont Fleuri
Victoria, Seychelles

Sierra Leone
Sierra Leone Football Association
S.Stevens Stadium, Brookfields
PO Box 672
Freetown, Sierra Leone

Singapore
Football Association of Singapore
Jalan Besar Stadium
Tyrwhitt Road
Singapore 0820

Solomon Islands
Solomon Islands Football Federation
PO Box 140
Honiara, Solomon Islands

Somalia
Somali Football Federation
Ministry of Sports
C.P. 247
Mogadishu, Somalia

Spain
Real Federacion Espanola de Futbol
Calle Alberto Bosch, 13
Apartado Postal 347
E-28014 Madrid, Spain

Sri Lanka
Football Federation of Sri Lanka
No. 2, Old Grand Stand
Race Course - Reid Avenue
Colombo 7, Sri Lanka

St. Lucia
St. Lucia National Football Union
PO Box 255
Castries, ST. Lucia

St. Vincent-Grenadines
St. Vincent and the Grenadines
Football Federation
PO Box 1278/130
Kingstown, St. Vincent

Sudan
Sudan Football Association
PO Box 437
Khartoum, Sudan

Surinam
Surinaamse Voetbal Bond
Cultuuruinlaan 7
PO Box 1223
Paramaribo, Surinam

Swaziland
National Football Association of
Swaziland
PO Box 641
Mbabane, Swaziland

Sweden
Svenska Fotbollfoerbundet
Box 1216
S-17123 Solna, Sweden

Switzerland
Association Suisse de Football
Laubeggstrasse 70
B.P.
Ch-3000 Berne 32, Switzerland

Syria
Association Arabe Syrienne de Football
General Sport Federation Building
October Stadium
Damascus - Baremke, Syria

Tahiti
federation Tahitienne de Football (F.T.F.B.)
A l'Att de M. Napoleon Spitz
B.P. 650
Papeete, Tahiti

Tanzania
Football Association of Tanzania
PO Box 1574
Dar es Salaam, Tanzania

Thailand
The Football Association of
Thailand
c/o National Stadium
Rama 1 Road
Bangkok, Thailand

Togo
Federation Togolaise de Footgall
C.P. 5
Lome, Togo

Trinidad and Tobago
Trinidad and Tobago Football Association
Cor. Duke Scott-Bushe Street

Tunisia
Federation Tunisienne de Football
2, rue Hamza Abdelmottaleb
El Menzah VI
Tunis, Tunisia

Turkey
Turkish Football Association
Zincirlikuyu Caddesi 17/3-4
Yeniulus-Istanbul, Turkey

Uganda
Federation of Uganda Football Assns.
PO Box 20077
Kampala, Uganda

United Arab Emirates
United Arab Emirates Football Assn.
Post Box 5458
Dubai, United Arab Emirates

Uruguay
Asociacion Uruguaya de Futbol
Guayabo 1531
Montevideo, Uruguay

USA
United States Soccer Federation
1750 East Boulder Street
Colorado Springs, CO 80909
(719) 578-4678

USSR
USSR Football Federation
Luzhnetskaja Naberzhnaja, 8
119871GSP-3 Moscow

Vanuatu
Vanuatu Football Federation
PO Box 266
Port Vila, Vanuatu

Venezuela
Federacion Venezolana de Futbol
Avda Este Estadio Nacional
El Paraiso Apdo. Postal 14160
Candelaria Carcs, Venezuela

Vietnam, Socialist Republic of
Association de Football de la
Republique du Vietnam
No. 36, Bouldevard Tran-Phu
Hanoi, Vietnam SR

Wales
The Football Association of Wales, Ltd.
Plymouth Chambers
3 Westgate Street
Cardiff-South Glamorgan CF1 1DD
Wales

Western Samoa
Western Samoa Football (Soccer)
Association
Min. of Youth & Sports Culture
Private Bag
Apia, Western Samoa

Yemen Republic
Yemen General Football Association
PO Box 908
Sana'a, Yemen Republic

Yugoslavia Football Association
PO Box 263
Terazije 35
1000 Beograd, Yugoslavia

Zaire
Federation Zairoise de Football Assn.
B.P. 1284
rue Dima No.10
Kinshasa 1, Zaire

Zambia
Football Association of Zambia
PO Box 33474
Lusaka, Zambia

Zimbabwe
Zimbabwe Football Association
PO Box 6343
Causeway
Harare, Zimbabwe

International Ice Hocke

International Ice Hockey Federation
Bellevuestrasse 8
A-1190 Vienna, Austria
(43.1) 32 52 52

Australia Ice Hockey
Federation
PO Box 715 Civic Square
Canberra 2608 A.C.T.
Australia

Austria
Osterreichischer Eishockey
Verband
Prinz-Eugen-Strasse 12
A-1040 Vienna
Austria

Belgium
Federation Royal Belge
Ice Hockey Federation
Sint Jacobsmarkt 59
B-2000 Antwerp, Belgium

Brazil
Brazil Ice Sport Union
Rua F - Lotes 65-79
Cep 25 645 Bairro
Maua Petropolis - R.J.
Brazil

Bulgaria
Bulgaria Ice Hockey
Federation
18 Tolboukhin Blvd.
BG - 1000 Sofia
Bulgaria

Canada
Canadian Amateur Hockey
Association
1600 James Naismith Drive
Gloucester, Ontario K1B 5N4
(613) 748-5613

China
Ice Hockey Association
of the Peoples Rep. of China
9 Tijuguan Road
Beijing, China

CSSR
Czechoslovak Ice Hockey Federation
Na Porici 12
115 30 Praha 1, Nowe Mesto, CSSR

Denmark
Dansk Ishockey Union
Idrottens Hus Brondby-Stadion 20
DK-2605, Brondby, Denmark

Finland
Finish Ice Hockey
Association
Radiokatu 12
00240 Helsinke
Finland

France
Federation Francaise de
Sports
Comite de Hockey Sur Glace
42 rue du Louvres
75001 Paris, France

Germany
Deutscher Eishockey Bund
Betzenweg 34
D-8000 Munchen 60, Germany

Great Britain
British Ice Hockey Assn.
40 Hambledon Road
Bournemouth, Dorset BH7 G8Q
Great Britain

Greece
Greek Ice Skating Federation
11 Kratinou Str.
GR-105 52 Athens
Greece

Holland/Netherlands
Niederlandsche Ijshockey Bond
PO Box 292
2740 AG Zoetemeer
Holland

Hong Kong
Ice Hockey Federation
B8-9F Causeway Center
Hong Kong

Hungaria
Hugarian Icesport Federation
Istvanmezei UT 1-3 Kisstadion
1146 Budapest, Hugary

Italy
Federazione Italiana Sport
Ghiaccio
Via Piranesi 44 B
201 37 Milano, Italy

Japan
Japan Ice Hockey Federation
1-1-1 Jinnan Shibuya-Ku 150
Tokyo, Japan

Korea DPRK
Ice Hockey Association of the
Democratic Peoples Republic of
Korea
Moonsin-dong 2
Dongdaiwon Distric Pyongyang
DPRK Korea

Korea
Korean Amateur Ice Hockey
Association
International PO Box 1106
Seoul, Korea

Kuwait
Kuwait Olympic Committee
Sheik Fhad Al Ahmed Al Sabah
PO Box 795
Kuwait

Luxemburg
Federation Luxembourgeoise
de Hockey Sur Glace
8 Rue Heine
1720 Luxembourg
Luxemburg

Mexico
**Asociation Metropolitana de
Deportes Sobre Hielo**
Seccion Hockey
Ramires BEL, Castillo 248 A

**New Zealand
New Zealand Ice Hockey
Federation**
239 Wairakel Road
Christchurch 5, New Zealand

**Norway
Norges Ishockeyforbound**
Normansgatan 47
N-0655 Oslo, Norway

**Poland
Polski Zwiazek Hockeja Lodzie**
UL.Zielenickea 1 Stadion X-Lecia
03901 Warsaw, Poland

**Romania
Federatia Romana De Hockel**
Pe Gheata
Vasile Conta Street 16/17 139
70139 Bucharest, Romania

**South Africa
South African Ice Hockey Assn.**
Mr. O Hertz Box 1323
Pretoria 0001
South Africa

**USSR
Ice Hockey Federation of USSR**
USSR Sports Committee
Luzhnetskaja Naberezhnaya 8
119270 Moscow
Soviet Union

**Spain
Spanish Winter Sports
Federation**
Ice Hockey Committee
Claudio Coello 32
Madrid 1, Spain

**Sweden
Svenska Ishockeyforbundet**
Box 5054
S-121 05 Johanneshov
Sweden

**Switzerland
Swiss Ice Hockey
Association**
Hadloubstr. 135
CH-8044 Zurich
Switzerland

**Taiwan
Chinese Taipei Amateur
Skating Association**
7Fl. No. 70 Hsi-Nigh S Rd.
Taipei, Taiwan

USA Hockey
2997 Broadmoor Valley Road
Colorado Springs, CO 80906
(719) 576-4990

International Field Hockey

**International Hockey
Federation**
1-Avenue des Arts
Bruxelles, Belgium

Continental Organizations

African Hockey Federation
PO Box 365
Dokki - Giza 12311
Egypt
(2) 3475956

**Asian Hockey Federation
National Hockey Stadium**
Ferozepur Road
Lahore, Pakistan
(42) 871447

European Hockey Federation
Edeby House, Luiksestraat, 23
2587 AL The Hague
Netherlands
(70) 3512774

Oceania Hockey Federation
Level 9 Fawkner Centre
499 St. Kilda Road
Melbourne, Victoria 3004
Australia
(3) 8664031

Pan American Hockey
Federation
231 Handsart Blvd.
Winnipeg, Manitoba R3P 0C6
Canada

National Associations

Afghanistan
National Hockey Association
of Afghanistan
Prime Minister's Office
Kabul

Argentina
Asociacion Amateur Argentina
de Hockey
San Jose 364 P 2
1076 Buenos Aires

Australia
Australian Hockey Association
Level 9 Fawkner Centre
499 St. Kilda Road
Melbourne, Victoria 3004

Australian Women's Hockey
Association
PO Box 182, Crows Nest
N.S.W. 2065

Austria
Osterreichischer Hockey
Verband
Prater Hauptallee 123a

Bangladesh
Bangladesh Hockey Federation
Hockey Stadium (outer stadium)
Dhaka 1000

Barbados
Barbados Hockey Association
PO Box 66 B
Brittons Hill, St. Michael

Belgium
Association Royale Belge de
Hockey
Bd du Regent 55 (Bte 4)
1000 Bruxelles

Bermuda
Bermuda Hockey Association
PO Box 683
Devonshire DVBX

Bermuda Ladies Hockey
Association
PO Box 741
Devonshire - 4

Brazil
Federacao Paulista de Hoquei
Av. das Nacoes Unidas, 10989
3 andar - Cep 04578
San Paulo

Brunei
Peti Surat 2906
Bandar Seri Begawan
Brunei Darrussalam

Canada
Canadian Field Hockey Assn.
1600 Prom. James Naismith Drive
Gloucester, Ontario K1B 5N4

Canadian Women's Field Hockey
Association
1600 Prom. James Naismith Drive
Gloucester, Ontarion K1B 5N4

Cayman (Islands)
Cayman Islands Hockey Club
PO Box 1543
Grand Cayman, B.W.I.

Chile
Federacion Chilena de Hockey
Av. Vicuna Mackenna 40
Officina 1, Santiago

China
Association Chinoise de Hockey
9, rue Tiyuguan
100763 Beijing

Chinese Taipei Hockey Assn.
12F, 196 Sec.2.,
Chun Chin n. Road
Taipei

Cuba
Federacion Cubana de Hockey
Calle 13 N 601 Vedado
La Habana zona 4

Cyprus
Cyprus Hockey Association
PO Box 5345
Nicosia

Czechoslovakia
Czechoslovak Field Hockey
Federation
Na Porici 12
11530 Praha 1

Denmark
Dansk Hockey Union
Bryggerstien, 7
Tune
4000 Roskilde

Egypt
Egyptian Hockey Federation
44 Kasr El eini Street
Cairo

England
The Hockey Association
S16 Northdown Street
London N1 9BG

All England Women's Hockey
Association
51 High Street
Shrewsbury
Shropshire SY1 1ST

Fiji
Fiji Hockey Association
PO BOx 1402
Suva

Fiji Women's Hockey Association
PO Box 621
Suva

Finland
Finnish Hockey Association
Radiokatu, 12
SF - 00240 Helsinki

France
Federation Francaise de
Hockey
64, rue Taitbout
75009 Paris

Germany
Deutscher Hockey Bund
Theresienhohe
5030 Hurth

Ghana
Ghana Hockey Association
National Sports Council
PO Box 1272
Accra

Gibraltar
Gibraltar Hockey Association
44, City Mill Lane
Gibraltar

Great Britain
Great Britain Hockey Board
Coventry Farmhouse
Hankins Lane
Mill Hill
London NW7 3AJ

Guyana
Guyana Men's Hockey Board of
Control
c/o National Bank of Industry
and Commerce
38/40 Water Street
PO Box 10440 - Georgetown

Hong Kong
Hong Kong Hockey Association
G.P.O. Box 4982

Hungary
Hungarian Hockey Association
XIV Dozsa Gy ut 1-3
1442 Budapest

India
Indian Hockey Federation
106 National Stadium
New Delhi 110001

Indian Women's Hockey
Federation
11 Abbas Road
411 001 Pune

Indonesia
The Indonesian Hockey Assn.
Persatuan Hockey Seluruh Indonesia
Jalan Pulo Mas Raya N 31
Jakarta

Iran
Hockey Amateur Federation of
Islamic Republic of Iran
Physical Education Organization
Dept. of International Affairs
Park Shahr
Avenue Shahid Dr., Fayazbakhsh
PO Box 11365-8617, Tehran

Ireland
Irish Hockey Union
7 Barnhill Avenue
Dalkey, Co. Dublin

Irish Ladies Hockey Union
"Waltonmere"
Cross Douglas Road
Cork

Israel
The Israel Hockey Assn.
31/10 Shlonski Street
Tel-Aviv 69400

Italy
Federazione Italiana Hockey
Viale Tiziano 70
00196 Roma

Jamaica
Jamaica Men's Hockey Assn.
PO Box 115
Kingston 7

Jamaica Women's Hockey Assn.
PO Box 203
Kingston 20

Japan
Japan Hockey Association
Kishi-Memorial Hall
1-1-1, Jinan, Shibuya-Ku
Tokyo 150

Kenya
Kenya Hockey Union
PO Box 42602
Nairobi

Korea
Korea Hockey Association
Room 602, 88 Olympic Center
88 Oryun-dong, Songpa-ku
Seoul

Democratic People's Republic
of Korea Hockey Association
Munsindong-1, Dongdaewon District
Pyongyang

Luxemburg
Hockey Club Luxembourg
Sportif
Boite Postale 1824
L-1018 Luxembourg

Lybia
General National Hockey
Federation
PO Box 879
Tripoli

Macau
Macau Hockey Association
PO Box 797

Malawi
Hockey Association of Malawi
PO Box 5266
Limbe

Malaysia
Malaysian Hockey Federation
710 Jalan Rasah
70300 Seremban, N.S.

Malaysia Women's Hockey Assn.
PO Box 6505
Kampong Tunku
47307 Petaling Jaya
Selangor

Malta
Hockey Association Malta
59, St. Dominic Street
Sliema

Mexico
Federacion Mexicana de Hockey
Venida del Conscripto Y Anillo
Periferico (COM)
Delegacion Miguel Hidalgo
Lomas de Sotelo
11200 Mexico D.F.

Morocco
**Federation Royale Marocaine
de Hockey**
Boite Postale n 384
Casablanca-Principal

Namibia
Namibia Hockey Union
PO Box 1011
9000 WINDHOEK

Nepal
Nepal Hockey Association
National Sports Council
Tripureswor, Kathmandu

Netherlands
**Koninklijke Nederlandse
Hockey Bond**
Postbus 1250
3980 DE Bunnik

**Netherlands Antilles
Nederlands Antilliaanse Hockey
Bond**
PO Box 3557
Curacao

**New Zealand
New Zeland Hockey Federation**
PO Box 24024, Royal Oak
Auckland 3

**Nigeria
Nigeria Hockey Association**
National Stadium
PO Box 6460
Suru-Lere, Lagos

**Norway
Norges Bandyforbund**
Hockey Section
Hauger Skolevei 1
1351 Rud

**Oman
Oman Hockey Association**
PO Box 5363
Ruwi

**Pakistan
Pakistan Hockey Federation**
National Hockey Stadium
Ferozepur Road, Lahore

**Papua New Guinea
Papua New Guinea Hockey**
Federation
PO Box 1359
Port Moresby

Paraguay
Associacion Amateur Paraguaya
de Hockey
Antequera 611 Of.8 (Altos)
Box 925
Asuncion

Peru
Comision Nacional de Hockey
Apartado 270043
Lima 27

Poland
Polish Hockey Association
Stary Rynek 76
61 - 772 Poznan

Portugal
Federacao Portuquesa de
Hoquei
Rua Antonio Pinto Machado 60
4100 Porto

Puerto Rico
Federacion Puertorriquena
PO Box 8
San Juan 00902

Romania
Federation Roumaine de
Hockey
Str. Vasile Conta, nr.16
Buccuresti

Scotland
Scottish Hockey union
Caledonia House
South Gyle
Edinburgh EH12 9DQ

Seychelles Islands
The Seychelles Hockey
Federation
PO Box 580
Victoria, Mahe

Singapore
Singapore Hockey Association
2, Taman Permata, Singapore

Solomon Islands
Solomon Islands Hockey
Association
PO Box 459
Honiara

South Africa
South African Hockey Union
PO Box 46112
Orange Grove 2119

Spain
Real Federacion Espanola
de Hockey
Calle Goya
Madrid 28001

Sri Lanka
Sri Lanka Hockey Federation
N 10, Zaleski Place
Colombo 10

Sri Lanka Women's Hockey
Association
1, Harrischandra Mawatta
Colombo 6

Sudan
Sudan Hockey Federation
PO Box 467
Karthoum

Sweden
Swedish Hockey Association
Storgatan 28B
S-753 31 Uppsala

Switzerland
Ligue Suisse de Hockey
sur terre
Postfach 305
6048 Horw

Tanzania
Tanzania Hockey Association
PO Box 4307
Dar-es-Salaam

Thailand
Thai Hockey Association
67/4 Charan Sanidwongs Road
10700 Bangkok

Trinidad & Tobago
Trinidad & Tobago Hockey
Federation
PO Box 3240
Diego Martin

Trinidad & Tobago Women's
Hockey Association
21 Chateaux Valley
Petit Valley

Uganda
The Uganda Hockey Assn.
PO Box 20077
Kampala

United Arab Emirates
United Arab Emirates Hockey
Federation
PO Box 87
Dubai

Uruguay
Federacion Uruguaya de
Hockey
Canelone 980
Montevideo

USSR
USSR Hockey Federation
Luzhnetskaya naberezhnaya 8
Moscow

USA
Field Hockey Association
of America
1750 East Boulder Street
Colorado Springs, CO 80909
(719) 578-4567

U.S. Women's Field Hockey
Association
1750 E. Boulder Street
Colorado Springs, CO 80909
(719) 578-4567

Venezuela
Venezuelan Hockey Federation
Apartado 61810
Chacao, Caracas 1060

Wales
Welsh Hockey Association
1 White Hart Lane
Caerleon
Monmouthshire NP6 1AB

Welsh Women's Hockey
Association
Welsh Hockey Office
Deeside Leisure Centre
Chester Road West, Queensferry
Clwyd Ch5 1SA

Western Samoa
Western Samoa Hockey
Association
c/o Ministry of Youth Sport &
Culture
Private Bag, Apia

Yugoslavia
Yugoslav Hockey Federation
Trg Sportova 11, Soba 12
41000 Zagreb

Zambia
Zambia Hockey Association
ZCCM Head Office
PO Box 30048
Lusaka

Zambia Women's Hockey
Association
ZCCM Limited, Mutondo House
PO Box 20172
Kitwe

Zimbabwe
Hockey Association of
Zimbabwe
PO Box 8046
Causeway - Harare

Zimbabwe Women's Hockey
Association
PO Box 450
Harare

International Rugby

**International Rugby Football
Board**
PO Box 902
Auckland, New Zealand
(01) 64.9 788 696

**Australian Rugby
Football League**
Box 4415, G.P.O.
Sydney, NSW 2001
Australia
(01) 612 231 4488

**Canadian Rugby Football
Association**
1600 James Naismith Drive
Gloucester, Ontario K1B 5N4
Canada
(613) 748-5657

**The English Rugby Football
League**
80 Chapeltown Road
Leeds LS7 4HT
England
0 532-624637

**French Rugby Football
Federation**
30 rue de l'Echiguier
75010 Paris, France
(01) 331 4800 9256

**New Zealand Rugby
Football League**
C.P.O. Box 712
Auckland, 1
New Zealand
(01) 649-366 3957

**Papua New Guinea Rugby
Football League**
PO Box 1095
Boroko, Papua New Guinea
(01) 675 259 733

USA Rugby
3595 E. Fountain Blvd.
Colorado Springs, CO 80909
(719) 637-1022

US Rugby League
PO Box 56153
Madison, WI 53705
(608) 274-9325

Minisoccer (FIFUSA)

**Federecao Internacional de
Futebol de Salao**
Rua 7 de Abril, 386
13o Andar
Conjunto 133
Telefone 255-7213 CEP: 01044

**South American Confederation de
Futbol de Salon**
Av. Brasilia, 1985
Esq. Tte. Frutos 2o Piso
C.C. 2272
Assuncion, Paraguay

**Argentina
Confederacion Argentina de
Futbol de Salon**
Talcahuano, 316-7op. Of: 702-703
Republica Argentina

**Australia
Australian Amateur Indoor
Soccer Federation**
PO Box 135
Revesby, N.S.W., Australia

**Bolivia
Federacion Boliviana de
Futbol de Salon**
Santa Cruz de Lasierra
Correo Central, Casilla, 4185
La Paz, Bolivia

Brazil
Confederecao Brasileira de
Futebol de Salao
Rua Cet.Ferraz, 52 Conj.301
6000 - Fortaleza - CE
Brazil

Canada
Canada Minisoccer Federation
660 Lambert Street
Nanaimo, B.C., V9R 5L9
Canada

Colombia
Federacion Colombiana de
Futbol de Salon
Carrera 18 No. 33-80
Bogota, Colombia

Costa Rica
Associacion Costarricense de
Futbol de Salon
Apartado, 179
San Jose, Costa Rica

Czechoslavak Indoor Football
Committee
Mlady Svet 112 22
Panska 8
Praha 1, Czechoslavakia

France
Federacao Francesa de Futebol
de Salao
B.P. 112, 13269 Marseille
Post 241 Cedex 2
France

Israel
Israel Football Association
12 Carlebach Street
Tel Aviv, Israel

Italy
Lega Italiana Calcetto
Via Acquedotto de Peschiera, 22
Roma Italy

Japan
Sergio Eshigo, Ishikawa Loshaki
Kansai Shinsaibashi
Building 704 - 12 - 8.4 Chome
Minami Semba Minami - Ku
Osaka, Japan

Mexico
Federacion Mexicana de
Futbol de Salon
Abraham Gonzalez, 74
Mexico, Mexico

The Netherlands
Cockevel 9a
5672 AE Nuenen
The Netherlands

Paraguay Federacion Paraguaya de
Futbol de Salon
C.Correo 1972
Asuncion, Paraguay

Puerto Rico
federacion Puetorriquena de
Futbol Sala
Ing. Juan A. Davila, 403
Urb Roosevelt
Hato Rey, Puerto Rico 00918

Spain
Federacion Espanola de
Futbol Sala
Dr. Fleming, 32
Madrid 16, Spain

Sweden
Gasagagen 28
422 48 Gothenburg, Sweden

Uruguay
Federaacion Uruguaya de
Futbol de Salon
Canelones 978
Montevideo, Uruguay

Venezuela
Organizacion Trigal Norte
Calle Saturno 90 131
Valenia, Venzuela

Sports Clubs & Teams

Listed in this section are the clubs & teams from leagues & first divisions throughout the world.

Football Club Addresses

ARGENTINA
Association Del Futbol
Viamonte 1366/76
1053 Buenos Aires

Boca Juniors
Brandsen 805
1161 Buenos Aires

Club Estudiantes de la Plata
Calle 53
620 1900 La Plata

Club Ferro Carril Oeste
Cucha Cucha 350
1405 Buenos Aires

Club Atletico Huracan
Avenida Caseros 3121/59
1263 Buenos Aires

Club Atletico Independiente
Mitre 470
1870 Avellaneda

Provincia de Buenos Aires
Club Atletico Newell's Old
Boys
Parque Independencia
2000 Rosario

Provincia de Santa Fe
Racing Club
Mitre 934
1970 Avellaneda

Provincia de Buenos Aires
Club Atletico River Plate
Avenida Figueroa
Alcorta 7597
1428 Buenos Aires

Club Atletico Rosario Central
Avenida Genova y Bvd
Avellaneda
2000 Rosario

Provincia de Santa Fe
Club Atletico San Lorenzo
de Almargo
Avenida La Plata
1250 Buenos Aires

Club Atletico Velez Sarsfield
Avenida Juan B Justo 9200
1408 Buenos Aires

AUSTRIA
Oesterreichischer Fussball-
Bund
Praterstadion, Sektor A/F
Meiereistr., Postfach 340
A-1020 Wien

FK Austria-Memphis
Wr.Stadion-Sektor D
Meiereistrasse
1020 Wien

FC Admira-Wacker
Johan-Steinbock-Strasse 1
2344 Maria Enzersdorf

GAK-Ring Schuh
Korosistrasse 56
8010 Graz

Lask
Koglstrasse 14
4020 Linz

SK ALCA Austria Klagenfurt
Siebenhugelstrasse 105
9020 Klagenfurt

SK Raika Sturm Graz
Maiffredygasse 1
8010 Graz

SK Rapid Wien
Keisslergasse 6
1140 Wien

Wr. Sportclub
Hernaiser Hauptstrasse 214
1170 Wien

FC Swarovski Tirol
Resselstrasse 18/11
6020 Innsbruck

Foto Nettig Vienna FC 1894
Hohe Warte, Postfach 3
1194 Wien

VSE Egger St. Polten
Spratzener Kirchenweg 25
3100 St. Polten

SK Leiner Vorwarts Steyr
Grillparzerstrasse 3
4400 Steyr

BELGIUM
Union Royale Belge Des
Societes De Football Assn.
Avenue Houba De Strooper 145
B-1020 Bruxelles

R.S.C. Anderlecht
Avenue Theo Verbeeck 2
1070 Bruxelles

R. Antwerp F.C.
Oude Bosuilbaan 54/a
2100 Deurne

K. Beerschot V.A.V.
J. De Geyterstraat 133
2020 Antwerpen

K.S.K. Beveren
Heiveldstraat 73
2750 Beveren-Waas

K.S.V. Cercle Brugge
Olympianiaan 74
8200 St.Andries-Brugge 2

R. Charleroi S.C.
Boulevard Zoe Drion 19
6000 Charleroi

Club Brugge K.V.
Olympiastadiod
Olympialaan 74
8200 St.Andries-Brugges 2

K.V.Kortrijk
Meensesteenweg 84
8500 Kortrijk

R.F.C. Liegeois
Stade de Rocourt
Chaussee de Tongres
4420 Rocourt

K.S.C. Lokeren
Daknamstraat 91
9100 Lokeren

K.V. Mechelen
Lieresteenweg 34
2800 Mechelen

K.R.C.Mechelen
Geerdegemdries 32
2800 Mechelen

R.W.D. Molenbeek
Rue Charles Malis 61
1080 Bruxelles

R. Standard de Liege
Stade de Sclessin
Rue de la Centrale
4200 Sclessin

K.S.V. Waregem
Regenboogstadion
Westerlaan 2
8790 Waregem

K.St. Truidense V.V.
Halmaalweg 62
3800 Sint-Truiden

K.R.C. Genk
Weg naar As 19/bus 16
3600 Genk

K. Lierse S.K.
Voetbalstraat 4
2500 Lier

BOLIVIA
Federacion Boliviana de
Futbol
AV. 16 de Julio NO.NO782
Casella Postal No. 484
Cochabamba

Auroa
Jordan 3797
Cochabamba

Blooming
24 de Setiembre
Santa Cruz de la Sierra

Bolivan Independiente
Unificada
Ed Litoral
Calle Colon
La Paz

Deportivo Chaco Petrolero
YPFB
La Paz

Guabira
Igenio Azucarero
Guabira
Santa Cruz de la Sierra

Club Jorgan Wilsterman
San Martin S-0348
Cochabamba

Deportivo Municipal
Honorable Municipalidad de
la Paz
Oriente Petrolero
YPFB
Santa Cruz de la Sierra

The Strongest
Comercio esq Colon 512
LaPaz

BRAZIL
Confederacao Brasileira de
Futebol
Rua da Alfandega, 70
PO Box 1078
20.070 Rio de Janeiro

Club Atletico Mineiro
Avenida Olegario Maciel 1516
Lourdes
Belo Horizonte

Esporte Clube Bahia
Rua Carlos Gomes 85
2nd andar, Centro
Salvador

Botafogo de Futebol e
Regatas
Rua Xavier Curado 1705
Rio de Janeiro 21610

Sport Club Corinthians
Paulista
Rua Sao Jorge 777
Tatuape
Sao Paulo 03087

Cruzeiro Esporte Clube
Rua Guajaras 1722
Barro Preto
Belo Horizonte

Clube de Regatas do
Flamengo
Praca Noss Senhora
Auxiliadora, Gavea
Rio de Janeiro

Fluminense Futebol Clube
rua Alvara Chaves 41
Rio de Janeiro 22231

Gremio Foot-Ball Porto-
Alegrense
Largo dos Campeoes
Azenha
Porto Alegre

Guaranti FC
Estadio Brinco de Ouro
Campinas

Sport Club Internacional
Avenida Padre Cacique
Menino de Deus
Porto Alegre

Sociedade Esportiva
Pallmeiras
Rua Turiacu 1840
Agua Branca
Sao Paulo

Santos Futebol Clube
Rua Princesa Isabel
Vila Belmiro
Santos, Sao Paulo

Sao Paulo Futebol Clube
Praca Gomes Pedrosa
Jardim Leonor
Sao Paulo

**Clube de Regatas Vasco da
Gama**
Rua General Americo de
Moura 131
Rio de Janeiro

BULGARIA
Bulgarian Football Union
Gotcho Gopin 19
1000 Sofia

FC Beroe
I.Aleksiev 10
6000 Stara Zagora

FC Etar
Karaminkov 19
5000 Veliko Tarnovo

FC Lokomotiv
Bul. Tolstoy 23
1220 Sofia

FC Locomotiv
Otez Paisly 31
4000 Plovdiv

FC Lokomotiv
Vassil Aprilov 26
5100 Gorna Oriahovitza

FC Minior
Fizkulturna 1
2300 Pernik

FC Pirin
Dabravska 1
2700 Blagoevgrad

FC Slavia
9-ti-Septemvri 128
1618 Sofia

FC Sliven
G. Dantschev 2
8800 Sliven

FC Spartak
Warnenska Komuna 1
9000 Warna

CFKA Sredetz
Stadion Narodna Armia
1504 Sofia

FC Dounav Rousse
Kvartal Zdravetz
Stadiodn Dounav
7000 Rousse

FC Trakia
D. Blagoev 10
4000 Plovdiv

FC Vitoshia (Lousky)
Todorini Kukli 47
1517 Sofia

FC Wratza
Jordan Lutibrodsski
3000 Wratza

FC Tcherno More
Stad.on Tchnero More
9000 Varna

CHILE
Federacion De Futbol De Chile
Calle Erasmo Escala No.1872
Casilla No. 3733
Santiago de Chile

Club de Deportes Cobreloa
Atacama 1482
Casilla 156
Calama

Colo Colo
Cienfuegos 41
Santiago

Everton
Viana 161
Vina del Mar

Deportes Huachipato
Parque Araucaria
Talcahuano

Desportes O'Higgins
Avenida Brazil 1079
Rancagua

Palestino
Avenida Pte Kennedy 9351
Santiago
Union Espanola
Carmen 102-110
Santiago

Union San Felipe
Prat 320
San Felipe

Club de Deportes
Universidad Catolica
Avenida Andres Bellol 2782
Santiago

Universidad de Chile
Marin 0525
Santiago

Wanderers
Lira 575
Valparaiso

COLOMBIA
Federacion Colombiana De Futbol
Avenida 32, No. 16-22
Apartado Aereo No. 17.602
Bogota, D.E.

Club Deportivo America
Calle 24N 5B-22
Apartado 1383
Cali

Club Atletico Junior
Barranquilla
depto Atlantico

Club Deportivo Cali
Calle 34N 2 bis-75
Apartado 4593
Cali

Club Independiente Santa Fe
Avenida 39 15-22
Apartado 4593
Cali

Club Deportivo Millonarios
Calle 39A-No 15-32

Club Atletico Nacional
Carrerea 76 48A-11
Medellin

Deportes Tolima
Ibaque
Depto de Tolima

CZECHOSLOVAKIA
Ceskoslovensky Fotbalovy Svaz
NA Porici 12
11530 Praha 12

TJASVA Diukla B. Bystrica
Stadion SNP
97401 banska Bystrica

Banik Ostrava OKD
Bazaly
71000 Ostrava 10

Bohemians CKD Praha
SNB 31
10 000 Praha 10

Dukla Praha
Postfach 59
16 044 Praha 6

Ruda Hvezda Cheb
PS 15
35 025 Cheb

SK Slavia IPS
Stadion Dr.V. Vacka
10 005 Praha 10

Skoda Pizen
Stadion Struncovy sady
30 526 Pizen

Slovan CHZJD Bratislava
Junacka 2
83 215 Bratislava

TJDAC Dunajska Streda
Sportova ul. 491/16
92 901 Dunajska Streda

Sparta CKD Praha
Obranacu miru 98
17082 Praha 7

Spartak TAZ Trnava
Sp. TAZ-Stadion
91760 Trnava

Sektion Fussball
Stadion
80 603 Ostrava-Vitkovice

Internacional Slovnaft
ZTS Bratislava
Vajnorska 100
83 284 Bratislava

Plastika Nitra
Jesenskeho 2
94901 Nitra

Spartak ZVU Hradec Kralove
PS 37
50 009 Hradec Kralove

TJ Sigma Olomouc
Stadion Miru - PS 145
77 111 Olomouc

DENMARK
Dansk Boldspil-Union
Ved Amagerbanen 15
DK-2300 Copenhagen

Aalborg Boldspilklub af
1885 (AAB)
Hornevej 2
Oster Uttrup
9220 Aalborg Ost.

AArhus Gynastikforening af
1880 (AGB)
Terp Skovvej 1
8260 Viby J

Brandbyernes
Idraetsforening
(Brandby)
Klubhuset
Branoby Stadion 26
2605 Brondby

Bronshoj Boldklub
(Bronshoj)
Terrasserne 10
2700 Bronshoj

Boldklubben 1903 (B 1903)
Lyngbyvej 270
2900 Hellerup

Herfolge Boldklub
Herfolge Stadion
4681 Holfolge

Ikast Forenede Sportsklubber
Stadion Alle 4
7430 Ikast

Kjobenhavns Boldklub (KB)
Peter Bangsvej 147
2000 Kobenhavn F.

Lyngby Boldklub af 1921
Lyngby Stadion
Lundtoftevej 52 B

Naestved I.F.
Rolighedsvej
4800 Nykobing F

Odense Boldklub (OB)
Sdr. Bouldevard 172
5000 Odense C

Randers Freja FC
Viborgvej 92A
8900 Randers

Silkeborg Idraets Forening
Ansevej 110
8600 Silkeborg

Vejle Boldklub
Vejle Stadion
7100 Vejle

GERMANY
Deutscher Fussball-Bund
Otto-Fleck-Schneise 6
Postfach 710265
6000 Frankfurt/Main 71

Hertha BSC Berlin
Reichsstrasse 17
1000 Berlin 19

VFL Bochum
Castroper Strasse 145
4630 Bochum 1

Werder Bremen
Weser-Stadion
2800 Bremen 1

Borussia Dortmund
Strobelallee
4600 Dortmund 1

Fortuna Dusseldorf
Flinger Broich 87
4000 Dusseldorf

Eintracht Frankfurt
Am Erlenbruch 25
6000 Frankfurt 60

Hamburger SV
Rothenbaumchaussee 125
2000 Hamburg 13

F. FC Kaiserslautern
Postfach 2427
6750 Kaiserslautern

Karlsruher SC
Adenauerring 17
7500 Karlsruhe

A. FC Koln
Postfach 100768
5000 Koln 1

Bayer 04 Leverkusen
Postfach 120140
5090 Leverkusen

Borussia Monchengladbach
Bokelstrasse 165
4050 Monchengladbach

Bayern Munchen
Sabener Strasse 51
8000 Munchen 90

1. FC Nurnberg
Valznerweiherstrasse 200

FC St. Pauli
Auf dem Heiligengeistfeld
2000 Hamburg 4

VFB Stuttgart
Mercedestrase 109
7000 Stuttgart 50

Bayer Uerdingen
Postfach 110
4150 Krefeld 11

SG Wattenscheid 09
Lohrheidestrasse 82
4630 Bochum 6

Republic of Ireland
The Football Association of
Ireland
(Cumann Peile NA H-
EIREANN)80, Merrion Square
South Dublin 2

Athlone Town
55 Auburn Heights
Athone

Bohemians
44 Woodbine Drive
Raheny, Dublin 5

Cobh Ramblers
75 Norwood Park
Cobh
Co.Cork

Cork City
Flushing Meadow
Crossbarry Road
Gortnaglough
Ballinhassig
Co. Cork

Derry City
18A Queen Street
Derry BT48 7EF

Dundalk
183, Ard Easmuinn
Dandalk

Galway United
34 Upper Abbeygate Street
Galway

Limerick City
c/o Famous Fried Chicken
Rhebogue
Dublin Road, Limerick

St. Patrick's Athletic
49 Edenmore Gardens
Raheny, Dublin 5

Shamrock Rovers
47 Sefton
Rochstown Avenue
Sunlaoghaire
Co. Dublin

Shelbourne
11 Northbrook Road
Leeson Park
Dublin 6

Waterford United
"Hilton"
Sweetbriar Park
Tramore
Co. Waterford

ROMANIA
Federatia Romana de
Fotbal
Vasile Conta 16
Bucharest 70130

F.C. Arges
Horia, Closca si Crisan 15
Pitesti

S.C. Bacau
Pictor Aman 94
Bacau

Flacara Automecanica
Str. A.I. Cuza 9
Moreni

Corvinul Hundedoara
Mihai Viteazu 10
Hunedoara

FC Olt
Corn. Scornicesti
Olt

Otelul
Str. Scintelli, 12
Galati

FCM Brasov
Str. Mihai Viteazul nr. 168
Brasov

C.S. Rapid
Calea Giulesti 18
Bucuresti
Steaua
B-dul Ghencea 35
Bucaresti

C.F. Sportul Studentesc
Stefan Furtuna 140
Bucuresti

Dinamo Bucuresti
Sos. Stefan cel Mare 7-9
Bucuresti

F.C. Universitatea Craiova
Str. Gh. Doja 2A
Craiova

CSU Universitatea
1-3, Piata Pacii
Cluj-Napoca

Victoria Bucuresti
Calea Grivitei, 71
Bucuresti

ASA Tirgu Mures
B-dul Lenin 5
Tirgu Mures

F.C. Inter Sibiu
Aleea Eminescu nr. 1-3
Sibiu

F.C. Bihor
Str. Iosik Vulcan 11
Oradea

F.C. Constanta
B-dul Republicii 24
Constanta

SCOTLAND

**The Scottish Football
Association Ltd.**
6 Park Gardens
Glasgow G3 7YF

Aberdeen
Pittodrie Stadium
Aberdeen AB2 1QH

Celtic
Celtic Park
Glasgow G40 3RE

Dundee
Dens Park
Dundee DD3 7JY

Dundee United
Tannadice Park
Dundee DD3 7JW

Dunfermline Athletic
East End Park
Dunfermline K12 7RB

Heart of Midlothian
Tynecastle Park
Gorgie Road
Edinburgh EHII 2NL

Hibernian
Easter Road Stadium
Edinburgh EH7 5QG

Motherwell
Fir Park
Motherwell MLI 2QN

Rangers FC
Ibrox Stadium
Glasgow G5I 2XD

St. Johnstone FC
McDiarmid Park
Crieff Road
Perth PHI 2SJ

St. Mirren FC
St. Mirren Park
Love Street
Paisley PA3 2EJ

SPAIN
Real Federacion Espanola
de Futbol
Calle Alberto Bosch, 13
Apartado Postal 347
E-28014 Madrid

Athletic Club
Alameda de Racaide 34
48 009 Bilbao

Club Athletico de Madrid
Estadio "Vicente Calderon"
Paseo Virgen de Puerto 67
28 005 Madrid

Club Athletico Osasuna
Plaza del Castillo 30-31
31 001 Pamplona

F.C. Barcelona
Aristides Maillol s/n
08 028 Barcelona

Cadiz C.F.
Canovas de Castillo, 21
11 001 Cadiz

Real Club Celta
Avda. de Balaidos s/n
36 210 Vigo (Ponteredra)

Elche FC
Jose Antonion, 3 ac.
03 280 Elche (Alicante)

C.D. Logrones
Breton de los Herreros, 17
26 001 Logroco

Real Oviedo
Marques de Santa Cruz, 9
33 007 Oviedo

Sevilla FC
Estadio "Sanchez Pizjuan"
Av. Eduardo Dato, s/n
41 005 Sevilla

Real Betis Balompie
Estadio Villamarin
Av. Heliopolis, s/n
41 012 Sevilla

Real Club Deportivo Espanol
Maestro Villa, s/n
08 017 Barcelona

Real Madrid C.F.
Av. Concha Espina 1
28 036 Madrid

C.D. Malaga
PO Martiricos, s/n
Estadio "La Rosaleda"
29 009 Malaga

Club Real Murcia
Ronda de Garay, s/n
Campo de la Condomina
30 003 Murcia

Real Sociedad de Futbol
Paseo Arbol de Guernica, 24
20 006 San Sebastian

Real Sporting de Giyon
Plaza Monte de Piedad, 2
33 201 Gijon (Asturias)

Valencia C.F.
Artes Graficas, 44
46 010 Valencia

Real Valladolid Deportivo
Macias Picavea 9
47 003 Valladolid

Real Zaragoza C.D.
Ponzano 10, I
50 004 Zaragoza

SWEDEN
Svenska Fotbolfoerbundet
Box 1216
S-17123 Solna 1

AIK
Box 1408
171 27 Solna

IK Brage
Box 69
781 21 Borlange

Djurgardens IF
Box 26062
1004 41 Stockholm

Gais
Box 4100
42104 Vastra Frolunda

Hammarby IF
Box 20056
10460 Stockholm

IFK Goteborg
Drottninggatan 36, V
411 14 Goteborg

IFK Norrkoping
Box 12067
600 12 Norrkoping

Malmo FF
Box 17301
200 10 Malmo

GIF Sundsvall
Box 311
85105 Sundsval

Vastra Folunda IF
Naverlursgatan 26
421 44 Vastra Frolunda

Orgryte IS
Box 52025
400 25 Goteborg

Osters IF
Storgatan 12
35231 Vaxjo

SWITZERLAND
Association Suisse de
Football
Laubeggstrasse 70
B.P.
CH-3000 Berne 32

FC Aarau
Postfach 383
5001 Aarau

AC Bellinzona
Casella postale 1023
6501 Bellinzona

Grasshopper-Club
Fussball-Sektion
Postfach 217
8037 Zurich

Lausanne-Sports
Case postale 175
1018 Lausanne 18

FC Lugano
Casella postale 96
6904 Lugano

FC Luzern
Postfach 2918
6002 Luzern

Neuchatel Xamax FC
Case postale 78
2000 Neuchatel 8-Monruz

FC St. Gallen
Postfach 14
9009 St. Gallen

Servette FC
Case postale 12
1219 Chatelaine

FC Sion
Case postale 401
1951 Sion

BSC Young Boys
Papiermuhlestrasse 71
3000 Bern 22

FC Wettingen
Postfach 110
5430 Wettingen

TURKEY
Turkish Football Assn.
Zincirlikuyu Caddesi 17/3-4
Yeniulus-Istanbul

Altay SK
Alsancak Stadt
C Blok Alsancak-Izmir

Adana DSK
Cevat Yurdakul Cad.
Adana

Ankaragucu Kulubu
Tandogan
Ankara

Besiktas SK
Akaretler Spor Cad. No. 92
Besiktas-Istanbul

Bursapor Kulubu
Bursa

Adanaspor K.
Ataturk Cad. No. 181
Adana

Boluspor K.
Bolu

Karsiyaka S>K>
Yali Cad. No. 396
Izmir

Eskisehirspor K.
Eskisehir

Fenerbahce S.K.
Kiziltoprak
Istanbul

Galatasaray S.K.
Hasnun Galip Sokak
Istanbul

Konyaspor K.
Zafer Meydani Zafer Carsisi
Kat 3
Konya

K. Marasspor Kulubu
Kahramanmaras

Sakaryaspor K.
Sakarya

Malatyaspor K.
Malatya

MKE Ankaragucu K.
Tandogan-Ankara

Rizespor Kulubu
Rize

Samsunspor Kulubu
Samsun

Sariyer S.K.
Sariyer-Istanbul

Trabzonspor K.
Trabzon

URUGUAY
Asociacion Uruguaya de
Futbol
Guayabo 1531
Montevideo

Club Athletico Bella Vista
Agraciada 3100
Montevideo

Danublo FC
8 de Octubre 4584
Montevideo

Club Athletico Defensor
Jaime Zudanes 2537
Montevideo

Club Nacional de Futbol
Avenida 8 de Octubre 2487
Montevideo

Club Athletico Penarol
Magallanes esquina de
Galicia
Montevideo

Club Montevideo Wanderers
San Fructuoso 1070

SOVIET UNION
USSR Football Federation
Luzhnetskaja Naberzhnaja, 8
119871 GSP-3 Moscow

Ararat Erevan
Pl. Lenina 2
Erevan

Chernomorets Odessa
Central Stadium
Odessa

Dinamo Kiev
ul. Kirova 3
Kiev

Dinamo Minsk
ul. Kirova 8
Minsk

Dinamo Moscow
Leningradskii pr. 36
Moscow

Dinamo Tbilisi
pr. Cereteli 2
Tbilisi

Dnepr Dnepropetrovsk
ul. Kirova 12
Dnepropetrovsk

Kairat Alma-Ata
Pr. Abaia 243
Alma-Ata

Lokomotiv Moscow
ul. Verkhnyaya
Krasnoselsjakyaya 3a
Moscow

Neftchi Baku
ul. Khagani 21
Baku

Shahter Donetsk
Avantgard Sports Society
Donetsk (340045

Spartak Moscow
ul. Verhniaia Krasnoselskaia
38/19
Moscow

Metalist Khar'kov
ul. Plekhanovskaia 65
Khar'kov

Torpedo Moscow
Avtozavodskaia ul. 23
Moscow

Zenit Leningrad
Aptekarskii pr. 16
Leningrad (194044)

Zhalghiris/Vilnus
Eidukiavichiaus str. 3/11
Vilnus

YUGOSLAVIA
Yugoslavia Football
Association
P.O. Box 263
Terazije Belgrade

FC Buducnost
Vaka Djurovica b.b.
81000 Titograd

FK Celik
Stadion "Bilino polje"
72000 Zenica

FC Crvena Zvezda
Ljutice Bogdana 1/a
11000 Belgrade

NK Dinamo (Z)
Maksimirska 128
41000 Zagrab

NK Hajduk
Stadion "Polijud"
58000 Split

FK Napredak
Stadion "Mladost" P.F.8
37000 Krusevac

NK Osijek
Sportska hala "zrinjevac"
54000 Osijek

FC Partizan
Humska 1 (stadion JNA)
11000 Belgrade

FK "Rad"
Crnotravska bb
11000 Belgrade

FC Radnicki
Sportska hala "Cair"
18000 Nis

NK Rijeka
Stadion "Kantrida"
51000 Rijeka

FC Sarajevo
Marsala Tita 40
71000 Sarajevo

FC Sloboda
Partizanska 2
75000 Tuzla

FK Spartak
Lenjinov Park 10
24000 Subotica

FK Vardar
Kej "13 Novembri"-kula 1
91000 Skoplje

FC Velez
Stjepana Radica 41
79000 Mostar

FK Vojvodina
Zarka Zrenjanina 8
Novi Sad

Enjoy Major League Baseball
6 to 11 Day Tours!
Each day watch a game with different teams playing in a different park. Travel in deluxe coach with sightseeing and shopping time, too. A family atmosphere for 8 to 80!
SEND FOR YOUR FREE TOUR SCHEDULE
Jay Buckley's
BASEBALL TOURS
P.O. Box 213, Dept GSP
La Crosse, WI 54602
(608) 788-9600

New National Olympic Committee Members

Bosnia-Herzegovina

**Olympic Committee of
Bosnia and Herzegovina**
(temporary address)
NOC for Germany
Otto-Fleck-Schneise 12
6000 Frankfurt-Am-Main 71,
Germany

Croatia

**Croatian Olympic
Committee**
Berislaviceva 2
41000 Zagreb, Croatia

Estonia

Estonian Olympic Committee
Regati 1
Tallinn 200103, Estonia

Latvia

Latvian Olympic Committee
49, Elizabetes Street
Riga 226050, Latvia

Lithuania

**National Olympic Committee
of Lithuania**
Vrublevskio Str. 6
2671 Vilnius, Lithuania

Namibia

Namibian Olympic Committee
P.O. Box 21162
Windhoek 9000, Namibia

Slovenia

**Olympic Committee
of Slovenia**
Celovksa 25
61000 Ljubljana, Slovenia

South Africa

**National Olympic Committee
of South Africa**
James and Ethel Gray Park
Athol Oaklands Road
Melrose, Johannesburg,
South Africa

Myanmar

Myanmar Olympic Committee
Aungsan Stadium
Mingala Taungnyunt Township
Yangon Division 11 221,
Myanmar
(formerly the nation of Burma)

A MODERN CLASSIC !

SPORTS HALL OF OBLIVION- A Guide to Defunct Pro Teams, *by Chuck Hershberger.*

This 112 page paperback contains sports history unknown even by experts!

This book features the past history of defunct leagues, teams, organizations & player records from over 20 professional sports. Included is the history of "phantom" leagues & teams that have never played a game!

Copies of the **SPORTS HALL OF OBLIVION** are in the Baseball, Basketball, Hockey & Tennis Hall of Fame Libraries.

THERE HAS NEVER BEEN A BOOK LIKE THIS BEFORE!

People across North America have this to say about Sports Hall of Oblivion:

****

"A great reference book for the sports collector and sport nut ! If ever you're looking for information on a defunct league or team-this is the book that tells all !"
GREENWATER, WA

"It is a very interesting and detailed work"
CAGUAS. PUERTO RICO

"It is about time someone took the time out to research such a unique portion of sports history"
FLUSHING, NEW YORK

"Very Interesting and Informative. Well worth the price." TORONTO, ONTARIO

"One-of-a-kind book" HONOLULU, HAWAII

****

ORDER YOUR COPY NOW!

Only $4.95 postpaid (U.S. & Canada)

Payable in U.S. Funds to: Chuck Hershberger
Box 69025B
Pleasant Ridge, MI 48069

FOREIGN ORDERS (Outside of Canada):
Book weight- 6 oz.
Check for appropriate postage.

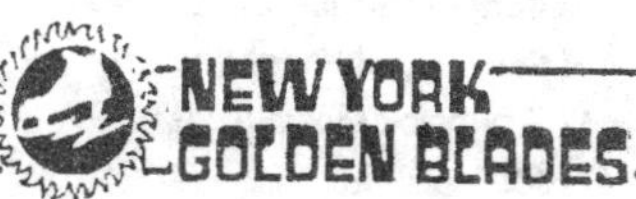

NOC ***********

Armenia

**Olympic Committee of the
Armenian Republic**
9, Abovian Street
P.O. Box 375001
Yerevan

Azerbaijan

**National Olympic Committee
of the Azerbaijani Republic**
98-A, Leningradski Prospect
Baku

Belarus

**National Olympic Committee
of the Republic of Belarus**
8/2 Kirov Street
220600 Minsk

Georgia

**Georgian National Olympic
Committee**
65, David Agmashenebeli Ave.
380001 Tbilisi

KAZAKHSTAN

**National Olympic Committee
of the Rep. of Kazakhstan**
Gorky Park, Spartak Stadium
480023 Alma-Ata

Kyrghyzstan

**National Olympic Committee
of the Rep. of Kyrghyzstan**
17, Togholok Moldo Street
720033 Bishkek

Moldova

**National Olympic Committee
of the Rep. of Moldova**
73, Stefan cel Mare Street
277064 Kishinev

Russia

All-Russia Olympic Committee
Kazakova ul. 18
103064 Moscow

Tadjikistan

**National Olympic Committee
of the Rep. of Tadjikistan**
18, Roudaki Street
734025 Dushanbe

Turkmenistan

**National Olympic Committee
of Turkmenistan**
44, Engels Street
74400 Ashkhabad

Ukraine

**Ukraine Olympic Committee
of Ukraine**
St. Esplanadnaj 42
Kiev 252 023

Uzbekistan

**National Olympic Committee
of the Rep. of Uzbekistan**
83, Tashkent Street
700029 Tashkent